CRITICAL ACCLAIM FOR
WHERE THE BUCK STOPS

"Tells it like it was. . . . 'Frank and honest' is an understatement."
—*Atlanta Journal*

*

"A fun read . . . it's rather like being invited to the former president's study—or even his kitchen table—to hear some homely lectures on this, that and the other thing delivered in the crisp Missouri diction that precisely matched Truman's autodidactic style."
—*Houston Post*

*

"I would recommend *Where the Buck Stops* for anyone who cares about politics and especially for students who find history boring. If I could, I would place it under the tree at the White House, hoping someone there would take it to heart."
—*St. Petersburg Times*

*

more . . .

"These personal musings of 'Give 'Em Hell Harry' confirm his reputation for taking positions on controversial issues with no equivocation."
—Houston Chronicle

*

"Offers both historical insights into political activities and challenges, and blunt comments on the making and perception of historical figureheads. No punches are pulled in his assessments of key political figures."
—Midwest Book Review

*

"A good, stimulating book."
—Chattanooga Times

*

"The most insightful, informative, direct and delightful book I've read in a long time. . . . You can hear Harry Truman saying these things in that machine-gun, Missouri speech of his."
—Austin American-Statesman

*

WHERE THE BUCK STOPS

THE PERSONAL AND PRIVATE WRITINGS OF
HARRY S. TRUMAN

EDITED BY
MARGARET TRUMAN

WARNER BOOKS

A Time Warner Company

Warner Books, Inc., 666 Fifth Avenue, New York, NY 10103

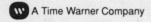 A Time Warner Company

Printed in the United States of America
First trade paperback printing: October 1990
10 9 8 7 6 5 4 3 2 1

Library of Congress Cataloging-in-Publication Data

Truman, Harry S., 1884–1972.
    Where the buck stops : the private and personal writings of Harry
  S. Truman / by Harry S. Truman; edited by Margaret Truman.
      p.   cm.
    ISBN 0-446-39175-1
    1. Presidents—United States—History.   2. United States—Politics
  and government.   I. Truman, Margaret.   II. Title.
  E742.5.T62   1989
  973'.0992—dc20   89-40366
                                                                        CIP

Book design by H. Roberts
Cover design by Paul Gamarello
Cover photo from the Harry Truman Library

My friend and agent, Scott Meredith, contributed far more to this book than his usual services as my literary agent, wide-ranging and essential as those services always are in themselves. For more than two years, spurred on by our mutual admiration for my father, we worked together virtually every weekend and many an evening, going over the stacks of pages and papers left by my father and shaping them into this book. I've been grateful to Scott for a long time. I'm even more grateful to him now.

Margaret Truman

CONTENTS

INTRODUCTION

My father began work on this book shortly after he left the White House and finished his basic material many years ago. He dictated a lot of it to his secretaries, and he wrote a lot of it on little scraps of paper, and he took some of it from things he'd said in interviews and speeches, and he also dictated a lot of it to my mother and me. I guess "told" is a better word because neither of us knew shorthand, and we just copied everything down slowly and laboriously. Eventually he ended up with what probably amounted to a couple of thousand pages, and from that material I've shaped the present book.

My father asked that the book not be published until he and my mother had left us. He decided this because he wanted to feel free to say things about people and events in his usual frank and honest fashion. No words minced; no punches pulled.

This is not a complex book, or a profound one. My father was a modest man and said frequently that he wasn't capable of writing a complex book even if he wanted to do so, but the fact is that he didn't want to write such a book. He wanted to leave behind him a book that would express, in plain and simple language, his viewpoint on the presidency, various presidents, the American government and the way it functions and operates, our history, and in general all of the things he had observed and thought about as a boy and young man and in his political offices. And he wanted to express himself in a manner that would be clear and comprehensible to most men and women—to the kind of person he considered himself to be, an average American. The single difference between himself and other men, he felt, was that, unlike most other men, he was, as he says in this book, "struck by lightning" one day and woke to find himself president of the United States.

ONE

Ordinary Men and
Three Great Presidents

I'VE often said that there are a million men in this country who could have done the job I did as president, or who were qualified for the job. I think that's true, but they didn't have the chance. A great many men who are well qualified to be chief executive have been passed up and overlooked. It takes luck, conditions that prevail at the time, and when the right moment comes, ability to meet that situation. Perhaps I shouldn't say that myself because I was finally nominated and elected president of the United States. But it's true.

Most men don't aspire to the presidency. It comes to them by accident. And don't think for a minute that the men who were defeated for the presidency were necessarily weaker men or less capable individuals than the men who beat them, or forget that it's an honor to run for the presidency even if you're defeated. There are places in history for many men who were defeated for the presidency. I can name them right down the line, and many of them were great men. Samuel Tilden was defeated by Rutherford B. Hayes in 1876—though "defeated" isn't exactly the right word, since Tilden had the majority of both the popular and electoral votes—and he was a great man because he let Hayes have the presidency in order to avoid seeing the War Between the States start all over again. Take James G. Blaine, who was defeated for the presidency and afterwards became a good secretary of state in the cabinet of Benjamin Harrison. Or take Charles Evans Hughes, who was defeated for the presidency and became Chief Justice of the United States. William Howard Taft was defeated for reelection and also became Chief Justice of the United States.

A great many of the men who were not elected to the presidency afterwards became good public servants and great citizens of the United States, and made a contribution to the welfare of the country. People who run for office and are defeated aren't rejected in the usual sense of the word. They're just defeated because they couldn't get enough votes that one time. It doesn't mean the public despises them. It's a preference for somebody else for that particular office at that particular moment, that's all. The examples I've given have shown that when those men were passed up, they were still highly thought of and were still great men. There were a good many like that. You take the Adams family. After John Quincy Adams passed on, there were Adams descendants in Lincoln's cabinet. They wrote important histories and things of that kind. Even in the states, some good men are governors who have been defeated previously in elections, even in previous tries for governor. If they don't become pessimists and decide to lay down and take it, if they get up and start over again, why, they don't have any trouble.

The defeated man I admire is one who can take it and like it. One of my favorite people is Francis Merriam Cockrell, who was a major general in the Civil War and was in command of the Missouri Brigades in Vicksburg. Then he came back home, and after the Reconstruction had fixed it so people could run for office, he wanted to be governor, I think in 1872. He was defeated by one vote at the convention. He stood out in the middle of the aisle in the old Capitol Building in Jefferson City, Missouri, and threw his old black hat up into the dome and said, "I'm still for the ticket." He was elected by the legislature of Missouri to the United States Senate and stayed there for thirty years. (I get a little envious as I write those last words. I think most people know that it's my opinion that Franklin Delano Roosevelt didn't seek a third term—events forced him into it. The same thing happened with a fourth term. And if the fourth term hadn't come about, I wouldn't have been president. I would have been in the Senate and would be there yet, where the happiest time of my life was spent.)

I'll have a lot more to say about all that in this book, of course, and a lot more to say about some of the men who became presidents and whose election was a good thing for the country, and about some of the men who were elected to the presidency and shouldn't have been, and about some of the men who weren't elected and should have been, and about presidents and the presidency and the government and the country in general. Among a lot of other reasons, I'm very anxious to get the truth about some of our presidents available to people in a plain-spoken manner, so that they can understand what it means to be the responsible executive of a great republic. A great many presidents have had biographers who've been very careful to give us a distorted idea of exactly what sort of a man the president was and how he turned out as the chief executive of the nation. They've been misrepresented both ways. They've been slandered, and they've been built up in some cases to a height to which they had no business to be built. And I think the second kind of portrait is just as bad as the first kind.

There are heroes in our history who have been set up on pedestals, and maybe they ought to have been, but it's my opinion that those who've been deified were just ordinary men trying to do the right thing and lucky enough to get it done. And then there are some that we've mistreated in history: for example, Andrew Johnson and two or three other presidents have certainly been misrepresented, because when the facts are revealed about what those men tried to do, it's clear that they tried their best to do what was right, most of them have. And it would be nice to get the facts straight so that people realize that nearly every one of the men in government in the United States—in any capacity, whether he was a general or the president or the governor—tried to do his best, and that when an ordinary man gets the responsibility, he really tries to do what's right. And essentially that's been the case in the history of our presidency, though some of the men haven't been good presidents because they were lazy and didn't like to work. That wasn't a terrible thing against them; I think the human animal is like that because none of us like to work too much. But most of us do the best we can. So I don't mind the fact that some men and women have been deified, but I don't want them to overshadow those people who have not and who have also made great contributions to the country.

I guess as good a way as any to start is to write out a list of the men I think were our best presidents, and a few who might possibly have been our worst, and I think I can put some new light on what they did and didn't do if I compare their work with what actually happened in my own experience as a president. And I think I can do it objectively because my perspective on the presidency and some of our past presidents changed a lot after I became president. Naturally that would happen. When you find yourself in a very responsible position, especially in the chief executive position, you begin to understand some of the things with which men were faced who were in the same position before that time. Sometimes you may not agree with them, but after you've been in the position yourself and understand what a man was up against, you look up the facts on all sides of the matter, and then you can change your mind on what he was doing. I think it's fundamental and basic, as I've said, that history is made in our country by men who have the welfare of the people in their minds, and they have to make frequent and difficult decisions in order to get that done. Sometimes those decisions are not exactly what they ought to be, but a man who's willing to make a decision in the first place can always make another one to correct any mistake he's made.

Well now, there are about six or seven men who understood the presidency for what it is: the chief executive, the man who runs the greatest republic in the history of the world. And there are at least that many who paid no attention to their powers and duties: that is, they didn't shirk the fact that they were presidents, but they didn't exercise the powers that were given to them under the Constitution, either. I'll name the strong presidents, in my opinion, and that doesn't mean that they're the only ones.

Washington, of course, was the fellow who set up the government, and he was one of our great and strong presidents. There isn't any question about Washington's greatness. If his administration had been a failure, there would have been no United States. A lesser man couldn't have done it. He had all the background that caused him to know how to make it work, because he had worked under the Continental Congress. Then he had one awful time with them trying to get things done when he was commanding general. He was always available. In his time, the first capital was in New York City and then in Philadelphia, but he was always on the job. Not only that, he went by stagecoach from one end of the country to the other to give people some idea of what the government meant. He went to South Carolina from New York by stagecoach and then back. Whenever it was necessary for him to appear on the scene, he did it, at his own expense and a lot of trouble. Some presidents have limited their roles to being administrators of the laws without being leaders. But Washington was both a great administrator and a great leader, a truly great man in every way.

I guess, in fact, that the only anti-Washington thing I can say is that he made a mistake when he established the precedent of the two-term limitation on the presidency, and even there he had a good personal reason for wanting that, at least for himself. He was attacked viciously by the press of his day; he was called so many terrible things that he told friends even during his first term that he wasn't going to run again. But Thomas Jefferson and James Madison and Alexander Hamilton persuaded him to go ahead and run for a second term, and finally he did. After he'd gotten through his second term, though, he made up his mind that he just wouldn't take it anymore, and he quit. That established the precedent, though of course it wasn't actually law until it became necessary for Franklin Delano Roosevelt to stay on for four terms because of the world war, and—I won't mince words here—the Republican 80th Congress took a sort of revenge on Roosevelt's memory because he'd made a lot of those people look bad by comparison.

The amendment limiting presidential terms, incidentally, didn't apply to me. I could be elected to the presidency as often as I wanted, even to succeed myself, as often as I felt like it, but I'd had enough, too. So it isn't for personal reasons that I say that the Twenty-second Amendment, the one limiting a president to two terms, is, excepting only the Prohibition Amendment, the worst thing that's ever been attached to the Constitution. In fact, I think the Constitution has had only two bad amendments, the Two-Term and the Prohibition amendments, and the Prohibition Amendment was finally repealed. There was even talk of limiting a president's term to one four-year term or two two-year terms, but four years just isn't enough. It's the continuation of a president's program that's necessary, and in most cases, it isn't possible to get measures through the Congress in two separate terms of two years or one term of four years. Therefore, if the president has a policy that's agreeable to the people, and he feels like working his head off for another term or several more terms, he's got a right to run for it. There are clearly times when more than two terms are both necessary and wise, and times when two terms are enough, and in my case I felt it was about time for the country to awaken to the fact that the people are responsible for the kind of government they get, and that somebody else should take over. (Unfortunately, the person who took over was Dwight Eisenhower, about whom I'll also have more to say later on. All I'll say now is that when the people elect a man to the presidency who doesn't take care of the job, they've got nobody to blame but themselves.)

The next great president, in my view, was Jefferson. I've heard it said that Washington is rated highly as the man who fought for independence and established a new government, Lincoln is rated highly as the liberator, and Jefferson is lost somewhere in between. Well, I don't think he is. Washington and Lincoln were involved in events that were more spectacular and dramatic, and there isn't any doubt in my mind that, if Lincoln hadn't saved the Union from being broken up, we'd have had four or five nations where just one is now established as one of the strongest of the great nations of the world, and we'd have no country at all without Washington. But Jefferson was just as important because he was working continuously for the preservation of free government as established by the Constitution. So let's simply say that the objectives the three men had in view were as follows: Washington's to establish the government, Jefferson's to maintain it, Lincoln's to prevent it from being broken up. And each did his job, every single one of them, as a man dealing with the period in which he lived.

Jefferson also had his share of press criticism and people who didn't like him, and I wonder how many people remember our history and realize how close Jefferson came to losing the election in 1800, and how close Aaron Burr came to being our third president, which would have been just as bad as electing Richard Nixon today.* In those days, the nomination of the president was made by congressional caucus. They usually nominated three or four men, and then the one with the highest number of votes was supposed to be president and the one with the second-highest total was supposed to be vice president. John Adams was popular in New England and got sixty-five electoral votes, but Jefferson and Burr dominated the southern states and the middle states and ended up with a tie of seventy-three votes apiece. This threw the election into the House of Representatives, and Hamilton, certain that the people clearly wanted Jefferson over Burr, whispered in a lot of ears and Jefferson became president and Burr vice president. That didn't satisfy Burr, incidentally, and he tried to take the southwest part of the country away from the United States because he was miffed about not being elected president, but more about that in my chapter on Jefferson.

Jefferson was also called a runaway president because he pushed through our purchase of Louisiana over a lot of opposition. I think that Jefferson's purchase of Louisiana was one of the best decisions ever made because, if we hadn't taken over Louisiana, then either Britain, France, or Spain would have owned it and our country would have ended at the Mississippi River, whereas the greatest part of our development has been by our ability to expand beyond the Mississippi River. I don't like this talk about runaway presidents, because the truth is that a president just does what he has to do.

Two of my other choices as great presidents are Andrew Jackson and Abraham Lincoln, and they were characterized as runaway presidents, too. Jackson had his troubles with the courts when he was enforcing the law, the tariff act that South Carolina decided they wouldn't pay. The old man wouldn't stand for nullification, South Carolina's attempt to nullify the tax, so he sent General Winfield Scott and a naval force to Charleston and they paid. And of course, Lincoln in his period suspended habeas corpus, allowing military authorities to arrest and try people ac-

*My father wrote these lines sometime before Richard Nixon was in fact elected president. He decided, however, not to change the sentence. He said his comments on Mr. Nixon would be unprintable. MT

cused of helping the South or impeding Federal troops, and he did several other things that he had to do in order to save the Union at the time. He dismissed the Circuit Court of Appeals and appointed new judges in the District of Columbia and extended the Supreme Court from seven members to eleven. But all of the former protections were restored when the emergency was over.

Jackson is my next choice as a great president after Jefferson, the next president who really did things. He was elected after a period of what they called in James Monroe's time "the era of good feeling." Well, when the era of good feeling got to feeling too good, meaning that the people and the government became too complacent and too lazy, why, the country went to the dogs, as it's always done. You have got to have opposition if you're going to keep a republic going. Old Jackson remedied that, and he did it in a way that was perfectly satisfactory to all concerned. Among a lot of other things I'll discuss when I have more to say about Jackson, the economic royalists, the favored few, had control of the government by controlling the finances of the country. A man named Nicholas Biddle and his Bank of the United States had all the government's money, and Jackson took the money away from him and in effect put all the dollar bills back into the Treasury of the United States, where they ought to be, by spreading all the funds around into various state banks. And of course, he was roundly abused for doing things of that sort, but all the great presidents had emergencies to meet, and they met them as best they could and usually came out on top. Not necessarily in their own lifetime, you understand. Admiration for Lincoln didn't come about for thirty or forty years after he was dead. Jefferson wasn't appreciated until he'd been dead forty or fifty years. It sometimes takes people a long time to find out exactly what past results were, and that's customary with all history.

There's also going to be some discussion in this book about why I think that military men make poor presidents. Before anybody asks me how I can say that and square it up with my admiration for old Jackson, let me point out that Jackson wasn't a professional military man. He was a volunteer military man. He had gone from North Carolina to Tennessee, and he became interested in the government of Tennessee and the organization of that state and helped to write its constitution. He was a private practitioner of law and was in the Senate of the United States. When the War of 1812 came along, he was a volunteer general of the militia and organized the people who fought the Battle of New Orleans. He wasn't educated as a professional soldier. He was a citizen soldier who learned his military affairs from the ground up on his own hook.

It's the fellows who go to West Point, and are trained to think they're gods in uniform, that I plan to take apart in that discussion.

My next choice for this list of great presidents is a man who usually doesn't get on lists of this sort, and it may surprise some of the people reading this book. But since this chapter is long enough already, I'll save it until you turn to the next page.

TWO

Five More Great Presidents

THE next man on my list of great presidents, a man who isn't much thought about these days, is James K. Polk. I won't say everything about him here because I'm going to say more about him later on, which he certainly deserves. For now, I'll just say that he's on my list, among a lot of other reasons, because of three accomplishments.

The first is that he exercised his powers of the presidency as I think they should be exercised. He was president during the Mexican War, and he was living in an age when the terrible burden of making decisions in a war was entirely in the hands of the president. And when that came about, he decided that that was much more important than going to parties and shaking hands with people. I know exactly how he felt, but in my time there were more able and informed people who were helping the president, and that made a difference. Polk not only had troubles with his generals, but he also had troubles with Congress. Every president, of course, always has his troubles with his generals and with Congress. If he's in the midst of a war, he'll have trouble with his generals, and every strong president always has trouble with the Congress whether there's a war on or not. But whenever the president knows what he's doing, and knows it's right, he can always convince the Congress that his ideas are the ones to be followed. All you have to do is bring in the leaders in the Congress, tell them what the situation is and why certain things have to be done. You never have any trouble with them after that. There have certainly been some stubborn men in the Congress, but they don't usually have control, thank goodness. The majority of the Congress is made up of men who are elected for sensible reasons and they're reasonable men. The stubborn men in the Congress are a natural corollary of free government, but when the president of the United States makes up his mind that he wants to do something that's right, he can always convince the majority of the Congress that he's right, and when he does, the stubborn men don't count. Weak presidents never seem to understand this, but fortunately Polk wasn't weak. He brought in the leaders of the Congress and told them what he wanted to do, and it was done.

The second important thing about Polk is that he bought the southwest part of the country for just about the same price that Jefferson paid for Louisiana. It was quite a bargain and really helped make us a great big country. We got California and the area between California and Texas, which was called New Mexico at the time, and which included the present areas of Nevada and Utah. Altogether, we acquired a total of about 918,000 square miles, and I don't think anybody's going to argue about the fact that that's a pretty impressive acquisition.

And the third impressive thing about Polk that I want to mention right now is that he did something that most of the rest of us who were presidents weren't able to do: he decided when he went in there that he would only serve one term, and that's what he did, exactly. I don't mean that he served one term and then was turned out by the voters with a lot of things unfinished. I mean that he was a man who knew exactly what he wanted to do in a specified period of time and did it, and when he got through with it, he went home. He was a chief executive of the kind we dream about, and very seldom see. He died three months after he got out of the White House; he retired on March 4, 1849, and died in June. He did what he promised, to serve one term and put his program over in one term. It was almost as though he knew his work was finished and he wasn't much interested in living a lot longer. He said a moving thing on his retirement, "I now retire as a servant and regain my position as a sovereign." He was right, absolutely right. I've been through it and I know.

* * *

There were a number of weak presidents after Polk: Zachary Taylor and Millard Fillmore and Franklin Pierce and James Buchanan. The last two were the presidents immediately preceding Lincoln, and Pierce was a nincompoop and Buchanan was just as bad. A president who's important in his period is one who has to meet a serious situation and does it with courage and ability. But there are times when that's not done, and one of those times, except for Polk's single term, was probably the period between the end of the Jackson administration and through the Buchanan administration, a time when things were allowed to drift as far as the chief executive was concerned. And then came Abraham Lincoln, a strong executive who saved the government, saved the United States.

Lincoln didn't even dream about the presidency until he was a prospective nominee. Before that, I don't think he ever had it in mind. He wanted to be a senator from Illinois more than anything he ever wanted in his life, and he was defeated. And when an opportunity came along to be nominated by his party, the Republicans, which was a minority party at that time, why, he set up an organization and got himself nominated. I don't think he ever had in his mind an ambition that he could ever be president of the United States any more than I did. I never thought I would be president. I never wanted to be, to tell you the honest truth, though maybe Lincoln did.

I think that, when he was nominated by the Republicans in Chicago, they were absolutely certain that they didn't have a chance to elect anybody. And of course, that helped him to get the nomination because the other Republicans felt it was meaningless and they didn't care much who got it. But he wanted the nomination and he worked for it, and he had the best organization that there was at that convention, some of the best politicians in Illinois and Missouri working for him. I don't believe he thought he was going to be elected, but he wanted to be nominated because it was an honor even if he was eventually defeated. And when he was elected, I think he was as much surprised as anybody else in the country. Interestingly, though, he didn't carry his home state.

My people didn't think much of Lincoln, but I thought he was wonderful. It took me a long time to come to that realization, however, because my family were all against him and all thought it was a fine thing he got assassinated. (Well, that's an exaggeration, but not by much.) I began to feel just the opposite after I'd studied the history of the country and what he did to save the Union. That's when I came to that conclusion, and that was a long time ago.

He was a president who understood people, and when it came time to make decisions, he was willing to take the responsibility and make those decisions no matter how difficult they were. A lot of people aside from my family didn't think much of him, even some of his cabinet; you'll see that if you read the cabinet viewpoint, and practically all of those fellows wrote memoirs. Some of them thought he didn't have much sense at times, some of them thought he was just a common old farmer from Illinois, and some of them thought he was just a baboon. He was all of those things, except the baboon. Most of all, he knew people. He knew how to treat people and he knew how to make a decision stick, and that's the reason his administration, which he carried through for the salvation of the Union, is considered one of the greatest administrations in the history of the presidency. He had a good head and a great brain and a kind heart. He'd educated himself to the point where he knew how a government should work, and he tried his best to make ours work that way.

Carl Sandburg and a lot of others have tried to make something out of Lincoln that he wasn't. He was a decent man, a good politician, and a great president, and they've tried to build up things that he never even thought about. I'll bet you a dollar and a half that if you read Sandburg's biography of Lincoln, you'll find things put into Lincoln's mouth and mind that never even occurred to him. He was a good man who was in the place where he ought to have been at the time important events were taking place, but when they write about him as though he belongs in the pantheon of the gods, that's not the man he really was. He was the best kind of ordinary man, and when I say that he was an ordinary man, I mean that as high praise, not deprecation. That's the highest praise you can give a man, that he's one of the people and becomes distinguished in the service that he gives other people. I don't know of any higher compliment you can pay a man than that. He was one of the people and he wanted to stay that way. And he was that way until the day he died. One of the reasons he was assassinated was because he didn't feel important enough to have the proper guards around him at the Ford Theater.

The president after Lincoln, Andrew Johnson, wasn't too bad, but he was overwhelmed by a hostile Congress. I'll write a little bit more about him and about that in my chapter on Lincoln later on in this book. Ulysses S. Grant was next, and he wasn't even a chief executive; he was another sleepwalker whose administration was even more crooked than Warren Harding's, if that's possible. Then there was Rutherford B. Hayes, who was elected by a fluke and knew it, and he did his level best to do a good job. Then along came James A. Garfield, who was assassinated six months after he was inaugurated. He was followed by Chester A. Arthur, who was vice president when Garfield was elected, and the only thing that stands out about Arthur is that he took all the wonderful furniture that had been brought to this country by Jefferson, Monroe, and several of the other presidents of that period and sold it in an auction for about $6,500. I think it was nine vanloads of furniture, any one piece of which would be worth more today than he got for the whole load. (I tried to get some of the pieces back when I was president, and they couldn't be obtained. People who had them wouldn't sell them at all. I don't blame them, either.) A bit more about some of these men later, too, but then the next great president showed up: Grover Cleveland. At least he was a great president in his first term; in his second term, he wasn't the same Grover Cleveland he was to begin with.

Some presidents in our history limited their roles to being administrators of the laws without being leaders. Cleveland reestablished the presidency by being not only a chief executive but a leader. In the period from Grant's administration through the administration of that fellow who sold all the furniture, the policy of the government was not for the welfare and benefit of the people but for the few who had access to the government and to major government officials. Cleveland spent most of his time in his first term working on bills that came from the Congress, and he vetoed a tremendous pile of bills that were passed strictly for the purpose of helping out people who voted for the Republican ticket or who promised to vote for the Republican ticket. He also saw to it that a lot of laws were passed, if he felt those laws were needed for the good of the general public, and even if the laws weren't popular with some members of the Congress.

In other words, Cleveland was a good president because he was familiar with the powers of an executive, and unlike some of his predecessors, he wasn't afraid to use them. He had been sheriff of Erie County, mayor of Buffalo, and then governor of New York State, and he knew how to use the powers of his various offices without abusing them. In Johnson's period in office, for example, a bill had been passed that prohibited presidents from firing members of their cabinets. Cleveland felt that this took powers away improperly from the presidency and succeeded in convincing the Supreme Court that that bill was unconstitutional. He also succeeded in placing some controls over the insurance companies, which were going pretty strong in those days. And Cleveland was really the first president to make anybody stop intruding into this hemisphere. The only reason the Monroe Doctrine had stood up in earlier days was because Britain was our ally and helped keep others out. But then, in Cleveland's time, we had to keep *Britain* out. The British tried to take over some territory in Venezuela to which they weren't entitled, and Cleveland told them that the Monroe Doctrine still worked. He sent a very strong message to Congress denouncing Great Britain's attempted intrusion into Venezuela, and the British backed off.

For the most part, however, Cleveland was a considerably less impressive man in his second term. He had been elected for the first time in 1884, but he was defeated by Benjamin Harrison in 1888; he had the majority of the popular vote but was defeated in the electoral college. He went to work for the Prudential Insurance Company and became one of the directors of Princeton University along with a lot of other businessmen, and when he ran for the presidency again in 1892 and was reelected, his viewpoint had substantially changed. The big corporations were then beginning to get control of the economic situation of the country; we were changing from an agrarian state to an industrial state, and if you remember, the big campaign cry in 1896, the period after Cleveland's second term, was for "a full dinner pail." Cleveland had a terrible time with strikes, and he called out the soldiers and they fired on the strikers. It was also during Cleveland's second term that a number of smaller companies got together and formed great big companies for the suppression of competition, companies like Standard Oil and the United States Rubber Company and United States Steel. These were formed not only to suppress competition but to exact higher prices from the buyer. And the administration did nothing about it: these things weren't corrected until Woodrow Wilson and then Franklin Roosevelt became president. That's why I say Cleveland was a great president only in his first term. In his second term, he didn't do so well.

Cleveland was a Democrat, but he didn't care for the 1896 Democratic candidate, William Jennings Bryan, so he supported William McKinley, a Republican. His son followed through with that and became the Republican leader in Baltimore. I don't hold that against either of them, but McKinley didn't turn out to be much of a president. Theodore Roosevelt was next and in my view, missed being a great president, though only by a narrow margin.

The trouble with Teddy Roosevelt is that, though he was the president who finally awakened to the fact that the welfare of the country was wrapped up in its physical assets—that is, in the forests and the mines and the other things the country owned—and he tried to conserve the situation as best he could, he had his troubles in the Congress and he had his troubles with the trusts, and he didn't get a heck of a lot done. He finally got to be called a trustbuster, but he didn't bust very many of them. I think he made a sincere effort to take the financial control of the government away from Wall Street and put it back in Washington where it belongs, as Andrew Jackson had done in his period and as Franklin Roosevelt succeeded in doing later on, but he ended up adding up to more talk than achievement. And some really bad things were allowed to happen during his two terms, one of which was his agreement with the Japanese under which they agreed that they wouldn't issue passports to laborers wanting to emigrate to the United States. That became the Chinese-Japanese Exclusion Act in the end. That was a part of it; the original Chinese Exclusion Act became law back in 1882, but Teddy Roosevelt's administration expanded and legitimatized it. This all happened just after the turn of the century, and I wasn't old enough to pay much attention to it, but a lot of people in California and the rest of the West Coast thought it was a good thing. They said they didn't want cheap labor competing with Americans in California or Oregon or Washington. The cry was, how can a man who has to have two dollars a day compete with a man who can live on two cents a day? Which is nonsense, because immigrants learn very quickly about the joys of living better. I wasn't old enough to do anything about that act, but afterwards, when the same situation came up, I did everything I possibly could to get the Japanese and the Chinese treated on the same basis that our own American labor force is treated. But there are still restrictions. It's economic. Purely economic. And it stinks.

So Theodore Roosevelt doesn't get on my list of great presidents, and neither does the man who followed him, William Howard Taft, a fat, jolly, likable, mediocre man. But the president after that, Woodrow Wilson, certainly does.

I've been asked which presidents served as models for me when I was president myself, and the answer is that there were three of them. Two were Jefferson and Jackson, and the third was Woodrow Wilson. When a fellow in modern times becomes the chief executive, it's his job to find out the relationship of the things with which he's faced with what has gone before. And then he has to try to project what he has to do in the future, and see whether the examples of past presidents are what he's looking for or whether he should set an example of his own. Every president has to act on his own, no matter what the situation may have been before he came along, but he has to have that background, that knowledge of past history, to be sure that he's doing what's right. And Woodrow Wilson served as a constant example to me of how to operate and function as president of the United States.

In many ways Wilson was the greatest of the greats. He established the Federal Reserve Board. He established the Federal Trade Commission. He didn't make a great publicity stunt of being a trustbuster, the way Teddy Roosevelt did, but the trust situation was never really met until Wilson became president. Wilson really felt that the monopolies ought to be controlled, and he controlled them. (That's the greatest thing Teddy Roosevelt ever did, incidentally: he contributed to the election of Wilson. Not intentionally, of course.) Wilson had no territorial ambitions, but when Victoriano Huerta seized control of Mexico and arrested some

American sailors in Tampico, and when Pancho Villa raided Columbus, New Mexico, and tore up an American flag, Wilson took quick action each time to make it clear that the United States expected respect and was going to get it. But he also made it understood that we were against those two murderers and not against Mexicans, and we've had friendly relations with Mexico ever since.

Wilson also established the League of Nations, which didn't succeed, but which served as a blueprint for the United Nations, which might succeed yet despite some built-in problems. He was a man who believed that the people ought to be kept informed on what the president wanted to do, and he reestablished the precedent of the president's going down and delivering his messages in person to the Congress. That hadn't been done, I don't think, since Jefferson's time.

Wilson was called a radical when he came in and organized all the reforms that were made in the financial setup of the government. But Jackson was also called a radical by his opponents, and Franklin Roosevelt was called a radical, and so was every other president who has done anything. Any man who does things for the welfare of the majority of the people is always called a radical. He doesn't necessarily have to be one. I'm going to try to avoid labels in this book because they're often misleading. Jackson was also called a liberal, and so was Jefferson, but some other presidents were called liberals, too, and they were mediocre presidents. All a good president tries to do is accomplish things for the good of the people, and if you want to call that liberal, then I'm with you. I guess the best way to describe Wilson, if I've got to use a label, is to say that he was a commonsense liberal. He wasn't one of these synthetic liberals who are always talking liberalism and who act some other way, and he wasn't one of these screaming liberals who aren't very liberal to people who think differently from the way they do. He was a genuine liberal who used his heart and his brain.

The final great president on my list is, as I'm sure you've already guessed, Franklin Delano Roosevelt. It goes without saying that I was highly impressed by him for a thousand reasons, but a main reason is that he inherited a situation that was almost as bad as the one that Lincoln had, and he dealt with it. And he was always able to make decisions. Presidents have to make decisions if they're going to get anywhere, and those presidents who couldn't make decisions are the ones who caused all the trouble.

I'm going to end this chapter right here because I'll be mentioning FDR many times in this book, of course, and saying a lot more about him. But anybody who's looking for any comments that are less than admiring had better go to the bookstore and see if he can get his money back.

PART I

Some Presidents We Could Have Done Without

THREE

Do-nothing Presidents—
Taylor, Fillmore, Pierce,
and Buchanan

THE purpose of these next few chapters is to flip the coin and write about some presidents of the opposite variety.

It's a remarkably varied thing, the way various presidents have handled the powers with which they're charged in the Constitution. Some of them haven't been interested at all in taking charge of things and operating as they should. It's a fascinating study, too, especially if a man happens to have lightning strike him and he becomes a president himself, as I did. He's suddenly the chief executive of the greatest country in the world, and if he wants to exercise that prerogative, he can do it. If he doesn't, he can sit still and take things as they come. I'd made quite a study of the presidency and I liked the work, and I hope people will agree that I worked hard. The history of the Republic is a struggle between the three branches—the courts, the executive, and the legislature. It's natural for a president to have problems with the Congress or the Supreme Court; in fact, it's my opinion that if a president isn't in an occasional fight with the Congress or the courts, he's not doing a good job. If the executive has the ability and the desire to make himself felt, he can run the government properly. If he doesn't, he can't.

A strong president is a president who carries on the operation of the United States as the Constitution provides, and has the willingness to decide what ought to be done and then put it over. Regardless of consequences. It doesn't make any difference whether or not the thing he decides to do is unpopular, or whether his doing it makes him unpopular for a while. If he does the right thing, the popularity will come. If he doesn't, well, then, too bad. And I don't think there's such a thing as too strong an executive, or that we've ever had too strong an executive in the White House. We're stuck with some men while they're in there, but that's all right and that's the way it should be; they've been elected and they should have their chance. But it's no danger because each man's term is limited. You can always put him out if he gets too big for his britches.

The United States has never suffered seriously from any acts of the president that were intended for the welfare of the country. It's suffered from the inaction of a great many presidents when action should have been taken at the right time. I don't think there's ever been a president who really did damage because he wanted damage to be done. I don't think any of them willfully and maliciously tried to get the country in trouble; I think you'll find that most of them were anxious to see useful things done. But some of them didn't act as they should in their position as chief executive, and that brought about some of the country's difficulties.

I've been asked if I really believe that most or all of our presidents had the welfare of the people in mind, or if that's just a myth. Yes, I do, and no, it isn't. I think the vast majority of the presidents were always as anxious as they could be to serve the people to the best of their ability. I believe that all of our presidents, good or bad, were genuinely interested in the welfare of the American people. You won't necessarily find that in inherited monarchies where the chief executive inherits the job. You'll find that some of the kings and princes and emperors and empresses were deliberately trying to increase their own power and their own welfare rather than the welfare of the people. That's what caused some of those revolutions. But that hasn't been true with the elected office of the president of the United States. Most—no, I'd say all—of the men who were elected president of the United States were willing and anxious to do what was right, if they knew what it was. Some of them didn't know, that's all, and some had an inkling or real knowledge but were just too lazy or too timid to do the work involved or take the flak that would come from opponents or the opposition press. That's why some presidents did a good job, some did a fair job, and some didn't do any job at all, so I guess the best way to rate presidents would be to call them great, near great, and do-nothings.

Zachary Taylor was one of the do-nothing presidents. Benjamin Harrison was that sort of president, too, and I think that Rutherford B. Hayes was almost that sort of president, although he lived in especially turbulent times and did manage to get a thing or two done. A couple of others were Franklin Pierce and Millard Fillmore. Ulysses S. Grant was a pretty bad president, too. In our own days, Calvin Coolidge is the nearest example to a sit-still president that we've had, except possibly Dwight Eisenhower.

Zachary Taylor was the president immediately after Polk, and from the beginning of his administration in 1849 until the end of James Buchanan's administration in 1861, we had the same sort of situation, a period of stagnation. The four presidents in that period were Taylor, Millard Fillmore, Franklin Pierce, and James Buchanan. I think it was one of the worst periods the country ever went through, and it brought on the War Between the States.

Taylor was a field general, one of the great ones. He was on active service when Texas was already in the Union, but there was a big question about the state's southwestern border; Texas said it was the Rio Grande and the Mexican government said it was the Nueces River. Polk ordered Taylor to cross the Nueces River and take over the disputed territory, and when Taylor did that and Mexican troops attacked, Polk and his Congress said that Mexico had in effect declared war and told Taylor to move deeper into Mexico. At the same time, a sea and land expedition headed by General Winfield Scott captured Mexico City, and Americans in California proclaimed their territory part of the United States, and Mexico quit and Polk made his deal that got us all those western areas.

But when Taylor became president of the United States, I don't think he knew what to do. I can't be charitable and say that he failed to carry out his program; he didn't have any program to carry out, so he couldn't fail because he had no program.

He was elected just as a military figure, and he spent his year in office behaving like a retired general. We've had that happen time and again, for example in the cases of Ulysses S. Grant and the occupant of the White House after me. Most generals have the idea that as commanding generals they're going to retire someday to a nice post and sit there and wait for their term to end, and some of them think they can retire to the White House as commander in chief and do the same thing. But they can't. The administrative job of the president is the hardest job in the world, and there's no general or anybody else who has any job that approaches the responsibility and the work that the president has to do to make the job work properly.

The things, of course, that test the effectiveness of a president are the special conditions and problems that exist, domestically and in foreign affairs, during his term or terms in office, and the things that determine whether or not a president is a good president are his ability to have ideas for the welfare of the country, and—most important of all—his willingness to work hard to turn his ideas into action and make things happen. He must have ideas and imagination as to what's needed for the good of the country, and he can create conditions that will make him great, or he can take things as they are and do nothing, like Taylor.

Taylor certainly became expert at doing nothing. There was a corruption scandal involving some members of his cabinet, but he delayed and delayed firing any of them. He was a slaveholder himself and in fact, briefly the father-in-law of Jefferson Davis (his daughter died of malaria a few months after her marriage to Davis), but he just looked the other way on the slavery question, making noises one day that sounded proslavery and noises the next that sounded antislavery. And when Stephen A. Douglas and Henry Clay were putting together the Compromise of 1850, which proposed that California come in as a free state, that Utah and New Mexico become territories without requiring them to become either for or against slavery, and that Texas, which already had slaves, be compensated for some of its area that had been given to New Mexico, the betting was about even on whether Taylor would sign the bill or veto it because nobody could tell how Taylor felt about it or even if he'd thought about it. Nobody ever found out, because Taylor stayed out in the sun too much and ate too much on an especially hot July Fourth in 1850, and he became very sick and died five days later. The Compromise of 1850 was passed after Taylor's death. It was one of Clay's greatest achievements, along with his Missouri Compromise, which allowed Missouri to enter the Union as a slave state while simultaneously allowing Maine to separate from Massachusetts and come in as a free state, but prohibited slavery forever in the upper Missouri Valley. If these compromises had been able to stand up, I doubt if the Civil War would have come in 1861. Of course, after the fact, it's always easy to decide what ought to have been done, but the Missouri Compromise and the Compromise of 1850 were eventually repealed, and I think those were among the things that really brought on the War Between the States.

Millard Fillmore was Taylor's vice president and, of course, became president when Taylor died. He was another of those detached, do-nothing presidents.

Fillmore was a lawyer from Buffalo, New York, who entered the House of Representatives in 1832 and became a kind of protégé of Henry

Clay's. He was proposed by Clay for the vice presidency in 1844, but didn't get the nomination. Then Clay and his people supported Fillmore when he ran for governor of New York that year, but he lost that one, too, and he returned to private law practice. Finally, in 1848, when Taylor was nominated for president, Clay, who didn't like Taylor very much, insisted that Fillmore get the vice-presidential spot, and this time Fillmore made it. He had no regular viewpoint on anything. He started in politics as an anti-Mason, one of those people who thought the Masons were going to take over and ruin the country and possibly the world; he was a Whig as vice president and president, but later became a member of the National American Party, the Know-Nothings, because he decided one day that his defeat as governor back in 1844 happened because foreign-born voters didn't like him; and toward the end of his career, he supported the Democratic candidate, General George B. McClellan, against Abraham Lincoln in 1864. He was a man who changed with the wind, and as president of the United States he didn't do anything that's worth pointing out.*

Fillmore kept losing support during his term because of his invisibility, then lost more when Clay died in 1852, and he was defeated for the Whig renomination by General Winfield Scott, the fellow who became popular when Polk sent him out against the Mexicans. But another general, Franklin Pierce, opposed him on the Democratic ticket, and the Democrats won. Neither Scott nor Pierce did any real campaigning as candidates; Scott moved around a little, but Pierce just stayed home and said he supported the policies of his party, including the Compromise of 1850, and apparently that was enough.

Pierce was a Democrat from New Hampshire, and he was a very popular man in the North and a compromiser with the South, so he was overwhelmingly elected by both northerners and southerners. But although he was a compromiser, he ended up being the man who signed the bill repealing Clay's two important Compromises, which really brought on the Civil War. It was Pierce's foolish notion that he could cool down the slavery question and make people forget about it by doing two things: filling his cabinet with people of differing viewpoints, and

*My father once mentioned something to me that he said typified Millard Fillmore and summarized Fillmore's presidential career in a nutshell. When my father was working on this book, he said he referred occasionally for dates and other data to a number of history books, among them two particularly popular and intelligent books, *A Basic History of the United States* by Charles A. Beard and Mary R. Beard and *A Pocket History of the United States* by Allan Nevins and Henry Steele Commager. In the Nevins and Commager book, Fillmore is mentioned in a single line as "the dim and forgotten Millard Fillmore." In the Beards' book, Fillmore doesn't appear in the index at all. MT concentrating almost entirely on foreign policy and territorial expansion instead of slavery problems. But the net result of those ideas was that his cabinet members kept bickering with each other and didn't accomplish much, and Pierce's moves in other directions didn't distract people's attention from slavery problems for a minute.

Pierce was a well-educated man who graduated from Bowdoin College, in a class that included Nathaniel Hawthorne and Henry Wadsworth Longfellow, and then went on to law school. His father, Benjamin Pierce, was a Revolutionary War veteran who became governor of New Hampshire in 1827, and when old Ben Pierce ran for reelection and made it, Franklin Pierce ran for the state legislature and was elected, too. He was reelected three more times and eventually went on to the House of Representatives. He wasn't even thirty years old at the time, and he married a woman named Jane Appleton just before his thirtieth birthday, but the trouble was that his wife didn't like politics or Washington, and she didn't go with him when he returned to the capital after their honeymoon. That, of course, was a great handicap to him, because a man shouldn't have the distraction of attempting to live a celibate life when he's trying to concentrate on helping to run the country. And judging from pictures of the lady I've seen, she was also good-looking enough and smart-looking enough so she might have become a great hostess when Pierce became president, maybe even as good a hostess as Dolley Madison, who was the most glamorous of the First Ladies. (I could say excluding Mrs. Truman, but Mrs. Truman never had any idea of being glamorous.) And being a hostess and throwing parties is important in Washington, because a great many important things are transacted at these functions that might otherwise never have been discussed.

Pierce went on to the Senate in 1836, the youngest man in that group of fogies, but his wife kept bothering him to give up Washington and come on home to New Hampshire, and finally, six years later, he did. His life in Washington hadn't exactly been exemplary; he did so much hard drinking with other bachelor and sort-of-bachelor legislators like himself that he developed an alcoholism problem that stayed with him all his life. He became state chairman of the Democratic Party and the United States district attorney for New Hampshire, but he refused other things that would have taken him away from home, including an invitation from Polk to become his attorney general. But then the Mexican War came along and he became a colonel and then a general, and he was back in the national public eye again and headed toward the presidency.

Pierce wasn't the Democrats' first choice for the nomination; the contest was pretty much between James Buchanan and a fellow named Lewis Cass. But Buchanan and Cass kept canceling each other out, neither one getting the two-thirds majority, and Pierce's name was entered as a dark horse possibility on the thirty-fifth ballot. He finally got the nomination on the forty-ninth ballot. Mrs. Pierce fainted when she heard the news, and Pierce, who'd gone to the convention in Baltimore because he and his supporters had the notion that what did happen might possibly happen, had to lie to her and tell her that he hadn't had the slightest notion he was even a possibility.

Pierce had even features and curly hair and was one of the best-looking men ever in the White House. He was also one of the most vain men ever to occupy the White House, which I guess was on account of the fact that he was so good-looking. But though he looked the way people who make movies think a president should look, he didn't pay any more attention to business as president of the United States than the man in the moon, and he really made a mess of things. He had those two foolish notions I've already mentioned, and even though he was a northerner, he believed in slavery, pretty much, and once said in a speech, "I believe that involuntary servitude, as it exists in different States of the Confederacy, is recognized by the Constitution." So when Pierce finally turned attention to the seriousness of the slavery problem, he allowed Senator Stephen A. Douglas to influence his thinking in favor of the Kansas-Nebraska Act, and even helped Douglas get the thing through.

The Act threw out the Missouri Compromise and allowed Kansas to come in as a slave state if the local voters wanted it that way, and a lot of tough characters moved in from Missouri, which was already a slave state, and saw to it that Kansas went proslave. This, of course, increased the bitter feelings even more between North and South, and that was, for all intents and purposes, the end of Pierce as a national figure. At the 1856 convention, he wasn't proposed for renomination, and the nomination went to James Buchanan. Pierce went back to New Hampshire and became more and more unpopular by doing things like proposing that the man who had been the secretary of war in his cabinet, Jefferson Davis, be nominated as the Democratic candidate for president in 1860, and by opposing Lincoln's Emancipation Proclamation and saying it was unconstitutional. The suggestion about Davis wasn't quite as silly as it sounds, since Davis was probably the best-informed man in the government at the time, but it was certainly unwise and unpopular at a time when the North and South were on the brink of war. And when Jane Pierce died in 1863, Pierce turned more and more to that best friend of his back in Washington, the bottle of booze, and continued to slip so much in popularity that, when he himself died in 1868, nobody in New Hampshire was even willing to put up a statue of Franklin Pierce for half a century.

* * *

James Buchanan was one more do-nothing president. I think he was the most obvious one in his time for that sort of attitude, and the worse thing about that is that he came just before the Civil War and had a lot to do with bringing it on. In emergencies, the chief executive is the only one who can operate to meet those emergencies. Buchanan was president from 1857 to 1861, and he hesitated and backtracked and felt that his constitutional prerogative didn't allow him to do things, and he ended up doing absolutely nothing and threw everything into Lincoln's lap.

He also wrote a message on the veto of the first land grants and the first land grant colleges that's a comic masterpiece. The whole question of land grants came up because railroads were extending into the Mississippi Valley and making it easier for colonists to get into the western territories, and Congress tried to encourage colonization of these territories by selling the land for just $2 an acre and then reducing this to $1.25 an acre. But even those low amounts were just too high for poor laborers in the East and poor farmers and farm workers in the South, so the idea began to grow that the land ought to be given away free to people who were courageous enough to travel to the West and claim it. This plan was backed by a lot of people—most particularly by Andrew Johnson, who was a great friend of poor people in both farm and urban areas—and also by Horace Greeley, who also supported the idea strongly because he, too, wanted to help poor people. On the other hand, many of the manufacturers in the East opposed the plan because they didn't want to lose a lot of their workers, and many southerners opposed it because they were afraid this would cause too rapid growth of free states, and free states would soon outnumber slave states. This put Buchanan in a terrible dilemma because he was more or less for free land grants himself but didn't really have the guts to go against its opponents, so he simply vetoed the bill and put it off into the indefinite future. That was in 1860, and I think he suspected that he'd be out of office by the end of the year anyway.

That wasn't so comic in itself; the thing that was comic was that he also had to veto land grant colleges, and he justified this by explaining that the country didn't require further education of people. In fact, the old fool went on to say, educated people were too hard to handle, and he thought there were too many educated people already. Well, this was in 1860, and of course he was out in 1861, and they finally passed the land grant college bill. The first land grant college is up in Michigan, and it's a good one. The one out in Utah is the same sort. All the agricultural colleges around the country are land grant colleges, and they're all good.

* * *

Fortunately, the next president was Abraham Lincoln, one of the greatest, and the president after Lincoln was another very good though much-maligned man, Andrew Johnson. I'll talk about all of the good presidents in more detail later on. For now, let's move on to the next chapter and some more of the Presidents We Could Have Done Without.

FOUR
All About Grant

ULYSSES Simpson Grant's period in office seems to prove the theory that we can coast along for eight years without a president. Well, of course, we've also recently done it with Eisenhower.

Ulysses Simpson Grant wasn't really his name. He was named by his parents Hiram Ulysses Grant, but he dropped the Hiram and took the name Simpson so his initials could be U. S. He later claimed that he lost the Hiram and got the Simpson when someone made some mistakes on his registration form at West Point, and that he didn't say anything about it because he preferred initials standing for United States to his old set of initials, which caused his friends to call him Hug, but that's a kind of doubtful story. I can see a clerk dropping someone's first name by mistake, but not adding a name like Simpson out of the blue.

He was born on a farm in Point Pleasant, Ohio, in 1822 and went into West Point when he was seventeen. He hadn't had much real education before that, so his years at West Point were a kind of struggle for him, but he managed to graduate twenty-first in his class of thirty-nine, and he also said later on that his four years at the school gave him an additional and very important bonus. Fifty of the men he knew at West Point later became Civil War generals—on both sides, of course—and Grant later told friends that his knowledge of the personal strengths and weaknesses of these men helped him command and helped him win his battles.

He fought in the Mexican War under both Zachary Taylor and Winfield Scott and rose to the rank of captain. He married a woman named Julia Dent in 1848, the sister of one of his friends at West Point, and eventually had four children, three sons and a daughter, but his pay was so small that he couldn't afford to have his family with him when he was sent to various western posts after the war, and like Pierce, he started drinking heavily. He became an embarrassment to the Army, and he had to resign his commission in 1854.

There were very lean years after that. He tried farming, but he was drunk so much of the time that he lost the farm, and then he failed at selling real estate, and didn't do much better as a clerk in a store owned by a couple of his younger brothers. When the Civil War came along, he got a job at a salary of $3 a day as a clerk in the outfit in Springfield, Illinois, which was putting together Illinois's volunteer regiments, but the governor of Illinois knew about his West Point education and his military experience and put him in charge when nobody else around seemed to be able to get the regiments to shape up. He did so well at it that he was commissioned a brigadier general, and he came out of the war as a lieutenant general, the highest rank in the Army in those days.

I've read some books that criticize Grant's ability and decisions as a soldier, but I don't agree with these writers; I think Grant did what he had to do and did it well. He was very tough when he and his men were fighting to capture Fort Henry and Fort Donelson in Tennessee, and he got one more nickname, Unconditional Surrender, when he told the general in command of Donelson that he wouldn't accept anything less than that, but he won the battles and took 20,000 Confederate prisoners. He and his soldiers were taken by surprise when there was a big Confederate attack at Shiloh, and he was accused of being off on a bender and maybe he was, but he hung on and drove off the Confederate forces. And of course, it was Grant's personal decision to go after Lee, instead of waiting to see what Lee might do, and keep chasing him and attacking him until Lee surrendered.

Grant also behaved the way he should have, in my view, when Lee surrendered. He came to accept Lee's surrender with the mud still on his uniform, instead of acting like a god and a conqueror the way Douglas MacArthur sometimes did when I was vice president and president, and he ordered the horses to remain with the Confederate troops and told the southerners to keep their sidearms and go home and take care of themselves. He was really a kindhearted and decent man, I think. It was the people around him later on who caused him all the trouble. His administration was one of the most corrupt in our history, but he didn't even know all the crooked business was going on when he was president of the United States. It's hard even to imagine that, but it's true.*

Grant was one of the most popular men in the country when the Civil War ended. People in New York started a campaign to get some money into his pockets by private donations and presented him with a gift of $105,000, a lot of money in those days and not too bad right now, either. A house was built for him in Galena, Illinois, where his brothers had their store, and another house was built and given to him as a gift in Philadelphia. A new rank was created for the first time by Congress, general of the armies, and given to him. Andrew Johnson made him secretary of war, as it was called then, and a lot of people in the Republican Party began to think it would be pretty easy to get him elected as the next president.

He was invited to the Republican Convention, nominated unanimously on the first ballot, and campaigned against another fellow nobody remembers today, a man named Horatio Seymour who'd been governor of New York. The popular vote was surprisingly close, 3,013,421 for Grant against 2,706,829 for Seymour, but Grant received 214 electoral votes to 80 for Seymour and became our eighteenth president. (I have a feeling that a lot of people don't really understand this business of popular votes and electoral votes, because I didn't at one time, and I'll explain the way it all works in one of the later chapters.)

Grant's period as president was one of the low points in our history. It was after the most terrible war that the country had ever suffered, and after any sort of a turmoil like that, there's great difficulty and often a bad president. There's bound to be, just as there was after the First World War and following a very great president, Woodrow Wilson, and it happens in nearly every instance. It's just happened again with Eisenhower, as I can't resist repeating, if you want to refer to a modern situation. And it certainly happened with Grant.

I don't think Grant knew very much about what the president's job was except that he was commander in chief of the armed forces. That was the thing, I think, that impressed him more than anything, and he was pretty naive or ignorant about everything else.

When the Civil War was still going on, Lincoln and Grant wanted to approach peace and the South in a manner of forgiveness: come back and be good fellows and behave yourselves from now on. But Lincoln

---

*I wish my father were around today to give me his views, and tell me what he believes, or doesn't believe, about the Reagan administration and Irangate. MT

and Johnson were in the moderate wing of the Republican Party, and there was another part of the party known as the Radical Republicans, and one of the men in that group, Thaddeus Stevens of Pennsylvania, was the leader of the House of Representatives and felt completely different about everything. Thad Stevens and his crowd wanted to approach the thing in a manner that would cause the people who tried to break up the Union to be punished by prison and by hanging. In fact, they put Jefferson Davis, who became president of the Confederate government when the war started, in prison for a while, and they did everything they could to get a great many leaders in the South executed. They even went so far as to want to put Robert E. Lee in jail, but I'll say this for Grant: he wouldn't stand for it. He was president at the time, and for once he said something definite; he got up and said that if they did that, he'd quit. He did, though, prove a disappointment in just about everything else regarding the peace.

Grant's politics were an unknown quantity; he showed practically no interest in politics at all before he was invited to the Republican convention, and he admitted to some of his friends that he had only voted one time in his life—as a Democrat. But somehow the word had gotten around that Grant was going to be easier toward the South than the tough series of Reconstruction Acts dictated, probably because Grant sometimes backed Johnson when he was in Johnson's cabinet and the President was fighting with Congress, which was practically all the time, and most of Johnson's problems were the result of the fact that he was more interested in healing the breach between the North and the South than in vengeance against southern leaders. This notion about Grant was reinforced by the fact that the most significant part of Grant's acceptance speech was believed by many people to be one line: "Let us have peace." Unfortunately, it didn't turn out that way at all.

Johnson's plan was to welcome the South back into the Union and allow southern leaders to return to their former positions, so he announced an amnesty for most southerners and issued proclamations permitting the southern states to start setting up civil governments. He felt, as Lincoln did, that the southern states had never really left the Union and were still part of the Union. His attitude was that southerners ought to be treated as bad children and be allowed to rehabilitate themselves on the same basis as people who were Union people—that the South should be taken back as soon as they were willing to confess that they'd been wrong and taken the oath of allegiance, and go on from there, because the slaves had been freed and there wasn't any reason to do any of the things that used to be done in a conquered country. But old Thad Stevens didn't believe in that; that didn't sit well with him and the other Radical Republicans. He wanted to keep the South as a conquered territory and set up territorial governments under the control of the Federal government, with southerners having no rights at all, especially no right to vote. Stevens was a bitter old man who was involved in a hatred program toward all the South, and there's a theory that this was because he owned an iron and steel mill in Gettysburg and it was destroyed by the Confederate soldiers when Lee was in the neighborhood, but that's only part of the story. The biggest part of it was that the Republicans were a minority party, and Stevens and company wanted to keep the Radical Republicans in control of the Congress of the United States, and they were very much afraid that if the southerners, who were mostly Democrats, were allowed to start electing senators and representatives again, they'd turn the Radical Republicans out of office in the next few elections.

Johnson tried to get his point of view across; he even toured the country making speeches urging a sensible and gentle reconstruction program for the South. But it didn't help; a tough series of Reconstruction Acts were passed that threw out Johnson's civil governments and replaced them with military governments. Federal troops were sent in to patrol and control the South, and northern carpetbaggers were encouraged to pack those bags of theirs made out of old carpets and emigrate to the South and join with blacks* in running local southern governments. That wasn't what Johnson had in mind for the former slaves, or what Lincoln had in mind, either; I think what Lincoln and Johnson planned was the proper education and rehabilitation of the slaves so they could become useful citizens and in time take their place in government. But that wasn't the idea at all of Thad Stevens and the Radical Republicans; they wanted the South to be oppressed by the people who had been slaves, and that's what brought about a lot of the bad feelings between the races. They put the blacks in charge right after their emancipation, which wasn't fair to the blacks or to anybody else because they lacked education and experience. It was one of the worst things that was ever done for the rehabilitation of the slaves. It's taken years and years to get the thing worked out so that people will understand that education and experience are the best things that can happen to any race or color that hasn't had experience beforehand, and it's only now that things are starting to straighten out between the races. (We've still got a distance to go, but we're finally starting to see some real improvement with more and more black leaders in government, and I'm sure we'll have black presidents one day.) I think Johnson understood that, and he tried to veto the tough Reconstruction Acts, but they were passed over his veto.

Well, the hope was that Grant would change things back to more

---

*I've made a change here. My father used the word "Negroes" throughout, but I've changed all references to "blacks" because that's the word that African Americans now commonly employ. My father always had a desire to be modern and up-to-date, and I'm sure he would approve. MT

temperate policies toward the South, but exactly the opposite happened. Grant certainly *looked* good: he was just forty-six years old when he became president, which made him the youngest president in the nation's history up to that point, and he was very determined and very much the commanding officer in his appearance when he gave his inaugural address. But even that speech was marked with some of the poor thinking, or lack of thinking, that showed up all through his whole administration. He didn't like a lot of the laws, Grant said, but he was going to enforce them because—if you can believe this—he felt that that was the way to get rid of them. "I know no method to secure the repeal of bad or obnoxious laws so effective as their stringent execution," he said, which is like telling people to go out and do a lot of lynchings or murders so that the public can see that lynchings and murders are bad. And with that Grant pushed the Reconstruction Acts harder and harder, widening the breach more and more between the North and the South. The worst thing that went on during Grant's administration was that vicious and alleged reconstruction of the South, and that will never be forgotten as long as people write about him because he was president when the worst part of it was going on.

I think it's even possible that, in his own muddleheaded way, Grant was for carpetbagging. He was a general, and he'd conquered the southerners and he might have thought that the conquered should pay the bill. A lot of people have had that idea since the Battle of Waterloo, when Napoleon was exiled and imprisoned. That idea has never worn off, and some people felt that same way after the Civil War. It was the same thing, if you remember, after the Mexican War, when Santa Anna was defeated: why, we made the Mexicans pay through the nose. We made them turn over a whole lot of land to us, though we did give them fifteen million dollars for it. The theory is that the victor should make the loser pay every time. In World War I and World War II, though, we didn't follow that sort of program, though I guess there was a little of that sort of thing after World War I. There was some attempt to make the Germans pay a penalty, but Germany was never really injured by the First World War. We never got inside their borders with our armies, and the Russians then had their revolution and made their separate peace. So there wasn't anybody to put the screws on Germany except France, and they got Alsace-Lorraine back and that's all they wanted. Down in Africa, in the colonies, the British took over all the African colonies, and we became the managers of one of their colonies in the Pacific, and we still have it—the Marshall Islands.

The other way in which Grant showed his lack of ability as a president was when he set up his cabinet. I don't think there were any good men in Grant's cabinet, or at least not many. I don't know a lot about his cabinet members because I've never read their histories; I've never tried to keep up with them because I didn't like what they did and I never went into it very carefully. I do know, though, that the first thing Grant did was appoint two of his old buddies from Galena, Illinois. One of them died during Grant's first year in office, which wasn't anybody's fault, but the other one found that job so hard that he resigned right away. Then Grant appointed a banker as secretary of the navy, and the man tried it for three months and quit because his duties in Washington were taking too much time away from his real interest, making money for himself. And then Grant made a big-time contractor his secretary of the treasury, and the fellow had to resign after just a few days because his business activities were in obvious conflict of interest with his official activities.

The result of all this, of course, was an administration so corrupt that it held the record until Warren Gamaliel Harding came to the White House and brought his poker-playing cronies along with him. Officials in the Navy Department gave contracts to manufacturers based on what they received in kickbacks and not because the manufacturers had more experience or bid lower than others. Officials in the Department of the Interior gave land to speculators on the same basis. Officials in the Indian Bureau ignored the needs of the Indians and practically sold trading posts on every street corner. Grant's own brother-in-law got into trouble when it became known that he was giving Jay Gould, the financier, inside information so Gould could pull some Wall Street coups and cut him in, and a couple of cabinet members and five federal judges had to quit or be thrown out and possibly jailed for fraud and for accepting bribes and a lot of other things. And there was also a terrible depression during Grant's administration.

Despite all this, Grant still managed to get himself elected for a second term. He even did better than the first time; his opponent was Horace Greeley, the editor of the *New York Tribune,* who was favored by both the non-Radical Republicans and by the Democrats, but Grant received 3,596,745 votes and 286 electoral votes to Greeley's 2,843,446 votes and 66 electoral votes. Well, Grant was a colorful figure, except that he was only about five feet six inches tall. And of course the black vote was crucial to his second election. He was elected by an overwhelming majority of the black vote. All the black vote went for him; I think it was something like seven hundred thousand votes. If it had not been for that, he would not have been elected, but those votes fulfilled the objective of old Thad Stevens and the rest of his people. They wanted to keep the Radical Republicans in control of the government of the United States, and they succeeded up to 1877.

But there's no question about the fact that if it hadn't been for the black vote, Grant wouldn't have been elected, and by 1877 the people began to get tired of the Radical Republicans just like they do any organization that stays in too long. Grant thought a little about running for a third term, but the Democrats had gotten control of the Congress in the middle of his second term, which I guess he considered handwriting on the wall, so he quit and even almost admitted that some of the corruption and the bad management was his own fault. "It was my fortune, or misfortune," he said, "to be called to the office of chief executive without any previous political training. Under such circumstances it is but reasonable to admit that errors of judgment must have occurred." Those sentences might even be the most noticeable presidential understatement of the nineteenth century.

The two men who had a try at the office after Grant were Rutherford B. Hayes and Samuel J. Tilden. Tilden was the former governor of New York and had become famous because he was the man who broke up the Tweed Ring, and you can tell how people were beginning to feel about Grant and the Republicans by the fact that, even though Tilden wasn't all that well-known around the country, and Hayes was a handsome fellow with red hair and blue eyes, and had been a popular general in the Civil War, it was Tilden who got a majority in both the general and electoral voting. Tilden got 4,284,265 votes to Hayes's 4,033,295 votes, and as for the electoral margin, Tilden ended up with 203 votes and Hayes received 166. But the Republicans weren't going to give up all that easily, even though they no longer had Grant to do their bidding, so they claimed the electoral votes in Florida, Louisiana, Oregon, and South Carolina, saying that a lot of black men had been prevented from going to the polls and that Hayes would have taken those states if the voting had been on the level. There was some question about whether or not Hayes would accept this interpretation of events, since he was a rigidly moral man who prayed on his knees each morning and sang hymns each night. (He and his wife were also strict teetotalers, which I don't admire all that much because I think a drink now and then is good for some people provided they don't overdo it. His wife was known as Lemonade Lucy because she prohibited liquor at the White House, and Hayes's last official act as president was to ban the sale of liquor at Army bases.) But Hayes looked the other way, and though the Democrats could have objected and demanded a recount or something, Tilden decided not to do this. Tilden was an old bachelor anyhow and never worked very hard, and when the time came for him to make a decision on the dispute, he just said, "Oh, well, there's no use fighting for it. I don't care anything about it, anyhow." Then he repeated Henry Clay's famous statement—he would rather be right than president. Incidentally, I never thought much of that statement. Why not try to be both?

Grant then had one more shot at the presidency himself. He was invited by some foreign governments to tour their countries, and he and Mrs. Grant went on a trip through Europe and Asia that lasted for three years. Everybody liked the glamour of heads of states in those days, and I think Grant visited them all; he met with Queen Victoria and Pope Pius IX and a lot of other people. There were parades and reviews, and he rode a horse and he wore the insignia of a four-star general, which was the highest rank there was in those days, and I think he enjoyed it very much.

The American press covered his trip so enthusiastically that, when the 1880 elections came along, a number of people at the Republican convention thought he'd make a good candidate again. Hayes obviously didn't stand a chance for reelection because the depression had gotten even worse during his administration, and he'd done a number of things that were unpopular even though they might have been good for the country, including withdrawing troops from the South and trying to reform the civil service and get rid of some of the corruption. (One of the things Hayes did was fire Chester A. Arthur from his job as collector of the Port of New York, a political-plum kind of position because the collector controlled about a thousand jobs at the Custom House and also got a very large salary from his share of fees collected. Arthur had been appointed by Grant, and Hayes wanted him out because Hayes was trying to make the civil service totally nonpolitical. But the move was unpopular because Arthur was well-liked, and of course, later became our twenty-first president.) Hayes also said he didn't want a second term anyway, so it looked as if Hayes might be out and Grant back in again, but a deadlock developed between Grant and a man named James G. Blaine, and the nomination finally went to James A. Garfield. It was a sad turn of fate for Garfield, as you know if you remember your history, because he was shot, just four months after taking office, by a disgruntled office-seeker named Charles J. Guiteau, and died, after suffering for eighty more days, on September 19, 1881.

Grant went into business after that, taking his life savings—about $100,000—and opening a Wall Street banking and brokerage firm with a man named Ferdinand Ward, and with one of Grant's sons as a partner in the company. Grant's savings would have been enough to support him in those days, but there's always been some sort of a feeling among some professional military men that the obtaining of a lot of money is the most important thing in a man's life. They graduate as lieutenants and go on through the military setup and they become socially conscious, and being socially conscious, they're very anxious to have the wealth to back it up. You can't really blame them for that; it's the system that causes it, and their salaries are not large enough to support the condition to which they think they're entitled. They're not all that way, of course; there have been a great many who have no ideas in that direction, and I can name two particularly. One of them was Robert E. Lee and the other was George C. Marshall. Marshall certainly doesn't belong in that group, and there are dozens of others who don't, men who were very much interested in the welfare of their country and not their own personal welfare. But Grant was one of those who wanted a lot more money than he had, even though what he had was enough, and this venture was another disaster. Grant didn't know anything about Wall Street and how the Stock Exchange worked in that day, which was wide open and had no regulation whatever, and Ward was a crook. It wasn't long before other people had everything that Grant had and a lot more besides, and Ward went to jail.

Grant then went to work and wrote his memoirs. He was broke now, and he had cancer and knew he had only a short time to live, so he worked on his manuscript every minute he had the strength for it, because he wanted to earn some money to leave for his family's support. He finished his manuscript about a month before he died, and a magazine ran his memoirs in serial form and Mark Twain bought the book rights as a patriotic act and published the memoirs in book form. Twain later delivered $500,000 to the Grant family, which made the family okay, but Twain spent the rest of his life working to pay off the debts he acquired in financing the publication.

FIVE
Harding and Coolidge

BENJAMIN Harrison was our twenty-third president, and he's next on my list. I tend to pair up Benjamin Harrison and Dwight Eisenhower because they're the two presidents I can think of who most preferred laziness to labor. They didn't work at all. Harrison was a general in the Army of the United States and in the Civil War, and he just wanted to retire as a general, just as Eisenhower did. Harrison was the grandson of a former president, of course, William Henry Harrison. But old William Henry Harrison had been in command at the Battle of Tippecanoe and two or three other battles in the Northwest and in the War of 1812, and he insisted on riding to the White House on a white horse and in his uniform and no overcoat on a cold day, and a month later he was dead of pneumonia. Benjamin Harrison was a member of one of the two families that had a family connection with the presidency for two or three generations, the other family being the Adamses, so there was some hope for him, but he got into office and spent his time like a retired general, and the only thing that's remembered about him today is that he had a billion-dollar Congress during his term in office. I don't know what people had said if they had had a $70 billion Congress like today. Anyway, Harrison came into office in 1889, after Cleveland's first term, and then the voters turned Harrison out and put Cleveland in again, and there's not much else you can say about Harrison except that he was president of the United States.

I didn't give much space to Benjamin Harrison, as you see, and I'm not going to give a lot more to Warren Gamaliel Harding. His administration was the most corrupt in our nation's history, and it was a lot worse than Grant's because there's no question about the fact that Grant took no part in the corruption that was going on all around him and received no personal gain from it. I think that's probably also true in the case of Harding, and so do most other people, but it's by no means a certainty.

Harding, like Grant, grew up in Ohio, and he entered the newspaper field as a reporter on the *Democratic Mirror* in Marion with a weekly paycheck of $1 per week. But he was such an outspoken and ardent Republican that he got himself fired, and this turned out to be a good break for him because his next move was to team up with two friends and buy another Marion newspaper, the *Daily Star,* which was dying, for $300. The two friends gave up soon afterwards, but Harding bought them out and turned the paper into a success, and he went on from there into politics, first as a state senator and then in the United States Senate.

Harding really liked his life as a senator in Washington, just as I did, and had no real interest in going any further, again like me. But most of Harding's political career had been masterminded by a lawyer named Harry M. Daugherty, and Daugherty practically scared Harding into trying for the presidency by telling him that he'd never be elected to a second term as senator unless he drew more attention to himself by being talked about as a potential presidential candidate. Harding's career as a senator certainly hadn't been distinguished. As a young man in Ohio, he'd spent a lot of time playing poker and shooting pool, and he did a lot of the same thing as a senator. He was absent at nearly half of the roll calls in the Senate, and when he *was* around to vote, he voted in a way that he hoped would make him popular with other people in his party even when his personal convictions ran the other way. He was a heavy drinker and liked his liquor more than he should have, but he voted for Prohibition because he knew that's the way his buddies wanted him to vote. He was a womanizer even though he was supposedly happily married, and later on whatever was left of his reputation was tarnished further because of it, but he didn't think much of women's intelligence or of their ability as political thinkers. So he didn't really like the idea of women voting, but nevertheless, he voted for it because he knew that would please the people who were important to him politically and socially. And he felt he didn't stand a chance as a presidential candidate, but he tried for it because Daugherty told him to try.

He did poorly in three primaries: he beat General Leonard Wood by a small number of votes in his home state, but lost heavily in Indiana and practically went unnoticed in Montana. That made Harding and a lot of other Republicans sure that the much more sensible candidates would be Wood and Frank Lowden, the popular governor of Illinois. But neither Wood nor Lowden took the nomination after nine ballots at the Republican convention in Chicago, and a number of important Republicans began to think more and more about Harding. He was a very handsome man, he was pretty good at making speeches, and he'd always voted the way his friends and advisors wanted him to vote. But there was one big question, because rumors about his dubious personal life had begun to spread, and Harding was finally called in and asked if there was anything in his personal activities that might emerge and injure his reputation. Harding assured his questioners that there wasn't, and he took the nomination on the tenth ballot with Calvin Coolidge as the vice-presidential candidate.

They were running against two first-rate Democrats, Governor James M. Cox of Ohio and a young fellow named Franklin Delano Roosevelt, who'd been assistant secretary of the navy, but the Republicans won easily and with a bit of irony involved. Despite Harding's only partially hidden indifference toward women everywhere except in the bedroom, it was the first time that women had the right to vote, and far and away the largest percentage of these votes went to Harding and Coolidge—some people said strictly because of Harding's matinee-idol looks. Harding won in every northern state and even in Tennessee at a time when the South was solidly Democratic, receiving 16,152,200 votes to Cox's 9,147,353 and 404 electoral votes to Cox's 127. The 16,000,000+ votes was twice as many as any previous presidential candidate had ever received in an election, and he probably would have received even more except that nearly a million non-Democrat votes went to the Socialist candidate, Eugene V. Debs, who was in prison at the time because he'd opposed our entry into World War I.

But the principal reason for Harding's election, and his landslide victory, I believe, was the fact that Woodrow Wilson, the president before him, had been a great president, and a great president demands great sacrifices and many other things from the people. People just felt that they'd had enough of what was starting to be called, not in a complimentary way, "the Wilson idealism"; and when people elect a weak man to follow a great president, they think maybe they'll have some relief from the pressures they have to go through when a great president is in office. I'll say more about that in my chapter on Wilson, but meanwhile let's leave it that the public was happy when Harding said he'd give us "normalcy," which isn't even a real word. That's what he called it, but that didn't mean a thing. If it meant anything at all, I guess, it meant to go back instead of forward. It meant that we became a sort of isolationist nation, because an evident attempt was made to discredit what Wilson had done in arranging a League of Nations, even though Harding, in his preliminary address, said that he was for the League of Nations. Then he did everything he could to break it up.

Harding's cabinet looked pretty good; it included Herbert Hoover as secretary of commerce, Andrew W. Mellon as secretary of the treasury, Charles Evans Hughes as secretary of state, and Henry Wallace as secretary of agriculture. But it also included a man named Albert B. Fall, a former senator from New Mexico and a fellow who was known as being too friendly with oil and other special interests, as secretary of the interior, and included Harding's special friend Harry M. Daugherty as attorney general. And anyway, the real heart of the government wasn't in the White House so much as it was in a place at 1625 K Street, which was known as the Little Green House, where Harding and his cronies caroused and played poker and started to put together a lot of private deals.

Harding became president in 1921, and the rough stuff started to come out a year later. A man named Jesse Smith, who was one of Harding's poker-playing friends and had the reputation of being the person to see if you wanted a job in government, and was so close to Harding and Daugherty that he once shared an apartment with Daugherty and split the rent and other costs, was suddenly suspected of taking bribes and a lot of other illegalities and was told to get out of the capital. Instead, he let himself into Daugherty's apartment and shot himself to death. Then it became known that the Veterans Bureau had been selling war surplus items at far below cost and value and replacing many of the items at far above cost, and the Bureau's attorney, Charles F. Cramer, another Harding pal who'd bought the President's house when Harding left the Senate, also killed himself. Then the head of the Veterans Bureau, Charles R. Forbes, who was both another poker player at the Little Green House and a Medal of Honor winner in the First World War, was told to resign and in fact to take a nice long vacation in Europe.

Albert Fall's turn was next. Harding was off on a tour of the United States, trying to make speeches that would restore the public's diminishing faith in his administration, when Mrs. Fall came to him and told him that her husband was suspected of accepting bribes for leasing oil fields, fields that were being held in reserve for naval use, to private oil companies. Fall was suspected of taking the bribes because he'd made big and expensive improvements on his properties in New Mexico even though he didn't have any legitimate income other than his salary as secretary of the interior. This was, of course, the start of the Teapot Dome scandal, and Fall was subsequently indicted and arrested along with two oilmen, Harry F. Sinclair and E. L. Doheny, from whom Fall had apparently received nearly a half million dollars in bribes. Fall went to jail and Sinclair and Doheny were acquitted, but Sinclair also went to prison for six months for contempt of court.

Then attention began to be turned toward Harding himself and toward Harry Daugherty, but this was diverted by Harding's unexpected and continuing illness. He was still on his speaking tour and was on his way back from Alaska on July 27, 1923, when he became sick in Seattle from what his doctors thought was indigestion caused by eating too much crabmeat. He got better and went on to San Francisco, but came down with pneumonia there, and again his doctors said he was on his way to recovery when he died suddenly on August 2. He was in bed at the time and his wife was reading to him, and the doctors were divided; some thought that indigestion in Seattle had really been a heart attack that had finally taken him off, and others thought a blood clot might have traveled to Harding's brain. But a rumor began to grow and spread that Harding might even have been poisoned so that he wouldn't testify about some of his present and former buddies, and the doctors finally asked for an autopsy so that it could be determined once and for all if there was any truth in the rumors, though they felt there probably wasn't. Nobody ever found out for sure because Mrs. Harding wouldn't allow the autopsy, and Harding was buried back in Marion, Ohio.

The next year, with Calvin Coolidge now president, Charles R. Forbes, back from Europe, was indicted along with one of the executives of one of the companies he'd favored, John W. Thompson. The charges were bribery and conspiracy, and both men got two years. Then Daugherty, who was still attorney general, was asked why he hadn't had a hand in developing prosecutions against all those poker friends of his, and when he wouldn't appear before a Senate committee or give them any of his records, he was told to resign. Shortly afterwards, he was indicted along with a man named Thomas W. Miller, who had been the Alien Property Custodian. It had been discovered that a German-owned company that had been seized during the war had gotten a $7,000,000 settlement, and it was believed that some top government people had gotten $400,000 of that money to allow the settlement. Daugherty took the Fifth Amendment and refused to testify, but hinted strongly that he was doing this only because he wanted to protect the reputation of the former president and that Harding was also involved. Miller went to jail, but Daugherty got two hung juries in a row and wasn't tried again.

Harding was a man who didn't really understand the responsibilities with which he was faced. I don't enjoy one bit making detrimental remarks about a man who had been president of the United States, but he never did know what the presidency was all about. His work as a senator and as a newspaper publisher just didn't seem to give him any insight into the job. I don't think there's any point in editorializing on the Teapot Dome scandal and the other scandals of the Harding administration, either. They speak for themselves. I'm not going to assess any blame to Harding personally for the scandals, but he didn't seem to know anything about what had happened in the country before he became president, or at least didn't pay much attention to it, and that always means trouble for any president who goes in without any background of the history of the United States. In Harding's case it was both the lack of knowledge of the history that went before him and lack of knowledge of how to use the powers that he had as president. I guess it was lack of knowledge and lack of capacity and lack of interest as well. You can translate that any way you want. He just wasn't interested in anything except setting the country back to what it had been before World War I and having fun with his friends. Anyway, his administration left no lasting damage. At least, I hope not.

Calvin Coolidge took over, of course, when Harding died in office. He was quite a character, and there are a lot of funny stories about him, but I guess pretty nearly the only thing I like about him are those stories. Otherwise, his ideas about being president were exactly in the same line as the president who preceded him. He believed that the less a president did, the better it was for the country, and I don't agree with that at all. He sat with his feet in his desk drawer and did nothing. He just sat there and signed bills when they came up, and vetoed a few, and that's all there was to it. Coolidge didn't think the president ought to interfere in any way with the policies of the legislative branch, and yet the president is the man who makes policy, or should make policy, for the whole country.

Coolidge's entrance into national politics was his decision that the police strike in Boston was against government and they couldn't do it. That was what set him up in the whole thing. This took place in 1919, when the police wanted to form a union and affiliate themselves with the American Federation of Labor, and the mayor of Boston said they couldn't, and the police responded by not showing up for work. As you can imagine, this brought on a lot of looting, and the mayor got into a panic and called Coolidge, who was governor of Massachusetts at the time, and Coolidge sent out the state militia and put a stop to the looting and the strike. I don't think anyone will disagree with the fact that I'm very much prolabor and always have been, but I thought that Coolidge was right in his stand regarding the Boston police back in 1919 and still do. When a man or woman takes the oath to support and defend the government of the United States or any of our governments within the United States, that's his first loyalty. No union or anything else can have anything to do with it. I don't think that a man or woman engaged in civil service or police protection has the right to strike. I don't think anybody has the right to strike against his government, local or federal or anywhere else. The men and women have sworn to protect and defend their government, and that's what they have to do. They have no other loyalty. And it isn't true that civil servants have no protection if they can't strike. That isn't true because they have congressional and other representation that will protect their interests.

In that sense Coolidge's beginning in national politics was as sound as it could be. He represented a viewpoint that the nation approved. And his own state. That's the reason that the Republican Party eventually put him on the ticket as the candidate for vice president.

Coolidge was born in Plymouth Notch, a little village in Vermont, on July 4, 1872. (He was the only president born on Independence Day, but the day had special, and sad, significance for other presidents. Both John Adams and Thomas Jefferson died on July 4, 1826, and James Monroe died on July 4, 1831. In fact, you might say that the whole month of July was a sad one in the history of the American presidency: Zachary Taylor died on July 9, 1850, Martin Van Buren died on July 24, 1862, Andrew Johnson died on July 31, 1875, and Ulysses S. Grant died on July 23, 1885. And as I've mentioned earlier in this book, James A. Garfield was shot by Charles J. Guiteau on July 2, 1881, though he lingered on until September 19, and Warren Gamaliel Harding was first stricken on July 27, 1923, with the illness that carried him off on August 2. But that's all pretty morbid, and let's go back to Coolidge's history.)

Coolidge was born John Calvin Coolidge but didn't like his first name and dropped it early in life. His father was the fairly prosperous owner of the general store in Plymouth Notch, and Coolidge had the ambition to get his education at Amherst, but he failed the entrance examination and had to take a year of study at St. Johnsbury Academy. On his second try, he made it, graduated from Amherst with honors, and then went on to practice law across the state line from Vermont in Northampton, Massachusetts. He entered politics in 1898, serving first on the Northampton City Council and then as city solicitor, then became a member of the state legislature, mayor of Northampton, state senator, lieutenant governor of Massachusetts, and finally governor.

He wasn't an especially outstanding politician: when he was city solicitor, for example, he held the office twice but was defeated when he tried for it a third time, and when he ran for governor in 1918, he was elected but got one of the smallest majorities in Massachusetts's history, under 17,000 votes. But his action on the Boston strike put him on the national map, and Republicans began to think about him at their convention in Chicago in 1920 as a good possibility for the second spot. He wasn't the first choice; the preference was for a man named Irvine L. Lenroot, a senator from Wisconsin. But Coolidge came to the convention as a favorite son of the delegation from Massachusetts, and then a delegate from Oregon nominated Coolidge for the vice-presidential spot, and Coolidge defeated Lenroot 674 to 146 and was elected with Harding.

There's an old joke that the vice president's principal chore is to get up in the morning and ask how the president is feeling, and I guess that's about all Coolidge did when Harding was still alive. And after he became president himself, he didn't do a lot more. He received the news of Harding's death just after midnight, got out of bed and awakened his father so that the senior Coolidge, who was a notary public, could administer the oath of office, and then both men went back to bed. And the new president then pretty much slept through the next six years, earning himself the reputation of the man who got more rest than any previous president.

Congress passed a bill giving bonuses to the veterans of World War I; Coolidge vetoed it, and Congress had to go back to work and override his veto. I remember being angry at Coolidge and happy with the Congress on that one myself. Congress passed another bill increasing pensions for all veterans of all wars, and Coolidge vetoed that one, too, though this time his veto held. Congress passed a bill giving control and management of the big new power plant in the Tennessee Valley to the government, instead of turning it over to private companies as the friends of Big Business wanted, and Coolidge took care of that one with a pocket veto. (A pocket veto is where a president gets a bill within the last ten days of a congressional session and just puts it in a drawer and doesn't do anything at all until Congress adjourns, so that this has the power of a veto without having to do any work to accomplish the veto. That kind of thing must have appealed mightily to Mr. Coolidge, accomplishment without work.)

Then Congress tried to get a bill through that would give some relief to the farmers, who were suffering terribly in a period in which the rest of the country was enjoying prosperity. There was no longer the big demand for food products that had built up during the war years, so prices for farm products kept dropping lower and lower, while at the same time the things that farmers needed to operate, things like farm machinery and fertilizer, remained high because a tariff had been placed on these products during Harding's administration. Farmers by the thousands began to lose their farms to banks when they couldn't meet loans and mortgage payments, so Congress came up with the idea of shipping food goods at low prices to countries that really needed the food, and adding to the monies realized and giving farmers a fair profit with what was called a government "equalization fee." Coolidge, however, vetoed the bill without suggesting anything to be put in its place. Congress tried again the next year, and Coolidge vetoed that one, too.

These weren't actions, of course; they were stopping or canceling actions. Despite this, Coolidge ran for the presidency himself in 1924, after he'd finished Harding's term, and won. He was helped by the fact that the leading Democrats of the period were Governor Alfred E. Smith of New York and William G. McAdoo, the secretary of the treasury in Wilson's cabinet, and Smith was a Catholic, which Americans weren't ready to accept at that point in history, and McAdoo was rumored to have the support of men in the Ku Klux Klan. Coolidge was helped further by the fact that a third party, Theodore Roosevelt's old Progressive Party, had been brought back to life with Senator Robert M. La Follette of Wisconsin as its candidate. In the end, neither Al Smith nor McAdoo got the Democratic nomination; it went, after more than a hundred ballots, to a sort of obscure Virginian, John W. Davis, who'd been our ambassador to Great Britain, and Coolidge beat both Davis and La Follette without much trouble. He got 15,718,211 votes to Davis's 8,285,283 and Bob La Follette's 4,031,289; 382 electoral votes to Davis's 136 and La Follette's puny 13. So he went back to sleep for four more years.

I'm sure everybody remembers or has read about Coolidge's famous statement in 1927, a one-sentence statement, which he handed to reporters when he was on vacation in August of that year in the Black Hills of South Dakota: "I do not choose to run for president in 1928." I think he was always sorry that he made that statement, because he liked to live in the White House; I think he just wanted to be coaxed and was sure that he would be. But all the members of his own party were perfectly willing to take him literally at what he said, and he wasn't renominated. He'd been perceived by his fellow Republicans and by other voters as a man of strength in the police strike, but he wasn't really a man of strength. He just proved to be a man who met a situation when it appeared. But when it came to the point where things had to be done as president, I think that, if he'd been forced to do things, he would have, but he was never forced to do things while he was president. He just relaxed in the office of president and did nothing. Just like our Mr. Eisenhower. And General Grant as president.

Coolidge turned up at the Republican convention in Kansas City all right, still expecting to be coaxed, and talking in a kind of not-too-nice way about Herbert Hoover, who was now the chief contender since Coolidge was supposedly out of the picture, as "that wonder boy." But Hoover got the nomination on the first ballot, and Coolidge went home to Massachusetts and had a heart attack and died four years later, on January 5, 1933. He was not quite sixty-one years old.

As I've said, there are a lot of good stories about Calvin Coolidge, and most of them deal with his dour conservatism, some of which take the form of just plain old stinginess. There's one in particular that I've always remembered about a friend of his from Massachusetts staying all night in the White House, and this friend got up and had breakfast with Mrs. Coolidge and told her that he was a collector of cigar bands, and she told him to go on over and ask Coolidge for a cigar band. Coolidge always went over early to look through the mail and be sure he knew everything that was going on, and when this fellow arrived, he told the President what he wanted. The President took out his cigar box, took the band off one of the cigars, and handed it to the fellow. Then he put the cigar carefully back in the box.

Another time, when Coolidge was governor of Massachusetts, another of his friends came to see him in Boston. They sat and talked awhile, and Coolidge asked him if he would have a drink. He said he would, so Coolidge got out a couple of glasses and a bottle and he poured a drink for both of them and they had it. And they sat there talking after Coolidge had put the bottle and the glasses away. Pretty soon another member of the Coolidge court, as I think they called the fellows surrounding Coolidge up there, came in, and the fellow who'd come in first told the governor that he thought his friend would like to have a drink. Well, Coolidge got out a glass and the bottle and poured him a drink, and the second fellow said, "Doesn't my friend want a drink?" Coolidge said, "No, he's had one."

Coolidge was pretty good at saying things in a few words but making his point at the same time. When he stopped that police strike, he got an angry telegram from the head of the American Federation of Labor, Samuel Gompers, who argued that he wasn't being fair to the police. Coolidge answered with a telegram of his own, but it was only one line long: "There is no right to strike against the public safety by anybody, anywhere, any time." He was appalled by the things going on with the Harding gang, and when he took over the presidency, he gave his orders to prosecutors in a single sentence, too. "Let the guilty be punished," he said. And since he didn't like the idea of giving extensions to the Allied governments on the $10 billion we'd loaned them for rehabilitation after the First World War, he also shook off arguments with a single sentence: "They borrowed the money, didn't they?"*

And then there's the time a man named Rupert Hughes wrote a debunking book on George Washington, and it was reported to Coolidge. He looked around and said, "Well, his monument is still there." That's the best answer to the debunkers. The debunkers of the early twenties showed up because it was a period of cynicism and people wanted something on which they could pin the notion that the greatest of the great were not as great as the historians pretended that they were. The main objective of some of the debunking writers, I suppose, was to give us a truthful approach, but it was overdone like everything else that gets into a groove of that sort.

I know I'm going off on another tangent here, but I just can't help saying that, though freedom of the press is one of the greatest things we have in this country, it's really more abuse of the press than freedom of the press when some writers attack people strictly because gossip and nastiness is more juicy and sells more copies than when nice things and honest things are said about people. I'm referring both to books like that Rupert Hughes book and to some newspapers that are guilty of abuse both for its own sake and because they're pandering to influential advertisers who don't happen to agree with the policies of the current administration. And in fact, I feel so strongly on the subject that I'm going to end this chapter right here and give some space to the press in the next one.

---

*This is a slight misquote; Mr. Coolidge actually said, "They hired the money, didn't they?" But "hired" is an old-fashioned usage, and as I've already reported, my father liked to be strictly up-to-date. MT

SIX

Freedom—or Abuse?— of the Press

THAT sort of thing has been around since the beginnings of our country. Washington set up the United States government so it continued to work, but he had a great many difficulties with it because he was attacked maliciously in the press of his day. If you'll go to the Library of Congress and read what the papers of that day had to say about him, you'll wonder how he continued. Well, he didn't want to continue, and one of the principal reasons he quit at the end of his second term was because the press was so vicious in its treatment of him.

Lincoln was an equally great man, there's no doubt about that, but he wasn't considered a great man by everybody, not by any means, when he was in the White House. At the Gettysburg celebration, Edward Everett, the great man of the day, made a speech for two hours, and Lincoln spoke for about four minutes. He got very little space in the national papers, and the *Chicago Tribune* made the statement as a sort of postscript that the President of the United States also spoke and made the usual ass of himself. Today nobody remembers that Edward Everett, that old preacher, was on that platform, but everybody knows that Lincoln was there, and they think he made the principal address, though he didn't. And the only words that are remembered from that Gettysburg celebration are Lincoln's Gettysburg Address, so that shows how far the papers can be wrong at the time things happen. The newspapers also continually made slurring comments about Lincoln's lack of "decent attire." Well, I think he had decent attire.

Washington was attacked because he was president of the United States. That's customary whenever a fellow is in power; it doesn't make any difference who he is. The establishment of the freedom of the press in this country was a precedent and had just about never been done before anywhere in the world, and some of the editors of the time were small men and went haywire on the subject. They worked it to death and might have been suppressed under other conditions, but Washington and Jefferson believed in a free press.

The press in Revolutionary times was partisan and much more liable to attack people personally even than newspapers are today, and the men in the Continental Congress and in our first government, that great body of men, realized that if they were going to reach agreements and run the country, they had to do it in such a way that they could get things done and then explain to the people exactly what it meant. If the thing had been argued day by day in the press of the country, we wouldn't have had any Constitution or any country.

The Constitutional Convention had a good situation in which to work because the men who were discussing things weren't afraid that they were going to have their hides torn off by some smart aleck newspaperman. I mean that for just what it says because that's what we have today, and any committee in Congress right now, today, that doesn't work with the same attitude as the Constitutional Convention never gets anything done. Otherwise, the members of the committee are always posing for television and looking out of the corners of their eyes to see what people think of them back home, and you can't do that. A fellow in government's got to have a viewpoint for the welfare and benefit of the whole country, and at the present time, for the whole world. And if he gets to posing for television or a radio set or a bunch of newspapermen, it just can't be done. Those fellows in Revolutionary days knew what they were doing, and they had a chance to discuss openly exactly what they thought and give the other people a chance to do the same thing, and then they got together with the best out of both arguments. Their purpose was to get things done rather than to try to set up a publicity stunt for the people.

We're supposed to have a free press today, and I guess we do in many ways, which is wonderful because, if you have a free press, there's no way in the world for anyone to get by with the subversion of the country. It's also very good because sometimes newspapers dig up things that ought to be dug up, crookedness on the part of public officials and other things like that, and the newspapers make a great stir about those things and they're usually corrected. You take Horace Greeley, James Gordon Bennett, and old man Dana, Charles A. Dana—they were as mean as they could be in their papers now and then, but they made a real contribution to the freedom of the press. But the press today really isn't free in some ways, not really. The press in early times was more personal; editors owned their papers and were responsible for them and sometimes got shot for things they said about people (not that I'm advocating that, you understand). Today the press isn't the individual editor's press that it was in times past; it's a publisher's press, a commercial proposition that sells advertising on the basis of circulation, and any approach that will increase the circulation for the purpose of increasing the advertising income of the paper is the fundamental concern. And there are very few newspapers in the country, even most of the so-called great ones, where the editorial policy is carried on by the editor. A lot of them even hire columnists on both sides of the fence, and you can never tell what they stand for. But most of the time, the policy of the paper is set by the publisher, and he sets his policy either to please his advertisers, the special interests who are his real customers, or to say things that will sell more papers.

One of the favorite methods of selling more papers is to abuse the current president even if he hasn't done anything wrong. Just about every president has been roundly abused by the press in recent times. And when you take the top man in a great republic and throw bricks at him, you know the people are going to buy the papers and read them, and you can sell more advertising. That's principally what's behind the publishers' attitudes. I don't think any of them have any serious principles that they want to enforce. I don't mind at all when a publisher says something in his paper that he obviously truly believes; publishers have their right to their opinions as any other part of the population has. But that's rare. The press always claim that they're on the side of the people, but they're really on the side of the people who support them, and that's usually the advertisers, so what we have isn't exactly a free press.

But every president who does anything has that sort of experience, and as you'll see by Washington's and Lincoln's history, they didn't lose anything by the attacks of the press. And no man who's in a place of responsibility can pay any attention to what the editors of the papers have to say about him, because if he does, he'll never have a policy and he can't continue it. Those presidents who knuckle down to the press usually wind up being just ordinary presidents or worse, and we've had too many of them like that. A good president just can't pay any attention when the press tries to abuse him; the papers often abuse him when he's right because they believe—wrongly—that he ought to do something else, and if he knows he's right and goes ahead with it, things work out and it doesn't matter how much they've abused him. Or, as I say, they've abused him just to sell papers, and he certainly shouldn't pay any attention to *that*.

It's hard, I suppose, to define what a free press really is. In the old days, I guess, from about 1840 or 1850 to about 1890, the papers were operated by the editors who wrote the editorials (they didn't hire people to write them like they do today), and they had their own opinions and they fought each other as much as they fought the government. Well, that was free press. Today—well, the country press in Missouri and Kansas and Iowa and places like that, where there are still small-town newspapers, that's the free press right now. The editors own their papers, they have their own opinions just as the old-time editors did, and they have the right to express them. The metropolitan press is a different proposition entirely. The great publishers control that press and they're in cahoots with their friends and advertisers, other special-interest types like themselves, to make sure that people see what they think they ought to see, instead of giving them a complete set of the news.

There are only a few papers in the country that give unedited news to their customers: the *New York Times* and the *Washington Star* are the best examples of that that come to mind. Well, of course, they sometimes get mixed up too much in politics, and then they're progaganda sheets just like any other paper. But it doesn't really matter; it's been shown somewhere that in presidential elections, the recommendations of the press as a whole have been disregarded by the voters more than 60 percent of the time. That's because the people don't really trust the press. The great metropolitan papers think they can fool people by propaganda, but they don't fool them, as that 60-percent statistic proves conclusively. One of the ways to avoid being fooled, incidentally, is to read the back pages of the papers. The prejudices of the publishers often appear on the front page and in headlines, and sometimes in garbled news, but if you turn the paper over and read the back pages, then you'll often find out what really goes on. Of course, I'm probably a little prejudiced about all this myself, but I really do feel that big city newspaper publishers have abused the ability they have to give people ideas, when they set their presses to work. And though one of the things that's brought publishers somewhat under control has been radio and television, where there's a freer approach, that's gradually being controlled by the same outfits.

Editors and publishers don't really know a heck of a lot of politics when you get right down to it, anyway. One of the most vivid examples of what happens to editors when they get into politics is Horace Greeley. He was nominated by the Republicans and he was endorsed by some

Democrats and he made a campaign for president in 1872, and he was thoroughly and completely whipped, and after that was over he lived around three months and laid down and died. He couldn't take it. I think that's what would happen to most editors and publishers if they'd get into politics.

The good thing, anyway, is that most presidents don't really care what the newspapers say about them. Lincoln certainly didn't. I don't think he paid a great deal of attention to the press at all. I ran across one of his statements one time about a vicious editorial that had been written about him one time by, I think, James Gordon Bennett, and somebody asked him about it, one of the other newspaper people. He said, "Oh, well, if I spent my time fooling with things of that kind, and trying to reply to every lie that's told about me, I wouldn't have a chance to run the government." That's not his exact language, but it expresses his relations with the press.

And though I'm not trying to compare myself with Lincoln in any way, that's precisely how I feel. I used to read as many critical editorials as the other kind. Sometimes I had to get up early and go over and see the papers myself because my staff were sometimes ashamed to show me some of the mean things that were said about me. It didn't bother me. When the newspapers are against any man in public life, it's an asset in most instances, because in the long run it'll be shown that they had an unfair prejudice. It doesn't bother any man in office who wants to do the right thing. He goes ahead and does it no matter what the newspapers may say. I never cared anything about what they said about me as long as they didn't jump on my family. If they did that, then they got in trouble.

SEVEN

Eisenhower and Generals as Presidents

WELL, I didn't mean to go on so long about the press in the last chapter, but I read newspapers a lot and do a certain amount of thinking about them. My favorite bit of newspaper reading, of course, is that one with the famous headline saying DEWEY DEFEATS TRUMAN.

We come now to the final president in my no-enthusiasm category, Dwight David Eisenhower, and I've sprinkled enough comments throughout the pages before this one so that you know that I'm not one of Eisenhower's admirers. I'm sure he has some, perhaps many, though for the life of me I can't tell you why.

I guess I've also made it clear that I just don't think military men make good presidents, though I'm not entirely clear on why I feel that way, either. It's not that I see any real danger in a military man becoming president, because I don't. With our Constitution and its built-in limitations, and our system of checks and balances, we never hesitate to get rid of a bad man, or have any trouble doing it when the time comes. I suppose my reason, as much as anything, is that history has proven that professional military men have trouble in running a free government, because a military man is used to being a sort of dictator in his military job. The occupant of the White House after me understood this himself, and he once wrote a letter to that old fellow who had that newspaper in Manchester, New Hampshire, Leonard Finder, that said the thing more clearly than almost anybody else has ever done. This was when Eisenhower was saying over and over again that he'd never run for president, before he turned around and ran, and he told Finder, "I could not accept nomination even under the remote possibility that it would be tendered me." Then he explained, "The necessary and wise subordination of the military to civil power will best be sustained when lifelong professional soldiers abstain from seeking high political office."

The thing, you see, is that the professional soldier is educated in an institution that creates the idea that an officer in the Army is better than the private, the corporal, and the sergeant, and when he becomes the chief executive, he can't get it out of his mind that he's way above everybody else in intelligence and character and everything. He thinks the whole civilian population is inferior to him, when in fact they're his equals and maybe better. You don't have to have any special quality being an officer. Not necessarily.

The other thing wrong with the professional soldier as president is that he doesn't have any experience with the problems we civilians have throughout our lives because he's pretty much protected as a military man. And the president of the United States is a man who should be able to understand what the ordinary, common man thinks about and worries about. A military man can't do that. (I'm referring to professional military men. Not men of military experience, just professional military men who've spent their lives as military men or retired as generals. That's where the difficulty lies.) I wouldn't, you understand, exclude any environment or background as a possible source of a good future president. Not even the military. I just don't think most of them have made or would make good presidents.

But they certainly make attractive candidates. The fact that people elected Grant, and then reelected him after a terrible first administration, and then almost elected him a third time after an even worse second administration, is a simple example of hero worship. All the people, no matter where they come from, like a winner, like a hero. That's worked nearly all the way through the history of our government. Jackson was a hero at the Battle of New Orleans. He won the only battle that was won in the War of 1812 and became the most popular man of his time —North, South, East, and West. Even Harvard had to confer a degree on him whether they wanted to or not. That was true of nearly every one of these generals except Winfield Scott. He was called Old Fuss and

Feathers and he was kind of a strutter, so people weren't too crazy about him for that reason. The hero of the Mexican War was Zachary Taylor, because he was an ordinary, everyday fellow like everybody else, and yet he won the Battle of Buena Vista and one or two others. The same was true of Sam Houston in Texas. He won the Battle of San Jacinto with less than half the people that Santa Anna had at the battle. He was a hero and continued to be a hero until he was against secession in Texas, and then they almost hanged him for that.

Well, the same thing was true of General Grant. He was a hero of the War Between the States. He was in at the surrender of Lee and he caused the opening of the Mississippi River, and he turned out to be a great field general, and that's the reason he was so well thought of. You'll find that there were a great many other generals who were well thought of at the time. There was a great big old six-footer who was in command of the XI Corps in Gettysburg, General Winfield Scott Hancock—I wouldn't be surprised if he was named after Winfield Scott—and he was so popular that he was nominated on the Democratic ticket in 1880, but the fellow who ran against him had also been a major general in the Federal army, Garfield, and they elected Garfield instead. I think Hancock was six feet four inches tall and weighed 230 pounds. He was one of the finest-looking men in the United States, but he was just a lazy, fat man. He didn't make any effort to win but he came very near to it.

In 1888, it was Benjamin Harrison, you'll recall, who beat Grover Cleveland for reelection, and Harrison was also a major general in the Federal army. They charged that Grover Cleveland didn't go to war because he paid some other fellow to go for him, though whether he did or not I don't know. It goes to show how far glamour and how far a military record can carry a man. William McKinley was a major in the Civil War. He was elected as Major McKinley on the Republican ticket. It isn't necessarily confined to the United States of America, either. Old Lord Wellington was made prime minister on the grounds of winning the Battle of Waterloo, and he was a perfect dumbbell when it came to government administration. Napoleon III was put on the throne of France because he knew how to wear his uniform and because they thought he looked like the real Napoleon. It's no different today; many people still like that kind of glamour. I can't answer that question of why that's so, but I know it's true. I know absolutely that a military career, no matter on what small basis it stands, is the best asset a man can have if he wants to be elected to office in the United States of America, anything from constable to president.

There have been exceptions to that attitude, of course. There was nothing more thoroughly looked down on by many people than an old soldier, for example, from about 1886 until about 1900, when the Spanish-

American War came along. I've heard my mother and father talk about the old Bluecoats and the old Fuzz and Gray, and how they were stealing from the Treasury as long as they lived. That's an attitude people sometimes take, but when the emergency comes along, then there's nothing too good for a man in uniform. Then people feel that the military was willing to be shot and didn't mind going up and standing between us and what was coming. I know, having been a private and a corporal and a sergeant and a captain, but the truth is that, in present times, the most dangerous place that a man can be is behind the lines and not in front of them. But a military man still has a lot of glamour.

Fortunately, we've had some pretty good men with military backgrounds. One of the greatest of the great presidents, George Washington, was a field general, and he set up the government and knew how to make it run. Jackson was another one who was a field general and knew how to make the government run, who was a chief executive in fact as well as in name. I even think it helps to have *some* military background, because a president is also the commander in chief and he ought to have a certain amount of knowledge of how the military works. I had very little. I was only a captain in the First World War, but I'd studied the military from start to finish and knew something about it, and it helped. But there were so many military men like Grant, men who were perfectly willing to fill chairs and let the Congress run the government if the Congress wanted to run the government—and sometimes the Congress did and sometimes the Congress didn't. The bad presidents weren't intending to do damage to the structure of the government. I don't think Grant, for example, intentionally tried to do what was wrong, but he didn't intentionally try to do what was right, either. He was just unsuited for the job, and inept. And that's my opinion of the man we've just elected twice.

Eisenhower's personal history is recent enough so that I'm sure everybody knows it, at least in broad outline, but I'll just sketch it in anyway since I'm doing that for other presidents in this book. His family were Kansas people, but Eisenhower himself was born in Denison, Texas, on October 14, 1890; his father had been working in a general store in Hope, Kansas, but the store failed and the elder Eisenhower was offered a job in Denison and moved where the work was. He was given the name of David Dwight Eisenhower, but switched the first two names around early in life to avoid confusion because his father was also named David. Eisenhower was one of six brothers; a seventh brother died in infancy. All six of the Eisenhower boys were nicknamed Ike when they were kids, but the name stuck only with the man who followed me into the White House.

When Eisenhower was two years old, his father got a better job in a dairy in Abilene, Kansas, and moved back there, and that's where Eisenhower grew up. He graduated from high school but couldn't afford to go to college, so he went to work at the dairy alongside his father for about a year. He had no thoughts in his early life about becoming a soldier; what he really wanted was a good general education. In fact, he became a soldier entirely by accident. He heard about the chance for a college education without cost; examinations were being given in Topeka for entry into Annapolis, so he applied quickly and might have ended up as a sailor. Which would have been a sad turn of events for the country, because our army was the somewhat more important factor in World War II than the navy, and there's no question about the fact that Eisenhower was one hell of a good soldier. On the other hand, we wouldn't have ended up with eight years of a mediocre presidency, either, because I doubt that he would have been elected president, or even suggested as a candidate, if he'd been an admiral in the war. We've never had an admiral for a president, of course. I don't know why, but I guess it's because we've never had an admiral who was glamorous enough to get himself nominated for president. And I guess it's also because the people didn't understand sea power until the last two or three administrations, and then, finally, they began to find out what it was all about, and also because people don't really think about us as a sea power the way the world used to think of England. We tried to flaunt our sea power all the way back in the War of 1812, and we got licked—there was only one victory in the whole war, and that was Andrew Jackson at New Orleans—but even now, with our position on the seas very different indeed, I don't think there'll be an admiral in the White House in the near future.

Anyway, it didn't matter, because, when Eisenhower got to Topeka, he found out that the test was for both Annapolis and West Point. He passed the test, but since he was over twenty years old at the time, he was told that he was over the entrance age for Annapolis, and he was sent to West Point. He was just an okay student: he graduated 61st in a class of 168 men in 1915. And he went on to appear to be just an okay soldier. He spent World War I at training camps in this country teaching soldiers how to use tanks, even though there weren't any tanks at the camps and he had to work out of a textbook, and he spent the years between the wars in Panama and in the Philippines working with the Philippine Air Force and in other jobs like that. Eisenhower's importance as a commander began to show up when we entered the war in 1941. He was a brigadier general by this time, in charge of the Third Army in Texas, and General George Marshall called him to Washington to work at the War Department because of his knowledge of the Pacific theater. He was so good at what he did there that General Marshall gave him the important assignment of setting up the plans for a second front in France, and then sent him there personally to run the European Theater of Operations. As everybody knows, he did a wonderful job, and President Roosevelt made him supreme commander of all the allied forces. And after the war, I used him myself when I was organizing the Department of Defense and working on my plan to put all of the armed forces under one command; and when he quit the Army in 1948 to become president of Columbia University, I asked him to come back into service in 1950 as supreme commander of NATO. But then that fellow Dewey, Governor Thomas E. Dewey of New York, the fellow who beat me for president back in 1948 according to the *Chicago Tribune*, began to push Eisenhower hard to run for president on the Republican ticket, and that's the sad part of the Eisenhower story in my view. It wasn't a new idea, of course; a lot of people thought he'd taken the job at Columbia as a step toward the presidency, to show people that there were more sides to him than just a one-note soldier, and he was so well liked by people that important people in both major parties were mentioning him often as a presidential possibility. But Eisenhower kept saying over and over again that he just wasn't interested, and even his personal preferences were sort of like at Topeka, where he could have ended up as either a sailor or a soldier; nobody even knew whether he was a Republican or a Democrat because he just wouldn't say, and there's doubt in my mind, and in the minds of a lot of other people, if he ever went to the polls in his life before 1952 and voted for anybody in either party. But Dewey obviously convinced him that he was a Republican and that he ought to run, and he did and won 33,936,234 votes to Adlai Stevenson's 27,314,992 and 442 electoral votes to 89.

It wasn't much of a contest from the start. Adlai Stevenson was an extremely intelligent and capable man, and his grandfather had been vice president in Grover Cleveland's second term, but he wasn't all that well-known outside of Illinois, where he'd been governor, even though he'd also served in Washington in a number of important jobs. He was also being damned regularly by the Republicans—and, I've got to admit with regret, by a lot of Democrats as well—as being that truly terrible thing, an intellectual. I liked him a lot, and I believe I was primarily responsible for convincing him to make the run for the presidency, and I also had a lot to do with convincing Governor Averell Harriman of New York to drop out after the second ballot at the Democratic convention and turn over the New York delegation to Stevenson. But he didn't really have a chance against the man who was quite properly the great hero of the people after World War II, and he was beaten even more strongly when he ran again against Eisenhower in 1956—35,590,472 to 26,022,752 and 457 to 73 electoral votes.

EIGHT

Why I Don't Like Ike

I tried very hard to make the transition smooth and efficient. The objective I had in view, of course, was to avoid the confusion that occurs when one man comes in and another goes out. About a week after the election, I called Eisenhower and invited him to come over and sit with the cabinet, and I had each member of the cabinet report exactly what was going on and what had to be done. I also invited the President-Elect to send his budget directly to the White House, because I had to make up my last budget, with which he'd be associated. I also asked him to send over his prospective secretary of state, prospective secretary of defense, and all the rest of his cabinet, so that they could have their programs and approaches coordinated with my cabinet members, and to send in his people who were going to work in the White House so that they could be shown the various programs that had been followed and the functions of all the various people who were already there.

For the most part, it worked very well. The only time it didn't work at all is when Eisenhower asked if he could also send over Sherman

Adams, whom Eisenhower described as his personal assistant, the man who would be taking over the White House staff, but who later became so powerful and threw his weight around so much that a lot of people began to refer to him privately as the president in chief. (I'm sure everybody also remembers that, in 1958, Adams also got into trouble because he allowed a Boston industrialist, who had problems at the time with both the Securities and Exchange Commission and the Federal Trade Commission, to pay substantial hotel bills for Adams and his family, and for accepting a lot of big gifts from people, and Adams was forced to resign.) I turned Adams over to John Steelman, whose title was assistant to the president, and told Adams that he could find out exactly how things worked from Steelman. But Adams tried to take immediate charge. He actually wanted to take over! He didn't offer to function for me administratively; he tried to take over my administrative staff immediately and tell them what to do, and I called him in and told him he couldn't do that and that's all there was to it. I told him that I was still the President until the twentieth and he was there on sufferance to find out what he had to do when his time came, and that's all he was there for. And I said that if he wanted to find out what went on, all right, but if he didn't, then he could go out and sit down in the middle of Pennsylvania Avenue as far as I was concerned.

I guess it also didn't work too well with the man Eisenhower appointed as secretary of defense, Charles E. Wilson. Wilson had been the chairman of the board of General Motors, and I suppose that made him think that job gave him more knowledge than anyone else under the sun about everything. Wilson was briefed and told exactly what the situations were all around the world and what he had to do. Every outgoing president, of course, has certain projects in view at the end of his administration, and he's more in a position then to have good ideas about how to carry things out, for the simple reason that he's had the experience of being president and he's had the opportunity to observe and think about everything that's taken place. And naturally there are things that he'd like to see carried out but hasn't been able to accomplish or complete by the end of his term.

At the end of my term, there wasn't really anything, I'd say, of particularly strong importance except our positions and relationships in foreign affairs, in which I was vitally interested. For this reason, I felt that Wilson was of particular importance. But Wilson thought he knew more than the fellow who was briefing him, even though he hadn't even begun work on the job and my secretary of defense happened to be Robert M. Lovett, who was also a major industrialist and the head of a great bank. And that was that. For the most part, however, my invitations to Eisenhower and his people worked well. New cabinet members often have trouble taking over. But being briefed as they were, and being allowed to sit with the members of my cabinet and seeing what their functions were, Eisenhower's people didn't have any trouble. It was the first time in the history of the country that these things had ever been done, and it was the most orderly turnover in the history of the White House.

Even if I say so myself, I tried so hard to be pleasant and cooperative when I was turning the office over to Eisenhower, but he acted as if I were his enemy instead of the fellow who'd had the job just before him. I had a meeting with him right after he was elected and offered him some pictures that had been given to me by several governments, and he told me to keep them because he was sure those governments would give the new president new pictures. I offered him the globe map I used at the White House, one he'd used during the war and given to me when I saw him in Frankfurt before going on to Potsdam in 1945, and he took it but didn't even say thanks. But he was saving his worst behavior for the inauguration.

It's been the custom right from the beginning of this country that the new president comes over and picks up the outgoing president and takes him to the inauguration, but Eisenhower said he wouldn't do that; he wanted me to come over to his hotel, the Statler, and get *him*. Well, I wouldn't do it, of course. There have been only two times when a president didn't show the established courtesies to the former president: one was when John Adams behaved like a damn fool and sneaked out with Mrs. Adams at midnight so he wouldn't have to make a turnover to Jefferson, because he didn't like Jefferson and was jealous of him as well, and the other time was when Roosevelt didn't go up the stairs with Hoover—and that time wasn't discourtesy at all, but because Roosevelt was paralyzed and couldn't climb stairs.

So I wouldn't do it, and I said Eisenhower would have to come and get me the way every other new president had, and he finally, grudgingly, agreed. But he showed up at the White House and wouldn't get out of the car; he sat there as if he were carved out of stone, and I finally went down and got into the car, and we didn't talk much to each other on the trip. You get disgusted sometimes, and I certainly did, when a man has a chance to make an orderly and pleasant transfer and doesn't have sense enough to do it. But that's a reflection on my successor. It's interesting that a single thing, that great smile of Eisenhower's, gave him the worldwide and life-long reputation of being a sunny and amiable man, when those of us who knew him well were all too well aware that he was essentially a surly, angry, and disagreeable man, and I don't just mean to me, either.

None of that is important, of course; the important thing is that he didn't do a thing as president. Perhaps the people who talked Eisenhower into running for president knew this in advance; perhaps they knew Eisenhower would do nothing but look good up there. If they did suspect this, or possibly even planned it that way, I'm sure their thought was that that would accomplish getting the Democrats out of the highest office, and then the Republicans would also control the Congress, and the Congress would do all the work that's always needed, and Republican policies would be the order of the day. But it didn't turn out that way. For one thing, Eisenhower's personal popularity, the halo he wore from 1952 to 1960, didn't extend to the rest of the party. In the midterm elections in 1954, the Democrats took control of both the House and the Senate, and in 1956, when Eisenhower ran for the second time, the voters put Eisenhower right back in office but again elected more Democratic senators and representatives than Republicans.

And for another thing, it just doesn't work like that. It just isn't the case that when, as I believe Eisenhower did, a president thinks that he's a kind of monarch or king who should be above everything that happens in the world and in the country, the Congress will do all the work. That's bad not only for the presidency; it's bad for the country and the world. The chief executive has to transact the business of the country: he has to provide leadership, and he has to have a program and the guts and ability to put it over. And Eisenhower never made any effort to put forward the leadership to which he was entitled, and he didn't have any program.

I'll list some of the things Eisenhower didn't do when he was supposed to be performing the job of president and running the country:

In July 1955, a meeting was arranged in Geneva between Eisenhower, the leaders of Great Britain and France, and three important Russians, Nikolai Bulganin, the premier of Russia, Nikita Khrushchev, the head of the Communist Party, and Georgi Zhukov, Russia's defense minister. The word was that Eisenhower was going to arrange for world disarmament, at least in a limited way, arrange for the unification of the two Germanys, and ease the Cold War tensions between the United States and Russia, which had been growing for years. Eisenhower was also going to push a good idea that wasn't his own, of course, but had been suggested by Nelson Rockefeller and some other people: an open-skies agreement that would allow the nations at the conference to fly freely and do photographic reconnaissance freely over the other countries so that the countries involved could make sure that armament, and any agreed disarmament, was kept within promised limitations. However, there was no agreement on disarmament; there was no decrease in Cold War tensions; there was no unification of the two halves of Germany; and the open-skies agreement never happened.

On October 23, 1956, there was a revolution in Hungary, which the Russians had taken over by killing the head of the government, Imre Nagy, and thousands of other people, and the Hungarian people appealed to the United States for help. Eisenhower ignored the plea completely, and Russian tanks rolled into Hungary and killed many more people and the revolution was soon over. And the United States began to get a reputation for turning its back on its friends.

A few months before that, a serious disagreement developed between the United States and Egypt. The United States had promised Egypt a loan of $70,000,000 so that Egypt could build a dam at Aswan, on the Nile, but some of Eisenhower's people didn't care much for Gamal Abdel Nasser, and we suddenly and unexpectedly canceled the loan. Nasser was furious and announced that he was nationalizing the Suez Canal, which in turn infuriated Great Britain, France, and Israel, which needed free movement on the Canal for oil supplies, and in the case of the first two countries, also needed free movement on the Canal because of their dependencies in the Pacific and elsewhere. The three countries asked the United States for help, hinting that it had, after all, been this country that had started the thing by making a promise and then breaking it.

Eisenhower ignored this plea, too, and Great Britain, France, and Israel invaded Egypt. All that Eisenhower did about that was to join Russia in a cease-fire resolution at the United Nations, which, of course, Great Britain and France vetoed immediately. The three countries eventually left Egypt after Eisenhower's secretary of state, John Foster Dulles, assured them that he'd guarantee free access to the Canal. Nasser came through on this for Great Britain and France but not for Israel, a fact that Eisenhower and Dulles also ignored. I'd recognized Israel immediately as a sovereign nation when the British left Palestine in 1948, and I did so against the advice of my own secretary of state, George Marshall, who was afraid that the Arabs wouldn't like it. This was one of the few errors of judgment made by that great and wonderful man, but I felt that Israel deserved to be recognized and didn't give a damn whether the Arabs liked it or not. So as you can imagine, I wasn't very happy about what amounted to a double cross of the Israelis by Eisenhower and that stuffed-shirt Dulles.

I'll just mention one more situation where Eisenhower looked out of the window or played golf or read one of those Westerns by Luke Short he was always reading when he should have been taking decisive action on behalf of the country and perhaps the world. And that situation is, as you might have guessed, when Fidel Castro took over Cuba in 1958.

I was interviewed a while ago by a young fellow who was putting together a television show, and he asked me what I thought about Eisenhower's nonaction on Castro. I didn't mince words then and I'm not going to mince words on that subject in this book. I told that young man that nonaction was characteristic of Eisenhower as president because he'd proved to be such a dumb son of a bitch when he got out of his uniform, and that one of the dumbest things that happened during his administration was ignoring Castro when there was a good chance—and I'm certain there *was* a good chance—to get him on our side rather than Russia's.

I said that if I'd still been president when Castro started that revolution against Batista and won, I'd have picked up the phone and made friends with him, offered him financial aid and other kinds of help in getting Cuba on its feet. I don't think for a minute that Castro was a locked-in pro-Russian at that point; I think he turned toward Russia because when he looked at us, all he could see was a bunch of backs turned away from him. I'd have said, "Listen, Fidel, come on down here to Washington and let's talk." Maybe I'd have hinted that it would be nice if he took a haircut and a good shower before he came, but speaking seriously, I'd have seen to it that we had a sensible meeting and worked things out, and we wouldn't be worrying ever since that time about what's being cooked up between the Cubans and the Russians on that island just ninety miles away from Florida.

But as I said to that young television fellow, all that Eisenhower did was sit on his behind and hope that if he didn't seem to notice Castro and the other Cuban revolutionaries, they might go away, and naturally the Russians didn't sit on their behind and they got Castro nice and deep in their pockets. Good old Ike Eisenhower was probably sitting there waiting for a staff report from one of his people that would tell him what he ought to think, something he could look at with one eye and initial and buck over to somebody else. Maybe he's still waiting for it as I write these words.

Those were some of the do-nothing things in the Eisenhower administration. Now, let's take a look at some of the things that did happen while Eisenhower was president, usually instances where Eisenhower followed the advice or instructions of his people, and see how they reflect on the man.

Eisenhower got a big boost to his reputation, and undoubtedly a lot of votes in November of 1952, because he promised to go to Korea if he was elected president and end the war there. He did go, of course, and the war, thank the Lord, did end in Korea—but was that campaign promise a decent and honorable thing to do, and did his trip have much to do with ending the war? In my view, the answer is no, emphatically no, to both questions. On the question of whether it was a decent thing to do, or the opposite, I'll remind people that I was furious about the promise because, as I said at the time, if Eisenhower really had a solution to the Korean War, it was his responsibility to tell it to me, and to the American public, right then and there, so that not a single day would be wasted, and not a single additional life would be lost, before it was put into operation.

I asked Eisenhower why he hadn't suggested his solution to the Korean War when he was one of my advisors, pointing out that if he felt he knew a way to end the war when he was elected president, we could and should do it now and save a lot of lives. He didn't respond because, of course, there was no solution; it was just a grandstand play. He went to Korea in December, and the shooting war dragged on for six months after that, with the armistice being signed in Panmunjom on July 27.

And as for whether or not Eisenhower's trip had anything to do with the eventual armistice—well, since I'm obviously a prejudiced party here, I'll quote from a book I admire, a book I think everybody admires because it's so open-minded that I don't believe anybody could ever accuse it of prejudice, Allan Nevins and Henry Steele Commager's *A Pocket History of the United States:* "Eisenhower had promised during the campaign that he would halt the cruel, grinding Korean War. The task was made the easier by Stalin's death, and by Chinese war-weariness. But positive administration steps contributed to the declaration of a truce. The administration let the Communists know, through Prime Minister Nehru of India, that if the conflict did not soon end, UN forces would begin bombing Chinese supply lines. In other words, Eisenhower and Dulles were ready to make tactical use of atomic weapons in China proper, even at the risk of bringing Russia into the struggle and opening a third world war!" The exclamation point is Mr. Nevins and Mr. Commager's. I would have used ten exclamation points. Then the writers continue and conclude: "At this point the Chinese government yielded; perhaps because it really wanted a truce, perhaps because the new government in Moscow after the end of Stalin's blindly bellicose regime brought pressure upon Peiping, perhaps because Nehru's influence counted. . . . The truce was supposed to be followed at once by a political conference, a treaty, and a permanent peace, but these proved a mirage. The world got an end to fighting, but it did not get a settlement, and Korea did not gain unity. . . . When in 1954 a conference of nineteen nations met in Geneva . . . it resulted rather in losses than gains for the free world. Korea was shoved aside; agreement there was impossible . . .''

I'll add only that I feel that even these comments give the Eisenhower administration more credit than deserved; I believe that the time had come where the people fighting in the Korean War were ready for an armistice no matter who was president, and without the brinkmanship of atomic threats at a point in history when the Russians also had atomic weapons. Anyway, that's my view of Eisenhower and his advisors' cynical use of a terrible war situation for political purposes.*

Eisenhower also allowed his party and his advisors to make a man like Richard Milhous Nixon his vice president. That speaks so much for itself that I won't even comment further.

Another thing Eisenhower did was to allow the clock to be turned back so that there were giveaways of natural resources and essential natural properties, practices that almost totally destroyed many of the things Franklin Roosevelt and I had worked so hard to achieve. During my administration, the Supreme Court ruled that tideland oil resources, the deposits off the coasts of California, Texas, and Louisiana, were the property of the federal government, and I'd given them to the navy as a reserve, filling a need I felt was essential to our defense. The Eisenhower administration gave these to the states for transfer to private companies. I worked hard to support the Tennessee Valley Authority, and Eisenhower and his people cut TVA appropriations and turned hydroelectric development back to private companies. Eisenhower also gave federal grazing lands back to private firms. His people also threw out controls over natural gas, so that companies wouldn't have to worry about or be subject to federal regulations. And one of the few bills vetoed by Eisenhower during his presidency was a bill allowing the government to keep an eye on pollution of rivers by industrial waste.

As you can probably tell from some of these examples, there were really two basic things wrong with Eisenhower and his administration. One was that a major motivation in some of the things Eisenhower and his people did, or conversely, avoided doing, was to discredit the previous two administrations—rather than deciding on doing or not doing something on the basis of whether it was good or bad for the American people. When I was succeeded by Eisenhower, the simple fact is that a very serious attempt was made to reverse some of the basic policies established during my administration and Roosevelt's, and for no good reason—just the fact that we were Democrats and now a Republican was president.

---

*I described my father's reactions to the campaign promise in my own book, *Harry S. Truman,* published in 1973:

". . . Candidate Eisenhower let one of his speech writers put into his mouth words that completely infuriated my father. In a speech in Detroit, Ike announced he would 'go to Korea in person and put an end to the fighting.' As politics, it was a masterstroke. It was exactly what millions of Americans, unhappy and worried about the deadlock in Korea, wanted to hear. As a realistic policy it was a blatant lie. Equally famous was his promise that he would overnight arrange things so that the South Koreans would do all the fighting, and our troops could go home. 'While he is on the back platform of his train, holding out his glowing hope,' my father said angrily, 'his staff are in the press car pointing out to reporters that he has not said *when* he can do this. And he knows very well he can't do it without surrendering Korea—until the present Korean conflict is at an end.'' MT

Nobody had any reason to believe that Eisenhower, who had been through a lot of the programs with President Roosevelt and General Marshall and me, would attempt to reverse things and kill things just for the sake of discrediting us, but that's exactly what happened. And behavior like that is not just the result of political differences; it arises out of nothing more or less than boneheaded foolishness. It was just a program to make the fellows who preceded him look bad, and I don't think that's the right attitude for a president to have when he takes over the office. Any man who has been president, whether you like him or not, has got to be a reasonably intelligent man or he wouldn't have been president. Eisenhower's attitude was the pinheaded personal attitude of a man who doesn't know anything about politics.

Eisenhower had the best chance in the world of any president who has ever taken over to have a complete outline of all existing situations. If he wanted to change things he didn't like, there wasn't any harm in changing them. That would be his business. They would be his new policies. But he had the idea that if he could cause situations to arise that would reflect on his predecessors, that would be to his credit. It didn't turn out that way. And it really shouldn't be that way. The objective of an incoming president ought to be to find out exactly what the past policies have been and to anticipate what future policies should be. Then, when the new president takes over, he should leave good policies alone and change policies he doesn't like to the way he wants things to be. But what Eisenhower and his people had in mind was to upset the old apple cart and make it appear that Roosevelt hadn't been a good president and I hadn't been a president at all. Well, it didn't work.

The second basic fault in the Eisenhower administration is, of course, that Eisenhower really didn't want to *do* anything or *decide* anything. He passed the buck, down. Which can't be done. And he tried to let somebody else do the jobs that he should have been doing himself. He also made it clear on several occasions that he wanted some sign from Congress, or some vote by Congress, before he made his own decision. That's not presidential behavior. A president should make a decision and then ask Congress to endorse it, which they usually do. Fortunately, Eisenhower and his advisors had to make relatively few decisions during the Eisenhower administration.

Getting back to some of the things that did take place during the Eisenhower administration, did you think Eisenhower had nothing to do with the Vietnam War, that it all came about long after he was out of office? A lot of people have a memory gap there and think that's the case, but it isn't. In 1954, when the French were still in Vietnam and fighting at Dien Bien Phu, the French government asked the United States for help in the form of air support. The Eisenhower administration, typically, didn't provide any help; they did nothing whatsoever. But after the French left, it was Eisenhower who sent in "military advisors" and "military observers," those two terms used dishonestly and so often for soldiers and other fighting men. I doubt that Eisenhower and his people thought the whole thing through; I doubt that they gave any thought to the far-reaching consequences. To quote Nevins and Commager again, "When, in 1954, the French departed, the Americans moved in, though neither their interest nor the nature of their commitment was entirely clear. And soon the Americans were confronted with all of those problems which had confronted, and confounded, the French." And that was the start of it all.

And I wonder if any of the people reading this book have ever given much thought, or any thought at all, to the little Middle East country of Lebanon, where I think more and more trouble will be showing up in the years to come. That was Eisenhower, too, who first got us involved with that country, a country I see as a time bomb waiting to explode, by sending a Marine outfit to the capital city of Lebanon, Beirut, in 1958, to help out the government.*

But I think the ugliest and the dumbest thing that Eisenhower did during his administration, and while he was campaigning before his first term, was the cowardly way he ducked the whole question of McCarthyism even when good, decent people around him were being hurt more and more by that awful and horrible man. McCarthy first began to make himself noticeable during my administration, and I recognized him immediately as a fake and a phony and as a real menace to our country and our principles of freedom and decency. I realized that he didn't really believe that stuff he was spouting about Communists taking over the country any more than I did, and that he was just whipping up hysteria without any evidence at all because it was getting him headlines and the hope of maybe taking over the country himself. (Fat chance he had of *that,* because the American people were just too smart to let him stay around for too long.) And I let my staff and the Congress and the rest of the world know how I felt about McCarthy every chance I got. I vetoed, in 1950, a bill put together by McCarthy's friend, Senator Pat McCarran of Nevada, and by Richard Nixon, the McCarran-Nixon Bill, which required members of the American Communist Party and members of so-called Communist front organizations to register with the Justice

---

*This was prophetic on my father's part, though he had no idea how prophetic it was. He was no longer with us when Lebanon became one of the world's most war-torn countries, and when American and other hostages were taken. Or when, in October 1983, American and French military headquarters were bombed by Arab terrorist groups and 241 Americans and 58 French soldiers died, and not long afterwards, the Americans left Lebanon. The slaughter in Lebanon, of course, continues. MT

Department, even when the connection of some of these organizations with communism was extremely doubtful, and placed many restrictions on people labeled in this way; I felt that this bill was even more un-American than communism, but it was passed over my veto. I also vetoed, in 1952, the McCarran Internal Security Act, which put ridiculous restrictions on immigrants, including prohibiting people who'd been communists in their teens and then disavowed it, from entering the country. But this, too, passed over my veto, and all these things made McCarthy more and more brazen, and he began to call the Roosevelt administration and mine "twenty years of treason."

McCarthy was joined by other individuals of the same ilk, men like Senator William Jenner of Indiana, and then by a few well-respected politicians like Senator Robert Taft of Ohio, men who either believed his big lies or more likely, felt that they might get some political advantage out of appearing to be his pals. Taft even gave McCarthy some advice that was so downright low that it could have come from McCarthy himself, telling McCarthy something along these lines: "Keep talking, and keep accusing people. And if a charge doesn't stick, accuse someone else, until you get a charge that does stick."

A lot of people began to be afraid of ruffling McCarthy's feathers or the feathers of his admirers. In 1952, I was doing some campaigning for Adlai Stevenson, and when I went to Boston to make a speech there, a couple of Massachusetts politicians asked me to go easy on McCarthy. They didn't like McCarthy any more than I did, but John F. Kennedy was running for the Senate that year, and a lot of other New England people, of course, were running for other offices, and the men who said that to me were afraid that people who liked McCarthy would end up voting for the opponents of the Democrats I was trying to help. Well, I refused absolutely, and when I gave my speech, I called McCarthy a gangster and a purveyor of the big lie and a lot of other things which, at that, were probably a little kinder than I should have been. It didn't seem to do any harm, since Kennedy was elected to the Senate all right, and most of the other people who were running also won. And it may have helped some people see McCarthy for what he really was, people who were fooled by his bluster and his unsubstantiated accusations before I said what I said.

Eisenhower, on the other hand, was also asked to say nothing against McCarthy, and he obeyed orders and didn't say a word against him. He even got up on a platform with McCarthy's mirror image, Jenner, and put his arm around the man and looked as though he were aching to kiss Jenner's rear end.

But Eisenhower's cowardice about McCarthyism really became evident, really became shameful and disgraceful, when he was told to cut out a statement about General Marshall in a speech he was about to give. This involved a few lines written by one of Eisenhower's speech writers, a fellow named Emmett John Hughes. By this time, McCarthy and Jenner were so arrogant that they were attacking just about everybody; I believe they'd have called the Almighty Lord a Communist if they'd happened to think of it. And one of their targets was General Marshall, whom they called a traitor, actually using that word, and saying that the Army was loaded with Communists and Marshall was soft on communism and looking the other way. Well, a man like George Marshall didn't really need defending from the likes of McCarthy and Jenner, but Hughes had written in those few lines anyway, having Eisenhower say that he'd known General Marshall for many years and that Marshall was a loyal and patriotic American (as if anyone, including McCarthy and Jenner themselves, could possibly think otherwise).

But Eisenhower was told to cut out those few lines because McCarthy might not like a statement defending a man he was attacking, and Eisenhower dropped that section from his speech as quickly and meekly as if he were a private taking orders from a chief of staff. I'm talking about a statement concerning *General George C. Marshall,* you understand, who was not only one of the most decent and honorable men this country has ever produced, and the creator of the wonderful Marshall Plan that helped save Europe and put it back on its feet, but also the man who had done more for Eisenhower than anyone else on earth. Every major promotion that Eisenhower got during World War II, every major assignment, came about because George Marshall recommended it or ordered it. And yet Eisenhower cut out those few mild lines in defense of General Marshall because he was told that Joe McCarthy wouldn't like it.*

There's been some speculation since then that Eisenhower dropped those lines about General Marshall because he was paying Marshall back for a big fight that the two men had had at the end of the Second World

---

*In my book about my father, I described Dad's reaction to these events in this way: "What troubled my father was the fact that Eisenhower was attacking the policies he had helped to formulate and carry out. This seemed to Dad to be the worst kind of hypocrisy. But what really drove the Truman temperature right off the thermometer was Ike's endorsement of Senators William Jenner and Joe McCarthy, men who spent hours in the Senate vilifying Ike's old commander, George Marshall. Without General Marshall's help, Ike would have remained an obscure colonel, at most a brigadier or major general, commanding a division before the war ended. When Ike appeared on the same platform with William Jenner, and deleted a personal tribute to General Marshall from a speech he planned to make in Milwaukee because Senator McCarthy would have been offended by it, my father just about gave up on candidate Eisenhower." I'm going to have to admit now that that phrase "just about gave up on . . . Eisenhower" was the understatement of the century. My father never used salty language in the presence of my mother or me, but he came very, very close to it when he talked about Eisenhower in those days. MT

War.* That isn't the case. Eisenhower admitted to a number of people that he dropped the statement about Marshall strictly because he was told to drop it since it might irritate McCarthy. The truth is that Eisenhower was too chickenhearted to be vindictive. He was just a weak man cowering at a mental image of McCarthy's pugnacious face and rasping voice.

Eisenhower's behavior toward McCarthy and McCarthyism didn't improve after he became president. Another of McCarthy's targets was the State Department, and McCarthy began to say in his speeches that overseas libraries funded by the United States were full of Communist and pro-Communist books. So a number of cowardly fellows in the State Department immediately started destroying a lot of books, just as Hitler had done a few years earlier. Eisenhower mumbled a few words about how terrible this was, but he didn't do a thing to stop the book banning and book burning. Then McCarthy went after a professor at Johns Hopkins, a man named Owen Lattimore, whom he described as "Russia's top espionage agent in the United States." Lattimore was hit with all sorts of charges that were, in the words of Nevins and Commager, "pressed with vindictiveness by the Eisenhower administration," and his life was made a living hell, but he ended up being cleared completely. And then McCarthy focused on Dean Acheson, my secretary of state from 1949 to 1953, saying that Acheson, like Marshall, was soft on communism, and that there were 205 Communists in the State Department. (This number kept changing in McCarthy's different speeches.) And again Eisenhower and his people said nothing and did nothing, and not a single Communist was found in the State Department.

It took a man who wasn't even connected with the government, Joseph Welch, who was hired as the Army's chief counsel when the Army decided to respond to McCarthy's charges, to bring McCarthy down. Welch showed his contempt for McCarthy, and showed that McCarthy was contemptible, and as everybody remembers, McCarthy was finally censured by the Senate in 1954. McCarthy slunk away after that and died of cirrhosis of the liver in 1957.

---

*My father gives no details and mentions no names here, and even threw out the correspondence between Marshall and Eisenhower on this matter, as a courtesy to Eisenhower, when Dad left the Oval Office. But of course he's referring to the relationship between Eisenhower and Kay Summersby, the British WAC who was Eisenhower's driver and then his romantic partner during the war. Eisenhower wrote Marshall at the end of the war, asking to be returned to the United States so that he could divorce Mamie Eisenhower and marry Kay Summersby. Marshall responded with fury, telling Eisenhower that his conduct was disgraceful and that, if he went through with his plans, Marshall would kick him out of the Army and harass him in other ways for the rest of his life. None of this is secret now because, in 1975, Kay Summersby told the whole story in a book, *Past Forgetting: My Love Affair with Dwight D. Eisenhower*. Eisenhower dropped Kay Summersby after his correspondence with General Marshall. MT

* * *

I'll end these comments on Eisenhower by mentioning that, in 1962, when Eisenhower's activities or nonactivities were still fresh in people's minds, a poll was conducted among leading historians on the relative qualities of thirty-one of the men who'd served as presidents up to that time. Eisenhower was rated twenty-second in the list of thirty-one, and in an associated list of twelve "average" presidents, he was rated eleventh.* This places him somewhat above Coolidge, who was rated twenty-seventh on the main list and fourth on an associated list of six "below average" presidents, and somewhat above Harding, who was rated thirty-first on the main list and second on an associated list of two presidential "failures." (The other man on the "failures" list is Grant.) I guess that's about right. I've been quoted a number of times as saying that Eisenhower didn't know anything when he became president, and in his years in office, he didn't learn anything. I guess that's about right, too.

---

*For the record, my father was rated ninth in the list of thirty-one presidents, and fourth in an associated list of "near-great" presidents, just above John Adams on the "near-great" list. I think he'd rank even higher in a poll conducted today. I also think Eisenhower would rank lower. MT

PART II

What It Takes to Be a Good President

NINE
Making Up
Your Mind

I'VE been thinking about a way to start the next section of this book, which will deal with the presidency rather than individual presidents, and with the qualities and qualifications that make a good president and a good presidential administration rather than a poor one, and then after that I'll have some things to say about how I think a government should operate and how it shouldn't. I'll be getting back to some individual presidents later on because, now that I've said quite a lot about our bad presidents, I want to balance things out with some facts and comments on our great presidents. But let's deal with the presidency in general first.

I'll become a bit more serious later on, but I believe I'll start out in a lighthearted way by saying that I certainly don't think a man has to be big and tall, has to have a commanding appearance and impressive height, in order to be a good president. I'm saying this because I enjoy history and have been reading books of history all my life, and I keep coming across statements by historians, men who are smart enough to know better, to the effect that Washington and Lincoln became great presidents because they were so tall that people had to look up to them and tended to respect them for that reason, and therefore they were able to lead and get things accomplished. What total baloney! I guess I'm slightly sensitive about that subject because, though I never let myself be bothered by anything the press said about me, I could never understand why some sections of the press kept referring to me as "that little man in the White House." (Well, maybe I let it bother me a bit, but it really *is* nonsense.)

Washington and Lincoln were certainly tall: Washington was six feet two inches tall, and Lincoln was our tallest president, towering over everybody at six feet four inches. But on the other hand, our worst president, Warren G. Harding, was also tall, six feet in height or slightly taller, and some of our nonentity presidents were also tall: Millard Fillmore was six feet tall, James Buchanan was about six one, and Chester A. Arthur was six feet two. And before you start building theories about that, wondering if Washington and Lincoln were the only good *tall* presidents, and that a president has to be small and quick to serve well in the Oval Office, keep in mind the fact that another of our bad presidents, Ulysses S. Grant, was such a little fellow that he almost missed being accepted for West Point because the minimum height requirement was five feet, and though he grew a bit after that, he was five feet seven inches at his tallest. And old Cal Coolidge was five eight. But none of that had anything to do with their being bad presidents.

As for me, I suppose I make a smaller appearance or something like that, but to use that phrase that people in politics like so much, let me state for the record that I'm five feet ten inches tall. I'm shorter than Franklin Roosevelt, who was six one, though I guess people didn't realize this since of course he had to lean on something when standing and rarely stood or was photographed standing, but I'm taller, for example, than Teddy Roosevelt, who was five eight like Coolidge, and I'm exactly as tall as Eisenhower, who is also five ten.* I might also have looked shorter than I am because I weighed 185 when I became president, though I got rid of ten pounds in office, or perhaps the pressures of the office got rid of the excess weight for me. And that's enough about me in that context.

Anyway, I don't think Washington's and Lincoln's commanding height had much to do with why they were respected. I think their lead-

---

*Height is often deceptive among presidents. Perhaps it's the way they're photographed, or before photography came along, the way their portraits were painted. Among recent presidents, I've discovered in conversations with friends who hadn't ever seen Lyndon Johnson in person that he's sometimes thought of as a man of average height, but I remember so well that my father and mother and I used to look way up at him, though not necessarily politically. He was our tallest president after Lincoln, standing six feet three inches. Many people think John Kennedy was taller than Johnson because he was so slim, but he was actually just slightly over six feet. Jimmy Carter is often believed to be quite short, but he's about the same height as my father and Eisenhower were. And I believe most people think of Ronald Reagan as exceptionally tall, but he's tall but not exceptionally tall; he's six one. He looks very tall because a lot of the people around him are rather short. I don't think that was planned or intentional, but who knows? MT

ership came from what was inside them. Of course, a wonderful appearance of a public leader is a great asset if he has something behind that public appearance to go with it. Otherwise it isn't worth anything; otherwise it's just deceptive like Harding's handsomeness or Eisenhower's smile. A president has got to have qualifications to do the job that he's supposed to do. He has got to be honest. Particularly, he's got to be intellectually honest, and if he isn't, it doesn't make any difference what kind of appearance he makes. In the long run, his good looks or good public presence doesn't amount to anything because he'll do a bad job and he'll be found out. Or even worse, as I've been pointing out in this book, some presidents go into the presidency and don't do any kind of job at all. A good president has to be a man—or as of course will come in time, a woman—who works for the people in a way that makes a great impression on the period in which he lives, and so far, there have only been about seven or eight presidents who've done that. The others have, to some extent, been presidents who were not truly interested in the events that were taking place and their part in it. In a sense, they retired from active life into the presidency, and that doesn't work.

The thing most people wonder about, of course, when you start discussing good presidents and bad presidents, is how to find the best available man. How, people ask, do you know if you're voting for the right man, or if you're someone like me and get to the point where you have some power in a political party, how do you know if the fellow you're pushing to be your party's candidate is the best man in your party at that time for the job. Those are difficult, possibly impossible, things to answer. You never can tell what's going to happen to a man until he gets to a place of responsibility. You just can't tell in advance, whether you're talking about a general in the field in a military situation or the manager of a large farm or a bank officer or a president of the United States. You can never tell if a man is going to be a figurehead or a leader when you nominate him and elect him president. You've just got to pick the man you *think* is best on the basis of his past history and the views he expresses on present events and situations, and then you sit around and do a lot of hoping and if you're inclined that way, a certain amount of praying.

You've just got to think hard and make your choice and not look back later on and wonder if you should have voted for Mr. Smith instead of having voted for Mr. Jones the way you did. When you contemplate things like what another man would have done as president, the plain truth is that you just never can tell. That's the kind of hypothetical question that can't be answered. You never can tell what anybody else would have done as president until he's in there and has a chance to act, so you've got to live with what you've got and hope for the best.

The one comforting factor in this whole question of the selection of presidents is that I feel absolutely sure that the vast majority of past presidents wanted to do the right thing, and that this will be the case with the majority of future presidents as well. But I honestly think that most presidents really *try*.

I'll admit that my view of the history of the presidency in general, and the way I want to express it in this book, is to give the men who were president—as much as I can—the best of it. But I do want people to understand that these men were leaders in their time or they wouldn't have been there, and that these men could never have been presidents of the United States unless they had something to offer, no matter how bad or how disappointing they turned out when they got there.

You can't breed or teach leadership; it comes about naturally. You can start a bunch of youngsters off in any program you desire, whether it's a local civil government, whether it's a local organization to raise wheat and make flour out of it, or any other thing you want to do, and there'll be certain men of talent who come to the top naturally. It doesn't make any difference what it is, whether it's a farm or a great corporation or a government: somebody has to have the brains to lead and to outline plans that will make the thing a success. There always has to be a man at the top who understands, or thinks he understands, where he's going or what he wants to do. There always has to be a leader, whether it's in the concentration of wealth or running a state or a country or whatever it is.

This isn't an aristocratic viewpoint. In our form of government, the ordinary fellow has the same opportunity to rise in the world as the fellow who started out with the handicap of too much money or being part of a famous family or any other thing you want to name. The poorest of poor men have gone straight to the top because of our type of government and philosophy. That happens in every line in this country. The reason it didn't happen much in Europe until recent times, of course, is that there was an aristocratic fringe at the top who were supposed to rule the people. Well, that was upset in the United States, and it's a great thing that there's no such thing as an aristocratic fringe at the top in our country. Any man from the bottom to the top of the financial ladder can become a leader if he has the abilities. I don't mean to say that there's any such thing as a classless society here, because people naturally gravitate to the place and the point where they think they can do the most for themselves. But it makes no difference whether they're rich or poor, or whether they *start out* rich or poor. When they show ability under our form of government, they have a chance to get to the top.

And that applies to our presidents, of course: it didn't really make such difference whether they grew up rich or in poverty. The presidents were, after all, just men like all other men, and those who had or seemed to have talent and ability, and were or seemed to be hard workers, were the ones who came to the top. A man's background is something to talk about and perhaps help get yourself elected, but in the final analysis the thing that makes you a good president or a bad president is your character and your understanding of what makes a free government, meaning your knowledge of the history of government and your knowledge of the powers of the presidency and how they should be exercised.

Let's take a look, then, at the things I believe a man has to have as president.

First and most important, in my view, is the fact that a president must be strong, particularly where there's the temptation, as there so often is, to look the other way and do nothing because the matter at hand is unpopular or unpleasant or difficult to attempt or accomplish. It may well be true that the best government is the least government, but when it comes to the point where an emergency arises, or when something has to be done (and sometimes in a hell of a hurry), then you want somebody in charge who knows how to do the job and can take over and see that things happen.

And that means, of course, a president who can make up his own mind, who isn't afraid of controversy, who doesn't allow himself to be held back by some of the limitations other people try to place on the presidency, and who doesn't even allow himself to be held back by certain limitations in the Constitution. I'll explain what I mean.

The ability to make up your mind sounds as if it speaks for itself, but it really isn't as simple as all that. First of all, the president has got to get all the information he can possibly get as to what's best for the most people in the country, and that takes both basic character and self-education. He's not only got to decide what's right according to the principles by which he's been raised and educated, but he also has to be willing to listen to a lot of people, all kinds of people, and find out what effect the decision he's about to make will have on the people. And when he makes up his mind that his decision is correct, he mustn't let himself be moved from that decision under any consideration. He must go through with that program and not be swayed by the pressures that are put on him by people who tell him that his decision is wrong. If the decision is wrong, all he has to do is get some more information and make another decision, because he's also got to have the ability to change his mind and start over. That's the only way in the world that a man can carry on as chief executive.

As far as controversy is concerned, a strong president can't avoid controversy, and shouldn't, either. The more controversy you have, the better it is for the big issues, because then the president can go before the public and explain what the people who are against him stand for and what he stands for. I think that controversy is always a good thing, because, when programs come up about which not everybody is in agreement, the man who's the leader has the chance to tell openly and specifically what he thinks ought to be done, and then go and do it. He's got to keep reminding the people of the nation, and the people in government, that our country has never suffered seriously from any acts of the president that were truly intended for the welfare of the country; it's suffered from the inaction of a great many presidents when action should have been taken at the right time. He has to keep reminding people that a good president must do more than just believe in what he says—he must also act on what he believes. If he's a weak man, a president sometimes can't control things; if he isn't, then he can meet the situation that he has to meet by getting the people who really count to go along with him. Reasonable people will always go along with a man who has the right ideas *and* leadership.

And as regards the necessity, sometimes, for a president to do what he has to do despite some limitations in the way the government operates and in the Constitution that seem designed to prevent him from doing them, the plain fact is that there is such a need on occasion, and a president who wants to do his job properly and fully has just got to recognize that. This isn't to say that there wasn't a good reason for the limitations having been put there in the first place, because there was. When the writers of the Constitution divided our government into those three branches, they knew exactly what they were doing. The reason for the separation of powers, of course, is that they'd been living under an absolute monarch, King George III, and the French also lived under an absolute monarch, and the people who made up the colonies didn't want an absolute monarch. They felt that by the division of the legislative, executive, and judicial powers of the country they'd be much less likely to have a dictator, and that's a main objective of the Constitution, to prevent a dictatorship. I don't know where they got that idea, but it's the right idea. It probably originated in this way—that those men knew the history of government. They were familiar with the Roman Republic and what happened to it, and the Dutch Republic and what happened to it, and they knew their own experience under the monarch in Britain and the experience of other people in Europe under other monarchs, and I think they decided that they'd try to get something that would prevent such things as an absolute monarch or a dictator from happening. It isn't a contradiction, their agreeing quickly that there ought to be a single executive and yet agreeing just as quickly that there ought to be a separation of powers. The object was to give him certain powers but limit them, that's all, limit them by the Constitution of the United States. The president has only certain powers set out by the Constitution, and the legislative branch of the government is in a position to overrule anything he does because they can pass a law by a two-thirds majority whether the president likes it or not. That's the limitation that created the situation under which you're safeguarded and can't have a dictatorship in this country.

I think our three branches are the best system, where the purse is controlled by the legislative branch of the government, where the executive operation of the government is, or should be, in the hands of a man who knows where he's going and what to do, and where the judiciary passes on the laws as to whether or not they're conforming with the Constitution. (The Constitution, incidentally, should be the only business of the high courts. Some people have asked me, hasn't the Supreme Court proved to be one of the greatest stumbling blocks in connection with progressive legislation? The answer is yes, but it's a good stumbling block. Because when legislation is considered, the Constitutional aspects are also considered, and then we have better government and better laws.) But none of that means that the president should be limited from doing good things for the country.

The writers of the Constitution decided that there had to be a single chief executive, but they didn't want an executive on the basis of the way Great Britain handled it because they'd had so much trouble with the political leaders of Great Britain, although some were their friends —Edmund Burke and two or three others. And besides, the British political leaders weren't really the top men; they were under kings who considered themselves appointed by the Almighty and in charge of everything. The Americans wanted a man who was elected by the people but was then really a chief executive, really running the government.

There've been efforts ever since then by the Congress and a lot of other people in the country to hand most of the powers of the executive over to the legislative branch of government. I don't believe in that at all, and I'm certain that isn't what the writers of the Constitution intended. The Constitution is one of the plainest-written documents in existence, and one of the truly unique things about it is, which puts it in a class by itself, is that there are only a few paragraphs on the powers of the head of the government. The writers of the Constitution didn't do much arguing on the office of the chief executive: they set it up in a way that it could be used for the purpose for which it was intended. Aside from those few paragraphs, there are implications in the rest of the Constitution on what a president can and must do to meet situations as they come up, and great presidents have always met situations in the ways they thought were best and would have the best chance of succeeding. Only about a half dozen presidents, of course, as I've said, have been great presidents, only about a half dozen capable of meeting emergencies; some others may have been conscious of emergencies, but they were either timid or indifferent or didn't care, and then there were some who tried. I believe I was one of those, and I did what I felt had to be done without worrying too much about limitations.

Obviously, the Constitution has had to be amended in certain places, such as when they had to take out certain things that were not practical after the government became an operative organization. The writers of the Constitution were also thinking of national development rather than world considerations, and that's all they could think about at that time. There were really only two great powers in that day, France and England, and they controlled just about everything in the world. Spain was on the way out; Spain had been a great country, and if Philip II hadn't sent his fleet against the British, why, Spain might still have been the greatest country in the history of the world, but down it went. Still, though a lot of thinking has had to change as the world changes, the Constitution remains pretty essentially the same as when it was written, and a president must abide by it but not be hog-tied by misinterpreting its intentions.

The thing a president has to do in order to meet a situation, in my view, is to read the law, read the Constitutional background for that law, and make up his mind what he wants to do and tell the lawyers what he wants to do and have them find a legal way to do it. And if they don't, do it anyhow, and then they'll find the legal way.

Well, it's the business of lawyers to interpret documents of government—bills, constitutions, and whatever else is before the courts—but they have the habit of interpreting every A and B and every comma and semicolon in a way with the idea of winning a case. But when it comes to the operation of government, the commonsense statements in bills and in constitutions are those that a chief executive has to follow, and it was my policy to tell the lawyers what I was going to do and instruct them to find the proper way to do it under the law, which they can always do when they want to do it.

The president has as much right to interpret the Constitution as have the courts or the legislative branch of the government, because it's a three-branch government, each independent of the other, and the president's interpretation of the Constitution is just as likely to be right as the interpretation of the Supreme Court. I think the first half-dozen presidents were all very strict constructionists of the Constitution, and there was no effort by any of them to overstep the boundaries as set out in the Constitution for operation of the government. But they were interpreting the Constitution in a very narrow way, and I don't believe that some of the presidents who came along afterwards and saw things differently were overstepping the restrictions that were placed on the presidential office by the Constitution, either. A great many of them were good presidents who made it perfectly plain that they knew what their rights were under Article II of the Constitution of the United States, and they were going to enforce it. That's the general policy, in fact—knowing my rights and expecting to get them—on which I've worked all the way through my lifetime, which has mostly been spent in that line of business.

TEN
Sticking to It

THE second important quality that I believe a good president must have is strength. Again you might think this is obvious, but it really isn't because the odd but true fact here is that there are times when the general public seems to prefer weakness in a president.

When Harding was elected, for example, the country had just lived through a major crisis, the First World War, and had had a very strong president, Wilson, who'd put pressure on the people and demanded sacrifices of them the way strong presidents sometimes have to do. And when the war was over and Wilson's terms were finished, people wanted to get away from the pressure; they wanted to go back to things as they were, as people always do after an emergency. People are always tired when a strong president is in office and tells them what they ought to do and makes them do it. They don't like it; they'd like to quit and relax.

Sometimes, too, it's made easier to give in to the temptation of voting for a weakling who looks as though he won't bother you much because it appears that neither party has a strong candidate. That was also the case when Harding was running, because neither the Democratic presidential candidate nor the vice-presidential candidate were particularly well-known countrywide at the time. It finally became clear, in retrospect, that there was strong leadership available at that period, because the man running for president on the Democratic ticket was, of course, Governor James M. Cox of Ohio, who was really a very good man, and the man running for vice president was a fellow named Franklin Delano Roosevelt, and you know how he turned out. He became one of the greatest presidents our country has had. But the people wanted a change, and they felt they could get back to the easy life without any effort on their own part. It didn't turn out that way. It finally cost us the Second World War.

There's also no question about the fact that a series of weak presidents also helped cause the Civil War. Some people believe that strong presidents usually come along after weak ones and save the situation, and we're always hopeful that will always happen, but whether it always will or won't we don't know. It certainly didn't happen with the fellow who came after Harding, old Cal Coolidge.

I happen to be in the minority in my opinion of the man who came after Coolidge, Herbert Hoover. I know most people think he was a poor president and practically caused the depression single-handed, but I think he was actually a president who tried hard and did the best he possibly could but was faced with difficulties that he just wasn't able to overcome at the time. I think he and his administration were blamed for things that were not their fault, things that were coming on ever since Woodrow Wilson left office and Harding became president in 1921.

Every president inherits the last administration's problem. Well, he can't help that; he does, and there's nothing he can do about it. But he's got to find out what he's inherited, assess it logically and realistically, and then see if he can meet the situation. Hoover assessed the situation as nearly accurately as he could with his background and experience, but one big problem was that his background and experience and general outlook weren't good enough or the right kind. You see, he'd been out of the country for quite a while. He was the man who fed all the starving people when Wilson was president, the man in charge of the Allied Food Council, which gave millions of tons of food to civilians in areas torn apart by the war, and before that he made his fortune as an engineer in Australia and China and other countries. He wasn't one of those fellows born with a gold spoon in his mouth, incidentally. His father was a blacksmith in West Branch, Iowa, and both of his parents died before he was nine years old, and he and his brother and sister were split up and sent to relatives. Hoover lived with an uncle in Newberg, Oregon, and he left school at fifteen and worked as an office boy and attended business college at night. And when he developed an ambition to become an engineer and applied to Stanford University in Palo Alto, California, because they were just starting up an engineering school, he was almost rejected because his academic background was weak, but he was taken on because he showed real brilliance in mathematics in his entrance examination.

But as I've said, he spent a lot of his adult life out of the country, and when he came back to the United States and became involved in politics, his only real political job before he ran for the presidency was as secretary of commerce in Harding's and Coolidge's cabinets. So, in my opinion, his thinking didn't start at the grass roots; he didn't really understand the American people, and the needs of the American people, and what had to be done to meet the needs of the people. His viewpoint was that the president was the executive to enforce the laws and had nothing to do with making the laws, with which I don't agree, of course.

I don't think we were a penniless nation after 1929; people just thought we were penniless, but when the facts became clear, we were not penniless and never would be, and I felt that Hoover could have enacted some laws to help things out as Roosevelt eventually did. But Hoover's philosophy and outlook didn't enable him to do that, and we had to wait for the next president to start to move out of the swamp. This was a shame, because, though Hoover's administration was generally conservative, he *was* capable of progressive action when he felt it was important. For example, when he believed in the necessity for an organization like the RFC, the Reconstruction Finance Corporation, which lent money to small businesses and to people buying homes, he didn't hesitate to organize it. And it was a great asset to the country—and not only in the latter days of the Hoover administration. It was also used up until my own administration, twelve years later.

We had very different viewpoints on most policies, and his viewpoint on politics was also very different from mine, of course, but none of this made any difference in our friendship. We were always friendly, and I was always very fond of him. As far as politics were concerned, we both felt that this was our own business, and we never made a personal matter out of it. And as far as his point of view on the presidency and the people of the United States was concerned, I think he was an honorable, straightforward person. When he was feeding the people of the world, he had no thought or interest other than the welfare of the people he was feeding. And when he was president, I don't believe he had any thought but the welfare of the country, of the United States, at heart.

It isn't easy, of course, to be a strong president. When John Adams was president, he functioned in a country that had about three and a half million people in it. Today, there are about a hundred and eighty million people, every one of whom must be considered and thought about every time a president makes an important move.* It isn't that the proscribed duties of the presidency have changed; they're exactly the same as they were under the first president. It's just that there's a lot more to do. And in the early days, the state governments were almost independent for the simple reason that communications were such that a state government had to act most times for itself in the interests of that state because it couldn't wait for the federal government to become involved, whereas today there's constant coordination between states and the federal government. And that sometimes makes it even more difficult for the president to act as president because sometimes state interests and federal interests aren't at all identical.

Sometimes it seems that the president has so much to do that there doesn't ever seem to be any time to get it done, but he can manage to do it if he works at it. I suppose there's even a temptation for a president who follows a strong president to take it easy, because a strong president who's accomplished a lot gives his successor a chance to coast along. The new president can always soothe his conscience with that business about the people being tired and anxious for a rest from the pressures of public concerns, and it's true that people *do* seem often to expect the successor to a strong and demanding president to go back to the easy way of doing things. But fortunately, it doesn't usually work out that way. For one thing, a number of strong presidents died or were assassinated before they came out of office, and the successors of these presidents had to carry through. I certainly never gave a thought to taking the easy route because the war was still on, and because that's just not the way I am, and that was the attitude of many of my predecessors. And for another thing, if a fellow has his heart in it, it's his greatest pleasure and his greatest satisfaction to work hard all the time to try to get worthwhile things done.

The thing that has to be remembered constantly is that it requires eternal watchfulness to preserve liberty, and the Constitution and the

---

*It's growing harder all the time, of course. The latest figures estimate the present population at just under 250 million people. My father would have been astonished at this, but pleased. MT

presidency and all the other offices are set up for the purpose of preserving the liberty of the individual. When people cease to understand that that's the case, and let things run and take care of themselves, then we're in trouble. It takes leadership all the way through, under any republic or any sort of government, to make it work.

An equally important thing that a good president must have is the ability to come up with new ideas and an understanding of how the implementation of these ideas will affect not only the present but the future. To put it a different way, a good president has got to have an understanding of history so that he's aware of how things were done in the past, develop ideas that fit in with the way things are different at present, and make sure at the same time that these ideas, though beneficial to present-day people, don't do injury to people of the future. That sentence is a mouthful, and if it also sounds like a handful to accomplish, it is. But it can be done.

Most good presidents knew the history of our government intimately and thoroughly, and the reason this is important, of course, is that knowledge of the past enables you to understand what makes good government and what doesn't. I think every one of our past presidents who made great names for themselves were men who knew history and through this knowledge, really understood the background of free government and tried to keep it established in this country.

Every single one of our past presidents, in some situation, made some good decisions that can be guides to what might come up ordinarily in the operation of a present government. Now, of course, as I've said, the ones that I think were the greatest in that line were Washington and Jefferson and Jackson, and the modern ones were Woodrow Wilson and Franklin Delano Roosevelt. But even the mistakes made by some of the ones in between are good guides on what not to do. The mistakes were also very important, vitally important, provided you take the time and make the effort to weigh one against the other. This man did this under certain circumstances and this man did this under the same circumstances, or what appeared to be the same circumstances, at another time. This one may have been wrong and that one may have been right, and you have to make up your mind which one is the right one and then try not to make a mistake like the fellow did who was wrong. But obviously, you don't have that opportunity to judge present events in context with similar or identical past events if your knowledge of past history isn't good enough.

In a sense, that's one of my main reasons for writing this book: to get people, perhaps some future presidents among them, interested in history and make them realize how important an understanding of the past is in dealing with the present and the future. My own period was an important and historic period, presided over for twelve years by Franklin Roosevelt when I took it over and carried it on. And I hope that readers will find the viewpoint of a president on what other presidents were up against, and what the presidency is all about, to be of some interest. The thing I have in mind is to try to interest people in the history of the presidency of the United States in a manner in which they'll make it a point, on their own hook, to go ahead and read other books on presidents and the presidency and American government in general. There have been very, very many definitive biographies written on the various presidents, and even more books written on the United States, and I have most of them. Some of them are written in such a way that you can't get the background of the man or the subject without reading the whole thing in a lot of dry language, but there are others that are interesting from the first word to the last, and these can be found if the reader works at it. Anyway, my hope is that this book will cause some people to go out and learn what I learned through a tremendous amount of study and reading of history, which began when I was ten years old.

If a president has sound knowledge of history and combines this with new ideas, he's going to do good and perhaps have some impact on history at the same time. And fortunately for our country and the world, men with new ideas always seem to come along in time to meet situations as they come up.

Cleveland had some new ideas. Among other things, he was probably the first president who was completely nonpolitical in his attitude toward government employees, and he absolutely refused to drop good workers from their jobs just because they were Republicans and he was a Democrat—despite tremendous pressure because he was the first Democrat elected since the Civil War, and there were 100,000 jobs up for grabs and Democrats were expecting to get practically all of them. He was the first president to try to do something about problems between labor and management, such as the growing number of strikes and a new idea—shocking to many businessmen—that people ought to work only an eight-hour day; his message sent to Congress suggesting a commission to deal with labor-management problems was the first message dealing strictly with labor sent by any president. He was the first president who tried to put some controls on big business; the Interstate Commerce Act, passed during his first administration (the good administration, as I've mentioned), created the first federal regulatory agency. (He was also the first president to get married in the White House—in fact, the only one thus far—when he was forty-nine and took as his bride Frances Folsom, aged twenty-one, the daughter of a former law partner. And the second of their five children, Esther, was the first child born in the White House. (I guess those aren't the kind of accomplishments I'm talking about. But these things certainly confirm the fact that he was an original thinker.)

Theodore Roosevelt had some new ideas, such as his creation of the Panama Canal and the Pure Food and Drug Act. Woodrow Wilson had many new ideas that were put into effect, including the Federal Trade Commission, the first child labor laws, and of course, the League of Nations, a concept in which I still have great faith despite some criticisms and some unquestionable flaws in the United Nations. And Franklin Roosevelt came along during a depression that was almost equal in difficulty to the problems that faced the Constitutional Convention when those men were creating a new nation, a new kind of nation, and he had a limitless number of new ideas and managed to put most of them into effect.

That continues indefinitely, and it brings about a continual reorganization of the government of the United States, which is exactly the way that marvelous document called the Constitution was intended. We're constantly up against situations where some reorganization is necessary even if it won't be satisfactory to all the people, and if you organize and reorganize as you go along, you'll deal with each problem as it comes up. Nobody knows that better than I do. Every problem can be met under the Constitution if an effort is made to do it, because we've been through every experience that a form of government can possibly go through from the time our government was formed up until now.

A president, of course, can't sit down and act as though the situation in 1789 or the situation in 1809 or the situation in 1840 or the situation in 1861 is the same as the one we're meeting now; there are always differences. He's always got to think of those differences and also be in the frame of mind to think ahead into the future as well. He's got to be a man who understands what may happen in the future and have the ability of a public relations man to convince Congress to do what he thinks is best for what's to come. Anybody can figure out what's happening after a law is passed, but somebody has to think about the future and that's the president's job. No president can afford to do nothing and let things happen around him. He's got to have a lot of ideas, and he's got to present his ideas, and if those ideas are genuinely for the welfare of the country, he'll get them over in the long run. He might be able to get them over in the first session of Congress, he might get them over in the second session of Congress, but he'll get them over sooner or later if he's always looking to the future welfare of the country based on the historical past. He's got to be the leader, and he's got to be looking toward the future all the time.

* * *

The next essential quality in a good president is the ability, as I've just said, to convince the Congress to go along with his ideas, and of course, also convince the general public that his ideas are good—particularly when, as often happens, a lot of legislators and a large segment of the general public don't think much of the ideas when they're first presented. And also with this quality must go the ability to be able to determine and understand exactly the way the people *are* thinking, so that you're not taken by surprise because you think everybody's for you and then find out that they're talking to each other about burning you in effigy, or worse.

As far as learning the public viewpoint is concerned, that's easy, but a president has to work at it all the time. He has to be in close contact with everything that goes on. He has to know what the newspapers are saying and what radio and television are saying every day of the year. I read the great newspapers of the day and looked at television and listened to radio, and once in a while I'd even read the editorials in some of the newspapers, but much more important, I had my own people's approach. I got a tremendous amount of mail and I read it all and I answered it all because I felt that a president really has to keep his ear to the ground on both local and national political situations and know exactly what people are thinking about in various states and various sections of the country. I used to get mail from thousands of people all over the United States, and I had a better understanding of what people thought and wanted than the newspapers did. Nine times in ten the newspapers don't tell the truth, anyway.

A president also has to be willing, indeed anxious, to talk to people. That's what a public man always has to do: talk to everybody and listen to what everybody has to say, so that he can gather up information and thinking from all segments of the population in order to make up his own mind. Obviously presidents these days aren't accessible to every visitor the way the early presidents were. The early presidents had no real staff; they had secretaries, no doubt, and military and naval aides, but the president was accessible to anybody who wanted to see him. That was true all the way up to James A. Garfield, but when he was shot in the back at the Baltimore and Ohio Station in Washington, they set up a guard for the president when he's on trips and in the White House, and that's been in effect ever since.

I wasn't sorry about that, needless to say, when two members of the Independence Party of Puerto Rico, Oscar Collazo and Girsel Torrasola, came to Washington and started shooting up the place. My family and I were living at Blair House because the White House was being renovated at the time,* and the Secret Service weren't happy about the security situation because Blair House was right out on a public street instead of being surrounded by grounds like the White House. The Secret Service people proved to be entirely right: Collazo and Torrasola, who wanted Puerto Rico to be an independent country even though most Puerto Ricans preferred either commonwealth status or statehood, got right up to Blair House, and there was only a screen door with an ordinary little latch between them and the inside of the house, where Mrs. Truman and I were in our bedrooms changing our clothes so that we could go and attend a ceremony. The Secret Service and the guards outside saw them, of course, but there were twenty-seven shots fired in the next three minutes, and Collazo shot and killed a young member of the military guard, Private Lester Coffelt, before Torrasola was also killed and Collazo was wounded and captured. I watched the whole thing from my window before some Secret Service men yelled at me to get away from there, and I wasn't really frightened; I said afterwards, and was quoted that way in the papers, "A president has to expect those things." And I felt then, and still feel, that Collazo and Torrasola were misguided fanatics and not really killers at heart, and later I commuted Collazo's death sentence to life imprisonment. But I certainly felt grateful to the Secret Service and my other guards.

Still, the president sees the general public when he's going around the country selling one of his programs or supporting someone politically, and he's using his head if he talks to everyone in sight and listens to everyone and listens hard. *That* isn't always easy, because people who don't agree with him will throw bricks at him and rotten eggs and everything else—the verbal kind, of course, but that doesn't necessarily make them easier to take. But then that shouldn't make any difference. If, once he makes up his mind, he's sure that what he's trying to do is right, then all he has to do is go ahead and make sure he puts it over. You'll find that the willingness to talk to people is true of all the great men in our history.

*I was indirectly responsible for our move to Blair House. The White House was really in terrible shape when we moved in in 1945. The place was infested with rats; my father once mentioned in a letter, for example, that Mrs. Roosevelt had told him that she was entertaining some women in the south portico when a rat ran right across the porch railing. The areas seen by tourists were kept freshly painted and decorated, but the paint in the private quarters was dingy, some of the furniture was falling apart, and one night, at an official reception in 1947, the color guard marched in and the old chandelier began to sway and it looked for a while as though it would collapse on the heads of everybody present. Another time, a man brought my father breakfast in his study, and the whole floor began to move as if it weren't connected to anything. My father also said in a letter that he'd learned that Coolidge was hit on the head one day by a piece of the roof, but that frugal man had the roof and the third floor repaired and left the second floor—where we lived—alone. But the coup de grace occurred when a little spinet, one of the two pianos in my sitting room, suddenly broke through the floor, and we were promptly moved across the street to Blair House until the White House could be put in shape. MT

The president's other main source of information, of course, comes from members of his staff, so he's got to make damn sure they're good people—and the right people. I think one of the reasons Washington was such a great president was that Jefferson and all the other brilliant men of the period were around him and being helpful to him. Any man who is in a responsible position like that, and who has able and brilliant men around him, is bound to be influenced by ideas presented at the meetings that they hold together, and I'm sure that the same thing applied at the first meeting of the cabinet of the United States under Washington as it does at the White House today. There's no man in the world, I don't care how much of a genius he is, who has a corner on all the ideas, particularly in government. And if he's interested in meeting his responsibilities if he happens to be president of the United States, he usually has himself surrounded with men who understand all the situations that exist at the time.

The president has to have an open mind. He has to get all the information he can possibly get, some of it difficult to obtain, the truthful facts behind a condition that's before him. For that reason, he must be willing to listen to all the ideas of the people in whom he has confidence. I certainly wouldn't say that the ability to listen to advisors is confined entirely to America, of course. The great prime ministers of Britain, and the great rulers of France, were also surrounded by men of brilliant minds.

You take King Henry IV of France, whom I consider among the greatest of the French kings. He had one of the best and most brilliant cabinets that any king ever had, and he had the best administration up to that time that any government of France had had. The same thing was true of those great political figures of Britain, Burke and a number of others—for example, Disraeli. They all had advice and help from the people with whom they surrounded themselves.

A president has to have people around him who are close to the various segments of the population and will give him frank statements of what goes on with those segments of the population. But he's got to have experience in judging people before he arrives at the White House, so that he has a pretty good chance of having picked the right people when he gets there. He's got to be able to understand what people are, what they mean when they say something or don't say something, whether or not they're essentially good people under the facade, and then he's got to trust them to a certain extent. If they fail him, then he has to get someone he can trust more, a more worthy person.

He can't have a man who's always expecting to get his picture in the papers and have a write-up about what he's going to say to the president. He's got to be a man who's willing to be anonymous and interested strictly in giving the president the information he needs to carry on the government. It's absolutely necessary to rely on people who aren't a formal part of the government. A president has got to have someone in the financial sector, in the farm sector, in the labor sector, in the various other sectors that have to do with the general welfare of the people. He's got to have people around him who can give him information without talking to the press and the public. Then he has to make up his own mind, and if something has to be said to the press and the public, it's the president's duty to say it. I certainly don't think that anything like that will lead to a secret government. If the president's got a will of his own, and most of them have, and it appears that the people on whom he relies are trying to work up a secret government for their own benefit, he's got a far more important duty: to fire them and get somebody else.*

---

*My father wouldn't have hesitated for a minute on what to do about Colonel North and Admiral Poindexter. But then I'm certain that he wouldn't have had them around him in the first place. MT

ELEVEN
Listening and Persuading

JACKSON was the first president to have a kitchen cabinet, and some people have compared me to Jackson because I did, too. Well, "kitchen cabinet" is the name they gave it, but all it means is a group of unofficial advisors in addition to the official advisors in his cabinet. Jackson felt that he had to have people to whom he could talk frankly and privately, people not in government but close to segments of the population, and who could tell him what was going on out there without thinking about their own public appearances in the press.

These advisors are people outside the publicity and the limelight that shines on the White House, and in many ways they're more essential to the president than the people in his cabinet, who are in front of the limelight all the time, because they can give the president information he needs very badly without ever stopping to think about themselves.

You can call these unofficial advisors what you please, but since Jackson, every president who knew what he was about has had them in one way or another, and I think they're absolutely essential. The thing a president has to do is listen to all the reports of his staff, and all the reports of his cabinet, and to what the newspapers and radio and television have to say, and then, after he's coordinated all of these things, he has to find out, from outside people on whom he can rely, exactly what the thinking is in each segment and section of the United States. He has to listen, read, and think all the time. He has to make up his mind whether or not this fellow or that is telling the truth and whether or not what he says is worthwhile, and that's also the case when he reads the papers or whatever else he does: he has to decide if he's in conformity with the newspaper articles or what people have said to him in those conversations.

It's not really hard to do. I had to do it constantly, of course, and got through it without too much trouble. And I think the presidents who got *into* trouble were the ones who didn't pay much attention to the information that was available to them, or didn't try to learn from other people or the newspapers, because they felt they had more important things to do. Or maybe it was because they felt *they* were more important than every other individual on earth, and smarter, too. Well, they weren't.

There's no question about the fact that it's a difficult task for a president to get the people around him, official people or unofficial, to understand him so completely that they'll carry out his wishes or get him the exact information he wants without trying to intrude on his decisions with their own notions. They're almost impossible to find, truly almost impossible to find, and yet you can find them if you work at it. Sometimes, when a fellow intrudes with some personal interest of his own and the president cross-examines him to find out what he has in mind, it may be all right for him to have that special interest. But if not, then the president simply has to tell him that that sort of thing doesn't belong here, and if he doesn't take the advice that the president gives him, then the president has to go somewhere else for his information, or get rid of the man. The president has to exercise his own judgment on policy, but he also has to be careful to analyze the people around him constantly and exercise his judgment in regard to them. And when it's necessary for one of them to leave, he's got to tell him to go.

But you've got to listen to all of them, special interests and all, and then make up your own mind as to what's right. And you've got to be a judge of men to determine if a man is honest. If he's honest and frank and fair with the president, it doesn't make any difference what his special interest is, it doesn't make any difference where he stands—he'll tell the president what he thinks is the truth. There's really no adjective that can define an honest man. An honest man is a man who is intellectually honest, who believes in honor and straightforwardness. He's either honest or he isn't, and if he's honest and doesn't believe with the president on a particular matter, he tells the president what he believes, and the president can either see the good sense in it and change his own mind, or disregard that advice and come back to the man for advice on other matters.

Naturally a president can be hurt by placing confidence in unworthy advisors. All presidents have been. There are people in every administration in whom the president has confidence and who break that confidence and cause him trouble. I've had them. I had plenty of them. They didn't affect me adversely at all. I used them to get one more point of view, and a lot of the time I was able to get information that way that I otherwise wouldn't get. And then I made up my mind on the basis of all the information, information from the people I trusted and from the people I didn't trust or suspected were stating viewpoints that weren't genuine but were designed to please me. That sort of thing doesn't have any real effect on the final policy of the president, because, when he has a program to put over, he wants to put together everything he can gather on the subject and make his own decision. And when he finds that one of his confidants isn't doing the right thing, he uses all that's worthwhile from the man and then gets rid of him.

And fortunately, there are plenty of good men around all the time if you look hard for them. I'd say that 96 percent of the men and women around most presidents are good people, even if they sometimes have interests that conflict with what the president may think is right for the country. The men and women have a right to that opinion, and if a president understands that there are all sections of the country and varied kinds of attitudes and opinions to be considered, then he can go ahead and take or not take the advice of the people who are around him.

A lot of the reports are not supposed to be advice, anyway, just information on what the situation is in different parts of the country. There's a distinction between advice and reports: a report is made by a man who gives the president an outline of what the situation is in certain sections of the economy and the people, and advice is when that fellow tries to make his report a part of the policy of the president. The president doesn't have to take that advice unless he wants to take it. He just has to consider everybody and everything and make what he hopes and believes is a good decision. And if it turns out that he's made a wrong decision, then he's got to be smart enough to realize it and brave enough to make another one.

My definition of a leader in a free country is a man who can persuade people to do what they don't want to do, or do what they're too lazy to do, and like it. Of course, you've got to have a program that you yourself believe is the best possible program you can get together. You've got to have that program in such a shape, or just one part of that program in such shape, that it will be for the benefit of all the people under the government. And you've got to have plenty of people around you whom you can trust to help you implement that program, whatever it may be, and whether or not they agree with that program, or all of it, themselves. And then you're in a position to wake the public up to the fact that "here it is, here's what we have to do to accomplish this. Now, come on, let's do it." And if you're persuasive, people will do things even if they don't like it or don't feel much like doing it, and you'll come out all right.

It really isn't much of a trick for a president to get people to go along with his programs and policies because the president has so many ways to present his viewpoint and pound that viewpoint home. The best medium that the president has had to date, and it's a relatively recent one, is the press conference, because he answers all sorts of questions and some of the papers print these things in toto. And the next best way is for the president to go from one end of the country to the other and tell the people what he thinks. That's a form of campaigning, of course, but the presidential office is a constant campaign to get your programs over. And a president, to get his programs over, must inform the people of exactly what he's trying to do and keep on informing them. The dictators of the world say that if you tell a lie often enough, why, people will believe it. Well, if you tell the truth often enough, they'll believe it and go along with you.

That's why I've always felt that a good president has to be the greatest public relations man in the world: because he's got to make the country believe that what he wants to do is the proper thing. The problem with some presidents was their inability to understand that the human animal can be convinced of right when it's right, and they didn't make any effort to convince people. And some presidents, at least some of the time, didn't really care whether people were convinced or not because it didn't really matter to them whether the program they were pushing actually got into operation; they just wanted, in a very cynical way, to appear to be backing certain attractive or popular things in order to get a lot of space and admiration in the newspapers. I don't like to charge presidents with trying to get themselves headlines, but the plain fact is that there have been some who loved press coverage more than anything else on earth, Teddy Roosevelt being as good an example of that as anybody. But I think most presidents were just anxious to do their duty, and most good presidents did believe in what they were trying to do and did make the effort to convince people of the value of their programs.

And if it turned out that the program the president was trying to put over wasn't as good a program as he thought it was, that was no great tragedy; the president just admitted his error and tried something else. Obviously, there are times when a president will make a wrong decision. Well, if he's a man of good sense, he'll listen to the arguments against what he wants to do, and if he finds that he's wrong, he'll go ahead in the other direction. That's merely a matter of laying the plans on the table and letting everybody have his say. I honestly believe that most presidents are pretty well-informed and convinced that the programs they want to follow are correct, but when they find out that they're not, then they're willing to admit that something else ought to be done.

I'm not referring to oratory when I say that a president has got to be a good public relations man. I don't think oratory is an advantage to a president. He's got to make himself understood, of course, and he's got to deliver his statements in a manner that isn't boring so that people will listen to him and be interested in what he has to say. In that case, he's orator enough; the greatest orators have been the men who understood what they wanted to say, said it in short sentences and said it quickly, and then got out of there before people fell asleep. They say the greatest orator in history was Demosthenes, and if you read his famous oration, which made him great, it's not long, and it's said in a way that you can understand, even in translation.

It doesn't really matter where the men who wrote the Constitution got the idea of the separation of powers, or whether my theories on how they got the idea, those theories I stated a while ago, are correct. It's the right idea. And the way to accomplish this is to limit the president's powers, that's all, and the president's powers are set out in the Constitution and limited by the Constitution. The legislative branch of the government is in a position to overrule anything the president does since the Congress can, by a two-thirds majority, pass a law whether he likes it or not. It's not easy for Congress to put together that two-thirds majority, but it has been done.

At the same time, there's an escape valve in a time of real emergency, which is the president's emergency powers. The Romans, whenever they got into trouble in their Republic, always elected a dictator to carry the Republic along and get through the emergency, but you don't have to do that with the Constitution of the United States. The president just exercises his emergency powers, which have to be okayed by Congress, but are just about always granted when they're really needed because most senators and representatives realize that, in an emergency, you have to have the power to go ahead and do what's necessary.

Decisions have to be made here and now—they can't wait. And though this may sound like a strange thing to say, a crisis can sometimes be a good thing for the country, because some men don't seem to be able to develop leadership when there's no crisis. That's been proven conclusively in the cases of those do-nothing presidents I've been naming to you, and the best actions of many presidents, I think, were brought about either by a crisis or the anticipation of a crisis. But under our form of government, you don't have to have a dictator in order to deal with the problems. (In fact, there's never even been a hint of possible dictatorship by any of our presidents because they're all elected for a certain term and a certain period. If the people don't like them, they know they can be thrown out.)

It also works the other way around, of course, since the president can also limit the power of the legislative branch if he doesn't like something that *they're* cooking up. This is done by way of the president's veto power, which is one of the greatest strengths that the president has. The president has a perfect right to analyze legislation when it comes up, just as he has the right to analyze whether a law is constitutional or not. And when he decides that it's not proper for him to sign something, or if it's against one of his policies and he feels certain that his policy is right, he vetoes it. And there's also that pocket veto, which a president can use if, as often happens, a bill he doesn't like comes to him late. If he doesn't sign it within ten days after Congress adjourns, as I've mentioned before, the bill is dead anyway.

Some people have the mistaken impression that presidential veto power is a fairly recent thing, but it's been going on almost as long as the country has been in operation. The first president to veto a bill, as a matter of fact, *was* the first president, George Washington. This took place in April 1792, and it occurred because a census taken in 1790 showed that, of the four million people in the country at the time, there were far more citizens in the North than in the South. This was because nearly a fifth of the southern population was made up of slaves, 700,000 men and women, and of course, they weren't citizens and couldn't vote. The legislative branch wanted to reapportion congressional seats and give more of them to northerners than southerners, but Washington came from Virginia, of course, and didn't care much for this idea and vetoed it. The Congress couldn't get up enough votes to override his veto, so they came up with a less drastic reapportionment, and this one Washington signed.

The Constitutional Convention, in fact, wanted to give the president the right of absolute veto, suggesting that "the National Executive shall have the right to negative any legislative act." But that brilliant and farseeing fellow, Benjamin Franklin, opposed this, as well he should have. He said he feared that "the Executive will be always increasing here, till it ends in a monarchy," and the delegates decided that the legislative branch should have the ability to kill a presidential veto in the same way they can kill one of his laws. So that, too, can be done with a two-thirds majority, though it's even harder to accomplish than the one to kill proposed new laws.

The point in all this is that that's the next thing it's essential for a good president to have: the ability to work with Congress, the varied and independent and sometimes unpredictable men and women who make up the Senate and the House of Representatives.

It goes without saying that this isn't always easy to do, or maybe a more accurate way to put it is to say that it's rarely ever easy to do. Even Washington found this out the first time he went down to Congress in person to talk to the men assembled there. Washington was one of the richest men in the country and never lost sight of that fact, and he also knew he was looked upon almost like a god by a large segment of the population because mobs of people kept cheering him and throwing flowers in his path when he rode his horse from Virginia to take up his duties in the country's first capital, New York City, so he was a pompous man in some ways. When he went to state affairs, for example, he wore velvet and satin and diamond knee-buckles and powdered his hair, things that were already going out of fashion among the plain people of the United States, and he had himself driven around New York in a fancy-looking coach with six horses and outriders.

But Washington was also an extremely modest man in his attitude toward himself as the first president, and in his nervousness about running a new and entirely different kind of country. His inaugural address was filled with references to his lack of experience in politics and administrative duties and his other flaws and deficiencies, statements that were sincere without a doubt; he wrote to General Henry Knox, his friend and his secretary of war (and the man for whom Fort Knox is named), that he felt "not unlike a culprit going to his execution"; and when he got to New York City, among the first things he did was to go to the Society Library there and read books like *Law of Nations* and *Debates of the House of Commons* in order to get some idea of what running a country would be like. So when he put together the first treaty he wanted the country to negotiate, which I think was one of his first attempts to get a treaty going with the Indian nations, he kept in mind the section of the Constitution which says that treaties should be made with the advice and consent of the Senate, and he hurried over there to do just that.

(The language of the Constitution, incidentally, is that the president can sign treaties but only with the approval of two-thirds of the Senate, and it doesn't include the House of Representatives. This became important in 1793, when the country's first Chief Justice, John Jay, prepared a treaty with Great Britain and the Senate okayed it. The treaty was very controversial; Jefferson and others hated it because Great Britain was at war with France, and the treaty seemed to be a betrayal of the friendship between the United States and France, which had helped this country during the Revolutionary War, and also because Jay's Treaty didn't attempt to rectify Britain's practice of boarding American ships and pressing all English immigrants into British naval service on the grounds that, as far as the Crown was concerned, they were still Englishmen. But Washington was convinced that the treaty would postpone further hostilities with England, which the Americans were in no position to undertake at that point—and it did, of course, until 1812, when America was better prepared. So when the House of Representatives grumbled about the treaty and asked to see all the related documents, Washington refused on the grounds that only the Senate had to approve the thing. Which I think he felt was more than enough.)

Well, getting back to the time Washington went over to the Senate, the senators didn't treat him very courteously. All he was trying to do was get the advice and consent of the Senate as specified in the Constitution, and they wouldn't give it to him. You see, the Congress was a successor to the Continental Congress, and they were already organized. They had committees and everything of that kind, so when Washington went down to discuss the treaty with the Senate, when he wanted to get their advice on the treaty, they told him they couldn't do business that way. They said that they had to have a committee, and they'd place the matter before the committee, and then they'd discuss it and get back to him, and they couldn't operate anyhow with the president sitting right there in the Senate and staring at them. The old man* got up and told them they could go to hell as far as he was concerned. He was worse than blunt. He called them a lot of interesting names, and he left in a huff and never went back. He was trying to advise and consent with the Senate and the damn fools wouldn't advise and consent, and after that treaties were just written up and then sent over for consideration.

Washington wasn't the only president who had his problems with Congress, of course, not by any means. Practically every president has had them: even Lincoln, as I've already discussed, when he was saving the Union and some people in Congress were trying to hamper him so he couldn't do his job as president, and he got tough because he wasn't going to let them do that. Franklin Roosevelt had his difficulties, too, particularly, if you remember, with what was called the matter of the nine old men,† the Chief Justice and the associate justices of the Supreme Court. The trouble was that the justices were mostly conservatives left over from previous administrations, and Roosevelt felt that they were hampering his efforts to improve conditions in the country at a time when

*This was a phrase my father used often and about many people, but nearly always affectionately and rarely in a pejorative sense. Washington wasn't an old man when he became president: he was fifty-seven, as compared, for example, to Reagan, who was seventy when he took office, or John Adams, who was sixty-two. My father was sixty-one when Franklin Delano Roosevelt died and he became president, and sixty-four when he ran against and defeated Thomas E. Dewey. MT
†This is an exception to the preceding footnote. Neither Mr. Roosevelt nor my father were being affectionate when they used that phrase. MT

we were in the grip of the worst depression in our history; among other things, they decided that both his NRA and his AAA were unconstitutional. (The AAA, the Agricultural Adjustment Act, was designed to reduce crop surpluses so that farm products would be less easily and cheaply available and farmers could take in more money for their products; and the NRA, the National Recovery Act, was designed to suspend antitrust and price-fixing regulations so that companies could work more closely together and hopefully improve business conditions, with participating companies agreeing as their part of the bargain to end child labor, reduce their workweeks, recognize labor unions, and improve conditions for employees in general.) Roosevelt's desire was to get rid of the men he felt were preventing him from accomplishing his aims, but in his effort to change the situation, the truth of the matter is that he went about things in the wrong way and caused a lot of the difficulties. The plan he proposed was that all Supreme Court justices be required to retire at the age of seventy instead of being allowed to stay on for their lifetimes if they desired, or if that wasn't acceptable, that he be allowed to appoint one additional associate justice, up to a total of six, for each justice who was then, or subsequently reached, the age of seventy and had a minimum of ten years of service. His plan didn't work because it brought protests from a lot of people, including some of his own supporters, that he was trying to "pack" the Supreme Court. In time, of course, many of the old men died, and he ended up with a Chief Justice and eight associate justices of his own selection, all of them far more liberal than the previous fellows.

But the interesting thing is that, even while the nine old men were still sitting on the bench, that conservative Supreme Court suddenly became a lot less conservative and passed a lot of the measures that Roosevelt wanted.

The one thing Roosevelt proved with the many measures he did get through is that the president is the boss and the only boss, and he can call the shots and not let himself be pushed around by the Supreme Court or Congress or any other body or individual. Every president becomes aware very quickly that there are congressional leaders, men serving at the same time as him, who are very anxious to move the power of the operation of the government of the United States into the legislative branch, but not every chief executive has been willing to get tough about it and say that that's all wrong. We've had presidents who sat back and let Congress take their powers away from them. It depends altogether on the leadership that both parties have at any particular time, but it makes no difference how strong the leadership in Congress may be—it shouldn't be allowed to happen. And if a president knows his powers and his duties, it won't.

As I've pointed out before, the president can overcome opposition if he exercises his leadership as chief executive by getting people in and explaining exactly what he wants to do. Most of them—even if they're in the opposition political party, or in the same party as the president but strongly opposed to some of his policies—will end up agreeing with him when he's right. I've had that experience, but it takes leadership to get these things done, and I've tried very hard to be a leader when I felt something was important and right but faced a lot of opposition. I had tremendous opposition from the South, for example, with the racial sections of my Fair Deal program, in which, among other things, I proposed an end to the poll tax, and even though the war was over, the retention of the Fair Employment Practices Committee so that black people could continue to be protected and get their share of jobs. But despite that, I don't think I'm being naive when I say that I don't think that southern leaders were unmoved by what I tried to accomplish. I think that, underneath it all, they're waiting for leadership to give them an out on which they can base a program for progress. And I'm very sure that they'll do what's right—what I pointed out was right—when the time comes.

TWELVE

Accepting the Past and Having Enough Time

THERE were three other presidents alive during James Monroe's two terms, which ran from 1817 to 1825: John Adams, Thomas Jefferson, and James Madison. Jefferson and John Adams both died on the same day, July 4, 1826, and Madison lived until 1836. I don't think Monroe consulted the previous presidents at all. I can't find any record that they were, and I suppose the answer is that Monroe just didn't care to talk to them. That's just my own opinion, but it seems logical.

And there were five other presidents alive when Lincoln was elected in 1860: Martin Van Buren, John Tyler, Millard Fillmore, Franklin Pierce, and James Buchanan. Van Buren and Tyler died in 1862, Buchanan died in 1868, Pierce in 1869, and old Millard Fillmore lasted until 1874. Here, at least, Lincoln had the good sense, as he had about most things, to try to use the knowledge and experience of these men in dealing with the situations that the country faced at that difficult time, and an effort was made to try to get the five men together. Four of them came to Washington, but Martin Van Buren wouldn't come, nobody knows why, and the conference broke up.

That brings me to the next important quality that a good president should have: the ability to continue and further the good programs of former presidents, and not try to abandon them simply because the previous president, or presidents before that one, belonged to a different political party.

Most presidents don't seem to want to talk to former presidents. And from my own experience, I know that it's pretty natural behavior. A new president wants to be president on his own hook and not have a former president around trying to give him advice. It's customary for the president, after he's elected, to want to run things himself. If he wants advisors, he usually wants to pick them out himself and then decide whether he wants to use their advice or not. And most of the people he picks are usually people who think along the same lines as he does.

But that's a mistake, and I tried very hard to avoid that mistake and worked constantly to get all the information I possibly could from people in whom I had confidence—whether we were in agreement or not on various things. Because of that, it was my privilege, and it definitely was a privilege, to ask the advice and get the help of a former president, Herbert Hoover, in the effort to keep people all around the world from starving. And he did a wonderful job of it. His own party had pretty much passed him up, of course. I don't know whether they "disowned" him or not, as some people say. They always had him at every convention, but I don't think they ever gave him any special consideration as a former president, or gave any thought to using his experience. He only had a chance with one Republican president after he went out of office, Eisenhower, and I know that one hasn't given him much consideration.

Well, if a new president comes in and decides to ignore all former presidents, that's his own business I suppose, even though my personal opinion is that it's shortsighted to do so. But the really terrible thing is when a president sets out actively to discredit the policies of the former president, and that's what happened when I was succeeded by Dwight Eisenhower.

Nobody had any reason to believe that Eisenhower, who'd been through the whole program with President Roosevelt and General Marshall and me, would attempt to do what he attempted to do. Well, he didn't succeed, thank goodness. He finally had to approve many of the things established by Roosevelt and myself as far as the foreign policy of the United States was concerned, although we lost or alienated some of our foreign friends when Dulles became secretary of state, and a poor one, and Eisenhower didn't work at his job. Anyway, they didn't manage to reverse things back to the time of Harding.

It was the same thing with Harding himself. Harding did, of course, succeed in reversing much of Wilson's program when he came in. The policy of the people who followed Woodrow Wilson was to decide that everything that Wilson had done was wrong, and the action of Harding and the others was purely political, an effort to have political advantage. And temporarily they did get the political advantage, but it was ruinous to the country in the long run.

We were coming out of isolationism into an entirely new period of international relations, and then along came Harding with his halfhearted statement that he'd support the League of Nations, followed by his abandonment of the organization. I don't think the people elected Harding because they thought he was returning to isolationism; I don't think they had any desire at all to return to isolationism. I think they elected Harding, as I've said earlier, because he coined that ridiculous word "normalcy," and he promised he was going to return the country to a normal condition of ease and comfort and no pressure. People do get tired after a while of being told what they ought to do, and of somebody who not only makes them want to do it but actually do it, and then they vote for some fool and have four years or eight years of rest period in which to think about how wrong they were when they voted as they did. As if it's *ever* possible to have ease and comfort without working for it, and without working *at* it!

But Harding and his people were full of promises like that, and the result was a situation that finally developed into a wild speculative period and caused the Depression, and an isolationism that caused another world war. They're to blame for all the youngsters killed in the Second World War, and I'll continue to say that as long as I live.

It took a president who understood the United States and the world, Franklin Delano Roosevelt, to come along and start to get the country back on its feet again, and also to make Americans remember that we're a world power and have to act like a world power.

Every president has to revitalize the public spirit to some extent. Wilson's great message to the American people was his Fourteen Points, a speech he made to Congress on January 8, 1918, and which he characterized as the only possible program for peace and an end to the World War. Among other things, he called for disarmament, the replacement of secret treaties by open treaties, freedom of the seas, the elimination of restrictive tariffs, and of course, "a general association of nations . . . for the purpose of affording mutual guarantees of political independence and territorial integrity to great and small states alike," meaning the League of Nations. And Roosevelt's opening message, when he was inaugurated on March 4, 1933, used exactly the same kind of direct, no-baloney approach to the problems we were facing at that time. (Incidentally, though not to get off the subject, this was the last time a president was inaugurated in March. After that, we were all put to work more quickly and began operating in January.)

Roosevelt's speech was, of course, the one in which he said, "Let me assert my firm belief that the only thing we have to fear is fear itself—nameless, unreasoning, unjustified fear which paralyzes needed efforts to convert retreat into advance. . . . Our greatest primary task is to put people to work. This is no unsolvable program if we face it wisely and courageously. It can be accomplished in part by direct recruiting by the government itself, treating the task as we would treat the emergency of a war, but at the same time, through this employment, accomplishing greatly needed projects to stimulate and reorganize the use of our natural resources. . . . I shall ask Congress for the one remaining instrument to meet that crisis—broad Executive power to wage a war against the emergency, as great as the power which would be given to me if we were in fact invaded by a foreign foe." Roosevelt said it in beautiful, inspiring language, but that's the gist of it. He wanted to hit people where they lived, and everybody went to work. There isn't any question about that. It's an intangible thing, but it has to be brought to life every time it looks as though our principles and ideals and constructive attitudes are going out the window. And if it isn't, why, then these things do go out the window, and we can have a dictatorship the way they did in Germany under Hitler.

We also, of course, got the United Nations as a result of Roosevelt's administration and mine, which is exactly what the League of Nations was supposed to be in the first place. I'm not saying that the United Nations is a perfect organization, or ever will be. It's far from flawless, and it's weak in many ways. But at least it's a start.

Whenever a president inaugurates a policy that's worthwhile, the chances are that it will carry through sooner or later for the simple reason that we're a two-party government and there are people in both parties with the intelligence to see both sides of a question. And whenever a president inaugurates a policy that is truly for the welfare and the benefit of the country, and his successor comes along and tries to overturn it, there isn't any likelihood that that successor president will succeed in burying it forever. We've had that illustrated very well in the two terms we've just gone through, so the practices of men like Harding and Eisenhower are not only bad for the country but not really worth attempting.

A good president is someone who can put aside political differences and try to carry forward the good programs of the past while simultaneously trying to introduce good new programs of his own. And if he can also manage to have a reasonably friendly relationship with Congress and a cabinet that will carry on the programs which the policies of his administration call for and also have the ability to turn over their functions, at the appropriate time, to their successors in a way so that the smooth functioning of the government can be carried on without any real interruption, then we've had a damn good president and a damn good government. You know what I mean. It's important to keep the government running in an orderly way, just as you'd carry it on if a new president came in to a great corporation. That's the idea. That's all there is to it, though I'm not saying that it's easy to do.

And the final thing that is essential to being a good president is for him to have the full opportunity to accomplish the things he sets out to accomplish. That places me squarely on a soapbox, because I feel very strongly that the Twenty-second Amendment, which limits presidents to two terms, is a terrible amendment. When the people who wrote the Constitution were working on it, they arranged it so that it could be amended, and it's been amended continually. But I think it's only had two very bad amendments. The dumbest of these was the Eighteenth Amendment, the Prohibition Amendment, the worst thing that was ever attached to the Constitution, and it was finally repealed. And the other dumb one is that Twenty-second Amendment limiting the term of the president.

My attitude isn't the result of personal frustration because the amendment limiting presidential terms didn't apply to me; the law was enacted to begin with the president who followed me. I could have run for the presidency as often as I wanted to run, including succeeding myself, as often as I felt like it. But I didn't want to go back because I'd had enough and felt it was time for someone else. (I hoped, of course, that it would be Adlai Stevenson, though it didn't work out that way. Well, as I've said several times before in this book, and will undoubtedly say again, the country has to awaken every now and then to the fact that the people are responsible for the government they get. And when they elect a man to the presidency who doesn't take care of the job, they've got nobody to blame but themselves. I know this is away from the subject of presidential terms, but I thought I should put it in.)

It was Washington who established the custom of a two-term limit, but it didn't happen because he felt that a president shouldn't be allowed to serve longer than that; I think the general attitude was that a president should serve as long as he wanted to serve if he felt he still had things to accomplish, and if he could get people to keep reelecting him. As far as Washington was concerned personally, he decided in his first term that he wasn't going to run again because he'd been attacked so severely by the press of his time, and Jefferson and Madison and Hamilton had to do a lot of persuading to get him to go ahead and run for a second term. But then, after he'd been through his second term, he just made up his mind that he wouldn't take it anymore and he quit, and that established the precedent. After that, it became a matter of custom for a president to be elected for two terms. And you'll find that, with just two exceptions, the two Adamses, every one of the first line of presidents all the way up to the seventh president was elected a second time.

John Adams wasn't popular enough to win a second term, but Jefferson was elected to two terms, and so were Madison and Monroe. Then, like his father, John Quincy Adams didn't make it a second time, either. Then Andrew Jackson was elected twice because he was a strong president, and after Jackson we had a whole row of one-time presidents all the way up to the Civil War. It's obvious from this that, in order to be reelected, a president has to carry out an administration that's for the welfare and benefit of the country as a whole, not only in home affairs but in international affairs, and when he doesn't do that, he doesn't get reelected. So why worry about it?

But there have always been people who felt that the length of time a president can serve should be regulated by law. There have also been those people who felt that a president should be limited to a single term, and that's dead wrong. A single term is simply not enough most of the time, and if a president feels like working his head off for another term, he's got a right to run for it. A single term is too brief for the simple reason that there are two Congresses in the one term of a president, and a president spends a lot of time getting acquainted with the members of those Congresses. And then, in an effort to get his program through, he usually runs for office again and tries to get his programs through in the next two sessions of Congress, which most of the time he's successful in doing. As I've mentioned, there has really only been one president who got his program through in one term and then was able to consider things finished and pack up and go home, and that was James K. Polk, but most of us need two terms and sometimes more.

It was necessary for Roosevelt to continue on account of the world war that was going on. The people themselves have to make up their minds when the time comes to elect and reelect a president, and they chose very wisely, in the case of Roosevelt, to elect him and reelect him three more times because he was needed. There are clearly times when two terms are needed, and times when more than two terms are both necessary and wise.

I'll tell you in plain language why the two-term amendment was passed. It was passed by a Republican Congress, the 80th Congress, a Congress with some particularly vicious members who wanted to discredit a president with the extraordinary achievement of serving and being elected to four terms. And it was ratified by the states while the people were still thinking about the wars they'd been through. But in my opinion, it was almost as bad a mistake as that absurd amendment that tried to legislate people out of drinking when they wanted to drink, and perhaps some sensible future administration and future Congress will repeal this one, too.

PART III

How America Got Started

THIRTEEN

Why People Came to America

I'VE written quite a bit about various presidents in this book, and I'll be saying some more later on. But I'm going to switch gears now and talk a little about our country, the country each of those men ran for a while. And I'd like to begin by taking a look at the way the United States got started.

Around the time of Columbus, there were an estimated five million people in the Western Hemisphere—two million on the North American continent and the rest in South America. Columbus didn't get proper credit for what he'd done until long after he was dead, when his son wrote a book about him and described his accomplishments to the world. As every schoolchild knows, Columbus and all the other explorers thought they were going to India, which they were nowhere near, of course, and the discovery of the Western Hemisphere, which was then open and free, was a pure accident. No one at the time even realized how big it was. Accident or not, however, it was still quite an accomplishment.

But another thing the book did was increase Europeans' lust for gold, which was always very strong. They were all equally that way—

British, French, and Spanish. They all thought, after the discovery of the Western Hemisphere by Columbus, that the right idea was to exploit that hemisphere and take everything and give nothing. And that's exactly what happened, especially after the Spanish found immense quantities of gold in Mexico and Peru and took it all back to Spain.

There's no historical information in the records of Sweden, Norway, or Denmark of Viking exploration; what the Scandinavians have are sagas, verbal accounts passed down from generation to generation, which say that Norsemen came to the area that is now Rhode Island. That's certainly possible, but the real exploration of our country, of course, didn't start until after Columbus. And eventually the Atlantic Coast area was settled by the British and the Dutch, the Spanish came to the South, and the French settled in the eastern part of Canada and all through the Mississippi River valley. The Russians also got into the act: they came in on the northwest corner of the continent and settled in Alaska and had claims as far down as San Francisco.

But the colonization of North America would probably never have happened as rapidly as it did except for all the troubles that were taking place in Europe. In England, there were two revolutions, one of which was in 1649 and against the King, when Charles I got his head cut off and Oliver Cromwell took over, and the other was in 1660, after Cromwell died in 1658 and the country went back into the hands of Charles I's son, Charles II, a couple of years later. When the first Charles was deposed, a lot of his followers came over here and settled in the South. And when Cromwell was replaced by the second Charles, a lot of Cromwell's followers settled in Massachusetts.

The men who settled in Virginia, South Carolina, and North Carolina were called the "gentlemen of Britain," though whether they were or not I don't know. I will say, though, that Virginia became the most progressive of any of the colonies in that time and period. Virginia was in the forefront of the American Revolution and one of the main reasons that the Revolution was a success, and of course many of our great leaders, and much of the leadership in thinking, originated in Virginia. When Jefferson was governor of Virginia, as a good example, his freedom of worship bill was passed by the Virginia legislature and was the first such bill in this country except for one in Maryland, and the Maryland bill was no surprise because Maryland was a Catholic colony and acting as a matter of self-preservation. If you study the history of that period, a great many of the progressive ideas in which we believe today originated in Virginia at that time. Virginia was also one of the last of the southern states to secede during the Civil War and didn't really want to secede even then. The colonists who came to Virginia were mostly of the royalist class, but when they came to Virginia after Charles I got his head cut off, they changed their viewpoint entirely, and they didn't become rabidly conservative until long after the War Between the States.

But getting back to England, eventually Charles II died, of course, and his brother, James II, took over in 1685. But by 1688 he was finished and running off to France, and his son-in-law William, the Prince of Orange, and his daughter Mary, became king and queen. William and Mary were brought in by the lords and the major merchants and other influential people of England, men who didn't want a return of the House of the Stuarts, once the ruling house of England. And even though James II was a Catholic, the new king and queen didn't think the same way and began to persecute Catholics, many of whom fled to Maryland.

William and Mary were as bad in their way as the Bourbons, once the ruling house of France, who never did a thing for the welfare of their country. (In fact, they were descendants of the Bourbons. The truth is that the only good king France ever had was Henry IV, who had an idea, a grand plan, for a league of nations, the first time this concept had ever come up in the world. But if he'd been able to put it through, it might have stopped a great many of the things that caused the settlement of the American continent, so maybe it's a good thing he didn't.)

Aside from Henry IV, however, most of the French kings were pretty terrible, and a lot of French Protestants were being persecuted by Catholics in the same way that Catholics were being persecuted in England by Protestants. And many French Protestants, the Huguenots, left their country and settled in South Carolina.

Then there were Dutch settlements in New York and New Jersey, and Swedish settlements in Delaware, and German settlements in Pennsylvania, and a lot of indentured people from England also came to Virginia and Georgia and other places. The indentured people came as servants, but they were servants only for a while. There was a time limit on their service, just long enough to pay for their transportation. After that, most of these people became landowners and helped to settle Tennessee and the Northwest Territories, all of the area up to the Mississippi River that was the western half of the United States at that time. Homesteading really began in Virginia. That's really where the idea started that finally made possible the settlement of the entire West.

And when you stop to think about it, there really wasn't any other known place for the colonists to go. The only other possibility was Africa, and that was no good because the Moors controlled the whole northern coast, which was the entrance to Africa from Europe. As I write this, the French are having the same trouble with the Moors that any group has that tries to go in there. The colonists' only outlet for a free approach to a new life was the new continent in the Western Hemisphere, where there was no opposition on the continent except a natural, and at that time very small, opposition by the inhabitants of that continent.

If I were selecting a place to begin to describe the history of the American people, it wouldn't just be the period of the settlement of the various colonies—it would also be the beginning of the formation and development of their common attitudes toward self-government. The people who made up early America, the British and the French and the Germans and the Dutch and all the others, brought with them different customs and different ways of dressing and different languages, but they had two really important things in common right from the start.

One of these was that so many of them had come to America to escape religious persecution. All the European countries oppressed people because, as I've said, they had a history in which it was believed that royalty, the kings and queens and emperors and empresses, were placed in their positions by God's direction, and that people who differed from them in religious beliefs—or any other kind of beliefs, for that matter —were going against the will of God. Well, I felt that was nonsense the moment I was old enough to read about it and start thinking about things of that sort. I happen to be a Baptist (though I attended a Presbyterian church and Sunday school when I was a boy because it was closer to where we lived than the Baptist place), and I'm certain that many Baptists and Presbyterians of the period, and many Lutherans and Catholics and Jews and other people who lived then and became Americans, felt the same way.

I think the men and women who worked so hard to escape from oppression, and left their homes and relatives and friends to make the long and dangerous move to America, did a lot of thinking about what really constituted human liberty, and about freedom and their own welfare and the welfare of the people around them. (There's no doubt about the fact that, after they got here, some people turned out to be just as oppressive as the people they'd left, but fortunately there weren't all that many of those.) To some extent, the vision of the four great powers, Spain, France, Holland, and Britain, the decision to open up the Western Hemisphere, might be said to be what really caused the United States, but the desire to escape from persecution is what sped it up and shaped and developed our country.

The second thing all the colonists had in common was the deep-seated, let's even call it urgent, desire of so many of the people to improve their financial status. The people who came here were transplanting some of the customs of the British and the Dutch and the Swedes and the others, but one thing they were determined not to transplant was the notion that they had to remain in the same economic class as they'd been in in the old country. Most of the people who came over were economically below the class of the people who were running the government, or at least below the people who had the ear and the friendship of the people running the government, and many of the men and women came to the Western Hemisphere with the idea of perhaps ending up economically in the same position as the ruling classes in Britain, Holland, Sweden, and the other places. Everybody felt he could better himself if he could go to a continent that had not yet been explored and settled and taken over by the great powers. It was all finally taken over by the great powers, anyway—Spain and France and Britain eventually controlled the whole Western Hemisphere, for all practical purposes—but there was still a very good chance for financial improvement and even wealth for any colonist who was willing to work hard for it.

They had to work plenty hard, all right. There were some parts of the colonial front on the Atlantic Ocean that were fertile and rich, but there were other parts that were not so fertile and rich, including Massachusetts, Rhode Island, and Connecticut. Truthfully, I don't see how in the world those people in those three places ever made a living when they first landed here. The same thing can be said about Georgia, where a lot of the poor people were taken out of the prisons of Britain and came here to farm but found exceedingly poor soil. The best soil on the Eastern coast at that time was in North Carolina, Virginia, and Maryland; and then later on, of course, people went over the Appalachian Mountains and found something they'd never even dreamed about, the richest part of the agricultural world. That area, from the Appalachian Mountains to the Rockies, and from the border of Canada to the Gulf of Mexico, is still the richest agricultural area in the world. But the people of Connecticut and Georgia and the other places managed somehow, and it made tough citizens of them, and they made a contribution to the country on that account.

So there they were, people from just about every European country and every type of European culture, speaking different languages but coming here for the same two important reasons. It was a melting pot in every sense of the phrase, and there's nothing like a melting pot to bring people together. They soon began to realize that the only difference between them *was* language, and it wasn't all that hard for people of other backgrounds to learn English when that became the official language of the country, and before we knew it we were an undivided nation. I think the uniqueness of the United States is due to the fact that our people came originally from every section of Europe but were essentially the same kinds of people with the same reasons for being here, and the fact that the people who eventually ran our first government were in many cases scholarly men who'd studied government through the ages and knew a lot—not only about all of the colonies and their similarities and differences, but about world history and the things we're taught by past events as well. And when we got to the point where we finally became a sort of unit, a unified group, with the Continental Congress, we had a group of men who knew more about the history of government than any group of men who've ever gotten together anywhere.

Keep in mind the fact that it took quite a while for these men to get together—from 1608 to 1760. That's a long time. Part of it, of course, was the result of the slowness of communication and transportation. It's improvements in communication and transportation that have made the United States what it is today, because we now have communications systems and transportation systems that are out of this world when you come right down to it. In those days it took five or six days to go from Baltimore to New York. Now you can do it in half an hour. But mostly it took all those years for the colonists to decide to form their own country because they really weren't ready for a long time, emotionally and psychologically, to break away totally from their homelands. There had to be plenty of injustice to put them in that frame of mind, but when they finally got there, they were so determined that they were immovable.

There's no way to arrive at a conclusion on the reasons for the existence of the American government, in the way in which it was set up, without an examination of the history of government long before that, because the idea of individual freedom and individual rights goes back to ancient times. You'll find thinking along those lines all the way back in the time of Hammurabi, who ruled Babylonia, the huge area of the Mesopotamian Valley in Asia around the Euphrates and Tigris rivers, about seventeen hundred or eighteen hundred years before the birth of Christ. (Babylonia was one of the kingdoms in the ancient region of Mesopotamia. Its capital was the city of Babylon. The Mesopotamian people were the ancient Persians; they were part of the Semitic race.) The fundamental basis for a just government, in my opinion, originated there in the Mesopotamian Valley long before the Greek and the Roman empires came into existence.

Hammurabi was no saint in a lot of ways; he's the fellow who popularized the phrase "an eye for an eye," and he meant it literally and carried it out lots of times. He also divided his people into three different and rigidly separated classes: the very rich merchants and landowners and priests, the poorer merchants and the artisans and peasants, and the slaves. Whenever the Babylonians conquered a place, they made slaves out of the people they conquered. And as I say, it wasn't exactly a classless society even aside from the slaves. Even in that upper group, they had nobles and people who were allegedly in charge of the government, but in all those countries, Egypt and the countries of Mesopotamia and the rest of them, the priesthood really ran things. That usually came to a violent end, as all those priesthood governments did. In the case of Babylonia, the Kassites, a nomadic tribe from nearby Elam,* took it over after a while, and then it became a subsidiary state of the Assyrian Empire.

But Hammurabi believed to some extent in the rights of the individual, and he wrote a code of laws that are absolutely astonishing when you read them now because so many of them are applicable to present times. They're concerned with the rights of the individual to live his own life as he went along, and the rights of property, and how to deal with murder and adultery and divorce, and just about everything else. Hammurabi had his codification carved on a diorite column, and it's a short document that says it all in just 3,600 lines of cuneiform. (Diorite is a type of rock, and cuneiform is an ancient form of wedge-shaped writing something like Egyptian hieroglyphics.) I believe the French got hold of the column in modern times and it can be seen in Paris. But you don't have to learn cuneiform and go there to read Hammurabi's laws; they've been published in book form, and it's just a little book, but it's fascinating. I've read the book over and over, and it's interesting to read every time.

There were also ideas about justice and the welfare of the individual in the Greek city-states, the colonies that the Greeks formed in the eighth through sixth centuries before Christ, and that were similar in some ways to the American colonies, except that the city-states also believed that there were classes of people, in their case two classes, those who didn't have to work and those who did. But at least they had some people with ideals on how fair government ought to be set up. You take the statements of Plato, who lived from about 427 B.C. to about 347 B.C., and Socrates, who lived from 469 to 399 B.C.; they always worked with the idea that the individual had his rights. (Unfortunately, they also believed that there were a certain set of individuals who didn't have any rights. But then, let's face it, so did we. At least until we got rid of slavery we did.)

The Romans had exactly the same ideas as the Greek city-states. They got their ideas, in fact, from the Greek city-states, and the basis of these ideas was, again, the freedom of the individual and the rights of the individual. The objective of the Roman Republic was to make people

---

*Babylonia is now part of Iraq, and Elam is now part of Iran. They were fighting then as now. As my father states in this book, he believed strongly in the lessons we can learn from the past and in the ways we can apply those lessons to present situations. He's quoted succinctly on this point in Merle Miller's book about him: "There's nothing new in human nature. The only thing that changes are the names we give things. If you want to understand the twentieth century, read the lives of the Roman emperors, all the way back from Claudius to Constantine. . . . Those people had the same troubles as we have now. Men don't change. The only thing new in the world is the history you don't know." MT

feel that the greatest honor that could come to a man was to be a Roman citizen, a citizen of the city of Rome, and the men there were willing to fight for the freedom of the city of Rome and of the individual. They had slaves, too, of course, but no matter whether a man was a slave or what he was, he had his rights under the law to make an appearance and get justice.

But then, naturally, the success of the Roman Republic, which became the Roman Empire and conquered the whole known world, was such that the people began to take it for granted and think that it would continue forever. The Romans began to grow fat and lazy, and the Empire was broken up from the outside. It wasn't broken up by a revolution or anything like that, it was broken up by the Gauls and all the rest of those savages; though I guess it would have broken up sooner or later in some other way, anyway.

In any case, the breakup of the Roman Empire was what eventually brought on European civilization—though let's call it so-called European civilization, since it sometimes wasn't too civilized. After the downfall of the Roman Empire, after it had been torn apart by the Vandals and the Gauls and all the other savages, there were a whole lot of little kingdoms, all of the kings always fighting with each other and killing each other. Then the Germans, across the Rhine, eventually began to settle down, and other places began to settle down, and in time the nations of Europe were formed more or less along the same lines as we have them today. They were on a very small scale as compared to the Roman civilization in the Mediterranean, but the countries on the western coast of Europe—Spain and France and Britain—were the great nations of the world at the time of the settlement of our own country. There were no sprawling empires in the Roman sense, huge territories next to each other being conquered and becoming a single land, but none of the European countries were adverse to the idea of owning lands all around the world and becoming an empire that way. And when everybody learned what Columbus had opened up, all of these countries were anxious to have a hand in the settlement and control of that part of the world.

I've just read an article, a day or two ago, on the policies of the Roman Catholic church, and the author made the interesting statement that, if the church had been more tolerant of Martin Luther, there wouldn't have been any Reformation, no real breaking away from the Catholic religion. But the church wasn't tolerant of Luther when he was the leader of the movement of Protestantism in Germany in the sixteenth century, and you might also say that the real Reformation, or at least the real advancement of the Reformation, took place when Cardinal Richelieu became chief minister of France in 1624. Richelieu, whose full handle was Armand du Plessis, Duc de Richelieu, was a prelate who became powerful politically as a protégé of Marie de Medici, second wife of King Henry IV of France. The marriage in 1600 was the great event of the turn of the century, and Rubens did a whole series of paintings about it, which I've seen in the Louvre and which are just beautiful; but then Henry was assassinated in 1610, and Marie became regent for her young son, Louis XIII, born in 1601. Marie continued to rule France for three years after her son came of age, and Richelieu eventually found himself in trouble when Marie became jealous of his increasing power and friendship with the young king; but then Louis exiled his mother in 1630 (remember what I said about so-called civilization?) and Marie ran to the Netherlands and died there in 1642 without ever returning to France. Richelieu pretty much ran the country after that as chief minister, a position equivalent to prime minister in England.

The Roman Catholic church was centralized in Spain at that time, and Richelieu was anti-Spanish, so even though he was a cardinal of the Catholic church, he became more and more allied with German and Dutch Protestants, and when the Protestant king Gustavus Adolphus of Sweden went to war with Spain, Richelieu financed Sweden's army. Gustavus Adolphus was killed in one of the battles, but more and more Scandinavians and Germans became Lutherans as a result of the war, and a large number of French people became separated from the Catholic church as well.

The move toward Protestantism in France had actually begun long before that, when the French theologian, John Calvin, born in 1509, rebelled against what he considered the too conservative teachings of the Catholic church and began to preach a philosophy that became known as Calvinist Protestantism in 1533. By 1598, this movement had grown so strong that there were actually two hundred French cities under Protestant control, and to keep peace in the country, King Henry IV issued a ruling that year, the famous Edict of Nantes, which guaranteed freedom of worship to the Protestants, royal subsidies of Protestant schools, courts made up of both Catholic and Protestant judges to deal with cases involving Protestants, and a lot of other fair-minded things. This held through his reign and the reign of his son, but then King Louis XIV came along, and he listened to the prejudiced mumblings of his anti-Protestant advisors and revoked the Edict of Nantes in 1685 and began to persecute Protestants in increasingly ugly ways.

One form of persecution was called the dragonnades because it involved billeting soldiers, usually the rowdy Dragoons, in Protestant homes without permission and then ignoring the outrages they committed, including rapes, robberies, and murders. Huge groups of French Protestants, the Huguenots—I can't tell you where or why they got that name because nobody seems to know, and every encyclopedia and dictionary

I've consulted just says "origin unknown"—began to leave the country, escaping to England, Germany, the Netherlands, Switzerland, and of course, to America in such large numbers that whole cities were depopulated. It was an act of massive stupidity on Louis XIV's part, and reminiscent in its way of Nazi Germany's persecution of Jews and their loss thereby of many of the country's leading scientists and other intellectuals. Most of France's best skilled artisans were Huguenots, and their departure caused severe damage to the country's economy. After a while, the only sizable number of Huguenots remaining in France were in a barren and unapproachable mountain area in southern France called the Cévennes; eventually a later ruler, King Louis XVI, gave the remaining Huguenots a sort of limited return to religious freedom by granting, in 1785, what he called "tolerance" and ending persecution, but full equality for French Protestants wasn't achieved until modern times, when church and state were separated in France in 1905. But meanwhile, of course, the wonderful Huguenot artisans who came to this country, and were typical of all the good but persecuted people who came here, did a lot to help *our* economy and growth.

And that little tour of world history brings us right back to our own beginnings, the beginnings of the United States. Religious and racial persecution is moronic at all times, perhaps the most idiotic of human stupidities. As I've said, however, the acts of stupidity through the ages did us a kind of unintentional favor—by driving so many different kinds of good people to our shores and merging them together as Americans.

This chapter has gotten to be a bit long. Let's continue in the next one.

FOURTEEN

What Led to the American Revolution

I don't think that the people who made up the colonies at the time of the American Revolution really wanted to tear themselves loose from the mother country. I think the people really wanted to stay in the British hegemony* if they had an opportunity to do so, and if they'd had a king who was a smart man, I don't think there would have been any secession from the British Empire. But the British monarch, George III, who was born in 1738 and took over the throne when he was twenty-two, was a very tough and mean person, and not all that bright, either, and he caused the Revolution to take place. From the American point of view, of course, the Revolution was a blessing, because it enabled the

---

*My father was a plain-spoken man and always said he preferred small words to big words. He also said that people sometimes forgot that the purpose of language was to convey thoughts to one another, and they used big words not to convey thoughts in the clearest way but to impress each other. My father, however, knew the big words and sometimes surprised people—and me, as in this case—by using an unfamiliar word now and then when it was the best choice. Some of the readers of this book may be ahead of me and know exactly what "hegemony" means when they come across it in that sentence, but I'll admit that I didn't and had to look it up. It's the right choice: it means "preponderant influence or authority, especially of a nation over others." MT

colonists to establish the principle that is still very much the essence of American political philosophy: that government must be by the consent of the governed. But from the British point of view, a lot of people knew even then that it could have been avoided.

There's really no question about the fact that the colonists could have been controlled if there had been some common sense used in Britain. A number of the great political leaders of the time, Burke and William Pitt, Earl of Chatham, and Charles James Fox and Isaac Barré and others, tried their level best to get things in shape so that there'd be no reason for the colonists to do what they eventually did, but it couldn't be managed. George III was an absolute monarch, and some of those absolute monarchs believed that God had given them all the knowledge in the world, and that therefore it wasn't necessary to listen to the advice or ideas of anyone else even when it would have been smart to do so. But as I've said, King George III wasn't smart, and he also began to show increasingly visible signs of mental illness, so he did a lot of stupid and unpopular things. (In fact, he became so unpopular that, even though he lived until 1820, he pretty much gave up running the government in 1783 and turned the reins over to his prime minister, the younger William Pitt, son of the Earl of Chatham. Then his periods of mental illness became more and more frequent, and in 1810 he was finally declared permanently insane and his son, George IV, took over as regent.)

Before the thirteen colonies joined together and became a single nation, the British colonies were, I believe, the best run of all the colonies anywhere in the world. Most of the other countries, such as France and Spain, appointed colonial governments run by governors with absolute power under the Crown, and the people were not represented at all in those governments. In the British colonies, the people weren't represented in the Parliament, but they had a definite say in local matters. Most of the British colonies had royal governors appointed by the British Crown, but they also had local legislatures, which acted on tax matters and things of that sort, and in the hundred and fifty years or so before the Revolution, they became very experienced in running local governments and did very good jobs in all of the colonies. I don't know if this method of operation was an innovation or not on the part of the British government, but I think it was because I believe these were the first colonies the British ever had; I don't think they had any elsewhere until much later. Anyway, even though some of the colonies in those days didn't even have the population that some of our counties have now, I think the local operation of the colonies, far away from the homeland and the centuries-old belief that the king knew what was best for everybody, made a lot of people determined to have a stronger hand in their own lives and welfare.

Although it's usually taken for granted, it's worth remembering that no important group of Englishmen, in the centuries before the Revolution, ever sought to settle themselves beyond and outside the influence of the chief executive of England—whether king, queen, or protector. Secession from the Empire waited for later generations and took place after there was so much provocation that things became unendurable.

The biggest problem was, of course, the thing that eventually became the battle cry of the Revolution, taxation without representation—in other words, the fact that, since the colonists had no representatives in Parliament, the taxes levied on them, and the rules under which they lived and operated, were established by strangers living thousands of miles away across the ocean, and not by people, their own people, who understood their needs and their ways of thinking.

The general British attitude was that Parliament acted for Virginia or Massachusetts in the same way it acted for Somerset or Kent; Virginia and Massachusetts had local legislatures to deal with minor local matters, but the king and his Parliament had the right without question to make all other decisions. They felt that Parliament exercised the same authority over the colonies as it did over local English towns, and that the only difference between the two places was distance; and they pointed out threateningly that the colonies were just "corporations" that could be limited or dissolved by the king and by Parliament at will. The colonists, however, felt that there was a far more basic and essential difference between the local English areas and themselves. Somerset and Kent had men in Parliament to represent them and express their views, and they didn't. As Commager and Nevins put it in their book on the history of the United States, they felt that therefore "the English Parliament had no more right to pass laws for Massachusetts than the Massachusetts legislature had to pass laws for England. If the king wanted money from a colony, he could get it by asking for a grant; but Parliament had no authority to take it by passing a Stamp Act or other revenue law. In short, a British subject, whether in England or America, was to be taxed only by and through his own representatives."

Some historians have interpreted all this to mean that the colonists were saying that they'd pay taxes to England only if their local legislatures levied the taxes and said they should pay them, but I don't think that's what the colonists meant at all. They were realistic enough to realize a fact that political leaders have known practically since the beginning of time: that people will pay local taxes more or less willingly, but are very grudging about paying taxes for other than local needs, and pay these only because there are higher authorities who make it mandatory that they do. I think that what they were saying was simple enough: that they were just like all the other English people even though they lived on another continent, and just as good as all the other English people, and deserved representation in Parliament just like all the others.

To put it another way, our Revolution was for the idea of representation in government, so that people could not be taxed except by their own consent. I think that what the colonists were saying, in effect, is that they were perfectly willing to pay the taxes if they had a chance to argue the question and find out whether the taxes were just or not, and I think they'd certainly have paid the taxes if they'd been given the representation they wanted. Most of the people who started talking revolution were the landowners and the small farmers and the small businessmen in the towns, and their objective, which was understandable enough, was a government in which they could have a voice. In a sense, the American Revolution was an attempted reorganization of the government approach to taxation and the ownership of property, a kind of capitalist revolution. It can't really be called anything else because every fellow who owns property is a capitalist, doesn't matter who he is. And capitalism shouldn't be a dirty word. It's abuse that's caused the problem; the very rich have made it a dirty word.

But mean old George III didn't see matters the way the colonists did, and a lot of things began to happen, some of them just plain silly and some of them very serious indeed. There was a thing called The Battle of Golden Hill in New York in 1770, in which some townspeople and soldiers stationed there began to call each other a lot of foolish names and people on both sides picked up guns, but fortunately nobody on either side fired the guns. That was one of the silly events. In the same year, however, there was a far worse confrontation in Boston. The soldiers stationed there were in the habit of performing on fife and drum every time they changed the guard, including when they did this on Sundays, and some of the local residents felt that this violated the Sabbath and began to yell at the soldiers and call them names, too. Then, on March 5 of that year, two soldiers were beaten up, and when other soldiers rushed out, a mob gathered and began to taunt the soldiers and pretty much dare them to shoot. The soldiers held on to their tempers, but then the mob knocked down another soldier, and when he stood up, his musket went off accidentally. This caused a general free-for-all, and then some other soldiers began to fire, deliberately though without orders from their commanding officer. Five people were killed, and the event became known as the Boston Massacre and inflamed people in every colony.

Then there was an incident that took place in Rhode Island when a British warship, the *Gaspee,* ran aground near Providence. It wasn't a very menacing kind of warship; it was just a little thing on which only eight guns were mounted, but the people of Rhode Island hated it because its sole assignment was to catch smugglers, and a lot of people in Rhode Island were involved in smuggling. So a bunch of people jumped onto the *Gaspee,* forced the captain and the crew to get off, and set fire to the ship, reducing it to ashes.

And then, of course, there was the Boston Tea Party. This famous event was the result of the fact that a new cabinet took over in England in 1767, and their strongest platform promise was that they'd reduce domestic land taxes. But the new chancellor of the exchequer, a fellow named Charles Townshend, had to get money for the treasury from somewhere, and naturally he came up quickly with the idea of getting it from those unimportant people in the Colonies. It wasn't the brightest idea in the world because the colonists had already shown how they felt about taxes—at least, how they felt about taxes imposed upon them without their approval and agreement—when a thing called the Stamp Act was passed two years earlier, in March 1765, for the alleged purpose of "defraying the expenses of defending, protecting and securing the British colonies and plantations in America." That law required that stamps had to be bought, at a cost of anywhere from a few pennies to a few pounds, and placed on everything from college diplomas, playing cards, liquor licenses, deeds, and mortgages to calendars and almanacs. And what made it even worse was that stamps also had to be bought and placed on newspapers and printed advertisements and broadsheets and the like, raising the costs of those things substantially. And of course, the colonial printers and publishers were often the best educated and most articulate men in the Colonies, and they did a lot, by way of their publications and local speeches, to anger the citizens about the law. There were so many riots in the streets, and so much boycotting of British products which required stamps, that the Stamp Act was repealed in 1766.

Before it was repealed, however, there was also another heavy cost placed on the colonists without their consent, and on which they hadn't even been consulted: the Quartering Act, which became a law of the land in 1765. This was a requirement that the colonists pick up one-third of the costs of quartering and feeding the 10,000 British soldiers stationed at that time in America—giving them lodging in inns, barns, taverns, and houses, supplying them with food, liquor, salt, candles, and other things, and furnishing wagons to haul their supplies. The cost to the Colonies came to about £360,000 a year, and the colonists felt it was adding insult to injury to have to pay this money because so many of the soldiers were strictly to keep them in line and make sure they obeyed unjust laws and paid unjust taxes. The Quartering Act was also soon repealed.

But there was still that necessity to bring in money, and so the Townshend Acts were passed, placing duties on tea, paint, glass, lead, and other products. Townshend and other officials argued that this was different from the Stamp Act because the Stamp Act imposed duties on many internal things, products created and consumed in the Colonies, whereas these duties were strictly external and placed only on things coming in from the outside.

Well, the colonists agreed that the new duties were different, all right—different and worse. They pointed out that many of the products came in from the outside because they weren't, and in some instances couldn't be, manufactured or grown in the Colonies, but that didn't make them any less desirable or necessary, and the new duties would in many cases put them out of reach for colonists with limited funds. This time there was an even greater uproar, and all of the duties were canceled with a single exception—the duty on tea. The boneheaded King George III and some of his advisors, particularly his prime minister, Lord North, insisted on continuing the tea duty, a tax of threepence on every pound of tea, saying it was necessary to leave one tax on the books as a "test of authority."

The colonists reacted exactly as might be expected. In New York and Philadelphia, ships carrying tea were sent back to England without being allowed to unload their cargo. In Charleston, a shipment of tea was seized by residents and locked up so that it couldn't be sold or taken back. And in Boston, as every schoolchild knows, the citizenry made its feelings known in a more visible—or as one historian has described it, a "more theatrical"—way, the Boston Tea Party.

The leading firebrand in Boston was Samuel Adams, who had already done a lot to unify the Colonies in their anger over taxation without representation and other thoughtlessly imperious acts by the British by forming "Committees of Correspondence," which circulated detailed descriptions of every unjust act to every colony. Adams, a second cousin of John Adams, and with John Hancock the organizer of a group called the Sons of Liberty, pledged to oppose "British tyranny," got together a group of fifty men. He dressed up the others and himself as Indians, and on the night of December 16, 1773, they climbed aboard a number of ships in Boston Harbor, broke open 343 crates of tea, and dumped them into the water. Some conservative local merchants felt that was pretty silly stuff, too, or possibly worse than silly—just too damn dangerous; but most other people, including Samuel Adams's more conservative cousin John, felt that the tea-dumping was a necessary and correct thing to do.

King George and his friends, of course, were furious, and they, in turn, decided that it was necessary and correct to punish the Bostonians. They closed the Boston port and said it would remain closed until the East India Company, which owned the tea, was compensated for its loss;

changed Massachusetts's charter, the document most dear to the hearts of the people in that colony, by removing practically all the personal liberties granted in it; "royalized" the colony by replacing Thomas Hutchinson as governor of Massachusetts with General Thomas Gage, commander of the British troops in America; reactivated the Quartering Act; insulted all colonists by stating that English officers accused of capital crimes in America wouldn't necessarily be tried by local courts but could elect to be sent back to England and tried by friendlier tribunals; and ordered the arrest of Sam Adams and John Hancock. All this was opposed by the more sensible British political leaders like Burke and Lord Chatham, who pleaded for gentler and more conciliatory action, but old George didn't listen to them. And the new acts, which colonists labeled the Intolerable Acts, backfired quickly.

Gage sent soldiers to arrest Adams and Hancock, but they evaded the soldiers and managed to escape; they then hid out and continued to fan the flames. John Adams and another colonist, James Wilson, wrote pamphlets questioning the right of Parliament, and by inference the King, to give them orders and place restraints on them without their consent. A Massachusetts group issued a declaration called the Suffolk Resolves, daring though unofficial, which called the Intolerable Acts null and void and proposed the formation of a local militia to protect Massachusetts against British soldiers if that became necessary. And finally Virginia leaders suggested a Continental Congress at which representatives of all the colonies would meet and discuss their grievances against the homeland.

The Continental Congress met at Carpenter's Hall in Philadelphia on September 5, 1774, with a man named Peyton Randolph, a Virginia lawyer and close friend of George Washington's, presiding. (Randolph was a very good man but isn't much remembered today because he didn't participate in the American Revolution; he became ill and died in 1775 at the age of fifty-four.) The Congress was attended by fifty-one men, delegates from every colony except Georgia, and issued a series of declarations in which they stated their "rights and immunities" and listed all the British acts that violated these rights. They also stated openly their support of the Suffolk Resolves, and most important to the British government from the economic point of view, reached an agreement to stop accepting British imports after three months and exporting American goods to Britain after a year, and continuing the boycott until Britain agreed to listen to their grievances and correct them. They also defined punishments for people who violated the boycott, including some uncivilized things, popular at the time, like tarring and feathering and public whipping of miscreants. It wasn't an easy step for many of the delegates to accept, since many of the colonies depended substantially on England for sale of their products; Virginia, for example, sold much of its tobacco there. But the colonists were determined to regain and achieve their rights, and in the end eleven of the thirteen colonies enforced the boycott, only New York and the absent Georgia failing to do so.

The delegates weren't yet talking about breaking with England and if necessary using force to do it, because there were, in effect, three different types of thinking represented at the meetings, and two of these three groups didn't advocate force at all. These were men who were totally against force under any circumstances, and men who didn't think force would be necessary because they felt confident that England could be made to see reason and treat them better without resorting to force. But there was a third group present whose members felt that force might be necessary and acceptable if all other means failed, and so the idea was, at least, planted at that time.

The Continental Congress adjourned on October 26, but agreed to hold a second Continental Congress if their complaints were ignored by the King and his advisors, and they forwarded their list of complaints and demands to England. For a while, the British government seemed to relent and relax, saying it would cancel all taxation of the Colonies provided that the colonies would in turn agree to help support British defense needs and also support the costs of maintaining British officers in America. A compromise might have been worked out along these lines, but then, in the same breath, Parliament became very emotional about the importance of enforcing British law in the colonies and added a whole new set of resolutions that restricted the liberty of the colonists even more than in the past. This encouraged British officers stationed in America to get even tougher, and on April 18, 1775, General Gage decided to send a force of eight hundred men to Lexington, Massachusetts, where he'd heard that Sam Adams and John Hancock were hiding out, and then on to Concord, where it was rumored that a cache of ammunition was stored.

Then, as all of us remember from our schoolbooks and from Henry Wadsworth Longfellow's famous poem, Paul Revere warned people that the British were coming, and a group of militiamen, men who were mostly farmers and called themselves minutemen, seized their rifles and were waiting at Lexington when the British soldiers, with Major John Pitcairn in command, arrived there on the morning of April 19. (Though it was really three fellows who did the warning. I'm not trying to take anything away from old Paul, whom history tells us was a fine, brave fellow, a great silversmith, a skilled printer and engraver and maker of bells, and even an expert dentist who made George Washington a good set of wooden teeth so he could eat properly and keep his mind on his work. But just to keep the history straight, it was certainly Paul Revere who saw two lights and not one in that churchtower and knew the British were coming by sea rather than land, but it was actually three men who set out to warn people, the other two being William Dawes and Samuel Prescott. In fact, old Paul Revere never completed the mission: Dawes and Revere were surprised by a British patrol, and Revere was captured. Dawes escaped but had to turn back, and only Prescott got through to Concord with word that the British were on their way.)

To this day, nobody knows for sure who started the shooting at Lexington. The leader of the minutemen was Captain John Parker, and he saw at once that his tiny group of men were hopelessly outnumbered by the British soldiers and ordered his men to withdraw. But while they were obeying his orders, admittedly very slowly, someone fired a single shot, and then a lot of British soldiers began to shoot—shoot *back,* they reported afterwards. The Americans insisted afterwards that it was a British soldier who panicked and fired that first shot, and the British insisted afterwards that it was a minuteman, and we'll never really know (though H. G. Wells, an Englishman himself, and a man who did intensive research and study of records when he wrote his admirable book *The Outline of History,* says unhesitatingly in that book that a British soldier fired the first shot). In any case, and sadly, there's no question about the fact that British soldiers fired a lot of shots after the first one, and when it was all over, eight colonists lay dead and nine wounded on the village green at Lexington.

That first shot was later called "the shot heard round the world," and when the colonists met again for the Second Continental Congress on May 10, less than a month after the massacre at Lexington, there was no longer much hope or interest in settling matters peaceably with the British. A final message expressing a hope for peace was sent to King George III, but it was frankly halfhearted, and the delegates simultaneously called for the organization of soldiers in Boston into an American Continental Army, and in a brilliant choice, appointed George Washington as commander of the soldiers. On the same day that the Congress started, May 10, a group of men from Vermont, headed by Ethan Allen and called the Green Mountain Boys, together with a body of Connecticut militia led by a man who later became a lot less popular with Americans, Benedict Arnold, moved against the British and captured Fort Ticonderoga, and two days later, Allen's cousin, Seth Warner, led another group of colonial soldiers and captured Crown Point, both of these in New York. The British under General Gage immediately moved to capture Boston, regarded, of course, by the British as the hotbed of American rebellion, and a month later, on June 16 and 17, came the Battle of Bunker Hill.

Let me, please, stop to correct this for the historical record, too, because the battle didn't take place at Bunker Hill. The American soldiers were ordered to occupy Bunker Hill and wait for the British, but they decided instead to fortify a place called Breed's Hill, slightly to the east of Bunker Hill and at a lower level. It doesn't really matter which hill it was; the colonists proved themselves to be formidable fighters, and even though the battle was a minor one in the context of the whole Revolutionary War, it had immense importance because it established the whole tone and mood of the war—established American determination and British fear of that determination.

The Americans had only 3,500 men, many of whom weren't even armed, and the much larger British army could have overcome them with ease by moving on them silently and from the rear. In fact, they could have won without a battle by simply occupying nearby Charlestown Neck with the help of their navy and waiting things out, cutting off the Americans' supplies and starving them into surrendering. But the British didn't wage war in that way in those days; they wanted to win only by what they considered a fair fight, and their idea of a fair fight was to march openly toward the enemy and with drums and martial music going full blast. General Gage had waited prudently for reinforcements after Lexington, and he was now joined by Generals William Howe, John Burgoyne, and Sir Henry Clinton, so he now became less prudent and (take your choice) more brave or dumber and decided to fight the battle in the established way. He ordered General Howe to take the hill with his men wearing their full-dress red uniforms (which is why the colonials referred to them derisively as "lobsterbacks") and carrying knapsacks and ammunition and three days' rations weighing perhaps a hundred pounds or more. He also ordered the British soldiers to advance in rank and warned them never to break rank. In short, he ordered them to move toward the Americans as the most visible targets possible on God's green earth, while the Americans waited for them silently and crouched and hidden.

The Americans waited until the British soldiers were about forty yards away, and then they fired, aiming at the British soldiers' middle. It was an awful, horrible slaughter, and finally the British retreated. Then they came on again, marching in rank in the same way, a brave but senseless act, and again the Americans cut them down, and again, after a while, they retreated. On the third assault, the colonists ran out of ammunition, and after firing their last two rounds apiece, surrendered.

But the British had lost 1,054 men to the Americans' 441, and not long afterward, Gage sailed back to England in disgrace. And General Howe, who took over command from Gage, was so appalled by the slaughter he'd witnessed that he was a weak and timid commander after that.

FIFTEEN

Washington— A General Without Experience

WASHINGTON took command of the American army, such as it was, in July 1775. He was forty-three years old at that time, and even though he was sufficiently well-known and popular among the delegates at the Second Continental Congress to have been given the job of leading the American military against the British, he was essentially a question mark as a commander. His total previous military experience had been as a colonel in the French and Indian War, and even that didn't happen because he liked the military life—but because he loved and admired his stepbrother Lawrence and wanted to follow in his footsteps.

Augustine Washington, father of George and Lawrence and five other children, had been married first to a woman named Jane Butler, but she died in 1730, and he married Mary Ball the next year, bringing two sons to his second marriage, Lawrence and Augustine, Jr., who was called Austin. George was born eleven months later. (As every American knows, the date was February 22, 1732. But in fact, the Gregorian calendar wasn't in use at that time; the Julian calendar was the one used, under which the date was February 11. Washington celebrated February 11 as his birthday all his life.) His stepbrother Lawrence was already fourteen years old, so George began to follow him around like a puppy; and when Augustine died in 1743, at which time George was only eleven but Lawrence was a grown man of twenty-five, Lawrence pretty much took over as surrogate father.

Lawrence was very much involved with the military: he served as commander of the colonial contingent in the West Indies and as adjutant in the Virginia militia. And when he built Mount Vernon, the plantation in which George later lived, he named it after his former commanding officer, Admiral Edward Vernon, chief of the British forces in the West Indies. Then, when George was fourteen, he suggested that George would do well with a career in the British navy and should join up as a midshipman, a suggestion George accepted eagerly because he accepted every suggestion made by his brother. But Mrs. Washington rejected the plan, and though a lot of young men ignored their parents' wishes in those days and ran away and joined the navy, George was a dutiful son and remained a civilian. He never really got along with his mother after that, however, and at sixteen he left the family home and moved in with Lawrence at Mount Vernon.

That wasn't the only reason George didn't get along with his mother. She was a strange woman in a lot of ways, including being so close to miser status that, although she was really quite rich, she complained all her life that she was destitute and that her children neglected her, and she kept embarrassing George by demanding money and other things from him, and then complaining bitterly and publicly even though he usually complied with her requests immediately. She even wrote to him once when he was serving in the French and Indian War to demand that he see to it that she got butter and one more servant, and I suspect that, when she died in 1790, during Washington's first term as president of the United States, he might have felt ashamed of himself for experiencing a sense of relief. (When I was a young man myself and first read about Washington's relationship with his mother, I couldn't help feeling a bit superior about my own relationship with my mother, Martha Ellen Young Truman, who was my dear friend until her death in 1947 at the age of ninety-four. Which isn't to say that we didn't disagree on some things ourselves. She was an intelligent, well-educated woman, one of the few women to attend college in those days, Baptist Female College in Lexington, Missouri. But she had her prejudices, and when she came to visit Bess and me at the White House, she was such a dedicated southerner that she refused to sleep in Lincoln's bed. These were usually little things, though, that I could laugh about or ignore entirely, and I sometimes felt pity for the young George Washington along with my sense of superiority.)

But Washington's failure to remain close to his mother made him even closer to his stepbrother. And then Lawrence died in 1751. His death came as no great shock or surprise, since he'd been gravely ill with tuberculosis for quite some time. He went to Barbados shortly before his death in hopes that the mild climate would help or cure him, taking George with him, the only time our future president stepped foot out of his country during his lifetime, but it didn't do any good. The only thing that changed was that George became ill himself with smallpox and nearly died, but he made a full recovery except for some scars on his face that remained all his life, and his thoughts after the loss of Lawrence turned more and more toward emulating his beloved brother and doing something along military lines.

He could have devoted himself entirely to managing his plantation and other holdings. His father had left him the family home, Ferry Farm, near Fredericksburg, Virginia, an additional two thousand acres, ten slaves (I don't even like writing those words, but as I keep saying, it was a fact of life in those days), three other lots, and a number of other holdings. And when Lawrence died, he became even richer. Lawrence had been left the bulk of their father's estate as the eldest son, but he had only one child himself, and his will directed that Mount Vernon and all his other holdings go to George if his daughter failed to survive, and that daughter died two years after Lawrence. So George was a very rich man, but he applied nevertheless for the job Lawrence had left, the post of adjutant in the Virginia militia. He got only a quarter of the assignment; the governor decided to divide the post into four parts, I guess because he was nervous about the youth and inexperience of all the applicants, and he made George adjutant of the southern portion of the colony on February 1, 1753. But he was now a military officer, Major George Washington at the age of not quite twenty-one, even though he didn't know the first thing about military command.

He learned a bit about warfare after that, of course. French soldiers had gone into the Ohio Valley, an area that Virginia considered it owned and where Pittsburgh is now located, and the governor of Virginia, Robert Dinwiddie, decided to send a message to the French to tell them to get out. Washington volunteered to deliver the message, and with six frontiersmen accompanying him, started out on October 31 on a trip to French headquarters, Fort Le Bœuf on Lake Erie, a distance of nearly one thousand miles and an extremely hazardous journey because of unfriendly Indians and conditions of extreme cold. It took Washington and his men two and a half months to get there. They had to make much of the journey on foot when their horses became too weak to carry them; the weather was so bad that Washington later reported that there hadn't been a single day from December first to the fifteenth when they hadn't suffered through either snow or icy rain; and Washington was also shot by an Indian, though fortunately the wound was superficial and he recovered quickly. And in the end the French simply rejected the warning, and Governor Dinwiddie set out to move the French out of the Ohio Valley by force.

This was the start of the French and Indian War, which is the American name for the war because we were fighting French soldiers and Indians when we were involved in it; but many European history books refer to it as the Great War for Empire because it was really part of a series of struggles for territory going on in many parts of the world. By the time Washington made his unsuccessful trip to the Ohio Valley in 1753, the British and the French had been at each other's throat in America for almost a century, starting with King William's War, which ran from 1689 to 1697 and consisted of many attacks by the French and their Indian allies on British colonies and including a couple of major battles at a key Canadian settlement, Port Royal, Nova Scotia, now called Annapolis Royal, which the British captured in 1690 and the French recaptured a year later.

The French and the British were traditional enemies—they declared war formally on each other four times between the last years of the seventeenth century and the time of the American Revolution—and they were also bitter rivals for territory not only in areas that became the United States and Canada but also in India and the West Indies and Africa. And each time there was a big formal war between the French and the British in Europe, there was pretty much a smaller war in America and Canada. King William's War was pretty much a sidebar of the War of the League of Augsburg, fought in Europe between military forces under William of Orange and King Louis XIV; Queen Anne's War, which ran from 1701 to 1713, was an offshoot of the War of the Spanish Succession in Europe; and King George's War, running from 1745 to 1748, was related to the War of the Austrian Succession. In America, both countries courted Indian tribes as allies, but the French used their Indian allies more savagely and successfully because they fought along with them in frontier fashion, firing from behind trees and other hiding places and not standing and posing in colorful uniforms as open and ridiculously visible targets.

The French and Indian War was the crucial one as far as the Western Hemisphere was concerned because it ended with the French being pretty much driven out of America and Canada, and Washington was involved in the war's first battle. He and his men ran into a French scouting party in southern Pennsylvania on May 27, 1754, and in the battle that followed, they killed ten French soldiers and captured twenty-one others, with only one loss on their side. Washington expected the French to retaliate and quickly built a small outpost that he called Fort Necessity, sitting where Uniontown, Pennsylvania, is located now. The main French force wasn't far away; the French had taken over a fort originally built by Virginians, also located near the present site of Pittsburgh, and had named it Fort Duquesne, and as predicted, several hundred French soldiers and Indians showed up on July 3. Washington had more men than the French, about four hundred soldiers, but the more experienced French and Indian fighters captured the fort the next day. They didn't do anything vengeful, however; they just sent the Virginians back to Virginia and even let them take their guns and their ammunition back with them.

Washington had been promoted to lieutenant colonel by this time, but then the British did one of those things that revealed their underlying contempt for the colonists: they decreed that any colonial officer of captain's rank or higher had to be demoted so that he wouldn't outrank any British captain or major or whatever. Washington quit immediately and went back to Mount Vernon, but then, when the French and Indian War grew hotter, he felt some patriotic stirrings—toward old King George at that time, of course—and offered to serve as aide-de-camp to Major General Edward Braddock, who was the commander in chief of the King's forces in America and was getting ready to attack the French at Fort Duquesne. Washington's offer was accepted, and he was quick to warn Braddock that frontier fighting was different from the battles fought in previous wars and that the French and their Indian friends couldn't be expected to meet British troops face-to-face and wearing uniforms as colorful as British dress gear. But Braddock shrugged off the advice and led his men toward Fort Duquesne in exactly the same way as Howe later sent his troops toward the Americans on Breed's Hill.

He marched his men, fourteen hundred regular British troops and seven hundred colonial soldiers, in beautiful order toward the French fort, looking so gorgeous that he would have gotten a lot of applause if he were doing it as part of a present-day international parade along Pennsylvania Avenue in front of the White House. He also used heavy transport for his cannons and other equipment instead of pack horses, totally contrary to the advice of Washington and other colonial officers, toward most of whom he was openly contemptuous. He moved so slowly and laboriously that he finally began to fear that the French would have plenty of time to send masses of reinforcements to Fort Duquesne, and then, when he was at a place called Little Meadows, with something like eighty more miles of rough country still ahead of him, he switched to pack horses and left his wagons behind with one of his two regiments, moving ahead with a force of 1,459 men.

But it was too late. The French and Indians didn't wait until the British reached Fort Duquesne; they waited, hiding behind trees and in ravines, until the British and American troops were struggling across the Monongahela River, and then suddenly descended on the troops, the French soldiers shouting and yelling and the Indians emitting bloodcurdling war whoops. There were only about nine hundred men in the French force—a small number of French soldiers and some Canadians, but a large number of Indians—so they were outnumbered by the British and colonial soldiers, but the battle became a quick and terrible slaughter of the British and the Americans. Despite the constant warnings of the colonial soldiers that frontier warfare should be expected, and not fancy face-to-face warfare by the book, the British were totally stunned and unprepared for the attack, and large numbers of the soldiers turned and ran, followed by Indians who killed them, paused only to take scalps, and then hid momentarily and returned to kill some more. Most of the British officers were braver than their men and stayed to fight, but they, too, were cut down because they insisted on remaining open targets while the French and the Canadians and the Indians fired at them from behind trees.

When the battle was over, the British and the colonials counted 977 dead or wounded, including 63 of the 89 officers present. The commander of the French forces, Daniel Hyacinthe Marie Liénard de Beaujeu, also died in the battle, shot down early in the fight, but then so did General Braddock; he had four horses shot out from under him and then fell wounded himself, hanging on for four days before he succumbed. Washington was luckier: he had two horses killed as he rode them, and four bullets passed through his clothing, but he was unharmed.

Shortly afterwards, Governor Dinwiddie asked Washington to return home and take command of the Virginia militia because he was afraid that the French and Indians would start attacking some of Virginia's more isolated western settlements; Washington refused at first, but then agreed, and was promoted to full colonel and regimental commander. The French and Indian War dragged on until 1760, the climactic battle taking place on the Plains of Abraham, a level area adjoining Quebec, in which both the British commander, General James Wolfe, and the French commander, General Louis Joseph de Montcalm-Gozon, Marquise de Saint-Véron, were killed. But the battle was a decisive victory for the British, who took Quebec, and the French gave up the next year and Canada became British territory.

Washington didn't remain in military service until the end of the war; he resigned his commission in 1758 to join the Virginia House of Burgesses, the colony's governing body. Thereafter, until he joined the

Continental Congresses and became commander of the American forces, he devoted himself to increasing his wealth; leading a nine-week expedition into the Ohio Valley in 1770 and claiming 20,000 acres for the soldiers he'd commanded, and himself, as compensation for their part in the French and Indian War; and to some romantic expeditions.

Some of these didn't amount to much. Back in 1752, when Washington was twenty, and a young woman named Betsy Fauntleroy, the daughter of a burgess and judge from Richmond County, Virginia, was sixteen, Washington fell deeply in love with her and pursued her vigorously, even managing to get her father to try to convince her that the marriage would be a good one. But young Betsy wasn't the least bit interested, and after a while Washington gave up, and in 1756, en route to Boston on a military matter, he stopped off in New York and met and fell in love with Mary Philipse, at twenty-six two years older than he was and the daughter of a man who owned a lot of New York land. He stayed in New York for a week and ended up proposing to her. Some cynical historians have speculated that what Washington really fell in love with was the fact that Mary was the heiress to 51,000 acres, but I doubt it; Washington enjoyed acquiring wealth and property, but he wasn't a fanatically mercenary and grasping type, and he *was*, on the other hand, clearly a romantic young fellow who fell in love easily and deeply. In any case, the New York lady wasn't ready to accept him any more than the Virginia lady, which turned out to be a good thing in a way because her sentiments became pro-Britain while Washington's, of course, turned more and more toward independence from the mother country. She later married Roger Morris, who was equally pro-Britain.

Washington's next love affair was with Sarah Cary Fairfax, who was called Sally and was eighteen when he first met her; but this one was totally hopeless because she was already married to his friend and neighbor, George William Fairfax. Sally was very beautiful, very intelligent, and very charming, and a romantic correspondence apparently went on between them for quite a long time, continuing even when Washington became engaged to be married himself, when he was twenty-six, to a twenty-seven-year old widow named Martha Dandridge Custis. Here some historians guess that the romance with Sally Fairfax never went beyond flirtation, while others, perhaps more romantic types themselves, believe it went a lot further than that. One thing that's sure is that, though Washington married Martha Custis on January 6, 1759, he was still writing love letters to Sally as late as September 1758, because one such letter has survived. Again, though, it's just as well that the relationship with Sally didn't take hold and become official, with Sally somehow ridding herself of George Fairfax and marrying George Washington, because she proved to be pro-Britain. In 1773, in fact, after the Boston Tea Party, the Fairfaxes became so alarmed with events in America that they left for England and remained there the rest of their lives.

Martha Dandridge, born in New Kent County, Virginia, in June 1731, had married a wealthy planter named Daniel Parke Custis when she was eighteen, and they had two children together. Custis died in 1757, leaving no will, but Martha inherited his 17,000 acres despite this fact, which made her the wealthiest woman of marriageable age and situation in Virginia. Her marriage to Washington therefore made him richer still, again causing speculation among some historians that love wasn't his only motivation in proposing, but Martha was reported to be a woman of considerable beauty, charm, and that not-so-common-quality common sense, and the marriage seems to have been a very happy one.

Washington was a big, healthy man who was, as I've said, six feet two inches in height and weighed 170 pounds in his prime and 200 pounds later in life, but he and Martha had no children together, possibly because his bout with smallpox in Barbados, or a siege with mumps that some people say he had as a boy, made him incapable. But he was very fond of Martha's children and treated them as his own, and he and Martha grew closer and closer through the years. Martha was never comfortable or happy away from him, and she made many difficult and dangerous trips to see him and stay with him at his headquarters during the Revolutionary War. And when Washington died on December 14, 1799, she became almost a recluse and died herself three years later.

Washington knew, incidentally, that he was dying. He made the mistake of traveling around his plantation through snow and sleet the day before, then came back to his house and dealt with some correspondence and had dinner without changing his wet clothes, and woke up the next morning with chills and a very sore throat. He thought that his aches and pains would go away, but they didn't, and three doctors were called: his friend and personal physician, Dr. James Craik, and two consultants, Dr. Gustavus Richard Brown and Dr. Elisha Cullen Dick. Naturally, the doctors practiced the primitive medicine of the period; they diagnosed his problem as quinsy, which is an abscess near a tonsil, and proceeded to treat the ailment by bleeding him four times, which made things worse. Finally, Washington dismissed the doctors, and at about ten o'clock on the evening of the fourteenth, he told his aide, Tobias Lear, "I'm just going." Then he gave Lear instructions for his burial, and as he was trying to take his own pulse, he died.

His will was forty-two pages long, written in his own handwriting five months before his death. He left his estate of about $500,000—an astonishingly high amount for those days—to Martha for her use during her lifetime, and he left very desirable tracts of land to his two grandchildren, George Washington Parke Custis and Nellie Lewis. He gave his personal servant, William, an annuity and freed him, and ordered that all the other slaves be freed after Martha's death. He was owed money by his brother-in-law, Bartholomew Dandridge, and by the family of one of his brothers, Samuel, and forgave these. He had stock in the Bank of Alexandria and in an outfit called the Potomac Company, and willed the first of these for a school for indigent children and the second for the start of a university. Tobias Lear got a rent-free residence for life; another brother, Charles, got a gold-headed cane that had been given to him by Benjamin Franklin; Dr. Craik got his desk and chair; and pistols taken from the British during the Revolutionary War went to Marie Joseph Paul Yves Roche Gilbert du Motier, Marquis de Lafayette. (I don't think Washington used the full name in his will, since that would have made it forty-*three* pages long.) And five of his nephews each got one of his swords, his will requesting that they never be used "for the purpose of shedding blood except it be for self-defence, or in defence of their country and its rights . . ."

Washington's only military experience before the Revolutionary War, in short, was his service during the French and Indian War, and it's a miracle that it proved to be enough. It would have been a miracle even if Washington had been the best-trained soldier in the world, because he had basically poor material to work with when he took on the difficult—some of his contemporaries thought impossible—assignment of going to war against the British.

First of all, it wasn't the usual kind of war, with one nation going to war against another nation. The thirteen colonies weren't really an integrated nation at all, not yet; due to the transportation of the time, the geographical distances between them made them almost like separate countries leading separate, and in many ways very different, kinds of lives, so much so that, until they started to get together in the Continental Congresses, many of the leaders from one colony barely knew the leaders from another colony—and in many cases didn't know them at all.

Second, a lot of them didn't like each other all that much. The soft-spoken, polite Virginians put a lot of stress on good manners, so some Virginians were appalled by the people from Massachusetts, considering their blunt, clipped speech and their attitude of "let's get down to brass tacks without a lot of bowing and scraping and formality" as boorish. Even Washington was heard commenting now and then on what he considered to be the bad manners of many of the Yankees. It was that way all around. Aristocratic colonists considered New Yorkers too steeped in business and too fanatic about making money, while New Yorkers considered the aristocrats lazy and indolent and living off the sweat of other people; city people considered the German farmers in Pennsylvania ignorant and the eighteenth-century version of rubes and hicks, and farm people considered town people the eighteenth-century version of city slickers; and in North Carolina, upland people hated lowland people and vice versa, and the two groups didn't want to have anything to do with each other. In other words, they were like people since the beginning of time, suspicious of and disliking each other's differences, and maybe a little more that way than most. Anyway, they certainly weren't people who fitted together naturally to do that job of winning the war.

Third, I hope you don't have the mistaken idea that most colonists rallied immediately to the cause of independence. I've mentioned some of Washington's friends and neighbors who decided in favor of the Crown, and they were by no means the exceptions to the rule. There were also a lot of people who wouldn't fight because of religious reasons. So Georgia stayed away because the people there were having their own troubles with the Creek Indians and were generally favorably inclined toward England because the King came through with funds to fight the Indians, and New Yorkers were about equally divided between men ready to join the Revolution and men loyal to old George III, and Quakers wouldn't fight at all. So when the Revolutionary War started, there were probably twenty-five thousand men who joined up on the British side, and a much larger number of Americans who stayed out of the fighting entirely.

SIXTEEN

Losing the Battles, Winning the Revolutionary War

WASHINGTON also had plenty of trouble with the men who did join the Continental Army. Many of his officers got their commissions by buying them, or by talking some of their neighbors and friends who'd joined up at the same time into appointing them as their commander, and the neighbors and friends soon got tired of being commanded by that fellow who'd lived down the road and refused to take orders from him. Other enlisted men just turned around and went home without leave when they received news of illness or other troubles back home, or when they learned that there was no one around on their farms to do the harvesting, or when they grew lonely for their wives and children, or even just because the weather was turning bad.

Washington never showed anything but a calm exterior throughout the war, but there's no question about the fact that he grew frantic at times and felt that the only way to keep things from falling apart completely was to adopt some harsh measures. He sent men out to bring departing soldiers back and got permission from the Continental governing body to punish disobedient soldiers, and soldiers who'd sneaked away and were brought back to duty, with as many as five hundred lashes, but it didn't help a whole lot. And there were times like the time he arrived in New York, in August 1776, and found that he had only eight thousand men to call upon, whereas the British had thirty-five thousand men there plus twenty thousand about to land on Long Island and join them.

Many of the battles after Washington took command in 1775 were what you might call informal skirmishes between colonists and British soldiers in different parts of the country, sometimes because they just happened to meet up with each other, and of course there had been no formal statement of independence at that point. But in March of 1776 the Americans captured and controlled Boston, and that was when General Gage sailed back to England with his tail between his legs. The victory, naturally, was encouraging and inspiring to colonists everywhere in the country, and it might be said to be the start of the more formal war.

For the first time, Washington and his men raised a new and different flag, a specifically American flag, and the Continental Congress, meeting regularly now in Philadelphia, asked the colonies to begin to disown their royal connections by declaring themselves to be independent states. South Carolina adopted a provisional constitution in March, North Carolina leaders reached agreement to declare independence on April 13, and Virginia decided on May 15 to ask the Congress to declare formal independence from Britain for all the colonies. On June 7, a member of the Virginia delegation, Richard Henry Lee, made that proposal, but Congress, still moving cautiously, agreed only to appoint a committee of five men to draft an independence document. Everybody knows that three of the men were Thomas Jefferson, Benjamin Franklin, and John Adams, though there's a tendency to forget the other two, Roger Sherman and Robert R. Livingston.

Well, maybe that's all right, now that I stop to think about it, because the first three I've listed did most of the work anyway. Jefferson did the basic writing and then he and Ben Franklin and Adams did the revising, and then the whole Congress did some more tinkering after that. (I probably shouldn't say "tinkering" because that sounds as though I'm saying that they messed things up, but the changes were really improvements for the most part. Did you ever see a marked-up copy of the Declaration of Independence, in which Franklin and the rest of those fellows made inserts? It looks just like one of my speeches when I write one and my people go to work on it, and those changes are usually improvements, too. It's a wonderful thing when you contemplate the Declaration of Independence, and the reason it's so wonderful is that it's such a beautiful document to read, almost like a great piece of poetry in its way, and its results have been so successful. Otherwise I guess it would never have been heard of. Jefferson became governor of Virginia after that, and the fine things he did on religious freedom and other innovative acts were, I'm sure, the direct result of his thinking on the Declaration of Independence. And of course he must have consulted all those fellows from time to time, particularly Franklin. Ben Franklin was the smartest man at that convention, and possibly in the country. I guess I have a special admiration for fellows named Franklin, last name *or* first.)

Congress finally adopted a resolution for independence on July 2, and the Declaration of Independence was adopted, of course, on July 4 —though not signed on that day as a lot of people seem to think. The official date for the signing of the Declaration of Independence was August 2; fifty delegates signed on that date, and six others weren't present and signed afterwards. Not everybody signed it, however; Robert R. Livingston, for example, never did, even though he was on that committee. John Hancock signed first because he was president of the Continental Congress, and I'm sure everybody knows the famous story about his signing nice and big so that his signature wouldn't be missed, which is why, of course, a signature is called a John Hancock today.*

So now it was all official, and Washington went to New York that month in hopes of taking New York City in the same way that Boston

---

*I might as well go ahead and do my first, and maybe last, footnote of this book and list the fifty-five other signers of the Declaration of Independence for the record. I'm not much on footnotes; I like to read right along when I'm reading a book and not keep dropping my eyes down eight or ten inches all the time. But I guess some footnotes are necessary, and particularly this one because it's amazing how many of these men are forgotten even though some have had streets and towns named after them. They were brave men who ought to be noted and remembered. Here are the names of the forty-nine men who signed right after Hancock signed: Josiah Bartlett, William Whipple, Samuel Adams, John Adams, Robert Treat Paine, Stephen Hopkins, William Ellery, Roger Sherman, Samuel Huntington, William Williams, William Floyd, Philip Livingston, Francis Lewis, Lewis Morris, Richard Stockton, John Witherspoon, Francis Hopkinson, John Hart, Abraham Clark, Robert Morris, Benjamin Rush, Benjamin Franklin, John Morton, George Clymer, James Smith, George Taylor, James Wilson, George Ross, Thomas Nelson, Jr., Caesar Rodney, George Read, Samuel Chase, William Paca, Thomas Stone, Charles Carroll, Thomas Jefferson, Benjamin Harrison, Francis Lightfoot Lee, Carter Braxton, William Hooper, Joseph Hewes, John Penn, Edward Rutledge, Thomas Heyward, Jr., Thomas Lynch, Jr., Arthur Middleton, Button Gwinnett, Lyman Hall, and George Walton. The six men who signed late were Oliver Wolcott, Elbridge Gerry, Matthew Thornton, Richard Henry Lee, Thomas McKean, and George Wythe.

Some autograph and document collectors spend a lifetime trying to assemble a set of signatures of the signers of the Declaration of Independence. The scarcest signature is Button Gwinnett's. Gwinnett was a delegate from Georgia; he was forty-one when he signed the Declaration of Independence, and he was killed a year later in a duel with a political rival named Lachlan McIntosh, who lived on to become a general in the Revolutionary War and then a congressman and a commissioner of Indian affairs dealing with the Cherokees and the Creeks. I gather that Gwinnett signed practically nothing other than the Declaration of Independence, and his signature is so valuable today that a friend who visited me in the White House told me a joke about it. Seems someone wrote and offered a collector a letter of minor importance, but he went ahead and bought it, and then had to go out of town and told his secretary to keep an eye out for the letter. When he got back, he found a memo from his secretary. "The letter arrived in good order," the memo said, "but it was practically worthless because some fool had written across the bottom of it, 'See me about this. Button Gwinnett.' But it's okay now. That stuff was written all the way on the bottom, and I cut it off neatly and threw it away, and the cut doesn't even show." HST

had been taken. But unfortunately it proved to be a terrible defeat, which is no wonder in view of the fact that he had less than one-seventh of the number of men the British had, and many of his men armed poorly at that. Washington and his men were badly beaten in a battle in what is now the Brooklyn Heights section of the borough of Brooklyn, and then they were chased into what is now Manhattan and managed to escape from there only because a sudden and heavy fog developed and they were able to slip away under its cover. They then moved up into White Plains, and then across the Hudson River into New Jersey, meeting the British frequently and being defeated by them each time. Washington and his men lost a lot of their supplies and ammunition, and a large number of men began to desert, so many members of the New York, New Jersey, Maryland, and New England militia running away that Washington soon found himself left with only about thirty-three hundred men.

There were only a few bits of good news for wives and children and the other people waiting at home. The British had had some trouble signing up a sufficient number of recruits to join the forces fighting the Americans, so they brought in a lot of German mercenaries, the Hessians,* to help them out, and on the night of December 25 and the morning of December 26, the Hessians were in Trenton, New Jersey, and were still celebrating Christmas. Washington and his men attacked suddenly while the Hessians were still full of Christmas spirit and schnapps, taking more than a thousand prisoners. As everybody knows from that famous painting, Washington crossed the Delaware River to do it, though I doubt like the dickens that he stood up in the boat doing it the way the painting has it, because he would have fallen right into the ice-cold water. And then on January 3, 1777, Washington again defeated the British and their friends at Princeton.

It's a mistake, incidentally, to believe that the Americans won the battles they won only because they continued to fight guerrilla style, shooting from behind trees and other cover, while the British continued to stand up there in ranks and making beautiful targets. It didn't work out that way: the British soon learned the error of their ways, and they also had Indian allies who were quick to tell them that it made no sense

*My father once told me that the Hessians were also a source of trouble to the Americans in a second way; they brought along with them, undoubtedly inadvertently, a destructive insect called the Hessian fly. I thought he was joking because he wasn't too crazy about the Hessians or any other soldiers who fought for money rather than principle, but I later looked it up and discovered that he was absolutely right. The Hessian fly is actually a gnat that attacks wheat, rye, and other grains by laying its eggs on leaves, and the larvae then consume the sap and the plants can't yield grain. The Hessian fly is a menace right up to the present time. It can be avoided to some extent by late planting, but if the insects manage to attack plants, the only thing that can be done is plow them under. My apologies to Dad, who commented a page or two ago (though in a footnote of his own) that he doesn't like footnotes, but I think some of these things off the main point are interesting. MT

to fight open battles on American frontier terrain. The Americans fought guerrilla style, really meaning Indian style, when it was suitable to fight that way, but they also managed to match the British and Germans in European style when that was the right way to do it, sometimes managing to rout the enemy by waiting until they got up very close and using smooth-bore muskets to deadly effect.

The best things the Americans had going for them was the fact that they were fighting on their own familiar terrain while the British were, as the saying goes, strangers in a strange land, and more important, the fact that that terrain was beloved to the Americans and they were fighting a war that meant everything to them while the British and their employees were just there to do a job. This was true of almost every American soldier, even the fellows who sneaked off to tend their crops and were brought back and lashed a hundred or five hundred times; when they went into battle, they fought with a fervor and a dedication that the other side just couldn't match. They were completely fed up with the British and the constant injustice of King George III and some of his advisors, and they had plenty of inspiration in the sight of Washington and others who had left wealthy and comfortable homes to lead them and fight along with them.

They also had the inspiration of a little book whose title and author I'm sure you'll recognize, *Common Sense* by Thomas Paine. Paine was an Englishman who came to America only two years before the start of the Revolutionary War; he was the son of a Quaker and aged thirty-seven when he arrived, and I guess you'd call him a radical of sorts because he was always in one kind of trouble or other through most of his life. He worked in the excise service in England and was fired twice, mostly because he was a kind of labor leader ahead of his time and kept agitating for higher wages and trying to get his fellow workers to agitate along with him. And after the war he went back to England for a while and wrote some things in favor of the French Revolution and against Edmund Burke that were so strong that they got him into trouble again and he had to leave the country and go to Paris, and then he got into trouble there and was in a French prison for nearly a year. And then he wrote some things against the Bible and against George Washington which made him so unpopular with Americans that, when he returned to this country in 1802, he found himself practically friendless and died in total poverty in 1809.

But he was a wonderful writer, and when he wrote *Common Sense* and it was published in January 1776, it sold more than 100,000 copies. And copies were constantly passed from hand to hand among the soldiers and helped tremendously to sustain their dedication during the darkest days of the war.

The soldiers needed the inspiration. After the small victories at Trenton and Princeton, there was a bad loss at Brandywine Creek in Pennsylvania on September 11, 1777. Washington learned that General Howe and his men were at Elkton, Maryland, and moving toward Philadelphia, and Washington stationed most of his men at a place called Chadds Ford because he knew that the British would have to cross the creek at that point. Howe sent a Hessian general, Baron Wilhelm von Knyphausen, and his men to Chadds Ford, making it appear that that was the entire British force, but moved with most of his men on the Americans' right flank. The Americans suffered many losses and were totally defeated and Howe moved on and took Philadelphia. Washington had to retreat to Chester, Pennsylvania, and that was the winter in which he and his men suffered terribly at Valley Forge.

There were other defeats, but also some important victories. One of the most important took place in northern New York on September 19, 1777. General Burgoyne, who was a fool in some ways, went home on leave and asked the King to allow him to go after the Americans around Albany when he returned, and the King bought it and the British War Office ordered it. Maybe it's hindsight when I say this, but I don't think so; I think it's obvious that that was exactly the wrong thing to do, and that the right thing to do was to bring all the British forces together, instead of separating them, and wipe out Washington and his men completely in New Jersey. The concentration of all the British forces against Washington's little group of men was what Washington himself feared most, and the destruction of his small army would have discouraged all other American soldiers completely and sent them home in total defeat. But instead Burgoyne went after the army in upstate New York, expecting that he'd be joined by Indians and loyalists and some of General Howe's men in lower New York.

It was the dumbest of moves. He left British headquarters in Montreal and marched his men a total of 185 miles into deepest wilderness, using up most of his supplies and making it necessary to send a force of about thirteen hundred men, mostly Hessians, to seize supplies from the Americans around Bennington, Vermont. He also had a secondary purpose: he felt that that area was a particular hotbed of American traitors and wanted to teach them a lesson. But for once, the Americans had the superior numbers. An army of two thousand men met the Hessians at Bennington, led by General John Stark, an experienced soldier who had fought in the French and Indian War, and the Americans easily defeated the Germans. And Burgoyne and his men, totaling about six thousand men, were met by a force of nine thousand Americans at a place called Freeman's Farm in Saratoga, and defeated there. Burgoyne and his men were then chased all over the place. His British and Indian and loyalist reinforcements never showed up, while more and more Americans arrived in northern New York, until the American force was up to about twenty thousand men. On October 17, Burgoyne surrendered at Saratoga to the American commander, General Horatio Gates.

The victory was important in an even more relevant way than American morale; it finally brought the French into the war on the American side. Benjamin Franklin had been sent to France as the American minister late in 1776, joining two other Americans there, Silas Deane and Arthur Lee, in efforts to persuade the French, as longtime enemies of the British, to help America win the war. The French, however, refused to help the Americans openly, limiting their assistance to loaning the Americans money secretly and persuading Spain, their allies and also traditional enemies of Britain, to do the same. Only a small number of Frenchmen like the twenty-year-old Marquis de Lafayette, who arrived in Philadelphia in 1777 and was appointed a major general, helped the Americans openly. And when news reached France of some of the Americans' earlier defeats, even the small amount of assistance slowed down to a trickle.

But when Gates defeated Burgoyne at Saratoga, and the news traveled across the ocean to France, Franklin rushed to tell the French foreign secretary, Charles Gravier, Comte de Vergennes, about it, and simultaneously, Franklin's close friend, Pierre-Augustin Caron de Beaumarchais, ran through the streets to tell King Louis XVI what had happened. Beaumarchais ran so fast and so enthusiastically, swinging his arms as he ran, that he later felt severe pain in one of his arms and discovered that he had dislocated it.

Beaumarchais wasn't a professional politician; he was a watchmaker turned dramatist who wrote a lot of things that you'll recognize, including *Le Barbier de Séville,* written in 1775, which Rossini turned into his famous opera in 1816, and *Le Mariage de Figaro,* written in 1784 and made into the opera by Mozart two years later. He was also a publisher who brought out, between 1785 and 1790, a seventy-volume edition of Voltaire's writings. But he was also an occasional secret agent for the King and enjoyed cloak-and-dagger operations, and he was enthusiastic about America and loved Franklin, so he was helpful to the American cause from the start. The principal supplier of French arms to the Revolutionary Army, in fact, was a company called Hortales & Cie., but there was really no such firm; it was Beaumarchais shipping guns and ammunition. (One sad note here, which probably ought to be a footnote, but which I'll put right in this paragraph because, as I've said, I don't like footnotes. Beaumarchais was supposed to be repaid his costs with tobacco and other American products, but the American government became so busy setting itself up that he didn't receive a dime in his lifetime. He died in 1799, and Congress didn't get around to paying his heirs until 1835. Which is just shameful.)

But the news about Saratoga fired up French enthusiasm again, and on February 6, 1778, the French government made it official and visible, signing a treaty with Franklin. They then sent over six thousand experienced soldiers to help Washington out, led by another very good man whose name takes up half a page, Jean-Baptiste-Donatien de Vimeur, Comte de Rochambeau. And the French also began to supply much more money and arms, and French ships started to harass the British on the seas.

The British didn't throw in the towel then and there, of course; the war dragged on nearly four more long years, until almost the end of 1781. The British now turned their attention to the South, planning to take over Georgia because there weren't too many American troops there and the place was loaded with loyalists, and they succeeded quickly. They captured the port city of Savannah and continued to move more and more deeply into Georgia and South Carolina, and when a general named Benjamin Lincoln, no relation to Abe, was sent with five thousand soldiers to try to recapture Savannah, assisted by a fleet of French ships under Admiral Charles Hector, Comte d'Estaing, they were beaten so badly by British forces headed by Sir Henry Clinton that Lincoln had to run to Charleston, South Carolina, and was surrounded there and captured with all of his men. Then Gates, who had done so well at Saratoga, was sent to the South; he was so popular because of his success at Saratoga, at a time when Washington wasn't doing all that well, that a thing called the Conway Cabal took place—a sort of unofficial movement by General Thomas Conway and some other American officers to remove Washington as commander in chief and replace him with Gates. But Gates only had three thousand men, half of them just brand-new recruits, and he was met at Camden, South Carolina, by Lord Charles Cornwallis and beaten so badly that two-thirds of his men were killed or captured.

The plain truth is that Gates and his men were so terrified that they turned and ran two hundred miles before stopping, and some historians report that Gates himself was a couple of miles ahead of his officers and men all the way. I don't know if that's true or not, but it's certainly true that he was replaced immediately by General Nathanael Greene and an inquiry was ordered into his conduct, though it never actually took place. He didn't get back into active service in the Army until after the war was over in 1782, and some of those historians are also now saying that it wasn't really Gates who was so brilliant at Saratoga but a couple of generals under him, Daniel Morgan and Benedict Arnold. (Well, we all know how we feel about Arnold's subsequent behavior, but there doesn't seem to be any question about the fact that he was a brilliant soldier and military strategist. And it's not too difficult to understand why he turned traitor after Congress promoted five other brigadier generals to major general and left Arnold in rank as a brigadier general despite the fact that the other men were junior to Arnold, and despite the fact that Washington kept pleading for a promotion for Arnold. This turned him into a bitter man, even though he eventually got his promotion, and his pro-British attitude increased after he married the daughter of a Philadelphia loyalist, Peggy Shippen. He was also bitter because he had some disagreements with civilian authorities and had to face a court-martial in order to be cleared of most of the charges. Though I agree that there's no acceptable excuse for traitorous behavior at any time and for any reason.)

Greene didn't do much better than Gates, or at least so it appeared at first; he was defeated in three battles in the Carolinas, at Guilford Courthouse, Hobkirks Hill, and Eutaw Springs. And there was deep depression among many American officers and soldiers when a British spy, Major John André, was captured and revealed that Arnold, then the commander at West Point, was in the process of handing over West Point to the British in return for some money and a British commission—and when Arnold escaped and joined the British and led his men in victories against the Americans in Connecticut and Virginia. (André was hanged, even though he seems to have been a decent fellow and a patriot like our Nathan Hale, but Arnold got away to Canada and then to England and lived in England until his death in 1801 at the age of sixty.)

Greene, however, was a better strategist and soldier than Gates, and probably better than most other American officers, and he kept regrouping after each retreat and harassing the British forces until he finally forced Cornwallis and his men back into Virginia. He was another true patriot and had to sign so many personal notes to get supplies for the Continental Army that, after the war, he was forced to sell his estates to pay off the pledges. I'm glad to say that the people of Georgia had the good sense to give him a plantation when that happened. And it can certainly be said that his victories in the South did much to demoralize the British and bring the war close to an end.

The end itself finally came in Yorktown, Virginia, near Chesapeake Bay. Lafayette and other officers, including General Anthony Wayne and General Friedrich Wilhelm, Baron von Steuben, a Prussian soldier who joined the Americans in 1777 and was with Washington during that terrible winter at Valley Forge, led their men in continuous attacks against the British in Virginia, and Cornwallis fortified Yorktown and settled down there to wait for reinforcements to come from Clinton, who was in New York. Washington and his French ally, General Rochambeau, were in New York, too, but they learned that Admiral François-Joseph-

Paul, Comte de Grasse, a French officer who had been ordered to help the Americans, had defeated a British naval force and captured Tobago in the West Indies, and he and his men were now free and available. Washington and Rochambeau asked de Grasse to go immediately to Virginia. De Grasse blockaded the York River and the James River, effectively locking Cornwallis up in Yorktown, and Washington and Rochambeau moved at once toward Virginia themselves, leaving only a small force in New York. It was a brilliant military move. Cornwallis had no idea whatever that Washington and his men were coming until a huge combined American and French force descended on Yorktown, a total of about sixteen thousand men. Cornwallis had half that number, and he tried to escape, but he was surrounded by the Americans and French on land and by de Grasse's fleet in the water. On October 18, 1781, he agreed to surrender, and the next day he sent along his sword. Washington instructed General Lincoln to accept it, and the war was over.

That old lunatic King George III couldn't believe his ears, and for two years he refused to regard his former colonies as a new country, entirely separate from England. But in 1783 a treaty was finally signed between England and America. John Adams, John Jay, and Benjamin Franklin represented this country in dealing with the British minister, William Petty Fitzmaurice, 2nd Earl of Shelburne, and Shelburne gave us all of the territory between the Alleghenies and the Mississippi without argument up to Canada on the north border and down to Florida on the south border, turning over Florida to Spain. A lot of British high-hats, as I sometimes like to call the aristocracy, felt Shelburne had been too easy and too generous, and he was pushed out of office that year. But that was that, anyway. The Thirteen Colonies had become the United States of America.

SEVENTEEN
Washington— A Great and Unpopular President

WELL, so now we were a country, and we needed some good men to run the country, men who were going to be called presidents rather than kings or emperors because they were going to be put into their jobs by the populace and not by accidents of birth, and who were going to follow a written set of rules, and who were going to be advised and to some extent controlled by legislators serving along with them.

I'm going to have things to say later on about that set of rules, our wonderful Constitution, and some more things to say about our government, and the way it's run in tandem with those legislators, the senators and the members of the House of Representatives. But since I've made comments throughout this book about some of our bad presidents, I think this is a good place to write a bit about the men who became our best presidents. And the proper way to start, it seems to me, is with our first president, George Washington. I've said some things about Washington in discussing the Continental Congresses and the Revolutionary War, but there's plenty more to say about him.

First of all, I guess I ought to remind people that, although most of us tend to assume that Washington was a very popular president because he's so much admired and idolized today, so legendary, as the Father of Our Country, the plain truth, unfortunately, is that this is far from the case. He was a very unpopular president; in fact, it's my opinion that he was more roundly abused than any other president who was ever in the White House.* As I've mentioned, he was abused constantly by the press, by the Congress, and by a lot of individuals like that bastard son of Ben Franklin's, William Franklin. William Franklin was a bastard in that way, too. He was a royalist; he stayed with the British side and was one of the worst heartbreaks in life for old Ben Franklin. Ben raised that boy and thought the world of him, but the boy, who was an attractive fellow and well liked by everybody at first, became the British governor of New Jersey and later did his best to keep the Colonies from becoming a free government.

I don't know why William Franklin behaved the way he did; I've read somewhere that it was because he loved the British aristocracy and the high-hat way of living so much, and I guess that's as good an answer as any. He was a terrible disappointment to Benjamin Franklin, and you never see the man mentioned in Franklin's memoirs at all. In 1776, after a terrible quarrel with his father, which didn't budge him an inch in his convictions, he was arrested by order of the New Jersey congress and imprisoned in Connecticut for two years. His father managed to get him released, but even after that he continued to favor the British, and in 1782 he moved permanently to England.

The two Franklins met in England in 1784 and had a reconciliation, but William Franklin never let up on his anti-American and anti-Washington statements and writings. He even wrote one really scurrilous piece when Washington was stepping down, saying thank God the monarchy is gone, that corrupt monarchy, and just to show the readers of this book the way Washington was treated by the press of the period, the article was picked up and published in all the papers. Old Ben Franklin didn't agree with any of that stuff, of course. The encyclopedias refer to William Franklin as Ben's "natural" son, which I suppose is a polite way of

*I suppose there's no way to avoid another footnote in order to say that that's just a figure of speech, since Washington never actually lived in the White House, either the original or the place that was rebuilt after the British set fire to the original building during the War of 1812. The cornerstone of the original building wasn't laid until 1792, and the first president to live in the drafty old barn, John Adams, didn't move in until 1800. It wasn't called the White House, even unofficially, for quite a while. When the plans were drawn up, it was called the Palace because it was natural in those days to think unconsciously in terms of monarchies, and monarchs lived in palaces, but that name was never really used. It wasn't called anything at all for a while, and then some people began to refer to it as the White House because it was painted white to cover up the smoke stains after the British set fire to it. But it wasn't called the White House officially until Theodore Roosevelt decided to stick it on his stationery one day. HST

saying it, but he seems pretty unnatural to me. He was the John Roosevelt of his day.*

But natural or unnatural, William Franklin was far from alone. There were a lot of people just like this Franklin boy who enjoyed turning loose their venom on somebody in power, that's all, just as there are people like that today. Even Thomas Paine followed up his brilliant *Common Sense* with an eventual not-so-brilliant "open letter" to Washington in 1796 that called him a "hypocrite in public life," accused him of commencing "your Presidential career by encouraging and swallowing the grossest adulation, and you traveled America from one end to the other, to put yourself in the way of receiving it," and added that "the world will be puzzled to decide . . . whether you have abandoned good principles, or whether you ever had any." And as I've said, the newspapers were equally nasty in their criticism. This comment, published the same year as Paine's outburst in a paper called the *Philadelphia Aurora,* is all too typical: "If ever a nation was debauched by a man, the American nation has been debauched by Washington. If ever a nation was deceived by a man, the American nation has been deceived by Washington. Let his conduct, then, be an example to future ages; let it serve to be a warning . . ."

As you can see, then, Washington wasn't as popular with every citizen of our new country as you might have supposed. Nor was he the most intelligent or knowledgeable man of his day. He probably wasn't as brilliant as Jefferson, nor as financially sound as Hamilton, although he knew how to keep his money and ended up, as I've mentioned, with a huge fortune for that day and age. His education wasn't too great, either. The information that's been left for us on that subject is pretty scanty, and historians differ in their statements, but it's pretty clear that he didn't get much formal education. One thing that's certain is that his widowed mother didn't send him to England for his schooling, as was often done with boys like him—though opinions vary on whether she just couldn't bear to be parted from him or whether, in keeping with her reputation for being pretty tightfisted, she just didn't want to spend the money. And opinions also vary on whether Washington was sent to an actual school in Fredericksburg or just given a smattering of basic education at home by an indentured servant.

Nor was he much of a reader. I'm not one to insist that a man can't possibly make it without a lot of formal education, since my own formal education pretty much stopped when I graduated from Independence High

*For the reader who's forgotten who John Roosevelt was, he was Franklin Delano Roosevelt's youngest son; born 1916, died 1981. He was the only Republican in his family and a constant source of aggravation to his father and to a lesser extent, mine. He was the chairman of Citizens for Eisenhower in 1952, and in later years supported Richard M. Nixon and Ronald Reagan. MT

School in 1901. And then there was a twenty-two-year gap, while I worked on a farm and as a railroad timekeeper and served in the Army and did a lot of other things, before I started to attend night classes at Kansas City Law School—and I left there in 1925 and never got a degree. But I've tried to increase my knowledge all my life by reading and reading and reading, and that wasn't the case with Washington. He once made a statement about reading that is quoted in many biographies—"I conceive a knowledge of books is the basis upon which other knowledge is to be built"—but he rarely followed that precept himself. He usually read books only when he felt it was absolutely necessary, and these were mostly confined to practical books related to his daily life and daily needs like books on farming.

I'll end this catalogue of Washington's deficiencies, or alleged deficiencies, with one more item. There were even critics then who said, and in fact there are historians to this day who say, that Washington never won a battle in the Revolutionary War and wasn't much of a commander, wasn't much of a soldier. Can you live with that one? I can't, and it gets me so mad that I won't wait past this paragraph for it to be refuted. I'll turn again to Nevins and Commager, who answered it beautifully and eloquently in their book, saying, "The culminating American advantage was that of leadership—for the Americans had George Washington. Chosen by Congress with little knowledge of his capacities, he proved all in all to the patriot cause its best guide and support. He can be criticized on narrow military grounds. He never handled an army larger than a modern division, he made many missteps, he was defeated again and again. Yet, taking command at forty-three, he became the soul of the war. This Virginia planter and frontier colonel was its informing spirit because of his unflagging patriotism, his calm wisdom, his serene moral courage; because in the gloomiest hours he never lost his dignity, poise, or decision; because he knew how to combine enterprise and caution; because his integrity, elevation, and magnanimity never failed, his fortitude never faltered."

I don't have their gift of language, so I'll speak my own piece more simply and briefly. So they say that Washington never won a battle, do they? Well, he outmaneuvered the British and won the war, and that's the thing that really counts.

Having dealt with that, I'll go on to say that in my opinion, and despite all those deficiencies or alleged deficiencies, Washington was probably the greatest president of them all. Maybe that's an overstatement, or too black-and-white a statement; maybe I'd be stating it more accurately if I said that Washington was one of our three greatest presidents along with Abraham Lincoln and Franklin Roosevelt. I still have some enjoyable arguments with friends over the order in which to rate these three men, and the reason it's enjoyable is that I have fun concealing my *real* opinion, which is that they just can't be rated one over the other. The truth is that they're really peas in a pod, three equally great men, and America is damn lucky that three such giants happened to come along. And the only reason I sometimes rate Washington first and Lincoln second and FDR third is that that's the order in which they arrived on the American scene.*

For a couple of other reasons, however, perhaps Washington should be rated as our greatest president, after all, and not just because he happened to be born before Lincoln and Franklin Roosevelt. The first is that he had to make many personal sacrifices, as a soldier and as an opponent to the ruling government and as president, which neither Lincoln nor FDR had to make. The second is that he had to proceed into unknown territories in ways that never faced the other two men—again both as a soldier in the first war for freedom on this continent, an entirely new phenomenon, and as the president of a brand-new country. And with none of those guidebooks, like his books on farming, to help him, he met the challenge. And he succeeded, and the country succeeded and became the greatest country in the world.

Take a minute or two to think about those sacrifices he had to make. When he attended the Continental Congresses, and when he accepted the job of chief officer and fought in the Revolutionary War, he ran the greatest risk of anybody because he was one of the richest men in the Colonies. He had his big house and his plantation and all that property all over the place, and he could have lived his life in peace and comfort and looked the other way when it became clear that a great soldier and a great leader was needed. He could simply have ignored the injustice going on around him because most of these things weren't touching him personally. No matter what happened to other people, he would have become and remained the leading citizen of Virginia. But he was perfectly willing to throw everything away for the welfare and benefit of all the other colonists by joining the protests against the British and then becoming the leading soldier in the war against them. He was interested in anything and everything that had to do with the welfare of Virginia and the welfare of the nation, of what became the nation, and he didn't have any partisan attachment to any part of the country. All he was interested in doing was making it all work together, and he made it happen. And let me tell you, it took a good man to do that at that time. I don't think anybody else could have done it in that period.

*Interestingly, the poll of historians lists the three presidents in exactly the same order my father sometimes did: Washington as our best president, Lincoln as second best, Roosevelt as third best. And perhaps for the same reason. MT

Some people have the impression that he was a cold man, but I don't agree with that at all. Some people also have the impression that he was an egotist, but he wasn't that either. He was certainly an aristocrat, but he wasn't one of those aristocrats who believed that he was better than anybody else in the United States. And he was certainly a tough old general, as you can find out very clearly for yourself by tracking down some of the things that don't appear in the more genteel books about Washington—such as the exact language he used to one of his subordinates, General Charles Lee, at the Battle of Monmouth in 1778.

The battle was going well and was a certain victory for the Americans until Lee, totally disobeying orders to advance, suddenly turned tail and retreated without any good reason, which enabled Sir Henry Clinton to counterattack. Washington was in a fury, and what he said to Lee was something to write home about. In fact, Lee became such an enemy of Washington's that he abused him publicly and at every turn, until a member of Washington's staff, Major John Laurens, challenged him to a duel in which, fortunately, neither man was hurt. Lee was court-martialed for his actions at Monmouth because he was disobeying orders, suspended from command for a year, and in 1780 thrown out altogether. Washington was as tough a bird as could be, and when he got wrought up, he used language that any artilleryman could understand, including an old artilleryman like me, but the important point is that his handling of the situation at Monmouth, like everything he did, accomplished a purpose. He ordered Lee to the rear, and with the help of von Steuben and Nathanael Greene, managed to reform Lee's soldiers and hold the British back until they retreated. And this allowed Washington to cross the Delaware, and there you are.

Mostly, however, Washington was just a good human being with the ability to make people do what they sometimes didn't want to do and like it, an ability he picked up and developed out of necessity because he had so much trouble running the war and winning it. And he was a man of his age with the unique qualities needed at that time to put over the Revolution and the war and the brand-new country. He knew how to command, and how far that command should go, and when to give up command, and that's what he did throughout his life. You don't find that very often. You don't find it very often at all; very few leaders know when to quit as Washington did. I think you have to go all the way back to Cato the Younger in the Roman Empire to find a similar example, and of course Cato's sudden retirement was different not only because he retired in a very drastic way, by committing suicide, but because, unlike Washington, he didn't retire at the time of triumph but because his enemy, Julius Caesar, was doing so well.

Life for Washington, on the other hand, was a series of triumphs, and the astonishing thing is how well he did at the very different things he undertook throughout his life. He was the commanding general of the forces that won the freedom of the colonies, and he was the presiding officer of the Constitutional Convention in 1787 when that great document was being drawn up, and between those two things and the fact that he set up the government as the first president, succeeding in his complex purpose of making the country operate and continue, shows how well his mind worked. As I've said, he may not have been as brilliant in some ways as Jefferson and Hamilton, but he knew how to make more brilliant men behave for the welfare of the country. I once described Washington as a doer surrounded by thinkers. He knew how to make the thinkers work for him, and only a truly superb politician and leader is able to do that.

It took me quite a while to understand that myself, because, like most kids, I grew up knowing very little more about Washington than the silly fairy tales that that lying old preacher Parson Mason Locke Weems put in his book *The Life and Memorable Actions of George Washington*. I didn't learn until much later that there's hardly a word of truth in the book because Weems fictionalized all his books "to increase their interest," and that even the story of Washington's chopping down the cherry tree didn't get dreamed up by old Weems until he was getting ready to publish the fifth edition of his Washington book. It took me a long time to find out what Washington was really like. I had to read dozens of books about him and part of the hundred and fifty volumes of his papers and records to understand him as well as I think I do now.

In a sense, you might say that Washington's series of sacrifices and successes began when he became a soldier in the Virginia militia and in the French and Indian War. His decision to become a soldier wasn't for entirely unselfish motives, but that's nothing against him; even people who spend their entire lives doing good for other people do so partly for selfish motives, although sometimes the selfish part of it is nothing more than the fact that helping other people makes them feel good and lifts their self-esteem a bit. In those days, it was necessary for every property owner to be ready to defend himself and his property against raids, and these attacks came from two forces, of course: the Indians and the French. Some Indian tribes were growing more resentful of the intruders who were taking over their lands, and the French were the longtime enemies of the British and therefore the enemies of the colonists, who were British subjects.

There were so-called "little wars" in America, which were not so little for the people involved in them, going as far back as 1689. This one was called King William's War, when the French and British, both with Indian allies, fought each other for eight years, mostly in New England and Nova Scotia, and the next was Queen Anne's War, which took place from 1701 to 1713, again mostly in New England and Canada. These wars were mostly skirmishes followed by periods of peace, but it was inevitable that the French and the British would eventually begin another war that would be even more bloody and continuous because both countries were determined to expand their territories in the New World (which is why some historians say the correct name of the French and Indian War is the Great War for Empire), and because they had conflicting claims on some of the territories.

The French, for example, felt that, based on the rights of discovery, they were the proper owners of Virginia, Pennsylvania, and a large part of New York, even though most of the settlers in these places were British. And they also felt they had military superiority, even though the British had more of their people living in America, because the French forces had more forts in key places than the British and because most of the Indian tribes who weren't against both groups tended to side with the French. The whole thing burst into flame in 1754, as I've described earlier, when Robert Dinwiddie of Virginia sent George Washington to tell the French to leave the Ohio Valley and they wouldn't go, and the war continued intensely for seven long years.

The necessity to be ready to defend his property was doubly important for Washington, both because he was a landowner himself and because all of his closest friends were landowners. Furthermore, he was already beginning to be perceived as a leader, and in addition to supervising his plantation and working his own land, the people who were sent to Virginia to work out their passage began to look to him to help them become landowners themselves once they were free of their debts. Washington believed very strongly in the protection of property and the protection of man's right to make as much as he possibly could in a financial way. Perhaps he was even a bit too strong on that subject because, later on, it was the main cause of the split between the Federalists, Washington's group, and the Jeffersonians. I think Washington felt that an asset in property showed that a man knew how to earn a living and that therefore he was a better man to have in control of the government of his local community, and nationally, too, than a man who didn't have any property. Whereas Jefferson believed that the people knew how to govern themselves if they had the facts before them, no matter whether they were rich or not. (Much as I admire Washington, I'm certain Jefferson was right on this point.) In any case, since each colony had its own militia trained to defend its own territory, it was certain that a man like Washington would join the Virginia militia, which he did, as mentioned previously, in 1754.

It was also certain that he would become an outstanding military man because he ran his plantation like the best kind of officer, meaning with an intelligent mixture of discipline and understanding. As a land-owner and farmer, he understood the necessity of getting people to work as they should, but he also treated the people we now call hired hands as people. He was decent to them; he saw that they were properly taken care of, and after they had worked out their debt for their transportation here, he helped a great many of them obtain land grants. And in his military capacity, he understood that a well-disciplined organization was necessary if they were expected to achieve victory, but he also understood his soldiers' feelings and rights.

He was the commanding general in the Revolutionary War and he acted like the commanding general; he believed in control of the army from the top, and when he gave an order that had to be carried out, he saw to it that it was carried out. And when it wasn't carried out, somebody got into trouble. But because he was considered the most honorable man of the period, there was both respect and affection in the attitude toward him on the part of soldiers and civilians. Washington's word was better than most men's bonds, and when he told people what he thought and why he thought it, they believed him and went along with him. I'm as sure of that as I'm sure that I'm sitting here, and that was why he was able to persuade the Continental Congress to give him money, and per-suade his troops to stay and fight when their terms were up and they wanted to go home. The things I've read make it clear that every person who served with him was exceedingly fond of him. He must have been a nice man as well as a tough one.

He served with distinction in the French and Indian War, starting as a major and ending as a colonel when he left to enter the Virginia House of Burgesses. He was a lot better soldier, for example, than that General Edward Braddock, who, as I've mentioned, tried to take Fort Duquesne and got himself and a lot of other men killed by ignoring Washington's advice after Washington urged him not to go where he did and in the way he did. Washington, you'll recall, was also largely re-sponsible for the rescue of that part of Braddock's army that wasn't slaughtered, bringing them back to a safe place after they were able to get away from the French and Indians. (Incidentally, I've been to Brad-dock's tomb. They've got a monument dedicated to him over there in Pennsylvania, though I'm not sure why.) And it goes without saying that Washington did an extraordinary job in the Revolutionary War, knitting the various militia organizations together and with the help of von Steuben and Lafayette and others, training the colonial troops and instilling dis-cipline into them—which made a wonderful army out of them or they could never have won the war. Together, these men went to work on the militiamen and other volunteers who came along, and when the war was over, the colonial army was as good as any army in the world.

But there were plenty of sacrifices and plenty of misery for a man who loved his home as much as Washington did, and I'm sure he was mighty glad to go back to Virginia and civilian life in 1758, and again when the Revolutionary War ended in 1783. And I'm equally sure he had every intention and expectation of living out his life quietly and in a settled way as a Virginia farmer each time he went back home. That's another recurring theme in Washington's life: his deep reluctance every time he was called upon for duty away from Virginia, followed immediately by his realization that he had to do what he was called upon to do. That was the case when he served in the French and Indian War, and when he was a member of the Continental Congresses, and when the Revolutionary War came along and he had to take command, and when he was asked to be the country's first president, and especially when he was asked to serve a second term. He had planned to serve for only a single four-year term, as you know, and you can hear his groans over that second term right down through the ages. But I think he realized fairly early in life that he was slated for leadership chores, jobs he didn't especially want, because he knew people in every colony and was associated with the men who were at the top of the government in every colony, and he undertook that second term just as he undertook everything else that he realized was necessary and needed.

He didn't even take any pay as president; he just put in bills for expenses whenever he paid out anything in the interest of the government. That was a firm decision he made when he decided to accept the presidency, and it wasn't easy at times because there was that big plantation of his back in Virginia—I believe he had something like 33,000 acres, and the cash crop was principally tobacco—and something like that doesn't run without plenty of costs. So he had to go to the banks from time to time to borrow money, which was another sacrifice because nobody likes doing that.

But he also knew that he was the certain choice for the first president, and in fact he was the only president in our history who was elected unanimously. The states voted by way of men who were called electors, and Washington was picked by the electors of all ten voting states—in alphabetical order, Connecticut, Delaware, Georgia, Maryland, Massachusetts, New Hampshire, New Jersey, Pennsylvania, South Carolina, and Virginia, Washington's home state. The three other states of the original thirteen, New York, North Carolina, and Rhode Island, didn't get into the act because North Carolina and Rhode Island hadn't yet ratified the Constitution, and New York was having some internal squabbles and never got around to deciding which electors to send. John Adams received the second-largest number of electoral votes and was elected vice president, but by the time he got around to running for president, there were two political parties of pretty nearly equal strength, and it became a close race with Adams getting seventy-one electoral votes and Jefferson getting sixty-eight. The two parties were Washington's party, the Federalists, which favored giving most of the ruling power to the central government, the federal government, and Jefferson's party, the Democratic-Republicans, which favored more power for the states. (More about that when I finish up with Washington and get on to Tom Jefferson. But isn't it a good laugh that there was once a single party called the Democratic-Republicans?)

Since I've mentioned electors, incidentally, this seems to be as good a place as any to explain how the electoral college works and why it exists. I'll do that in the next chapter and come back to Washington in the following chapter

EIGHTEEN
The Electoral College

YOU have to understand, of course, that there was no real precedent for the members of the Continental Congresses in the notion of *electing* a single individual to the job of running the country, since kings and emperors took over by birth or by capturing territory in a war. It was quite creative and inventive, therefore, when a thing called the Virginia Plan was introduced at the Constitutional Convention on May 29, 1787, by Edmund Jennings Randolph, Virginia's governor, a document that contained these words: "Resolved, that a National Executive be instituted, to be chosen by the National Legislature . . ." The length of the term was left blank, with some men at the Convention favoring a single term of seven years and others favoring three years, and there were a lot of other arguments and debates on how the members of the National Legislature should go about picking their man. Washington was the president of the Convention, and when five states voted for the seven-year term and four states voted against it, and the remaining state, Massachusetts, split on the subject, Washington decided that the seven-year term had won. But the question of how to decide on the right man was a lot tougher.

It was a fellow from Pennsylvania, James Wilson, who later became one of the original justices of the Supreme Court, who first suggested the idea of an electoral college, meaning a body of electors to be chosen by the people of each state. But this notion was defeated eight to two, and instead it was determined that Congress, the body of senators and representatives, would do the selecting of the man. Then Randolph spoke up and said that maybe the Virginia Plan wasn't such a good idea after all, and perhaps there ought to be three executives working together rather than one, because a single leader might start thinking he was really a king and start acting like one. But Wilson argued that that was a lousy idea because the three men would be squabbling all the time and never get anything accomplished, and he pleaded again for his plan for a body of electors chosen by the general population. The first part of his argument made sense to the men at the convention, but not the second, so the Virginia Plan was revised to read as follows: "Resolved, that a National Executive be instituted, to consist of a single person, to be chosen by the National Legislature, for a term of seven years, with power to carry into execution the national laws . . ."

Nothing was really settled at this point. New Jersey came up with a rival plan that again suggested government by a group of men rather than a single individual, but it left blank the number of men in the group and also left blank the number of years the group should serve, but specified that all of the men in the group could be removed by application to the Congress of a majority of the chief executives of the states. Alexander Hamilton came out against both the Virginia Plan and the New Jersey Plan, saying that neither really gave the federal government enough power, and suggested his own plan, which provided for "the supreme Executive authority of the United States to be vested in a Governor, to be elected to serve during good behaviour; the election to be made by Electors chosen by the people . . ." But there were violent arguments against the Hamilton Plan as well, with a Virginian named George Mason pointing out that a term of "good behaviour" could well mean a lifetime and a return to a monarchy.

It all went on for quite a while. James Madison of Virginia, a tiny fellow who was five feet four, weighed less than a hundred pounds, and spoke so softly that people complained constantly that they couldn't hear him, but who later became our fourth president because he had a darn good brain, argued that selection of a president by the National Legislature might tend to bring in men chosen less because they were great leaders than because they had a lot of buddies in Congress. Gouverneur Morris of Pennsylvania said pretty much the same thing, arguing that "if the people should elect, they will never fail to prefer some man of distinguished character, or service . . . If the Legislature elect, it will be the work of intrigue, or cabal, and of faction . . ." Then Oliver Ellsworth of Connecticut joined the argument in favor of electors and came up with a suggestion with specific numbers: states with population of under two hundred thousand should have one elector, states between two hundred thousand and three hundred thousand should have two electors, and states above three hundred thousand should have four electors. And Elbridge Gerry of Massachusetts came up with even more specific suggestions: that Connecticut have two electors, Delaware three, Georgia one, Maryland two, Massachusetts three, New Hampshire one, New Jersey two, New York two, North Carolina two, Pennsylvania three, Rhode Island one, South Carolina two, and Virginia three. Some of the smaller states objected, of course, but Gerry's suggestion was accepted by a vote of six to four.

The objections didn't really matter because Gerry's proposal didn't hold up very long. On July 24, William C. Houston of New Jersey began to argue again against the use of electors, saying that the system would be too expensive and that really good men wouldn't be interested in taking on the job. The delegates immediately reversed themselves and by a vote of seven to four decided again to let Congress pick the presidents. There were also further arguments on the length of presidential terms, on whether a president could serve for only a single term or for a number of terms, and various other things. And finally a committee of eleven men was set up to deal with the open questions, and the proposals of these eleven men were at last accepted.

The president and vice president were to be elected for four-year terms and could be reelected for an unlimited number of equal terms. They both had to be natural-born citizens of the United States, residents of the country for at least fourteen years, and thirty-five years of age or older. And they were to be chosen by electors in a system based on the numbers of senators and representatives from each state; each state would have a total of electors equal to the total of senators and representatives from that state.

As for that number of senators and representatives, it was decided that there would be two senators from each state, and that the number of representatives would depend upon population, with each state having at least one representative. That meant, of course, that each state would have at least three electors.* Population was defined as the number of

_____

*In 1961, the Twenty-third Amendment finally gave residents of the District of Columbia the right to vote in presidential elections. The amendment also gave the District of Columbia three electors. MT

"free persons" in each state, plus three-fifths of "all other persons," meaning slaves, but excluding "Indians not taxed." During Washington's first term, there were twenty-six senators, since there were, of course, thirteen states, and a total of sixty-four representatives; in my two terms, there were forty-eight states and ninety-six senators, and the number of members of the House of Representatives had grown to four hundred and thirty-five. (Incidentally, senators were at first chosen by each state legislature and representatives by popular vote, the votes of the general public, but in 1913 the Seventeenth Amendment changed that so that both senators and representatives are elected by general vote.)

This idea of an electoral college seemed like a sensible one at the time because it was assumed that the man chosen for president would be the same man chosen by the people in the general voting, but the system has come in for a lot of criticism through the years, and frequent attempts have been made to change it or discard it, because it doesn't always work out that way. The reason for this is that, though electors were originally also selected by each state legislature, so that electors came from different political parties and therefore didn't necessarily vote in a bloc for the presidential candidate of a particular party, this was also later changed so that today you vote for and elect your electors the same way you pick the men and women, and therefore the political party, running your state. This means that, if your state has a majority of Democratic or Republican electors, the members of the electoral college from your state vote, of course, for the Democratic or Republican candidate for president. But because of this the electoral college vote sometimes doesn't match the popular vote, since individual voters frequently cross political lines and vote for the man they prefer rather than the man given the electoral votes by their state's electors. But it's the electoral college total that elects the president, not the popular vote total, so you can see where there are objections to the system.

The result of all this is that there have been nine instances where the man who got in received fewer popular votes than his chief opponent, or fewer votes than his combined opponents, but more electoral votes. James Buchanan was the first; in 1856, he beat his two opponents, John C. Frémont and Millard Fillmore easily in the popular voting by getting 1,838,169 votes to Frémont's 1,335,264 and Fillmore's 874,534, but as you can see by doing a little quick arithmetic, Frémont and Fillmore together got 2,209,798 votes, or a total of 55 percent of the votes to Buchanan's 45 percent. In the electoral college voting, however, he got 174 votes to a total of 122 for the other men (Frémont got 114 and Fillmore 8), and he was the new president. The same thing happened to Abe Lincoln in his first term. Lincoln, the Republican candidate, got

1,866,352, or 40 percent of the votes, while the other men got 60 percent: Stephen A. Douglas, the Democrat, got 1,375,157 votes, 29 percent, John C. Breckinridge, of the National Democrats, the splinter party composed of southerners, got 845,763 votes, and 18 percent, John Bell, of a short-lived party called the Constitutional Union, got 589,581 votes, which is 13 percent. But in the electoral voting, Lincoln got 180 votes to the other candidates' combined 123. To give you an idea of how electoral college votes can differ from popular votes, Douglas was second in the popular voting, as you can see, but last in the electoral college. Breckinridge got 72 from eleven states, mostly in the south —Alabama, Arkansas, Delaware, Florida, Georgia, Louisiana, Maryland, North Carolina, South Carolina, and Texas; Bell got 39 votes; and Douglas got only 12. (In his second election, though, Lincoln had only one opponent, General George B. McClellan, Democrat, and beat him both ways, getting 2,216,067 votes, 55 percent of the popular vote, to McClellan's 1,808,725 votes, 45 percent, and 212 electoral votes to McClellan's 21. The Confederate states, of course, didn't vote in this election.)

The first candidate to lose the popular vote but get the presidency because of the electoral college was Rutherford B. Hayes, who received 4,033,950 votes to Samuel J. Tilden's 4,284,757 votes, but squeaked past him in the electoral college 185 to 184. Garfield was practically neck and neck with his opponent, Winfield S. Hancock, in the popular vote, beating Hancock by only 9,464 votes and picking up 48.3 percent of the votes to Hancock's 48.2 percent, but got 214 electors' votes to Hancock's 155. Cleveland got 49 percent of the popular votes in his first election to James G. Blaine's 48 percent, but beat Blaine 219 to 182 in the electoral college; and he got only 46 percent in his second election victory against his combined opponents' 54 percent, but took the electoral college votes 277 to their combined 167.

Cleveland, you'll remember, was president for the first time in 1884, and then took a break and was elected again in 1892, and the reason he wasn't president in 1888 is that old Benjamin Harrison beat him in that one. Not in the popular vote, though; Cleveland got 5,540,329 votes, 49 percent, to Harrison's 5,439,853 votes, 48 percent, but the electoral college gave Harrison 233 votes to Cleveland's 168. Woodrow Wilson didn't attain a majority against his opponents in either election, getting 42 percent the first time and 49 percent the second time, but he got 435 electoral college votes the first time against his two principal opponents' combined 96, and 277 electors' votes the second time against Charles Evans Hughes's 254.

Then there was another fellow about whom I'll say a word in a minute, and the most recent example is John F. Kennedy.* Kennedy defeated Nixon in the popular vote only 49.7 percent to 49.5 percent 34,227,096 votes to 34,108,546, but received 309 electoral college votes to Nixon's 219.

How do I feel about the electoral college system personally? Well, that other fellow I mentioned is me. I received the *most* votes in both categories when I ran against Dewey, but I didn't receive the *majority* of the popular votes. I got 24,105,812 votes, which was 49 percent of the votes cast, while Dewey got 21,970,065 votes, 45 percent, Strom Thurmond, the Dixiecrat candidate, got 1,169,063 votes, 2 percent, Henry A. Wallace, the Progressive candidate, got 1,157,172, also 2 percent, and the other 2 percent got scattered among other people. But in the electoral college voting, I got a stronger majority, 303 votes to Dewey's 189 and Thurmond's 39. (Wallace didn't get any electoral votes.) I got the majority of electoral votes in twenty-eight states—Arizona, Arkansas, California, Colorado, Florida, Georgia, Idaho, Illinois, Iowa, Kentucky, Massachusetts, Minnesota, Missouri, Montana, Nevada, New Mexico, North Carolina, Ohio, Oklahoma, Rhode Island, Tennessee, Texas, Utah, Virginia, Washington, West Virginia, Wisconsin, and Wyoming; the fellow with the little mustache got the electoral votes in sixteen states—Connecticut, Delaware, Indiana, Kansas, Maine, Maryland, Michigan, Nebraska, New Hampshire, New Jersey, New York, North Dakota, Oregon, Pennsylvania, South Dakota, and Vermont; and Thurmond got Alabama, Louisiana, Mississippi, and South Carolina. So it can certainly be said that I benefited personally, in a way, from the electoral college system.

Still and all, I don't think I'll abstain from this one; I think I'll come right out and say that, all things considered, I'm in favor of a change to

---

*This has happened a couple of times since. In Richard M. Nixon's first contest he received 43.4 percent of the vote, with the other candidates receiving the other 56.6 percent of the votes. Hubert Humphrey received 42.7 percent and George C. Wallace received 13.5 percent, but Nixon got 301 electoral votes to Humphrey's 191 and Wallace's 46. For his second term, however, against Senator George McGovern, Nixon got 61 percent of the popular vote and 520 electoral votes to McGovern's 17. Jimmy Carter had what might be called a draw; he received 50 percent of the votes with 40,825,839, and Gerald Ford received 48 percent with 39,147,770 votes, the remaining 2 percent going to other candidates. But Carter received 297 electoral votes to Ford's 240. These figures total 537, but there were actually 538 votes cast. The missing vote was cast by an elector from Washington State, who voted for Ronald Reagan, even though Reagan wasn't a presidential candidate at that time. Reagan beat Carter easily in the next election, getting 43,899,248 votes, 51 percent, to Carter's 35,481,435 votes, 41 percent, with 5,719,437 votes, 7 percent, going to John B. Anderson, a former Republican who ran on the Independent ticket, and Reagan absolutely overwhelmed Carter in the electoral voting, 489 votes to Carter's 49. Anderson received no electoral votes at all. Reagan did even better in his second run for the presidency, receiving 525 electoral votes to Walter Mondale's 13. Mondale's votes came only from his home state, Minnesota, and from the District of Columbia. MT

election of our presidents on the simple basis of putting in the man who gets the most votes from the people of our country. And I wouldn't want to see some silly clause stuck in that says he has to get the largest percentage of votes as compared to the combined percentage of the votes for all the other sixteen people running against him, if you count all the candidates put up by the various little parties. It just seems to be elementary logic that, since every citizen in the country has the right to vote for his or her choice for president, the man who gets more votes than any of the other candidates ought to be told that he's our next president. That's simpler, cleaner, and it makes the most sense.

PART IV

Our Great Presidents, and Some in Between

NINETEEN
Washington, Chief Executive

L ET'S get back to George Washington. He was now president of the United States, and let me tell you, he really worked at it.

As you can imagine, he was an unknown quantity as the first chief executive of a new country, and of course the country itself was an unknown quantity, made up of different kinds of people trying to work together as a single unit for the first time. It was one thing to fight together in an army against a common enemy, but an entirely different thing to function together in peacetime and create laws and systems that everyone would obey and follow. All Americans knew Washington as a tough general and as a patriot and as a man capable of running temporary organizations like the Constitutional Convention for brief periods of time, but nobody knew how he'd function at the long-range and complex job of running the country. Fortunately for all of us living in this country in later years, with all of its privileges and freedoms and blessings, he was good at it, good at the job of getting the country started and keeping it going.

In my opinion, that's the principal and outstanding thing in Washington's character, even more than his ability as a military strategist or anything else, his ability to become a chief executive in a new government and act like a chief executive. And even when some decisions were hard to make, he made them, and he carried them through. I think he realized from the first day that it was the business of the executive to enforce laws, and he enforced them. The Whiskey Rebellion, which took place in 1794, is a good example.

In 1791, Alexander Hamilton, who became the country's first secretary of the treasury, levied a tax on liquor to help pay off the debts created by the war and to bring in some revenue to run the government. A lot of people in Pennsylvania didn't care much for the new tax; many of the farmers made a practice of turning their corn crops into corn liquor and selling the liquor instead of undertaking the heavy expense of moving the corn long distances to sell it, and they felt that the new tax was discriminatory. They were mostly hard-bitten fellows of Scotch-Irish descent who enjoyed using up a little of their home product themselves, and they refused to pay the tax. Riots broke out in many places in Pennsylvania, and partly on Hamilton's advice and partly because he felt the same way himself, Washington decided to get tough about it. He believed it was necessary and important to establish, once and for all, the right of the Congress of the United States to levy taxes in any way it saw fit, since the taxes were being levied by the representatives of the people. He sent 15,000 soldiers into Pennsylvania and showed up in person to review the troops, a simple and pointed show of federal strength, and the rioting stopped and the people of Pennsylvania paid the tax like everybody else.

At the same time, however, Washington realized, the way a really good executive of any type should, that too much toughness isn't a good idea, either—that an excessive show of authority can easily degenerate into toughness for its own sake, just to show who's boss. So when Hamilton, who sometimes tended to behave on the autocratic side, wasn't satisfied even when the riots stopped and felt it was necessary to make examples of the rioters and had some of them arrested, Washington promptly pardoned the men.

As an executive, Washington was one of the best men who were ever in office. Some of the great, fundamental, basic laws that are still in force were passed in Washington's administration, and it took a man who was a first-rate administrator and had the energy and the intestinal fortitude to make those things work. If Washington hadn't been that sort of man, I don't think we would have had a government.

Naturally, there were accusations every time he felt it was necessary to put his foot down and do something tough, accusations that he was trying to act like a king. You'll find all of that in the newspapers that were published at the time. He was treated like a pickpocket by the press when he was president. He was always being abused by nitpickers. He was called a traitor and a royalist, and he was accused of wanting to establish a sort of royal line to take charge of the government. None of it was true, of course. Hamilton was also accused of acting like a king, and so were the other people around Washington. But Washington didn't want to be a king. He could have been if he wanted to be, too, because there was plenty of talk after the Revolution about establishing the country as a new kingdom with Washington as our first monarch. But Washington wanted the country to go according to the Constitution, which he had helped to write. He just wasn't the kind of man who spent time trying to promote himself, which is evident, or should be, from the fact that he tried to get out at the end of his first term. But they persuaded him to go with a second term, and it's a good thing that they did.

He just wasn't interested in absolute power or inherited power at all. He didn't want a monarch as head of the government. He wanted the United States to have a chief executive who had been elected by the people, or as nearly elected by the people as the rules about the electoral college in the Constitution will allow. And he consulted all the time with the men who surrounded him as advisors because he wanted the laws and operation of the country to be based on as many different viewpoints as possible.

There were only four cabinet posts in the first government: secretary of state, secretary of the treasury, secretary of war, and attorney general. That was it, only those four, but Washington managed all right under the circumstances. As the country grew, of course, and the situation developed where the president needed more help, where responsibilities piled up, why, they expanded the cabinet, and it's proper that that was done. But Washington did fine with what he had. Each member of his cabinet, naturally, had the help he needed to operate—I'm sure they all had secretaries—and Washington also had a staff just like any other president would have to have. He'd been in the habit of running an army, and he knew how to set up a proper staff. I don't know how often he met with the members of his cabinet. He met with them as often as was necessary.

Jefferson was Washington's first secretary of state; Hamilton, as I've mentioned, was his secretary of the treasury; Henry Knox was the first secretary of war; and Edmund Randolph, the fellow who came up with that Virginia Plan, was the first attorney general. But there were plenty of changes during Washington's two administrations.

Jefferson and Hamilton didn't get along at all, and they had some outstanding debates during cabinet meetings that practically turned into fistfights. Hamilton was far from content with sticking to financial matters and spent a lot of time talking about foreign affairs, in which he was essentially pro-British, favoring a return to friendship with the British now that we were an independent country, and he didn't care much for the French. The French were, of course, having their own revolution at that time, and surprisingly, or at least it surprised me when I first read about it, Hamilton was against that revolution despite his support of the American Revolution. Whereas Jefferson was pro-French and didn't trust the British. (I suppose the reason, as much as anything, is that Hamilton tended to be aristocratic in his outlook and admired the British ruling classes, and he was against the revolution in France because the lower-class people were taking over and executing the aristocracy. Jefferson, on the other hand, was a supporter of the belief of the equality of all people. You'd have guessed, thinking about the backgrounds of the two men, that it would have been the other way around, since Jefferson had an aristocratic background—he was a direct descendant of King David I of Scotland—and Hamilton grew up in humbler circumstances. He was the illegitimate son of James Hamilton, a West Indies planter, and of Rachel Faucett Lavien, the estranged wife of a doctor and part-time planter. But that's the way it was.)

The quarrels between the two men became so severe that, in 1793, Jefferson quit and returned to private life for a while and was replaced by Randolph, transferring from his job as attorney general. But Randolph lasted only until 1795 because he was disliked by both the Jefferson and the Hamilton factions, and he was replaced by Timothy Pickering, a lawyer from Massachusetts and a friend of Hamilton's, who kept everybody reasonably happy and continued in his job into John Adams's administration.

Hamilton served as secretary of the treasury until 1795, then resigned because he was starting to feel a financial pinch and knew he could make a lot more money as a lawyer and banker in New York than in government. (I should explain that he left the West Indies when he was seventeen to study at King's College, which later became Columbia University, and then established a law practice in New York City. He subsequently married Elizabeth Schuyler, the daughter of General Philip Schuyler, which made him part of an old and respected New York family. He was also one of the founders of the Bank of New York, which is still around.) But even as a private citizen, he remained close to Washington and kept a hand in the development of the country, continuing to give advice to his successor, Oliver Wolcott of Connecticut, and other government officials, and he also helped to write Washington's eventual Farewell Address. Wolcott continued as secretary of the treasury throughout the remainder of Washington's period in office and stayed on for a while for Adams.

In the secretary of war post, Knox stayed on until 1794, then was replaced by Timothy Pickering until Pickering became secretary of state; then James McHenry of Maryland, who was a surgeon during the Revolutionary War, took over the job and continued into the Adams administration. Knox and McHenry were both well liked; Knox got Fort Knox named after him, and McHenry got Fort McHenry in Baltimore named after him. I guess Pickering was okay, too, but after John Adams became president, he accused Pickering of scheming with his pal Alexander Hamilton to involve the United States in a quarrel and then a war with France, and fired him. So I can't find any record of anything important being named after Pickering, but he did go on to become chief justice of the Court of Common Pleas of Massachusetts and then a United States representative and senator.

In the attorney general's job, William Bradford, a former judge in Pennsylvania, took over after Randolph moved over to become secretary of state in 1794; he lasted only a year and was replaced by Charles Lee of Virginia, who held the job into the Adams administration. This wasn't the same Charles Lee who was a general in the Revolutionary War and behaved so poorly, you'll recall, at the Battle of Monmouth that he was thrown out of the army. This one was a brother of Henry Lee, better known as Light-Horse Harry Lee, a general who was an excellent officer during the Revolutionary War, and also commanded the troops that Washington sent into Pennsylvania during the Whiskey Rebellion. He was also the man who wrote that famous line about Washington, "First in war, first in peace, and first in the hearts of his countrymen." (And just to be a bit mischievous, let me take a line or two to tell you about another side of the man. He was also such a poor businessman that he failed to pay some bills and was thrown in debtors' prison for a while, even though he had plenty of money.) He was also the father of General Robert E. Lee of Civil War fame. I hope I'm not confusing you with all these generals and all these Lees.

As you can see, Washington had a lot of talent surrounding him during his years in the presidency, many of these people of high intellectual order. He was, himself, a practical man who had been through all sort of difficulties on the ground and knew how to act when problems came along; you might even say that he was a practical man surrounded by intellectuals. That's a good combination. You've got to have highly educated people who know history and who have a viewpoint, maybe, that's so idealistic that it won't work practically some of the time, and then you've got to have practical men to put it into effect. A good president is a man who's able to use the brains and ability of all the people that he can persuade to come and advise him. I don't think you can overemphasize the importance of intellectuals, because the intellectual is one of the best assets the country has; but you must also have a practical man around as a safety valve to show how the intellectual ideas can be put to work for the benefit of the people. That's all there is to it, and it's clear that Washington knew how to use his practical sense together with his advisors' intellectual abilities.

He was in touch constantly with all of the leading people in the government, the way any president who's going to make a success of his job has to be, and he also tried his best to consult with Congress whenever possible. *That* wasn't always as successful. You'll recall that that one time Washington went over to the Senate in person to discuss a matter—that time that they were so discourteous to him that he cussed them out and left—almost ended all discussions or appearances by the president forever. This was a voluntary approach by the president because he believed in advice and consent as stated in the Constitution; but even though he pulled out that time and never went back again, I'm sure he still had plenty of conversations with senators and members of the House of Representatives. You know, of course, that congressmen aren't hesitant about seeing the president if they want some special thing done in their part of the country. I'm certain that he met with senators and represent-atives whenever they wanted to talk to him, and I'm very sure that when he had important matters pending, he discussed the matters with individual congressmen. I don't know whether or not he ever appeared before a congressional committee, but I know that the chairmen of those com-mittees, and maybe the individual members, talked to Washington be-cause he had to sign the things. And they certainly didn't want him to veto anything, because he was so popular with the Congress in general that there was no chance that one of his vetoes could have been carried over his head.

The presidential veto power, incidentally, was another thing that was debated pretty fiercely during the Constitutional Convention. It was Elbridge Gerry who first suggested that the president should have the right to veto a bill or law that he felt was harmful to the people, but that the other legislators should also have the right to overrule him if enough of them felt that he was wrong; his exact language was that "the National Executive shall have a right to negative any legislative act, which shall not afterwards be passed by————parts of each branch of the National Legislature." (He left the amount blank that would be needed to overrule.) Hamilton and James Wilson felt that the chief executive's veto power should be absolute, and that the legislators shouldn't have the right to overrule him under any circumstances, but Ben Franklin and others argued that this would give the president *too* much power. Finally, it was agreed that the president should definitely have veto power, but that a presidential veto could be overridden if two-thirds of the legislators voted to override the veto. There was a subsequent effort to require the president to get the approval of some members of the judiciary in order to veto a bill, but this was shot down by a very narrow margin; with nine states voting, Connecticut, Maryland, and Virginia were for it, Delaware, Massachusetts, North Carolina, and South Carolina were against it, and Georgia and Pennsylvania were split on the subject. And that's the way the veto situation remains today.

Another way in which Washington worked hard was that he did a lot of traveling in order to talk to people and give them an idea of what the Constitution meant and what he was trying to do to make it work. He made tours all over the country at a time when it took months to travel from one place to another; he traveled by stagecoach and on horseback and he made it his business to visit every single state in the union. Whenever Congress wasn't in session, he went from Georgia to Massachusetts and from Delaware to Virginia, time and again, familiarizing the people with the government of the United States and with the presidential viewpoint. He was working to establish the government, the hardest thing any man can ever do, and I think he did more than any other person of the period to knit the country together as the United States of America.

He accomplished it by having meetings all over the place. He just talked to the people and explained things. And I suppose that, when he went on his trips, one or two of his cabinet officers came along with him and helped him do it. I don't know that for sure; I don't think there's any record of it. But I'm sure that when he went into the states where these men came from, they were there to receive him because he was so well liked and admired in every state. It couldn't have been otherwise or they wouldn't have argued him into being president that second time.

He wasn't a great orator, but he was able to put his thoughts across so that people could understand what he was talking about, and could understand what he was trying to do and leave the meetings convinced that he was capable of doing it. I've read a couple of books over the years that sneered at the way Washington talked and wrote, saying he was long-winded and flowery, but that's just nonsense. The formal and wordy way of writing, and to some extent speaking, was the customary style of the day, and they all did it. They all used long sentences in their speeches; go ahead and read some of Daniel Webster's speeches if you don't believe that. And they had a system of something they called polite correspondence; people were taught how to write letters and how to close letters and how to address each other, and there was a great deal of flowery language involved in those things, and some of it crept into Washington's speeches and correspondence and messages. We've got his messages here in the Truman Library, all of them, and I've read them many times, so I know what the nitpickers are talking about. But for heaven's sake, *everybody* wrote that way and talked that way to a certain extent at that time, and the simple proof of that is that, as the historical records show, a lot of the things he signed weren't written entirely by him. When he wrote a message to Congress, every one of his cabinet members made a contribution to it, and if he discussed a matter with members of the Congress, he sometimes inserted a paragraph or two in the exact language that somebody in Congress had suggested to him. We all do that when we have to do it.

I think every president ought to travel a lot, and I think every president ought to make it his business to give the people an exact outline of what his program is and why he wants it. That's a lot easier to do now because we have a far better transportation system and communications system, of course, than we had at that time. But Washington was a full-time president, and if it took travel by stagecoach or horseback to inform the people of his country of what was going on, then he jumped on his horse or got into a stagecoach and did it. He was a full-time president, all right, not like one or two of the lazy fellows we've had since his time.

I'm sure Washington felt that his travels were a plain and simple necessity because I'm certain that he had the same difficulties that all other presidents have when we're trying to get things done for the welfare of the country—at least what we're convinced is for the welfare of the country. As I've mentioned, he was attacked viciously in the press of that day on nearly every decision he made, but it didn't stop him because he thought that he was doing right and he was willing to try and carry things through. And as long as he got the proper support in the Congress, he did carry things through.

This isn't to say that those attacks by the press didn't upset him. They worried him and made him feel bad and sometimes discouraged him for a while. One time he even threatened to resign the presidency; and when the time came along for the second administration, as you know, they had to do a lot of persuading to get him to continue in the job because of those vicious and public attacks. He didn't like it very much, you may be sure; in fact, under ordinary conditions, and if he hadn't been president of the United States, there isn't any doubt that he would have fought some duels with the men who made the meanest remarks about him. But that doesn't make him an egotist; he just wasn't used to attacks like that because they didn't do that kind of thing when he was a general in the Continental Army. For the most part, his problems were essentially with the press. He didn't have much trouble with the major politicians of the day because many of them had served under him, and they liked him and thought he was all right. When he put forth policy, of course, there was sometimes opposition. Jefferson opposed some of his policies, and that's one of the other reasons Jefferson quit the cabinet. But Jefferson and the others had a perfect right to oppose policies when they felt the policies were wrong, and I'm sure Washington understood that and dealt with those situations calmly and sensibly.

He was a good executive, and a tough one when necessary, but I don't think he was the hard-boiled person some historians say except in his military career. When he was the commanding general, he acted like a commanding general, but I think as a president he acted like a servant of the people. And that's the reason he made those tours all around the country—to let people know what he wanted and why he wanted it, and to give them the chance whenever they wanted to ask questions about the various things he was doing or planning.

TWENTY

Isolationism: Our First Foreign Policy

THERE'S one other matter I want to take up, and that's Washington's reputation for conservatism and isolationism.

I don't think there's any question about the fact that Washington was about as conservative as it's possible for a man to be in many of his views, and it's natural that he was because, in those pioneer days, a man had to think more about staying alive and about the welfare of his family and his own welfare than about the needs of the rest of the world. And I don't think there's any question about the fact that Washington's administration was more conservative than anything else, and that conservatism rather than liberalism was the order of the day. In a way, the thing has been going on ever since Washington's time in the same sort of way, with the pendulum swinging from one side of the clock to the other and conservatives controlling the country part of the time and liberals (some of whom weren't so liberal) controlling the country the other part. But the thing you've got to keep in mind is that Washington and his people *had* to be conservative in order to start the country off; they *had* to think more about themselves and their needs and problems than about the rest of the world. And that doesn't mean that because that kind of thinking was proper and correct for the eighteenth century, it's also the right way to think now.

I've been asked if Washington would have been the same sort of conservative president during this period as he was during his two terms in office. Damned if I know. You never can tell; that's another of those hypothetical questions at which you can only guess the answer. But I doubt it. Washington, I'm sure, would have done what he thought was the right thing whether the people agreed with him or not. And if the country happened to be on one of those pendulum swings at the time where the conservatives controlled the thinking, whereas Washington felt, as I do, that we're now at the point where every resident of the world has to think of the well-being of every other citizen of the world, he would have been a liberal president and not a conservative.

The same thing applies to Washington's attitude of isolationism. Washington is often used as an example of America's minding her own business, and the first of our isolationists, and I'm afraid it's quite true. There's no question about the fact that Washington was almost an absolute isolationist. In his Farewell Address, Washington said very clearly and very specifically that we should detach ourselves from the rest of the world in every way except commerce, and it's that message that isolationists have always read in the Senate since that time. These were his exact words: "The great rule of conduct for us in regard to foreign nations is, in extending our commercial relations, to have with them as little political connection as possible. So far as we have already formed engagements let them be fulfilled with perfect good faith. Here let us stop."

Washington wrote the speech with Hamilton's help. They tried to get Jefferson in on it, but I don't think he had anything to do with it because he was concerned with freedom of the seas and other international problems, and he was a lot more interested in help from other nations than the other two men. Washington never actually gave the speech; he just had it printed in the *Philadelphia American Daily Advertiser*'s issue of September 17, 1796. But it was the greatest isolationist document that's ever been written, and every modern isolationist's point of view is the direct descendant of that Farewell Address. And when I was in the Senate, and I guess right up until recently, it was standard practice for someone to read that address on Washington's birthday.

Well, Washington's brand of isolationism was just good common sense on his part. It was a long way to Europe and we were defended by two oceans that were hard to navigate, the Atlantic and the Pacific, and that created the idea of an isolationist Western Hemisphere. And at that time, the three million Americans scattered from Maine to the southern boundary of Georgia were not in a position to become a loud voice in world affairs, anyway.

The strongest countries at this point in history were France and England, of course, and they were at each other's throat much of the time. During most of the Napoleonic period, it looked very much as if France would have absolute control of all Europe and wipe Britain out, but it didn't happen because the British controlled the seas. Spain was pretty much on the downgrade. The Spanish government began its downgrade when the Spanish Armada was wiped out by Sir Francis Drake, and they never really recovered from it; and then later on, Spain was controlled entirely by Napolean during the height of his success. So the two powers that really counted were Britain and France, and we were avoiding involvement with the two major powers because we were weak. We didn't want to get involved in a foreign war at that time. We couldn't afford it, and we didn't have the men to put in a foreign war in any case. Washington, therefore, was trying to reach a balance in American thinking regarding those two countries so as to protect the new government of the United States, and he thought that the less we meddled in the foreign affairs of Europe—that's all they looked at then, the foreign affairs of Europe—the better off we'd be.

But that was then, and this is now. We're no longer a small country that can't afford to get mixed up in foreign affairs; we're one of the great leaders of the free world, and that message of Washington's doesn't work anymore because he was faced with an entirely different situation. That's one of the things we've always got to keep in mind: that we've always got to meet situations as they shape up now with present-day considerations and conditions, and not base decisions entirely on situations of the past, which may be entirely different from today's conditions. It goes without saying that the Atlantic Ocean and the Pacific Ocean are no longer defense barriers. You can cross either one of them now in less than three or four hours, and it's going to be that soon we'll cross them quicker. Communication is instantaneous. We can talk to London, Paris, Moscow, Peking, or anywhere else in the world, just like that. It doesn't take any longer than the snap of the fingers to get hooked up to them, and we know instantly what goes on in every section of the world. And that means that the world has changed from a thirty-inch globe to a globe the size of an orange, or maybe even a grape.

Washington, of course, was afraid that the strong European countries, the royalists, would come in and try to take over the Western Hemisphere as they'd done before. But as time passed, it became more and more clear that you can't protect the country, you can't keep the United States safe, by pretending not to be part of the world. It took the

United States a long, long time to realize that we were part of the international community, and that we must be ready to oppose other countries
when necessary and help them when necessary, but we finally came
around to accepting that fact.

The first major example of our acceptance of these facts of life
occurred during the administration of our fifth president, James Monroe,
when it became clear that Spain, with the help of France, was planning
to seize some of its former possessions in Latin America and make them
Spanish colonies again, and that Russia was also thinking about insisting
that its territory in Alaska extended right down into what is now Oregon.
This worried both Great Britain and our own country, since both countries
had territorial claims in the Pacific Northwest at that time, and we also
both had good commercial relationships with the independent Latin American countries. Britain's foreign secretary, George Canning, suggested
that we join forces and warn off the European countries together, but
John Quincy Adams, who was then Monroe's secretary of state and later,
of course, became our sixth president, advised Monroe that we ought to
take our own stand and not, in Adams's words, look like "a cockboat
in the wake of the British man-of-war."

In 1823, therefore, Monroe made our position clear with some strong
statements that became known as the Monroe Doctrine, warning that we
wouldn't tolerate the establishment of any new European colonies in the
Western Hemisphere or any attempts to seize existing countries that were
already independent. The Monroe Doctrine wasn't a new American law
or anything of that sort, as most people who've forgotten their history
lessons seem to think; a doctrine is just a principle that someone proposes
or advocates, and Monroe made his statements as part of his annual
address to Congress. But in very plain language, he stated that all Western
Hemisphere territories were "henceforth not to be considered as subjects
for future colonization by any European powers" and that any movement
into the Latin American countries for the purpose of "controlling their
destinies" would be considered an act of unfriendliness toward the United
States, and his words were heard and understood very clearly. And that
policy has been the American position ever since that time.

It didn't always hold up, of course. During the Civil War, for example, when we had our hands full with a few other things, France moved
into Mexico and set up an empire there. But when our war was over,
the empire was broken up and Mexico became a republic. And in Cleveland's second term in office, toward the end of the nineteenth century,
there was that business with Great Britain's colony, British Guiana, and
the neighboring country of Venezuela, where some Americans became
convinced that Britain was trying to expand its territorial holdings by
insisting that part of Venezuela's acreage actually belonged to British

Guiana, and the United States sent Great Britain a note boasting that "the United States is practically sovereign on this continent" and implying that the Monroe Doctrine had been violated and insisting on immediate arbitration between Great Britain and Venezuela.

That one was more than a little bit hysterical, particularly since Cleveland referred to his communication publicly as a "twenty-gun note" and followed it up with a message to Congress demanding that this country "must resist by every means in its power" Britain's move to take territory from Venezuela. The British were offended at first by the high-handed note and did nothing whatsoever, but fortunately they were essentially good-natured about it; thirteen hundred British authors and more than three hundred members of Parliament sent messages designed to cool things down, and so did a great many Americans, and eventually arbitration between Venezuela and Great Britain took place. For the record, most of the arbitration was decided in favor of Great Britain.

But for the most part, Monroe's basic idea of preventing the expansion of European colonization in the Western Hemisphere has worked all right, and it's given us some very good neighbors. It's also resulted in the escape from bondage of some countries, such as when, after the Spanish-American War, the Cuban Republic and the Philippine Republic were set up and the proper freedom of Puerto Rico was established.

I don't have to be reminded of the fact that some Puerto Ricans don't like Puerto Rico's close ties with our country, since, you'll recall, a couple of Puerto Rican extremists showed up in Washington in 1945 with the idea of shooting me and I'm lucky they didn't succeed. And I don't have to be reminded that Cuba eventually became a very corrupt country and then a Russian satellite. But I'm certain that most Puerto Ricans are strongly in favor of our relationship, and this is borne out by the fact that, when I said, during a visit to San Juan on November 1, 1948, that the Puerto Rican people "should have the right to determine for themselves Puerto Rico's political relationship to the United States," and convinced Congress to enact laws enabling Puerto Ricans to elect their own governor and other officials and control all local affairs, most Puerto Ricans came out for commonwealth status and some for statehood. Practically nobody except a few extremists was interested in total separation from this country.

And as far as Cuba is concerned—well, I'm an optimist, and I still feel there's hope for that country as a totally free nation at some point in the future. We've just got to keep working at it. Whenever a foreign country like Russia tries to establish a position in the Western Hemisphere, they've got to be stopped just as they were in Monroe's time, and just as the French were in Mexico in Lincoln's time. And I feel that, sooner or later, that will happen.

We've always tried, as far as we can, to be of help to our neighbors. I think there's no country in the history of the world that's been as fair and has treated our neighbors as well as we have. (Sometimes we didn't treat our own inhabitants as well as we should have, but we're learning.) I think our policies, and in particular our love of freedom, has been good for Canada and for Mexico and a lot of other places. If we hadn't had our revolution, we'd be in the same position that Canada is in now, a commonwealth of the British hegemony, and that's not what was best for the world. I'll even wax religious for a moment and say that I think Almighty God straightened that out. Canada is all right, it's fine, but I believe that one of the reasons Canada has been able to grow is that they have a good neighbor south of them. I think we've contributed far more to Canada's growth and welfare than Britain has. There isn't any doubt about that because western Canada was mostly settled by people from the United States, and if the situation hadn't developed that Canada's government is along the same lines as our own, we would probably have annexed the whole west end of Canada. And they've got autonomy because they're alongside one of the great free nations of the world, a country that has always helped them to get that autonomy. And we're continuing to do that.

But the main point in all this is that we can't transact business today on Washington's program or Monroe's program; we've got to have a program of our own to meet conditions as they are now. In many ways, we stayed in the isolationism rut until after the First World War. We were still almost entirely isolationist up to that time, and there were still some isolationists left in the period between 1920 and 1932. But when we became a world power after the First World War and the Second World War, we could no longer be a country concerned only with ourselves. We had to get along with our neighbors in every part of the world, and that's what we've been trying to do ever since.

I can give you an exact parallel in ancient history, a situation that is exactly the same as now, and that's the Roman Empire, which by communications and transportation made the whole Mediterranean area into one great country. And as long as the Romans were interested themselves in the maintenance of that whole situation, they had no trouble. When they got lazy and fat, why, down it went. The world is now in that same situation. The whole world is now in a position to transact the business of the world just as we transact the business of the state of Missouri with one hundred and fourteen counties. Every one of those counties thinks it's an independent state, but it isn't. It's under the government of Missouri. Every one of our fifty states thinks it's absolutely independent and can do anything, but it can't. It takes the federal government with the power to act for all the people, and there may be a similarly powerful group of people who can, I hope, do the same thing for the whole world. It's my dream, of course, that that group will be the United Nations.

Now, I may be a nut on the subject, but I believe sincerely that the United Nations can work, despite its weaknesses and obvious problems, if we just have patience and give it enough time and don't become discouraged with it. I was strong for the League of Nations, too. I'm very well aware of the fact that it's been said often that war is an instrument of settlement when settlements can't be made without it, and that that's been the customary procedure since the beginning of the world, but it's my opinion that that can be overcome if we can succeed in getting a group of nations to work together in an organization to settle difficulties just as we've succeeded in getting it done among the states of the United States. It doesn't matter if the association of nations is called the United Nations or League of Nations or whatever you want to call it. When a war is over, life goes on, and then the important thing is to bring countries together and at the same time try to correct the things that caused the war in the first place.

If we can get a situation set up in world affairs such as was finally set up here after the War Between the States, with the states back together under a federal government, if we can get the world set up on the same basis, I think we can settle our difficulties without going to war by settling them through judicial approaches. When Kansas and Colorado got into a controversy recently over ownership of the Arkansas River water, Kansas sued Colorado. They didn't go to war. They didn't go to the National Guard. They let the courts settle it. And if we can do the same thing with all the countries that make up the United Nations, then maybe eventually we won't have anything but local border troubles that we can settle without having to go to all-out war as we did in 1917 and as we did in 1941.

I'm not saying that it's going to happen fast or be easy. The situation was a little different, a little better, even when I was president. We'd been working hard on friendship with Russia and China. Roosevelt had been working on it for twelve years, and I continued it for eight years more, and it had its effects. But when special interests get control of a country and really don't give a damn about the freedom of the people there, as has been happening more and more in those two countries and in other places, then you have tremendous difficulties.

But there's certainly nothing new about that. Even back in the early days of our country, when there was a display of Russian friendship toward us in our purchase of Alaska and the removal of the Russians from the west coast of the North American continent, the friendship was because the Russian government of that time was an enemy of Great Britain and was making overtures to a country that the leaders thought would be a thorn in the side of the British. You'll remember that the Russians owned Alaska; they settled Alaska and had fur trading places up there; some towns up there now still have Russian names. And they had claims in California, too, but their friendliness toward us when we settled with them was really unfriendliness toward Britain and to some extent toward France. We weren't naive about Russia then, and we're not naive about Russia and China and other places now. But you've still got to keep trying.

We did our best to help China. We sent immense amounts of money and immense amounts of equipment to China, but the people with whom we were doing business in China didn't have the right attitude toward their own people. In fact, the Communists in China used the equipment we sent to run the government of free China out of China, making the country surrender something like seven hundred million people to three hundred thousand Communists. They used the equipment we sent for the use of the free Chinese to chase the free Chinese out of China. And of course we've also done plenty for Russia. We loaned them $6.6 billion under Lend Lease, and they still haven't settled their debt. If it hadn't been for that Lend Lease, Hitler would have taken Moscow, and Leningrad, too. The Russians answer that by saying that we were only trying to save our own skin by doing it. We were not. We were trying to save Russia, and they've repaid us by attempting to discredit us before the whole world.

It just seems to be the objective of Russia and China at the present time, under their present governments, never to tell the truth. It seems to be their objective to promulgate the big lie and try to make it stand up. I really don't know how to offset that kind of propaganda. We're just not built on a basis where we like to tell a big lie and keep telling it and hoping somebody will believe it. We try to give people the right information as to what we really are, and we try to help other people of the world in the way we helped China and Russia. And we've tried to help all those countries in South America, and to a very large extent, we've been of great help to them in their development. I suppose there really isn't a thing you *can* do when you're up against countries with propaganda machines like Russia and China, countries that don't care anything about the truth or the facts. You can make anybody appear to be a no-good, no-account man if you lie about him enough. That's what the Russians and the Chinese have tried to do to us. I just don't know how you're going to overcome it, except just to go ahead and do the right thing as we've always done.

The big problem with Russia and China, of course, is that they're anxious to control the whole world all by themselves. No matter what they say, that's what they want. And they're willing to control the world by conquest. And that's what concerns, or should concern, the leaders of free countries, not the fact that they're Communists. Let me stick in my statement right here that communism isn't all bad, by any means, not when you spell it with a small "c" rather than the capital letter. In the first part of the Acts of the Apostles, in the King James version of the Bible, it says that the Christians in Palestine put all their belongings into a pool and handed the people the things that they needed when they needed them. That's the first example of real communism. In fact, if you remember, the Romans fought their wars to maintain the Roman Empire in every direction, and they always improved the countries they took over and adopted their gods. But the one instance in which they didn't do that is when they took over Palestine and didn't adopt the Christian religion, and I think the reason is that the Christians were practicing actual communism, real communism, and this was such a new idea that the Romans were afraid of it and were afraid it would develop as a worldwide program. Well, we've got to be careful not to be afraid of an idea just because it's new and radical, but the type of communism practiced by the Russians and the Chinese is a very different matter entirely. It's just a political organization on a totalitarian basis, and the leaders of those two countries seem perfectly willing to ignore the welfare and limit the freedom of their people in order to accomplish their aims.

And that's not what we want, not at all. We want to see a world control that will have every nation, large and small, properly represented so that justice can be obtained under every situation. My personal dream is for the development of the nations that now exist to a point where they'll have plenty to eat, plenty of room to live, and plenty of clothing and everything else it takes to make life livable and enjoyable in this day and age, and I believe that's the dream and the wish of most Americans. That may also be the dream of most Russian and Chinese people,* but many of their leaders have entirely different motives, and it's important that they don't succeed.

Well, they won't succeed as long as we stay together with our friends in the free world. And we do have many friends in the world in addition to our longtime allies in Europe. I think that we have a friend in Japan. We have a friend in the Philippines, and eventually, if things work out, we should have friends in Indonesia. And we know we have friends in

---

*I think my father would have liked *glasnost*, the new Russian policy of relative openness and relative freedom for the Russian people, though he would have wanted to see a lot more of it happening there before he'd be convinced that it was totally genuine. I hope it's still in existence and expanding by the time this book appears. MT

Australia and New Zealand. We're not exactly together with all of our friends in the free world as I write this, and there'll be plenty of other times when we'll be scrapping with some of our friends or facing similar disagreements with people with whom we agree most of the time.

We have our difficulties. We sit around and let the Communists come in and organize right next door to us when it shouldn't have happened. There's an article in *The Economist,* in one of the recent issues, in which the writer makes the statement that if the situation had gone along as it should have gone, Cuba might have been a state in the United States, and that it would have been so much better for Cuba if that had happened. A lot of presidents have wanted to take over Cuba as a possession of the United States, but that wouldn't have been right; the ideal thing would have been a voluntary joining with us on Cuba's part. That would be just like Hawaii, which wouldn't allow itself to be associated with anyone else and voted to come in as a state. Our best opportunity was back in the 1890s and the beginning of the twentieth century, but at that time we had some presidents who just weren't thinking along those lines. It would have been a wonderful thing if Cuba had been kept as our friend and had wanted to become a part of the United States. Or it could have been handled the same way that Puerto Rico was. Puerto Rico is, of course, now a free commonwealth of the United States, and I hope that the history books will give me a little credit for that. Well, at some time in the future, Cuba may still do that if they get rid of the present dictator.

It was the great king of France, King Henry IV, who first had the idea of an association of countries to keep the peace, a congress of European nations. He lived and died a long time ago—he was born in 1553 and died in 1610—but he was more modern in some of his thinking and more interested in the welfare of his people than most of the world leaders since his time. As I've mentioned, it was Henry IV who proposed and signed the Edict of Nantes, which gave a certain amount of religious freedom to the Huguenots, the Protestants, even though he converted to Catholicism himself, and he also did a lot of other things to improve and advance France like building roads and canals, increasing farming activity and productivity, encouraging the colonization of Canada, and signing trade agreements with England, Spain, and Turkey. He was also working all the time to improve living conditions for the poor people of his country; it was Henry IV, in fact, not President Hoover, who first used that famous phrase, though his wording was slightly different, "There should be a chicken in every peasant's pot every Sunday." So it isn't surprising that he was probably the first man in history to come up with the astonishing idea that perhaps nations ought to try to face each other around a conference table and work together for peace rather than face each other on the battlefield.

Unfortunately, he didn't get very far with it; he was on his way to try to put it in effect when he was assassinated by a religious fanatic named François Ravillac, and then it all went to pot. And then the idea pretty much disappeared until it was revived by Woodrow Wilson with the League of Nations.

The difficulty as far as the United States was concerned, as I've said, is that we were too wrapped up in ourselves at first, too busy getting ourselves on track, to do much thinking about the rest of the world. If it hadn't been for Thomas Jefferson and Benjamin Franklin, there's no telling when we might have started making our move toward relationships with other countries and toward becoming a world power. But Franklin went to France and spent enough time there to make them our friends, and Jefferson backed him up a little later on, and that's what really began to give us our foreign connections. Foreign policy, after all, is nothing more than the ability of a country to get along with its neighbors, and the ability to carry on trade with other countries, and that was the next step; inevitably, we began to deal more and more with other countries once we wanted them more and more as markets for our products and as suppliers for things we didn't make, or didn't make in large enough quantities, ourselves.

We didn't become a very great trade nation until we became interested in sea power. That started with Jefferson, too, when he was president and we were having a lot of trouble with the Barbary pirates and Jefferson decided to do something about it. The situation was that these pirates from Tripoli, Tunis, Morocco, and Algiers kept demanding tribute from ships in the Mediterranean Sea, and when a ship refused to pay, the pirates boarded the ship and looted it and shanghaied the sailors. The worst thing about it is that most countries paid the tribute, and even Jefferson went along with this for a while even though he hated paying the tribute; but then, in 1801, Tripoli increased its tribute demand, and that finally stiffened Jefferson's backbone and he refused. Tripoli immediately declared war on the United States, and when, in 1803, Jefferson sent a naval force, the pirates seized one ship, the *Philadelphia*, and drove the rest of the fleet away by firing the *Philadelphia*'s own guns at them. But then Jefferson really got mad and sent every ship he could put together into the Mediterranean Sea, and in 1805 Tripoli gave up and no longer demanded tribute. (I'm sorry to have to add that Tripoli continued to hold the crew of the *Philadelphia*, and Jefferson finally had to pay $60,000 to get them free. And we continued to pay tribute to Morocco, Tunis, and Algiers for another ten years.)

But it was a start, and our next move toward sea power was, of course, at the time of the War of 1812, when we were willing to go to war to maintain freedom of the seas because of the British practice of impressing seamen on American trading ships into their navy on the claim that the men were citizens of Britain no matter how free the United States considered itself. After that, we were able to move around pretty much as we pleased, and by the middle 1840s, we had those big clipper ships that ran between Boston and China and made a lot of millionaires up in New England. And by the time of the War Between the States, when Britain again began to interfere a little bit with our transportation across the Atlantic, we demanded heavy damages and they paid it.

TWENTY-ONE

Becoming a World Power, Dropping the Bomb

I'LL never be able to answer completely why it took us so long to become an economic power or a military power, and I don't think anybody else can. I guess, as much as anything, it was because we had some selfish stinkers during the early periods in our country who felt that the economic program at home was something they ought to control, and in controlling it, they dealt only with the countries that could benefit them and didn't need help themselves. It wasn't decided on ideological grounds, or because, at least after a while, they didn't want to get involved in anything outside our borders. It was strictly selfishness that made them interested only where they could get the most money. In South America, the development in those countries was very small and very light, and our fiscal trade for quite a while was pretty much confined to Brazil and on the basis of coffee. And then the United Fruit Company went into Central American countries for bananas and other tropical fruit that we could use, and that helped the development. But it took a long time for us to realize that the resources of those countries were just as great as the resources we have right here at home.

We also, of course, had a bunch of economic royalists who controlled much of the trade of the country and wanted to keep outside trade from coming in and giving them competition. In that line of thinking, too, it took them a long time to realize that, in order to maintain our status as a great commercial and world power, we had to carry on trade with the rest of the world. Cordell Hull, who was Roosevelt's secretary of state from 1933 to 1944, the longest period of service of any secretary of state in our history, helped a lot in that direction, with his Reciprocal Trade Act in 1934, which increased our trade enormously with other countries by allowing us to reduce tariffs on their goods in return for reductions on ours, and with his work on our Good Neighbor Policy, which increased our help toward our immediate neighbors, and strengthened our friendship with them and the united stand of the Western Hemisphere against our enemies in World War II. Hull received the Nobel Peace Prize for his work in 1945 and really helped us realize that equality is the only fair proposition—that what's fair for one country should be fair for all others, whether they're weaker nations or just as strong as we are. We finally made up our minds that the best way, the *only* way, to treat other nations is as equals, and we've been doing it ever since. And I hope we continue that policy even though there are still people around who would like to see it discontinued.

Wilson is the most outstanding example of a president who was guided by the lessons of history when he decided to try again to bring a group of nations together to work for peace in the same way that King Henry IV tried to do it in the seventeenth century. You can learn a lot by the study of history, and the politics in history is the most interesting study that's available, unless you're a nut on figures or something of that kind and want to go into mathematics, because the formation of governments in all parts of the world always shows you that things work only if people are treated fairly, and if they aren't, you have rebellions and destruction. We've come to the point in the twentieth century where the whole world is only about a tenth as large as it was when Columbus set out and discovered America, and I think Wilson realized, more than any other man in our history up to that time, that all parts of our great world can be used for the welfare and benefit of all mankind if we want to do it. And when Wilson went to Europe after the First World War to join David Lloyd George, prime minister of England, Georges Clemenceau, premier of France, and Vittorio Orlando, premier of Italy, in attending the Paris Peace Conference and putting together the Treaty of Versailles, the first American president ever to go to Europe while still in office, he was able to get included in the treaty an agreement for the formation of the body he called the League of Nations. The League's headquarters were set up in Geneva, and the new organization was empowered to deal with all matters "affecting the peace of the world," including the use of military force and economic sanctions if absolutely necessary. The League would also be associated with several important related organizations such as the World Court, also known as the Permanent Court of International Justice, and the International Labor Organization.

But Wilson made a lot of political mistakes at the same time. He had less than two years to go in his second term in office, and the Republicans had gained control of both the Senate and the House in the 1918 elections, but Wilson didn't include a single Republican in his American delegation. So when he returned to the United States, he found that many Republicans were objecting to the Treaty of Versailles in general and the League of Nations in particular, and so were some Democrats.

The Treaty of Versailles was in some ways a big territorial grab. France was given Alsace-Lorraine, formerly under German control; Great Britain and France took over all of the German colonies in Africa; Premier Orlando demanded a part of the Alps for Italy, even though the area included two hundred thousand German-speaking people, and when Wilson objected mildly to this, Orlando walked out in a huff; and Japan demanded the Shantung Peninsula in China, also formerly controlled by Germany. Wilson had made many public statements objecting to things like the Japanese takeover of the Shantung Peninsula, but in his eagerness to get the League of Nations going, he went along with them, feeling that the League would correct many of the problems.

But when he returned home, he found his popularity disappearing and he found himself attacked on all sides. Irish Americans didn't like the provision in the Treaty that gave Great Britain, British-controlled Ireland, Canada, Australia, New Zealand, and South Africa a vote apiece, feeling that that gave the British too strong control of the League. German Americans felt that the territorial transfers, the huge financial penalties levied against Germany, and the provision that prohibited Germany almost totally from retaining an army, navy, or air force were too harsh. People who were German-haters felt it was too mild. And others felt that the Shantung Peninsula should have been given back to China rather than to Japan. In general, a lot of people felt that Wilson had been pushed around in Europe and hadn't been strong enough in protecting America's position in the matter. And this feeling was strengthened when, in January 1919, a New York newspaper secured and published the text of some secret treaties between Great Britain, France, Italy, and Russia which revealed that they'd plotted to divvy up German territories long before the war was over.

Here Wilson made his next big political mistake. Some extremists were totally against the Treaty of Versailles and the League of Nations, but others, including Senator Henry Cabot Lodge, a Republican who headed the Foreign Relations Committee, were more moderate and were prepared to back Wilson if he'd agree to try to get some improvements in the Treaty when he returned to Paris for a second go-round. But Wilson turned stubborn and insisted that the Treaty be left alone, when in fact he agreed that there were serious flaws in the Treaty, and he could easily and with a clear conscience have gone along with the people who were ready to help him. The result was that a group of senators issued a "round-robin letter" denouncing Wilson and the League of Nations.

In September 1919, back in the United States, Wilson went off on a speaking tour to sell the idea of the League of Nations to the American people, a difficult and exhausting trip in which he traveled eight thousand miles in three weeks and spoke in twenty-nine cities. It was too much for him, and on September 25, in Pueblo, Colorado, as I mentioned earlier in this book, he collapsed from exhaustion and went back to Washington. And a week later, on October 2, he had that stroke which paralyzed his left side and kept him in a wheelchair or in bed for the remaining four and a half years of his life.

On March 19, 1920, the Senate voted down acceptance of both the Treaty and the League of Nations; the necessary two-thirds majority missed by eight votes. The United States never joined the League of Nations, and in the next presidential election, with James Cox and Franklin Roosevelt running on a platform that supported the League of Nations, they were, as you know, whipped soundly by that fellow Warren G. Harding. You know how I feel about Harding. Alice Roosevelt Longworth, Theodore Roosevelt's daughter, once said about him, "Harding was not a bad man. He was just a slob." I think she was being entirely too kind.

The League of Nations limped along, of course, under the control of Great Britain, France, Italy, and Japan. Bulgaria and Austria joined the League in 1920, Hungary in 1922, Turkey in 1932, and Russia in 1934. Germany joined in 1926 and left again in 1933, when Hitler was starting to strengthen in power. But without the presence of the United States, the League of Nations was weak and grew weaker and weaker, and by 1940 the League Secretariat in Geneva was nothing more than a skeleton staff. After the war, in 1946, it collapsed completely, and its Palais des Nations and other holdings were turned over to the United Nations.

Our failure to participate wasn't the only reason for the collapse of the League of Nations, of course, but I believe that some of the things that failed in the League of Nations could have been worked out and settled if the United States had been there as a strong voice speaking for the free governments of the world. The European powers that made up the League of Nations almost entirely weren't all that much concerned with things that didn't affect Europe, and Japan really didn't take much interest in it because Japan was on the road to doing what she did in the Second World War. But the outside influence of an objective viewpoint from the Western Hemisphere, I think, would have been a tremendous help to the survival of the League of Nations.

I've always thought that World War II might have been avoided if we'd joined the League of Nations, that the very fact that we were not in the League of Nations, the greatest free government, then and now, in the history of the world—our standing to one side—is one of the causes of the rise of Hitler and Mussolini and brought on the Second World War. But that's history now. Hundreds of years passed between the time of King Henry IV and the time of Woodrow Wilson, and when Wilson's dream was thrown out the window, it took another World War before another president was in charge who understood the history and the background of the world and what makes the world tick, and he set up the United Nations on the same basis as the League of Nations. Franklin Roosevelt believed, and I believe that our main hope for the future lies in that organization.

Roosevelt profited by Wilson's mistakes in this way: when it came time to bring the Second World War to a conclusion, he had the advice of all the sections of opinion in the United States. He had what we named bipartisan foreign policy, which included the two great parties of the United States. They were both represented in a major way, and of course, Wilson just didn't do that.

And now that we have the United Nations, I truly feel that it will succeed if we just give it enough of a chance. I feel this even though, obviously, each nation thinks mostly, and a nation or two entirely, of its own concerns. That attitude isn't very hard to understand, and it isn't so terrible when you stop to think about it. Every member of every nation ought to be proud of his country and spend his time trying to make it the best one on earth. It's no different in this country; there's an esprit de corps that starts in just about every village, every county, every city, and every state. Every citizen of the United States is proud of his state and thinks it's better than any other state in the union, but that doesn't mean that we go to war because we have the same free communications and the same commercial opportunities in every state. And one day, perhaps, we can come to the same conclusion about the world, and if we do, the patriotism toward your home country need never leave you. It can't leave you; it's born in you. It's competition without shooting each other that we're after. That's what we want.

I don't know how long it's all going to take. There's a selfish streak in all of us that we have to overcome in order to accomplish the things that we have to achieve. We have to make some sacrifices even to make our own good government work. It's going to take a lot of people who understand the situations around the world, and they're hard to find. And though the United States ought to be the leader in the whole program, it may not be because we've lost some of the respect the other people of the world once had for us. There was a time when all the free world had the utmost confidence in the government of the United States as an honest, fair government that didn't want to cause anybody any trouble, that wanted to help everybody. We've lost some of that standing now, and I hope we can get it back.

But there shouldn't be any permanent barrier to the success of the United Nations because of color or language or other differences. I think there are some eleven or twelve hundred languages and dialects around the world, and it would be wonderful if we had a universal language that everybody could understand because there wouldn't be so much misunderstanding, but I guess that'll never happen. So we've got to work to accept the fact that we're all the same despite some outward and minor differences and should be treated with equal fairness. It will take plenty of time, and there'll be plenty of frustrations and plenty of temptations to throw up our hands and give up, but we've got to keep reminding ourselves that it's something that won't come easily or quickly. And Americans in particular have got to keep reminding ourselves that the United Nations is still very young and will remain very young for quite a while, and that our own Constitution had to go through a great many difficulties for over eighty years before we finally settled down. And then we had to fight among ourselves for four more years before we made up our minds that we really wanted it to work.

Just about all the fighting in the world is caused by the lack of enough to eat and enough to wear and the lack of a good place to live, but if atomic energy is used the way it ought to be, it can save the whole world from fighting each other to get what's necessary for people to have. It can do unbelievable good for the world, truly a world of good, if people can be persuaded to get along by looking at examples of the times they didn't get along and were wiped out and destroyed because they couldn't get along. The same thing can happen now, except this time it will wipe out the whole population of the world if we go to war with this atomic energy, which we turned loose.

I was the president who made the decision to unleash that terrible power, of course, and it was a difficult and dreadful decision to have to make. Some people have the mistaken impression that I made it on my own and in haste and almost on impulse, but it was nothing like that at all.

If I live to be a hundred years old, I'll never forget the day that I was first told about the atomic bomb. It was about 7:30 P.M. on the evening of April 12, 1945, just hours after Franklin Roosevelt had died at 3:35 P.M., and no more than half an hour after I was sworn in as president at 7:09 P.M. Henry L. Stimson, who was Roosevelt's secretary of war and then mine, took me aside and reminded me that Roosevelt had authorized the development of a sort of superbomb and that that bomb was almost ready. I was still stunned by Roosevelt's death and by the fact that I was now president, and I didn't think much more about it at the time. But then, on April 26, Stimson asked for a meeting in my office, at which he was joined by Major General Leslie Groves, who was in charge of the operation that was developing the bomb, the Manhattan Project. The meeting was so secret that Groves came into the White House by the back door. And at the meeting, Stimson handed me a memorandum that said, "Within four months we shall in all probability have completed the most terrible weapon ever known in human history, one bomb which could destroy a whole city."

Stimson said very gravely that he didn't know whether we could or should use the bomb because he was afraid that it was so powerful that it could end up destroying the whole world. I felt the same fear as he and Groves continued to talk about it, and when I read Groves's twenty-four-page report. The report said that the first bomb would probably be ready by July and have the strength of about five hundred tons of TNT, and even more frighteningly, it went on to say that a second bomb would probably be ready by August and have the strength of as much as twelve hundred tons of TNT. We weren't aware then that that was just the tip of the iceberg. That second bomb turned out to have the power of twenty thousand tons of TNT, and the hydrogen bomb that eventually followed it had the explosive power of twenty million tons of TNT.

Stimson's memo suggested the formation of a committee to assist me in deciding whether or not to use the bomb on Japan, and I agreed completely. The committee, which we called the Interim Committee, was formed at once and consisted of Stimson as chairman, James F. Byrnes, who later became my secretary of state, as my representative on the committee, James B. Conant, who was the president of Harvard, Karl T. Compton, who was the president of the Massachusetts Institute of Technology, and Vannevar Bush, who was the head of our Office of Scientific Research and Development. The Interim Committee in turn called in, for advice and information, the scientists who developed the bomb: Arthur H. Compton, who was Karl Compton's brother, Enrico Fermi, Ernest O. Lawrence, and J. Robert Oppenheimer.

Then, on May 8, my sixty-first birthday, the Germans surrendered, and I had to remind our country that the war was only half over, that we still had to face the war with Japan. The winning of that war, we all knew, might even be more difficult to accomplish, because the Japanese were self-proclaimed fanatic warriors who made it all too clear that they preferred death to defeat in battle. Just a month before, after our soldiers and Marines landed on Okinawa, the Japanese lost 100,000 men out of the 120,000 in their garrison, and yet, though they were defeated without any question in the world, thousands more Japanese soldiers fell on their own grenades and died rather than surrender.

Nevertheless, I pleaded with the Japanese in my speech announcing Germany's surrender, begging them to surrender, too, but was not too surprised when they refused. And on June 18, I met with the Joint Chiefs of Staff to discuss what I hoped would be our final push against the Japanese. We still hadn't decided whether or not to use the atomic bomb, and the chiefs of staff suggested that we plan an attack on Kyushu, the Japanese island on their extreme west, around the beginning of November, and follow up with an attack on the more important island of Honshu. But the statistics that the generals gave me were as frightening as the news of the big bomb. The chiefs of staff estimated that the Japanese still had five thousand attack planes, seventeen garrisons on the island of Kyushu alone, and a total of more than two million men on all of the islands of Japan. General Marshall then estimated that, since the Japanese would unquestionably fight even more fiercely than ever on their own homeland, we would probably lose a quarter of a million men and possibly as many as a half million in taking the two islands. I could not bear this thought, and it led to the decision to use the atomic bomb.

We talked first about blockading Japan and trying to blast them into surrender with conventional weaponry; but Marshall and others made it clear that this would never work, pointing out that we'd hit Germany in this way and they hadn't surrendered until we got troops into Germany itself. Another general also pointed out that Germany's munitions industries were more or less centralized and that our constant bombings of these facilities never made them quit, and Japan's industries were much more spread apart and harder to hit. Then, when we finally talked about the atomic bomb, on July 21, coming to the awful conclusion that it would probably be the only way the Japanese might be made to surrender quickly, we talked first about hitting some isolated area, some low-population area where there would not be too many casualties but where the Japanese could see the power of the new weapon. Reluctantly, we decided against that as well, feeling that that just wouldn't be enough to convince the fanatic Japanese. And we finally selected four possible target areas, all heavy military-manufacturing areas: Hiroshima, Kokura, Nagasaki, and Niigata.

I know the world will never forget that the first bomb was dropped on Hiroshima on August 5, at 7:15 P.M. Washington time, and the second on Nagasaki on August 9. One more plea for surrender had been made to the Japanese on July 29, and was rejected immediately. Then I gave the final order, saying I had no qualms "if millions of lives could be saved." I meant both American and Japanese lives.

The Japanese surrendered five days after the bomb was dropped on Nagasaki, and a number of major Japanese military men and diplomats later confirmed publicly that there would have been no quick surrender without it. For this reason, I made what I believed to be the only possible decision. I said something to this effect in a letter to my sister, Mary: "It was a terrible decision. But I made it. And I made it to save 250,000 boys from the United States, and I'd make it again under similar circumstances." I said the same thing at somewhat greater length in a speech at a university in 1965:

"It was a question of saving hundreds of thousands of American lives . . . You don't feel normal when you have to plan hundreds of thousands of . . . deaths of American boys who are alive and joking and having fun while you're doing your planning. You break your heart and your head trying to figure out a way to save one life . . . The name given to our invasion plan was Olympic, but I saw nothing godly about the killing of all the people that would be necessary to make that invasion. The casualty estimates called for seven hundred and fifty thousand American casualties—two hundred and fifty thousand killed, five hundred thousand maimed for life . . . I couldn't worry about what history would say about my personal morality. I made the only decision I ever knew how to make. I did what I thought was right."

I still think that. But God knows it underlines the need for an organization like the United Nations to prevent another and probably final world war.

I'll come back to George Washington just long enough to say goodbye to him. He was a great man and a good man, and when his work was over as our great first president, he went back home to Virginia for his long-earned rest. Just three years later, on December 14, 1799, at the age of sixty-seven, he went to his final rest. As I described earlier, he went back to Mount Vernon and ran his place, and he went out in a bad storm and caught pneumonia and died. They bled him, as they often did in those days, and modern doctors say that if they hadn't bled

him he might have lived. But everything I've read about his death in-
dicates that he died peacefully, and perhaps he died because he'd accomplished his purpose. He knew that he'd done what was necessary
for his country, and there was no longer a need or a desire to live any
longer.

TWENTY-TWO
Jefferson the Populist

THE next president worth a lot of respectful attention is Thomas Jefferson. This means, of course, that I'm pretty much skipping over John Adams, the president between Washington and Jefferson, but I'm not doing that because I think that Adams was a terrible president. It's just that he wasn't very special, whereas Jefferson was special indeed in a lot of ways.

To understand the difference between Adams and Jefferson, you have to understand the differences between two other and very important matters: the development and evolution of our country's leading political parties and the essential philosophical differences between the two parties. Please forgive me if that sounds sort of stuffy and pedantic, but there's no other way to put it, and I'll try not to sound like a boring lecturer while I'm explaining it.

You have to realize, to begin with, that there was no thought at all about political parties when the Constitution was being put together. It was the idea of the people who wrote the Constitution that there would not be any partisan setup in the government because it was unnecessary;

the purpose of the government, as they saw it, was to create an organization of the colonies, the states, so that there wouldn't be any barriers between the states and they could transact business with each other and possibly with the rest of the world. And since it was intended to develop a government with a president and a Congress whose interest, principally, would be trade, there seemed to be no need, or even any likelihood, of differing political parties because everybody would want the same things.

But that was just foolish, or at least naive. The origin of political parties wasn't contemplated by the makers of the Constitution because they had no experience in free government independent of the British crown. And there was also the fact that, even though we were now an independent country, there was still an underground of perhaps as much as 30 or 35 percent of the population who were Royalists and had wanted to stay with Britain and wouldn't have minded returning to British rule, so it was much more important to think about the objectives that kept Americans together instead of the things that separated us. Nevertheless, our first leaders should have realized that, even if we all had the same idea of wanting trade and business and plenty of it, the different kinds of people who became our first legislators would have very different ideas about how to run the government that was being set up. But they didn't realize it, and that was, as I mentioned earlier, the cause of the basic rift between Washington and John Adams and Alexander Hamilton on one side and Jefferson and the people who thought the same way he did on the other side.

Washington's appointments weren't political appointments in the sense in which that term is used today, meaning people whose theories of government operation are exactly the same as those of the president who appoints them. His appointments were made strictly on the basis of the known abilities of the men who were appointed; he knew them well and was familiar with their backgrounds and their experience, and that's the reason he appointed both Hamilton and Jefferson. He was a man of good judgment, and I'm sure he was well aware that there were major differences in the thinking of the two men and that Jefferson felt differently about some things than Washington himself did, but he wanted both men in this cabinet because he was determined to establish the government so that it would survive and continue to run. And I'm also sure he had confidence in his ability to make people get along together.

He was right in this assessment of his ability, too, because he came to depend a lot on Hamilton during his administration, and he was just as dependent on Jefferson as he was on Hamilton. And though both Jefferson and Hamilton later said publicly that Washington didn't have a good intellectual background, he was smart enough to make both of them perform. In that way, he was like Lincoln, who also had the ability to make men who didn't want to get along get along together. That's true of all of our great presidents. When people with different viewpoints have something that can be used for the benefit of the government, the chief executive should make use of everything they have no matter what they believe, and he can get them to perform if he has the ability to make people understand that what he's trying to do is to run the government as it ought to be run. You've got to have an executive who has an urgent desire for the continuation of our great free government, and a man who has that desire ought to make use of every means at his command to keep that government running. That's what Roosevelt did, and in a way, it was Wilson's failing that he didn't. He was smarter than anybody else, but he knew it and he let the people around him know it even though he lost support that way. You can't do that when you're trying to run a government.

The big difference in Jefferson's and Hamilton's thinking, as I also mentioned earlier, was that Jefferson believed that our leadership should come from the general population whereas Hamilton felt that it should come only from the upper classes. The reasoning of the two men was basic and simple. Hamilton felt that there should be a ruling class, a sort of political aristocracy—that the rich and the educated should be the heads of government and control the country's finances and lawmaking because they knew more about most matters and would do a better job of running things. Jefferson's idea, on the other hand, was that the people, properly educated, would know how to run the government just as well as the aristocrats of the time. And he expressed concern that, if the rich ran the country, they would be interested mostly in the welfare of their peers and not in the welfare of people who worked in the fields and on farms and in other jobs that put calluses on your hands.

You've got to remember that Jefferson's point of view was a radical and revolutionary approach because just about all the governments up to that time had been monarchies with the idea that the king was the representative of Almighty God. The description of the king's authority was "the divine right of kings," and the word "divine" was meant literally in the dictionary sense of "pertaining to God or being a god," and not in the way one lady tells another lady her new dress is divine and means it looks kind of nice. But from about 1760, I guess, to about 1800, the point that Jefferson and others kept pounding home and reminding people like Hamilton of was that the idea of the United States was that government should not be by the divine right of kings but by the consent of the people. That's made very clear in the Declaration of Independence. It's right in the first line.

It's ironic that Hamilton became the voice of the aristocracy and Jefferson became the voice of the man on the street because, in a sense,

Hamilton had less right to try to develop an aristocratic class than anyone else in the country, whereas Jefferson was the son and grandson of wealthy landowners and the husband of Martha Wayles Skelton, a young widow who brought to the marriage a fortune equaling Jefferson's own holdings. The reason I say that Hamilton was an unlikely spokesman for the aristocrats is that, you'll recall, he was born in the West Indies without knowing who his father was. He came to this country without friends or family and deserves a tremendous amount of credit for making a success of his life by the use of his mind; he had a great brain, and one of the most terrible things that ever happened in this country is that his life ended when he was only forty-nine. He did a lot of good things for the country and would have done many more if he'd lived longer. But he had a viewpoint that was entirely different from Jefferson's, and for that matter mine, and in that line of thinking he was dead wrong. Jefferson's simple and logical belief that a country should be run by the people of the country has gone all around the world since his time, and the whole world has been in a sort of revolution ever since as a result of the Declaration of Independence and the Constitution of the United States. So there's no doubt, simply no doubt at all, about the fact that that makes Jefferson a great world figure as well as a great American.

And though it may be ironic that Jefferson became the voice of the people, it isn't really surprising because he knew history, the way so many of the members of the Continental Congress did, and learned a lot of the lessons that history can teach us, and he had a wide-ranging mind that made him seek out the right things in life even when they weren't the most popular things. He had the idea that knowledge was the most important thing that a man could have in life, and he tried to attain as much of it as he could. He was a brilliantly educated man, a graduate of William and Mary College and a lawyer, and he was also an architect, farmer, a musician, an inventor, and almost everything else you could be in that period except a doctor of medicine, and I'm sure he could have been that, too, if he wanted to be.

He was interested in everything. He had one of the best libraries in the whole Western Hemisphere, and whenever he went abroad, he added books to it that he thought were necessary for a man to understand and read. As a matter of fact, that library was finally the foundation of the Library of Congress; all of Jefferson's books are in the Library of Congress in toto. He brought a great many plants to this country from Europe and used them as a start of a separate agricultural program for the United States. He had a hand in starting a conservation program to save the soil of Virginia and keep it from washing into the Atlantic Ocean. He was very much interested in agriculture, and in fact you can't find anything in which the welfare of the people was at stake in which he wasn't interested. And the only reason that Virginia's soil isn't as rich as it was in Jefferson's time is that the generations that followed him weren't as interested in following that program as he was.

He had a wind gauge on his roof that registered down in the front hall of his mansion. He had his bed fixed so that he could pull it up and out of the way with ropes, which I guess was the first Murphy bed. He built a cart with special springs so that it was more comfortable when he rode back and forth to the Capitol. That cart is still there in his home, Monticello, in Virginia. He knew enough about architecture, incidentally, so that Monticello is based on a building in Italy, a building he saw just outside of Venice, and he also brought back the plans of a beautiful little temple in France and based the Virginia capitol building on that.

He also made our monetary system a decimal system. Jefferson was the man who made the tenth part of a dollar a dime, and the one-hundredth part of a dollar a cent—a one-cent piece they called it in those days, which I guess is still the proper name for it—and of course the other coins were half-dollars and quarters. It made it a much easier arrangement than the British pound sterling, which had all sorts of complications that were difficult to remember and figure out. The British are still sticking to that plan, and it's always hard to figure out what you have in British money when you try to translate it into American money. He also tried his level best to get the metric system of weights and measures adopted in this country, but didn't succeed in accomplishing that one.*

He was also interested in art and drawing and the music of the day, music we'd call classical today, and he was a fiddler himself. In his house back there at Monticello, they still have his stand where he stood practicing his violin. He was a very good violinist, as good as I am a pianist. Well, he wouldn't have to be very good to be that.

As I say, not all of Jefferson's ideas were popular, though most of them were absolutely right. When he was campaigning for the presidency, he was called a Jacobin, the name given the men who started the French revolution because that was the Parisian name for the Dominican order and the first revolutionary meetings were at the Dominican monastery. That was a pejorative term because many Americans felt the French revolution wasn't a "respectable" one like our own—it was sort of like calling someone a Communist today—but Jefferson didn't give a damn about that because he felt that the French were as much entitled to freedom as we were. He was also called an atheist because he didn't believe in a state church, an official church of the government, and in fact made it clear that he didn't much like any church at all, though he did admire

---

*The British, of course, have now adopted the decimal system, though it took them nearly a couple of centuries to get around to it. And we're still trying to popularize the metric system in this country. It's now the official system, but it continues to baffle and confuse the general public. MT

many, though not all, of the teachings of religion. He wrote that he was "a real Christian, that is to say a disciple of the doctrines of Jesus" because those doctrines were "the most perfect and sublime . . . ever taught by man," but also felt that the clergy had distorted the meanings of some of Jesus' teachings and that therefore the Bible should be read even more critically and analytically than any other book.

And you'll recall that it was Jefferson, as governor of Virginia, who wrote the Statute of Religious Liberty in 1786, which said that "no man shall be compelled to frequent or support any religious worship" but that all people "shall be free to profess . . . their opinion in matters of religion." He summed up very bluntly one time his view that no man harmed anyone else in choosing and practicing his own religion, or no religion. "It does me no injury," he said, "for my neighbor to say that there are twenty gods, or no god. It neither picks my pocket nor breaks my leg." But he showed his belief in what he considered the good teachings of religion by putting together an abridged version of the Bible himself, taking the directions for leading the proper kind of a life out of the Gospels and the Acts of the Apostles and some of the Epistles and collecting them together. I've got the book and it's very good reading.

He was also against slavery, you'll recall, even though he inherited a lot of slaves along with his plantation when his father died, and he tried to get an antislavery clause into the Constitution. But he didn't succeed and made it his business to free all the slaves on his plantation when he died himself. He also tried to launch a program to end the slave trade in America, but didn't succeed in that effort, either. Which is a shame indeed. In my opinion, as I've said before, if Jefferson had succeeded in getting that clause into the Constitution, and had succeeded in ending the slave trade in 1809, then slavery would have been eliminated gradually, and I don't think it would have been necessary for the War Between the States to take place.

All in all, he was probably the most versatile, and one of the most intelligent, men ever to occupy the White House. Some of his opponents called him a dangerous man, but they said the same thing about Andrew Jackson and Franklin Roosevelt and every other great leader. I suppose the people today who use the word "egghead" as a pejorative term, the way "Jacobin" was used in Jefferson's time, would call him one; but if he was an egghead, he was a practical egghead. He knew how to make things work on the ground as well as to read and talk about them. His particular talent was understanding free government and how it can be made to work, and I think that was the most outstanding contribution that Jefferson made to the history of the United States. He was responsible for the development of a government in the hands of the people, which the Constitution says is where the power of government should reside, and he succeeded in many ways in carrying out that principle in the Constitution. Sometimes presidents were both politicians and thinkers, and Jefferson was one of our greatest thinkers and also a great politician. If you want to call a man an egghead who has a knowledge of all sorts of things, who's well versed in history and everything else, and who's also a practical politician and can make good government work, then he certainly was an egghead.

The great and important thing that was accomplished by that major disagreement between Jefferson and Hamilton was that it created political parties in the United States. This is the way it happened, and this is why it's such a good thing for our country:

In the beginning, there was just a single political party, the Federalists. The name derived, simply enough, from the fact that it consisted of the people who had put together the concept of a centrally governed United States and therefore believed in strong control by the federal government over the thirteen former colonies. There were people around, of course, who believed in less control by the federal government and more autonomy for the states, their idea being that the United States should essentially be a loose league of the former colonies working together and helping each other when possible, and not a lot more than that. But they weren't organized in any formal way and didn't have a real party name; they were just called anti-Federalists.

But then those differences developed and kept growing between Hamilton and his followers and Jefferson and *his* followers, and it began to seem that they disagreed on everything. The basic difference was the disagreements between federal control and states' rights, but there were all those others. Hamilton believed that federal law should dominate at all times, and with the collaboration of James Madison and John Jay, he was the author of *The Federalist Papers,* a brilliant political work that started as eighty-five long newspaper articles and was then published as a book, and that did more than anything else to get the original Constitution accepted.

Jefferson believed that the states should have the right to overturn federal law when it was unfair, and when the government came out with the Alien and Sedition Acts in 1798, which gave the federal government the right to deport foreigners who talked against the United States and jail newspaper editors who published articles that attacked the government, the president, or the Senate or House of Representatives, Jefferson, also in collaboration with James Madison, wrote documents called the Virginia and Kentucky Resolutions in bitter opposition to these acts. (Jefferson's contention that states should be allowed to kill federal laws was never accepted, but his statements against the Alien and Sedition

Acts made their unfairness very clear, and the four items comprising the Acts were all dead by 1802.) Hamilton and John Adams and other Federalists hated the French Revolution and called it mobocracy; Jefferson hated the violence and bloodshed, but felt the revolution was necessary to get the French royal family out of power. Adams agreed with Hamilton that the upper classes were smarter and should govern; he wanted senators to be elected for life as a balance to agreeing that members of the House of Representatives should go on being elected by the masses. Jefferson felt that the people should elect all public officials.

And so, by the time Washington finished up his two terms, there were two formal political parties, the Federalists and Jefferson's party, now given an official name, the Democratic-Republicans. As I've noted before, it's amusing to realize, in these days when Republicans say that Democrats are dumb and Democrats say that Republicans are dumber, that one of our original political parties combined both names, but there it was. And though Washington was elected without opposition for his two terms as president, and John Adams ran similarly unopposed for those two terms as his vice president, the race for the presidency to follow Washington's was as bitter as any presidential contest today. The candidates were Adams and Jefferson for president, and Thomas Pinckney of South Carolina as the Federalist candidate for vice president and Aaron Burr, born in Newark, New Jersey, but now a resident of New York, as the Democratic-Republican candidate. And supporters of the two presidential candidates had plenty to say about the fellow who opposed the man of their choice.

Adams was called a royalist and a monarchist, and it was pointed out that, when he was Washington's vice president, he'd proposed that the president be called His Highness, and that the members of the Congress should stand in formal reverence when the president addressed them, the way that subjects of the king of England stood when the king talked to them. He was also, because he was fat, referred to as His Rotundity and His Superfluous Excellency. Jefferson's alleged atheism was stressed in that campaign and the one that followed four years later, and the Federalists' rallying cry was in the form of asking people which they wanted, "God and a religious president or Jefferson and no God." Adams, the Federalists went on to say, would teach decency and clean living; Jefferson would bring about "murder, robbery, rape, adultery, and incest." Jefferson later commented in a letter to his friend James Monroe, "It has been so impossible to contradict all their lies that I have determined to contradict none, for while I would be engaged with one they would publish twenty new ones." It's a wonder that no Federalist remembered Jefferson's interest in art and accused him of loading up the country with graven images.

Nevertheless, the race was a very close one, and there's no telling how it may have ended if Washington had remained silent. But much as Washington respected Jefferson, and much as he continued to depend on his help even after Jefferson left his cabinet and returned to being a private citizen in 1793, he felt that Adams was more likely to continue his policies and viewpoints than Jefferson, and he finally came out and endorsed Adams. It was enough to tip the scales—that and the fact that most of the people in government jobs had been put there by Washington and Adams and were more likely to be kept on there if Adams rather than Jefferson became the second president. And in the electoral vote, Adams got seventy-one votes and Jefferson sixty-eight; Adams carried the electors in Connecticut, Delaware, Maryland, Massachusetts, New Hampshire, New Jersey, New York, Rhode Island, and Vermont, and Jefferson got the electors in six southern states and one other state, taking Georgia, Kentucky, North Carolina, South Carolina, Tennessee, Virginia, and that one state that wasn't in the south, Pennsylvania.

And one other thing happened that seems weird to twentieth-century minds: Jefferson, Adams's opponent and the leader of the party opposed to Adams, became Adams's vice president. Keep in mind that, as the Constitution had it originally, the man who got the most votes became president and the man who got the second-largest number of votes became vice president, and remember also that our Founding Fathers weren't thinking much or at all about opponents and opposing political parties. As they saw it then, the fellow who got the most votes would be the fellow who was most popular and had the most popular viewpoint, and the fellow who got the next largest number of votes would be the fellow who was almost as popular as the first man because he thought along the same lines.

But the thing that happened here changed that kind of innocent thinking permanently. Alexander Hamilton didn't care much for either of the two men running for president—he thought Adams was unstable and too unpredictable, and you know the ways in which he differed with Jefferson—so, since he was a Federalist himself, Hamilton set out quietly to see if he could get both presidential candidates defeated and the Federalist running for vice president, Thomas Pinckney, in as president. Since Pinckney was a southerner, Hamilton began to campaign for Pinckney among southern electors, hoping that enough of them might move away from Jefferson to give Pinckney the largest number of votes. But instead it caused confusion and dissension among the electors. Pinckney came in third, and Thomas Jefferson was the new vice president.

Jefferson was a bit bored as vice president because he often felt he just didn't have enough to do, and I'm in sympathy with that feeling because I felt that way myself once or twice when I had the job, even though there was a lot more responsibility given to the office by the time I got it. Jefferson had so much free time that he sat down and wrote that book, *A Manual of Parliamentary Practice,* which is still being used today, but he also did whatever chores came his way and did them well and effectively, and he was an even stronger candidate when he ran for president against Adams again in 1800.

Burr was again the Democratic-Republican candidate for vice president, and this time the Federalist choice for the office was another Pinckney from South Carolina, Charles Cotesworth Pinckney. (Charles Cotesworth Pinckney was Thomas's brother, Thomas having decided not to run again. Both men were officers in the Continental Army. And to confuse you further, there was another Charles Pinckney around at the time. He had no middle name, and was Charles Cotesworth's and Thomas's cousin. He was governor of South Carolina from 1789 to 1792, and again from 1796 to 1798, and again from 1806 to 1808. He also served in the Revolutionary War. All three men were captured during the war, and I imagine the British had a hell of a time telling them apart.)

The results of the election were even more confusing. Adams and Pinckney took the majority of the electoral votes in seven states, Connecticut, Delaware, Massachusetts, New Hampshire, New Jersey, Rhode Island, and Vermont, and Jefferson and Burr got the majority of the electoral votes in eight states, Georgia, Kentucky, New York, North Carolina, Pennsylvania, South Carolina, Tennessee, and Virginia. Maryland's electors gave half their votes to Adams and Pinckney and the other half to Jefferson and Burr. However, when the individual votes were added up, Adams was third with a total of sixty-five votes, thereby becoming the first, but far from the last, president to be defeated for a second term, but Jefferson and Burr ended up with an identical seventy-three votes apiece. It should have been simple at that point; Jefferson, after all, was the presidential candidate and Burr the vice-presidential candidate, so Jefferson should have become president and Burr vice president. But Burr wasn't a sensible man, and he refused to go along with this obvious solution. This put the matter into the hands of the House of Representatives, and they voted no less than thirty-six times in the days between February 11 and February 17, 1801, before a decision was reached. Hamilton had a lot to do with the decision; he felt that his unpredictable colleague Adams was a pillar of wisdom and sanity compared to Burr, and since it was now strictly a choice between the two Democratic-Republicans, he went around urging electors, and politicians who had influence with electors, to support Jefferson. This time his efforts succeeded, and Jefferson took Georgia, Kentucky, Maryland, New Jersey, New York, North Carolina, Tennessee, Vermont, and Virginia, a total of ten states, and Burr took four, Connecticut, Massachusetts, New

Hampshire, and Rhode Island. Delaware and South Carolina were so undecided that they abstained completely from voting. Jefferson, therefore, was now president and Burr vice president.

It would have been bad news for the country if Burr had become our third president; there's no telling what might have happened to us. It's a big enough blot on our history that he was our vice president, and it's fortunate for that reason that vice presidents didn't have all that much power and all that much to do then, because he was really quite a terrible man.

It wasn't that Burr, who was born in 1756, was stupid, because he was certainly clever enough; the problem with him was that he was a driven man, so ambitious and so ruthless that he'd do anything to get what he wanted at the time he wanted it. He was a graduate of the College of New Jersey, which later became Princeton University, at the age of sixteen, then a brilliant law student until he left law school to become an equally brilliant soldier in the Continental Army, and after that a lawyer in New York who moved rapidly up the political ladder. In quick order, he was an assemblyman, New York State attorney general, and a United States senator. He also helped develop a patriotic club called the Tammany Society into a political organization that had a lot to do with creating the Democratic-Republican Party, and for a while also did some good fighting unfair practices like the imprisonment of people for debt and assisting immigrants in getting jobs. The organization also helped get some good men elected, including Andrew Jackson. (This was, of course, long before it degenerated into Tammany Hall, which was controlled by Boss Tweed and his cronies.)

All this made Burr an increasingly powerful national figure and got him on the ticket with Jefferson in 1800, but you've already seen how he behaved when he refused at first to concede to Jefferson even though he knew that everybody was really voting for Jefferson for president and for him for vice president. But the really terrible thing occurred in 1804, as most people will remember from their history studies, when Burr, who hadn't gotten along at all well with Jefferson during their four years together, was replaced by another New York lawyer, George Clinton, as Jefferson's running mate in Jefferson's campaign for a second term. Burr returned in fury to New York and ran for governor of his state, but Alexander Hamilton continued to fear Burr as a dangerous man and continued to talk out against him. Burr was defeated, and more frustrated and filled with hatred than ever, he challenged Hamilton to a duel.

Hamilton, unfortunately, accepted, because the stupid general attitude in those days was that a man was branded a coward if he didn't accept. The duel took place in a deserted area in Weehawken Heights, New Jersey, on July 11, 1804, and Hamilton was killed. He was only forty-nine years old, and it was an awful waste because he'd done many good things for the country, and I'm sure he would have done many more if he'd lived. He was a very important man of his period, and Burr had a chance to be, too, but he had those tremendous and terrible ambitions. I don't know what he would have done if he'd been chosen as president instead of Jefferson when there was that tie vote, but I have an idea that he would have done everything he possibly could to make the president an absolute monarch. That's what I've always thought in studying the events of that period, anyway, so maybe it's just as well that he was so clearly the kind of man he was and that this eventually brought him down completely.

The duel was the end of Burr's usefulness as a public man in the United States, but he had one more bad move to make. He organized a group of sixty well-armed men and headed into the South and the Southwest; it's never been exactly clear what he intended to do with such a tiny army, but the popular theory is that he intended to instigate some kind of war between Spain and the United States and while they were at each other's throat, grab some piece of land, either in the Louisiana Territory or perhaps down in Mexico, and set it up as an independent nation with himself as its president. (Or maybe even its king. I don't know what was going on in that strange man's mind.)

But Burr made the mistake of trying to enlist the help of a man named James Wilkinson, a sort of disreputable fellow who had been a brigadier general in the Revolutionary War and had the responsible job of being "clothier general" in charge of the Army's supplies, but resigned after he was accused of having irregularities in his accounts. The thing that Burr didn't know was that Wilkinson was a friend of the Spaniards, and in fact it later came out that he was working for Spain and had even sworn an oath of allegiance to Spain and was drawing a pension of $2,000 a year from them, which was later raised to $4,000. Wilkinson went immediately to Jefferson and told him what was happening, and Burr was arrested for treason and tried in Richmond, Virginia, with John Marshall, who was then Chief Justice, presiding.

Marshall decided not to make any more of the matter than was absolutely necessary and acquitted Burr, saying he hadn't actually committed "an overt act of treason." Burr moved to Europe for a while, then returned to New York and practiced law again, but never reentered politics. He died at the age of eighty in 1836. Wilkinson, the chief witness against him at his trial, reentered the American army and served in the War of 1812, but was such a bum officer that he was relieved of his command, and he retired and moved down to Mexico and died there in 1825.

TWENTY-THREE

Jefferson—
The Man, the President

JEFFERSON, meanwhile, had no trouble at all in being reelected for a second term. This time Charles Cotesworth Pinckney tried for the presidency rather than the vice presidency on the Federalist ticket, but he was easily defeated, drawing only 14 electoral votes to Jefferson's 162. Jefferson got the electoral votes of fifteen states, and Pinckney only the votes of Connecticut and Delaware. (Despite this, incidentally, Pinckney ran again as a Federalist in 1808 against James Madison and this time got 47 votes to Madison's 122. Pinckney then decided that politics wasn't for him and took a job as the first president of the Charleston, South Carolina, Bible Society.)

All that confusion during Jefferson's first election finally resulted, in 1804, in the Twelfth Amendment to the Constitution, which required that the president and the vice president be voted for separately, so that there'd never again be any question of which man should get which office if they happened to end up with an equal number of votes. But the really valuable thing that occurred during Jefferson's time, as I've said, was the arrival of the two-party system. And the two-party system is plenty valuable because, as I'm sure is obvious, it means that there'll always be an opposition group to yell and complain that the party in power is doing wrong; and if the people agree that the party in power really *is* doing wrong, that party gets thrown out. Opposition is good for a political party and for the country in general because there's never been a time in the history of any free country when one group could run the country successfully forever, so whenever that group gets to behaving foolishly or improperly, it's essential to have somebody around to point it out and tell the people what they're doing. And that group then usually gets overthrown and there's a new start. That's why you'll find, in modern times, that there's an opposition party in every free government and in every republic.

And our two-party system, our system of a Democratic Party and a Republican Party of almost equal strength, is, I believe, better than the systems in other countries. The British, for example, have two major political parties, too, the Conservative Party and the Labour Party, but the difference is that the Conservative Party is made up mostly of the people who control the finances of the country and the Labour Party is made up mostly of the working class. We don't have that. Our two main parties are made up of sections of every part of the population of the United States. It's true, of course, that it's the general policy of the Republican Party for the financiers to control the country, so they might be compared in a way to Britain's Conservative Party, and it's also true that the Democratic Party has a greater percentage of the people who have to work for a living, so we Democrats might be compared in a way to the Labour Party. But the big difference is that the Republicans have plenty of people who are interested in labor and the welfare of the country as a whole, and the Democrats have plenty of rich people, so there are different segments of the population and different types of people in the three branches that separate the powers in this country, the executive, the legislative, and the judicial branches. And that's a very good thing because, when a president is elected every four years, there's never any total turnover that will upset the government of the United States.

If you want to trace the development of the two major political parties in this country, and the origins and development of their differences, you have to remember that it was the notion of the Federalists to exploit, or at least to dominate, the ordinary man, and the refusal of the Democratic-Republicans to go along with this, so that their party was made up largely of the would-be exploited. That means, at least in my view, that the Federalists were like some of the modern Republicans and the Democratic-Republicans were like most of the modern Democrats.

As the years went along, the names changed here and there, with the Federalists fading out and their party next being called the National

Republicans and then the Whigs, and the Democratic-Republicans settling for just being called Democrats, but their viewpoints remained more or less the same, with the Democrats being the party of the common man and the Republicans being the party of the more aristocratic class. The two-party system collapsed for a while in 1824, when John Adams's son, John Quincy Adams, ran against Andrew Jackson and Henry Clay with no political designations for any of the three men, but the results were truly chaotic. Jackson got the most votes, ninety-nine electoral votes and 152,901 popular votes; Adams was next with eighty-four electoral votes and 114,023 popular votes; W. H. Crawford of Georgia was third, at least in electoral votes, with forty-one electoral votes and 46,979 popular votes; and Clay received thirty-seven electoral votes and 47,217 popular votes—but it was decided that no man had a clear enough majority, and it was up to the House of Representatives to do the final voting. Clay then had to drop out because he had the fewest electoral votes, and he decided to throw his support to Adams. The House of Representatives then gave Adams thirteen states, Jackson seven, and Crawford four, so Adams became our sixth president even though Jackson had done better than him in both the electoral and popular voting! Can you beat that?

You can be sure that, when Jackson ran against Adams again in 1828, the two political parties ran their men as the only two major candidates, and this time Jackson beat Adams even more decisively, 178 electoral votes and 647,292 popular votes to Adams's 83 electoral votes and 507,730 popular votes. And when he ran again in 1832, this time against Henry Clay, Jackson invented the convention system, bringing the members of his party together in a large meeting in Baltimore to pick their candidates. He also had another, equally important motive: he'd begun to realize that little caucuses, little special interest groups, in Congress and in the various legislatures were again controlling too many things, and he wanted to make sure that people of every persuasion within his party were present and being vocal and visible in expressing what they wanted in the party's policies and who they wanted as candidates.

The Whigs were still around as late as 1852, when Franklin Pierce, a Democrat, ran against John C. Frémont, the Whig candidate. Then in 1856, the Whigs and some of the other and weaker parties got together and called themselves the Republican Party. The original name of Jefferson's party came, of course, from the fact that they were a democratic organization in a republic, but now that Jackson's people were just calling themselves Democrats, the opposition took the other half. I think they had the idea of fooling the people a little bit. Anyway, as you know, Frémont didn't make it, but a very great president, Lincoln, was elected as a Republican. And after a while, I'm afraid, the Republicans went back to being Federalists in disguise all over again, too frequently forgetting the needs and desires of the man in the street.

That fellow Richard Nixon said recently that Jefferson wouldn't agree with the Democrats of the present day. Well, that's just nonsense. I'm just as sure as I sit here that if Jefferson were alive, he'd be right in line alongside the Democratic Party as it is today because it's fundamentally the basis on which free government is organized. As I've pointed out, the Democratic Party goes all the way to the time of Jefferson shortly after the Revolution, and it's based on the fact that the Constitution means what it says—that the power of the government is in the people. I'm certain, therefore, that Jefferson would be a good Democrat if he were alive today.

I haven't talked a lot about Jefferson's personal background, aside from the fact that he was descended from a king and a few other things like that. So let me do a little of that now because a man's background and upbringing often determines whether he becomes a good president or a bad one.

I'll have a bit of fun to start with and tell you that Jefferson was born on April 2 and April 13, 1743; that he was born in Goochland County, Virginia, and Albemarle County, Virginia; and that his full name was Thomas Jefferson and wasn't. What are the explanations for all that? Well, when he was born, the old style or Julian calendar was still in use, that funny old calendar that started the year on March 25 and did a lot of other things that look strange to us today, so his date of birth was April 2 at the time. But the Gregorian calendar, the one we use today, was adopted by Britain and the colonies in 1752, and that shifted things around and April 2 became April 13, so the "official" date of Jefferson's birth is now April 13, 1743. As for the other things, well, Jefferson was born in Goochland County, but the name was fancied up and changed to Albemarle County later on, and Jefferson never called himself anything other than Thomas Jefferson, but he was really Thomas Jefferson III, because he was named for his paternal grandfather, and his paternal grandfather was Thomas Jefferson II.

It's pretty clear that the aristocratic side of the family was the maternal side. Jefferson told friends that he really knew nothing about his father's family beyond the fact that the Jefferson family probably originally spelled the name Jaeffreson and probably lived originally at Mount Snowden, Wales, and probably came here early in the seventeenth century. Jefferson's mother, Jane Randolph Jefferson, however, was the one who could trace her family all the way back to King David I, who ruled Scotland from 1124 to 1153, and the Randolphs were one of the richest and most respected families in Virginia. But by the time Tom came along, the families were pretty equal in reputation and holdings; his paternal grandfather became a major landowner and judge before his death in 1731, and Jefferson's father, Peter Jefferson, increased the family's wealth substantially, owned about 7,000 acres of good Virginia land, and was also a surveyor, sheriff, an officer in the local militia, and a judge himself.

Thomas Jefferson grew up to be a tall fellow, nearly six feet three inches in height, with red hair and a face full of freckles. (A book I once read described him as looking like a taller Tom Sawyer, and I'd say that's a pretty good description.) He was extremely shy, which made him a very poor speaker when he went into public life, though he was okay when he was speaking to small groups and probably felt more at ease. And he didn't seem to give a damn about his clothes other than to insist that everything he wore fit loosely and comfortably, and more than once he shocked visiting foreign dignitaries by showing up for meetings in worn old clothes and house slippers.* He enjoyed good health all his life, except for headaches when he was nervous and tense, arthritis toward the end of his life, and after he was forty-three, a bad right hand because he tried jumping over a fence to impress a lady friend and fell and broke his wrist.

He was one of eight children; two sisters preceded him, and then there were four more sisters and a brother. One of his sisters, Anna, and his brother, Randolph, were twins. Another of his sisters, Elizabeth, was retarded. Both his parents died relatively young—his father at forty-nine of an illness that was never figured out and named, and his mother of a stroke at fifty-six. Jefferson himself, fortunately for the country, lived to the good old age of eighty-three.

Despite his shyness, he was quite a ladies' man. His first romance was with a sixteen-year-old girl named Rebecca Burwell when he was nineteen; and he attempted shortly afterwards to propose to her, but he was so nervous that he couldn't talk straight, and she ended up marrying a fellow named Jacquelin Ambler. The Amblers subsequently had two daughters, one of whom later married John Marshall, who became Chief Justice of the United States and the man who went easy on Aaron Burr.

Jefferson's next love was a married woman, Betsey Moore Walker, and that caused Jefferson a lot of trouble when he was president. In 1805, her husband, John Walker, wrote a long article in which he said that he'd

---

*My father's attitude toward dress was slightly different: the moment he could afford it, he switched from ready-made suits to clothes made up for him by the best tailors, and when he was a senator, he was on the list of the ten best-dressed men in the Senate. But he shared Jefferson's insistence on comfort at all times. He wanted to look good, but was much more concerned with feeling relaxed and comfortable. MT

trusted Jefferson and made him executor in his will and asked Jefferson to look after Betsey while he was away, and instead Jefferson had tried repeatedly to seduce his young wife. In fact, Walker said, Jefferson continued to try to seduce Betsey for eleven long years, even after Jefferson had gotten married himself, and had even jumped out of the darkness at Betsey a couple of times and tried to force her to give in to him.

Walker got so agitated after he wrote his piece that he ended up challenging Jefferson to a duel, but Jefferson admitted only that he had fallen in love with Betsey while he was single but denied all the other things, and he managed to convince Walker to meet him for a quiet talk at James Madison's house and cooled him down.

On January 1, 1772, as I mentioned previously, Jefferson married Martha Wayles Skelton, and their marriage was an extremely happy one but not very lucky. Martha became pregnant seven times, but only two children survived. These were two daughters, one also named Martha but nicknamed Patsy, and the other named Mary but called Polly. And on September 6, 1782, after ten and a half years of marriage, Jefferson's wife died. She was only thirty-four and had given birth to another daughter just four months before her death, but the child, another daughter, lived for only two years.

Jefferson promised his wife on her deathbed that he would never remarry, and he never did. But he continued to be attractive to, and attracted by, women for the rest of his life. One of his two more famous romances after Martha's death was with Maria Hadfield Conway, a well-known painter of the period and wife of another painter, whom Jefferson met in 1786, when he was minister to France. It was while he was taking a walk with Maria, at which point he was forty-three and she was twenty-seven, that he tried to get over that fence and ended up breaking his wrist, which was set poorly and gave him a deformed hand for the rest of his life. The romance subsided after Maria and her husband left Paris, but flared up again when Maria returned to France for a few months in 1787, and was confined only to passionate letters after that.

Jefferson's other romance has received even more attention from historians, who, I guess, were shocked because it was with one of the slaves on his plantation, Sally Hemings. In those days, it was commonplace for plantation owners to take female slaves to bed with them whether they wanted to go or not, but it's clear that Jefferson's relationship with Sally Hemings was a genuine love affair and not like that at all. Sally Hemings was the daughter of another slave, Elizabeth Hemings, but her father was John Wayles, who was also the father of Jefferson's wife, Martha, which made Sally the half-sister of Martha Wayles Skelton Jefferson. The history books record that Sally was an outstandingly beautiful woman and that Jefferson had several children with her, though some historians dispute the latter statement. The thing that's certain, in any case, is that, for some of the time Jefferson was in France, Sally was there, too, and took care of Jefferson's daughter Polly, and that the love affair with Sally lasted for thirty-eight years.

Jefferson's early education was with ministers; he boarded and studied first with Reverend William Douglas in Northam, Virginia, staying there except for visits home from the age of nine until he was fourteen, and then he studied until he was sixteen with Reverend James Maury in Fredericksville, Virginia. Jefferson didn't care much for Douglas and had already begun to develop his doubts about established religions and his general feelings that the best kind of religion was a belief in God and in doing good for other people, but he liked Maury, who also tutored two other men who later became presidents, James Madison and James Monroe. In 1760, Jefferson entered the College of William and Mary and went there for two years, then went on to study law for five years, and was admitted to the Virginia bar in April 1767. It was at William and Mary, incidentally, that Jefferson met Dr. William Small, a professor of literature whom Jefferson liked and admired and helped instill in him his love of books and reading and his lifelong interest in and curiosity about just about everything. Jefferson had always enjoyed books, but he became such a dedicated reader that, when the family home burnt down in 1770 and the fire destroyed all of his books, he set out almost fanatically to buy more books and ended up with a library of over sixty-five hundred volumes.

He was now twenty-four, and his father had been dead for ten years at this point, so, as the oldest son, Jefferson expected to spend the rest of his life practicing law in Virginia but mostly to devote his time to managing the family plantation and the Jefferson properties. As a matter of fact, not long after he married Martha, he reached a decision even to give up his law practice and spend his time as a farmer and with the books he loved so much. He had already begun to build the mansion that became his home for the rest of his life, Monticello, and it seemed to him that he already had all he needed and wanted in life. But he'd become a member of the Virginia House of Burgesses in 1769, a kind of standard assignment for young and prominent Virginians, and the other young men who became his friends there were outspoken about their feelings regarding British injustice.

One of his colleagues in the House of Burgesses was Patrick Henry, a fiery and self-educated young lawyer whose two famous lines, ''Give me liberty or give me death'' and ''If this be treason, make the most of it,'' did a lot to advance the idea of the American Revolution. Jefferson agreed with these views and in 1774 wrote his own brilliant statement of his opinions on the relationship between his homeland and the motherland, *Summary View of the Rights of British America*. He was also very active in the Committee of Correspondence in Virginia, that underground network of men, mostly very young men, who believed increasingly in freedom for America and kept their views alive by writing to each other constantly on the subject.

It was therefore inevitable, of course, that Jefferson became a member of the Continental Congress, and in a way, almost equally inevitable that Jefferson would be the man picked to write the first draft of the Declaration of Independence. As you're aware, those other men picked for the committee to prepare the Declaration were no dumbbells—you'll recall that they were Benjamin Franklin, John Adams, Robert R. Livingston, and Roger Sherman—but it was decided almost without discussion that Jefferson would write the initial draft of the Declaration all by himself because, despite that tendency to freeze up and give poor speeches before larger audiences, it was already more than clear from his correspondence and other writings that he was far and away the best writer of his times. Three of the other four men on the committee were older and more experienced than Jefferson; Adams, born in 1735, was forty-one, Sherman, born in 1721, was fifty-five, and Franklin, born in 1706, was already seventy. Only Livingston, born in 1746, was younger than Jefferson, but they all felt that Jefferson was best equipped to put their views down on paper. He went to work on June 11, 1776, and without ever going to other people's writings to assist him, had completed his draft of the Declaration seventeen days later.

The other men didn't accept the draft exactly as written, of course. They all went over it and made changes as needed, and if you take a look at the original draft, you'll find it pretty well scratched up with recommendations for its improvement. And they *were* improvements. Just to give a single example, take that wonderful sentence "We hold these truths to be self-evident." Well, that wasn't Jefferson's; nobody's absolutely sure today whose change it was, but it's generally believed to be Ben Franklin's. Jefferson's original sentence was, "We hold these truths to be sacred and undeniable," and then another man's opinion prevailed and changed it to the simpler and totally perfect sentence we all know today.

I'm sure that just about every American capable of reading this book, or any other book, has read the Declaration of Independence, but I'm equally sure that hardly anyone can quote even its superb language word for word. I think it's worthwhile, therefore, to remind people of some of the great words of our greatest American masterpiece by stating those words here:

We hold these truths to be self-evident.—That all men are created equal, that they are endowed by their Creator with certain inalienable Rights, that among these are Life, Liberty, and the pursuit of Happiness.—That to secure these rights, Governments are instituted among Men, deriving their just powers from the consent of the governed.—That, whenever any Form of Government becomes destructive of these ends, it is the Right of the People to alter or to abolish it, and to institute new Government, laying its foundation on such principles and organizing its powers in such form, as to them shall seem most likely to effect their Safety and Happiness. Prudence, indeed, will dictate that Governments long established should not be changed for light and transient causes; and accordingly all experience hath shewn, that mankind are more disposed to suffer, while evils are sufferable, than to right themselves by abolishing the forms to which they are accustomed. But when a long train of abuses and usurpations, pursuing invariably the same Object evinces a design to reduce them under absolute Despotism, it is their right, it is their duty, to throw off such Government . . .

It goes without saying that the words and the thoughts weren't entirely new and original. In the preceding century, a number of influential British writers and philosophers, men like Algernon Sidney and John Locke and James Harrington, had expressed similar views on mankind's natural right to freedom and happiness, and in Jefferson's own century a number of other writers in other countries had done the same thing, including Jean-Jacques Rousseau in France, Christian von Wolff in Germany, and Emerich de Vattel in Switzerland. De Vattel and Locke in particular had a great effect on American minds, De Vattel because his book, *Law of Nations,* was translated into English and published in America in 1760, a crucial time in which Americans were beginning to think hard about their treatment by their king, and Locke because his writings said much the same things that the early Americans began to believe more and more. As Nevins and Commager say in their excellent history of the United States, "Locke maintained that the supreme function of the state is to protect life, liberty, and property, to which every man is entitled. Political authority, he said, is held in trust for the benefit of the people alone. When the natural rights of mankind are violated, the people have the right and duty of abolishing or changing the government."

Nevins and Commager go on to analyze the Declaration. "What we have here, of course," they write, "is the philosophy of democracy, a philosophy which had never before been given so succinct or so eloquent a statement. There are certain things . . . that no reasonable man can doubt—self-evident truths. There is the truth that all men are created equal—that all men are equal in the sight of God and equal before the law. There were, to be sure, even as Jefferson wrote, many inequalities in America: the inequality of rich and poor, of men and women, of black and white. But the failure of a society to live up to an ideal does not invalidate the ideal, and the doctrine of equality, once announced, worked as a leaven in American thought . . .

"Another great truth proclaimed in the Declaration is that men are 'endowed' with 'inalienable' rights—among them life, liberty, and the pursuit of happiness. These are not rights granted to men by some benevolent government and held at the pleasure of that government. These are rights with which all men are born and which they cannot lose. This principle, too, worked as a ferment in the minds of Americans and others, changing their attitude toward authority; for, as the Declaration pointed out, it was precisely to secure these rights that governments were organized in the first place. What we have here is the 'compact' theory of government the theory that men once lived in a 'state of nature,' that in such state they were continually in danger, and that in order to protect themselves they came together and set up governments, granting to these governments just enough power to protect their lives, their liberty, and their property. In short, men made governments to do good, not evil; made it to protect them, not injure them. And the moment government failed of the purposes for which it was established, it no longer deserved the support or allegiance of men."

Jefferson and the other members of the committee submitted the Declaration of Independence to the Continental Congress on July 2, and following a few small further changes, it was, of course, adopted two days later. It was probably the most revolutionary document ever written, and it has affected many other nations in addition to establishing forever the policy and the philosophy of the United States. It was one of the reasons for the French Revolution and a reason since then for revolutions all around the world. The French Revolution's own Bill of Freedom has many similarities to the Declaration of Independence, and in fact some people believe that Jefferson had a hand in helping the French write that one as well.

During the Revolutionary War, Jefferson became governor of Virginia, following Patrick Henry into that job; and then, after we'd won the war, he was Washington's minister to France from 1785 to 1789, and then, of course, Washington's secretary of state from 1790 to 1793, and of course, Adams's vice president from 1797 to 1801. When Jefferson set out to oppose Adams once again for the presidency, I don't think he did a whole lot of traveling and campaigning. As I understand it, he did everything almost entirely by letters, just writing to all the people he knew. He developed relationships with the leading men in every colony via the Committees of Correspondence, and of course he knew everybody of consequence in Virginia as well, so I don't think it was necessary for him to do much campaigning aside from writing a lot of letters. He carried on a tremendous correspondence all his life. I found one letter of his not long ago in which he said he was a slave to his writing table. There are two full volumes of the letters that passed between him and John Adams alone, and that was only part of the correspondence that he carried on. He kept up with all his correspondence, and of course it was all in longhand, so I don't see how in the world he ever did it, but he did.

Of course he hadn't done much campaigning to become governor of Virginia, either. In Virginia in those days, the succession was carried on by cliques just like it is now under Harry Byrd.* Jefferson was in Boston and New York and Philadelphia all the time while the Continental Congresses were in session, but I don't think he did a great deal of traveling up and down the country while he was campaigning to become president. In any case, as I've said, he was picked over Burr and Adams that first time, and in that second contest against Charles Cotesworth Pinckney, he landslid all over Pinckney with those one hundred and sixty-two electoral votes to Pinckney's fourteen.

Jefferson did a lot of important things as president, but I guess the three that should be mentioned in particular, before I move on to Andrew Jackson, are his dispatching of the Lewis and Clark Expedition into the Northwest Territory, his purchase of Louisiana, and his bill putting a stop to the importing of slaves into this country.

That third one is undoubtedly the most important, or at least it would have been if the damn fools who opposed it or ignored it had just had the sense to obey it. As it turned out, opposition to the whole idea of an end to slavery in this country continued right up until the Civil War, of course, and even after Jefferson signed the bill in March of 1807 that prohibited people from bringing slaves into the country commencing January 1, 1808, slaves continued to be smuggled in for many years after

---

*For people who don't recognize this name, though I imagine everybody will, it should be explained that Harry Byrd was a prominent and powerful Virginian who was first elected to the Senate in 1933 and who died in 1966. His son, Harry Byrd, Jr., was a senator from 1965 to 1983. It should further be explained that there always seem to have been Byrds of the nonfeathered variety in Virginia. One of the first such Byrds was William Byrd II, who lived from 1674 to 1744 and was one of the first royal governors of Virginia, and who became so rich and powerful that he ended up owning 179,000 acres of even richer Virginia soil. One of his estates was so large that it included the entire area of what is now the city of Richmond. I'm not sure that Harry senior was part of that same family, since he was actually born in Martinsburg, *West* Virginia, back in 1887. But he certainly became a powerful Virginian and a powerful southern politician, and when Eisenhower and Stevenson were opposing each other, some electors in Alabama, Mississippi, and Virginia even gave Byrd a total of fifteen electoral votes. His brother, incidentally, was Richard E. Byrd, the explorer. MT

that. But at least Jefferson managed to get the idea of an end to slavery made more official, and it was an idea that he'd felt and expressed most of his life. Years before this bill was proposed, he wrote and managed to get passed a bill that prohibited slavery in five states getting ready to come into the Union—Illinois, Indiana, Michigan, Ohio, and Wisconsin; and he almost managed to get a bill passed that prohibited slavery in all future states. But that bill was defeated by a single vote, and he wrote bitterly afterwards that ''a single individual [could] have prevented this abominable crime from spreading itself over the new country. Thus we see the fate of millions unborn hanging on the tongue of one man, and Heaven was silent in that awful moment! But it is to be hoped that it will not always be silent, and that the friends to the rights of human nature will in the end prevail.'' It took almost another century, and the Civil War, of course, for that to happen, and there's still plenty of injustice to black people in this country. But as he said, it's to be hoped that right will prevail in the end.

The other two things were the direct result of Jefferson's lifelong opinion that land, the ownership of land, is the key to what you might call the good health or strength of both individuals and nations. He was always eager to acquire more territory for the United States so that small landowners could become bigger landowners, and so that people who owned no land at all could get some, and he jumped at the chance when Napoleon agreed to sell Louisiana to the United States.

Jefferson's investigation into whether or not some of that territory might be for sale, however, started because he was afraid that France, which was becoming the strongest nation in the world under Napoleon, might develop too strong a presence near our own country. France had originally owned Louisiana, but now, as the eighteenth century drew to a close, Spain owned it; and in 1795 our minister to England, who was one of those Pinckney boys of South Carolina, Thomas Pinckney, sent an envoy to Spain and established diplomatic relations between Spain and the United States. Among other things, the treaty signed that year allowed both Spanish and American citizens uninhibited use of the Mississippi River, and also allowed Americans to deposit grain and other farm products from the Ohio and Mississippi valleys at the port of New Orleans before selling them around the country. But in 1801 Jefferson learned that Napoleon had done some tough talking to Spain, a much weaker country at that point in history, and had gotten Spain to sign a secret agreement ceding Louisiana back to France. The next year, Spain canceled America's right to deposit products in New Orleans, and in alarm Jefferson instructed Robert R. Livingston, who was then our minister to France, to see if he could negotiate a purchase of part of that vital territory. He also sent his friend James Monroe over there as ''minister extraordinary and plenipotentiary,'' about as fancy a title as anybody could think up, to help with the negotiations, and he got Congress to give the two men a budget of up to $2,000,000 to make their purchase.

Jefferson was hoping to buy only New Orleans and a part of what is now the western section of Florida. But to his absolute amazement and delight, Napoleon offered to sell the entire Louisiana territory, an area of more than a million square miles, equal in size to the entire United States at that time, if we could come up with somewhat more than that two million dollars. Napoleon, Jefferson realized instantly, was in trouble and cash-poor and eager to refill the French treasury. France and England were not at war at that time, having signed the Treaty of Amiens. Napoleon knew it was a shaky peace and that the two countries would soon be fighting again, and in fact they *were* fighting again a year later. Napoleon was also feeling depressed at the fact that a revolution had been started over in Haiti, which France owned, by a black leader named Toussaint-Louverture, and that French forces there were in terrible trouble. (The French eventually managed to put down the revolution, but a combination of Toussaint-Louverture's men and yellow fever killed twenty-four thousand French soldiers.) And though Napoleon had always had the ambition to establish part of his empire in the Western Hemisphere, he realized all too well, after the great French losses at the battles of Aboukir and Acre, that his naval people weren't as good as the forces he had on land, and that he really had no way of controlling the oceans. So he allowed his foreign minister, Charles-Maurice de Talleyrand, to ask the Americans what they might be willing to pay for the entire French territory, hinting that eighty million francs, which was then the equivalent of fifteen million dollars, might do the trick.

Jefferson also realized two other things. One was that Napoleon's price for that entire huge area of land came to a mere three cents an acre, which made it one hell of a bargain for land anywhere in the world, but especially for all that rich farmland and all the other first-rate real estate. The other was that he might be tinkering with the Constitution if he said yes, because the Constitution contained no provision whatever for the purchase of foreign lands. There had already, in fact, been protests from many Americans, mostly Federalists, when Congress allowed Livingston and Monroe to show up on Napoleon's doorstep with two million dollars in their back pockets. Jefferson knew, therefore, that the proper thing to do was to go and ask Congress to allocate the additional money and okay the purchase, but he also knew that Napoleon, an erratic and temperamental fellow, might change his mind if he had to sit around and wait too long. On April 29, 1803, Jefferson told his envoys to tell France that they had a deal at eighty million francs, and *then* he went to work to get the money and Congress's approval.

TWENTY-FOUR

The Constitution—
Stretched or Broken?

SOME constitutional lawyers say that Jefferson stretched the Constitution until it cracked. And some people say that there's no point in having a Constitution if you're going to break it the way Jefferson did. I don't agree with these viewpoints at all because, as I see it, the Constitution wasn't broken by Jefferson because he never overstepped its provisions—though he certainly stretched it. You don't break the Constitution if you're a good president, as Jefferson certainly was. You just don't break it. But you do stretch it when necessary because the Constitution is a document *built* for stretching when emergencies or opportunities demand that it be stretched. And it's been stretched time and again by our best presidents.

The thing some people tend to forget is that our Constitution isn't just a revolutionary doctrine, something no other government in the history of the world had done up to that time; it's also an evolutionary document. If you'll read the preamble to the Constitution, you'll see that it's a document that's flexible enough to make the country run no matter whether the population is three million or three hundred million. The

Constitution, and we're lucky that it's the case, was arranged so that it could meet the changes in conditions as time went on.

I'm one of the greatest believers in the Constitution in the country, I guess, and one of the greatest admirers of what it says and the way in which it says it. I think it's far and away the best government document that's ever been put together by any bunch of men. It says things simply and beautifully; it's written in plain language, and it states exactly what's meant and isn't tangled up with any legal verbiage or any Latin inserts. And when you read it, you can understand it. I admire the Constitution so much that, when they asked me one time to go down and dedicate a monument to Patrick Henry, I wouldn't do it because Patrick Henry was one of the bitterest opponents of the Constitution of the United States. Maybe that was going overboard, because he certainly said and did some good things, but I just said I wouldn't go down there because there wouldn't be any United States if old Pat Henry had had his way.

On the other hand, I've been going around giving a lot of talks to youngsters, trying to get them to understand what they have and what they have to do to keep it. I think the people who wrote the Constitution were interpreting the wishes of the people themselves, and not trying to lure the people toward *their* ideas. The Constitution was conceived on a high intellectual basis, but it was written in such a way that people could understand it and argue with parts of it if they felt like it. That's the difference between our country and a lot of other countries.

But I'm a liberal constructionist of the Constitution rather than a strict constructionist. Some people label the two schools of thought ''strict constructionists'' and ''loose constructionists,'' but I won't use that second term because I don't believe there's anything loose or unformed or unsupported by logic about the way we interpret the statements in the Constitution. I think the right term is ''liberal constructionists,'' using liberal in the sense of not being excessively rigid and immovable in interpreting those statements. And I'm a liberal constructionist because it seems obvious to me that a president should interpret what it says in context with the needs and events of his own times, and not necessarily in context with things as they were in 1789. And I'm also a liberal constructionist because I believe that change is always good if the change being contemplated is a necessary change or one that will better existing conditions.

I'm sure the men who put together the Constitution realized that parts of it would have to be changed as the country grew and changed, and that's the reason, of course, that the Constitution is set up so that it can be amended. Which isn't to say that I believe it should be amended casually or lightly, and fortunately most of the lawmakers of this country have tended to have that same viewpoint.

You really ought to stop and read the whole Constitution yourself, and read it more than once, because the more you read it, the more informed you become about our theories of government and about what makes this country tick. But just in case you haven't read it recently or at all, let me remind you that the Constitution has a Preamble that makes it clear in the first seven words that it's everybody's document and not the document of a small aristocracy; those seven words, of course, are "We the people of the United States . . ." Then there are seven articles, the first three of which set up the government of the United States and separate it into its three branches. The first article sets up the legislative branch and gives Congress its powers to "make all laws which shall be necessary and proper" and puts the purse strings in the hands of the elected branch of the government; the second establishes the executive branch and the fact that the government will be headed by a president and a vice president; and the third sets up the judicial branch and assures all Americans of the right of trial by jury and other legal protections, and sets up courts that can check the legality of laws passed by the Congress. And then it occurred to somebody, and I believe Jefferson was the moving man in the thing, that the protection of the individual *from* his government had been overlooked—and that an individual must be protected against the encroachment of a government on his rights or we just have the same old go-round that they had in the monarchies in Europe. It's the fifth article that allows the Constitution to be amended, and Jefferson and his people pushed to get the first ten amendments passed because they're all amendments for the protection of the people *from* the government being set up, so people can't be persecuted and unduly prosecuted by their government.

The First Amendment, as most people know, guarantees freedom of speech, worship, press, and assembly. The Second guarantees the right to bear arms by state militias and the like. The Third prohibits the quartering of soldiers in homes without permission. The Fourth protects against unreasonable search and seizure. The Fifth, one of the best-known amendments, allows a person to refuse to testify against himself, and protects against double jeopardy and incarceration without indictment. The Sixth provides for an impartial and speedy trial in criminal matters (though unfortunately "speedy" is a relative word), and the Seventh provides for the right of trial by jury in common-law matters. The Eighth prohibits excessive bail, fines, and "cruel and unusual punishment." The Ninth makes it clear that the fact that the Constitution states some specific rights held by the people doesn't mean that they're denied or don't have other rights not specifically named. And the Tenth states that rights not granted to the federal government, as needed for the operation of the country, are reserved to the states.

The first ten amendments became law in 1791. And just to give you the complete picture, the Eleventh prohibits suits against a state by foreigners or residents of a different state; the Twelfth was the one set up after that mess between Jefferson and Burr and requires that a president have a majority of electoral votes to be elected; and the Thirteenth, Fourteenth, and Fifteenth were those especially important amendments that came after the Civil War and abolished slavery and guaranteed civil rights to all Americans. The Sixteenth enabled Congress to collect an income tax; the Seventeenth provided for popular election of senators rather than through state legislatures; the Eighteenth was that dumb one, the Prohibition Amendment; and the Nineteenth allowed women to vote as of 1920, and about time. The Twentieth moved up the opening of Congress to January 3 and the inauguration of the president to January 20 so that presidents and other legislators who were no longer in office wouldn't be around for four months, as they'd been previously, and have all that opportunity to push through bad last-minute laws; the Twenty-first was the sensible one that got rid of Prohibition; the Twenty-second provides that no one can be elected president more than twice; the Twenty-third allows residents of Washington, D.C., to vote for president, finally eliminating in 1961 the antiquated law that prohibited them from doing that; and the Twenty-fourth, passed in 1964, at last eliminated the poll tax and other types of discrimination against "poor people," which should never have been law in the first place.

I don't know whether or not you're aware of the fact that there have been somewhere between three and four thousand amendments to the Constitution introduced since Washington's time, and it's interesting that only the twenty-four I've described have actually been accepted to date.* That's because the basic Constitution is sufficiently flexible and sufficiently open to differing but sensible interpretations, so that a good president can succeed in doing (constitutionally) what has to be done— sometimes with a little bit of stretching, of course.

And it's equally interesting that only two of the amendments have been truly bad. The Eighteenth Amendment, the Prohibition Amendment, speaks for itself. You can't prohibit something the largest part of the population wants and enjoys; all you do is make people go underground to get what they want, and you create a whole army of gangsters to supply the need. And I've made it clear in many of my public statements and conversations with people, and in this book, that I consider the Twenty-

*There have been two additional amendments signed into law since my father wrote those lines. The Twenty-fifth Amendment, adopted in 1967, was the result of President Kennedy's assassination and allows presidents to fill the office of vice president instead of leaving it vacant. And the Twenty-sixth Amendment, adopted in 1971, changed the minimum voting age from twenty-one to eighteen. MT

second Amendment, limiting the presidential term, equally stupid and meanspirited. Someday they'll repeal that one, too.

The Constitution has often been called "a bundle of compromises," but what if it is? That's all any government is, a bundle of compromises, and when it ceases to be a bundle of compromises it becomes a dictatorship or goes to pot the way the Fourth French Republic did in 1958, with everybody thinking differently and pushing so hard to get his own way that nothing ever got done, and they had to drag old Charles de Gaulle in as president again for a while to see if he could sew the country back together. A series of compromises is just what they did in the Constitutional Convention; it's a discussion of every approach to a matter or a problem that's before a legislative body, or any other body that has to pass on things, and see if you can find an answer or a solution. The ablest men present at the time have to guess how the thing they're trying to do will affect both the present and the future, and it often takes a compromise to meet that situation. Nobody can predict the future; if you could, you'd be Isaiah or some other prophet. So what's often needed is an accommodation without surrendering the main principle of what's trying to be done.

Some of our "normalcy" presidents, like that fellow Harding who coined the word, used the normalcy excuse at every turn and more or less thrived on the limitations of the Constitution by doing nothing, by just sitting back and saying, "Well, the Constitution prohibits me from doing this or that." You'll find that in times of so called normalcy, people just don't pay attention to what goes on in government, and they get away with sleeping on the job for a while. And then Harding was succeeded by another man, Coolidge, who was equally indifferent to what his powers were and what he could do in that Oval Office. But fortunately people finally get tired of that sort of thing just as they get tired of a man who exercises too much power, and then there's a change and maybe another change and sooner or later we get someone who tries to get some things accomplished.

A lot of us had to stretch the Constitution at times. Jackson was a great believer in the Constitution, for example, when he made a statement that the three branches of the government were equally powerful—meaning that under the Constitution one branch couldn't override or overrule any other. Yet when the Chief Justice made a decision he didn't like, he said, "Now let him enforce it. I'm president of the United States. How can he enforce it?" Old Jackson also knew how to meet the situation when he was having his trouble with the United States Bank; he just vetoed the bank's charter and put the bank out of business. The same thing happened in a bigger and much more serious way under Lincoln during the War Between the States, when he suspended the right of habeas corpus and everything else of that kind. All those things certainly stretched the Constitution, but they were absolutely necessary at the time to save the republic.

Lincoln stretched the Constitution further than any other president because, of course, it was the only time in our history that our country was in danger of being split in half, but the truth of the matter is that that kind of thing has gone on continually. We all had to stretch the Constitution when the time came to do it. Theodore Roosevelt did what he had to do in 1907, when he was having his troubles with the depression and with Wall Street. He pumped money into banks that were failing and did a lot of other things to help business along, like canceling an antitrust action against United States Steel when it was acquiring the Tennessee Coal and Iron Company, even though he was usually so vocal about antitrust matters, because otherwise the Tennessee company would sink. And when Wilson came along, he met a financial situation that was equally bad, so what he did was set up the Federal Reserve Board and based our currency on production in the country so that it could expand and contract to meet all possible situations. Wilson did far more extreme things than that as well; he was the greatest constitutional lawyer ever to sit in the White House, but he did what he had to do when the First World War started up. And I'm sure most people are familiar with all the great laws and programs that Franklin Roosevelt put through in the first part of his administration, things that were again necessary to help and perhaps even save our people and our country.

I'll go into more detail about some of those things in the next few chapters on our greatest presidents, but the point is that, when these men did these things, they weren't stretching the Constitution until it cracked. They were stretching it in exactly the way it was meant to be stretched when it was first put together, because the Constitution is an expanding document designed to meet each new situation as it comes along. It's also an enabling document all the way through—to enable a president to do what's necessary to do. It's the greatest document of government ever written because it's an outline of government and only an outline, and it can continue to help every new president meet and deal with every new problem if he (or she) reads it and studies it and recognizes the fact that the implied things in the Constitution are of much greater use to a republic than those that are set down on paper as limitations to what can be done.

For instance, the most important implication is the power of the president. It's implied very clearly that the president must meet emergencies when they come up, and every good president has used all reasonable and sensible means at hand to do just that. In the same way that the Constitution establishes the executive branch, the legislative branch, and the judicial branch, it also gives those branches certain powers and certain duties to perform. There are a great many powers assigned to the Congress, and a great many assigned to the courts, and even more powers and duties assigned to the president of the United States for the operation of the government and the country. Any president who really wants to lead the country can do it under the Constitution, and he won't have to infringe in any way on the things that limit his power in the Constitution. He has plenty of power if he wants to use it.

There have been very few of the great presidents who haven't understood that and didn't follow through on what the Constitution provides and allows. A great many of the other kind of presidents just sat there and let Congress do as it pleased and felt they were only the executive who enforces the laws passed by other people. But as I've said before, a president has just as much right to decide what's constitutional as the Congress does or the Supreme Court does, when it comes to that, and that's what all the great presidents have done. In other words, when an emergency arises, it's necessary for men to meet that emergency by the practical method of sitting down and debating and taking measures.

I don't think any of the presidents ever considered the Constitution a burden. Some of them were kind of like a spirited horse when you put a bridle on him, but none of them ever tried to sidestep the Constitution and throw it out. We met the emergencies in periods when we were in trouble. I guess some presidents do get out of line. Sometimes they become a runaway horse, which I think is educational for those of us who follow them. But then a bridle is there in the form of the Constitution. The men who were sitting in that Constitutional Convention were completely familiar with all the pitfalls of totalitarian government and all other kinds of government; there wasn't a single member of that Convention, all sixty-one of them, who didn't have an idea of government and how government should be set up. And the result is that the Constitution lets us go as far as necessary but not too far. The idea of freedom of action within sensible limits has always been the basis of our constitutional approach to things. There's always a way to correct things without a bloodletting revolution, and that's the reason we've continued to work and to govern as we have. Everything's attainable under the Constitution. Everybody has the opportunity at some time or another to better himself, and perhaps even better his country, and that's the objective in the long run. The Constitution should be applied constantly, but let me put it this way: it should be applied constantly in an improved manner.

Sometimes, of course, some of us have found the courts' *interpretation* of the Constitution a burden, when the courts overstepped *their* limitations, such as when Franklin Roosevelt did the great things he had to do in his administration and the courts called a great many of them unconstitutional. But as in Roosevelt's case, when a court came along that could really analyze the situation, they found that the Constitution implied that the measures Roosevelt suggested ought to be done because the American people needed those things, and they were done in the long run. It's often said that the Supreme Court interprets the Constitution with an ear to the ground or an ear to public opinion. I think that's correct to some extent, but they can't interpret it out of existence; and usually when they interpret it too much, the next court will set it aside.

Obviously, a strong leader is necessary in times of emergency or need, and that's always been the big question with each president in times like that: whether he'll want to run the government for the welfare and benefit of all the people or whether he'll want to confine it to a groove and not let it run at all. But that's been our lucky situation, to have strong people around who were willing and able to handle each emergency as it arose. Whether it'll continue or not, we've got to wait and see, but I'm an optimist and have confidence in our strength and future, despite the fact that some people who are mediocre or worse get into power and impede our progress for a while.

Which brings us full circle back to Jefferson and his Louisiana Purchase and the fact that it was most certainly not in violation of the Constitution. Jefferson, in fact, brought up himself the question of whether or not the purchase was constitutional because he respected the document so much, and there are letters written by Jefferson to various people in which Jefferson comments admiringly on Washington's abilities as an administrator at the Constitutional Conventions because he was able to get a document like the Constitution out of it. But Jefferson wasn't about to let a foreign power gain strength and grow stronger and stronger on our borders. He had no intention of going beyond the limitations of the Constitution to the point of injuring it. His objective was to protect the United States, and eventually the Congress came in and agreed with him on the way he handled it.

Perhaps, as some historians say, Napoleon's principal motive was that he hated Britain and wanted to put a thorn in the side of the British. There were a great many lawsuits against the French government after he did it, but I don't think they would have stood up in court. I think he was mostly afraid that the British were just going to come down from the north and take all that territory anyway, and they probably would have done just that if the United States hadn't stepped in and bought it. In any case, it's certain that Jefferson didn't care in the least about Napoleon's motives. He jumped at the opportunity and didn't wait for legal maneuvering. The legal maneuvering was done afterwards because what he did was right.

There are certain circumstances where it's absolutely essential to move quickly. Roosevelt had the same kind of difficulties at times, and I had some of the same difficulties, and Lincoln had more difficulties than either one of us. That's why I always try to explain things when people say, as I've mentioned, that there's no point in having a Constitution if some presidents think nothing about breaking it. You don't break it at all. The provisions of the Constitution were never overstepped by Jefferson. The objective in a thing like that is to meet the situation with which you're faced, and then apply the Constitution to the program after it's over if you can't do it beforehand. The enabling legislation in the purchase of Louisiana was the appropriation of funds immediately for the purchase, and Jefferson had no problem getting that done. He just insisted that the money be given to him quickly, and as he wrote about the matter, "the less said about the Constitutional difficulty the better." After the fact, of course, everybody could see how good all that territory was for the welfare of the country. There wasn't any argument about it after it was all over.

You just have to move quickly sometimes to meet certain circumstances. The same thing happened when Roosevelt traded some of our obsolete destroyers for naval bases; there was plenty of noise about it until people realized what a good thing he'd done. That was the same as the Louisiana Purchase.

The chunk of territory that Jefferson acquired for those three cents an acre was almost too big to be believed; it stretched from the Mississippi River and Lake Pontchartrain on the east to Texas and the Rockies on the west, and from Canada on the north down to the Gulf of Mexico on the south. It's true that Napoleon had gotten hold of it from Spain by promising that he was going to hand one of the members of the Spanish royal family one of those little Italian kingdoms, and he never paid off on his promise at that, but it was still the greatest bargain in the history of the United States. In time, no less than fifteen additional states or parts of states came out of it: pieces or all of Arkansas, Colorado, Iowa, Kansas, Louisiana, of course, Minnesota, my own state of Missouri, Montana, Nebraska, New Mexico, North Dakota, Oklahoma, South Dakota, Texas, and Wyoming. It was mostly those good old Federalists who opposed it and yelled that it was unconstitutional, but the treaty between France and the United States was completed on April 30, 1803, signed a few days later, and finally ratified on October 21. The American flag went up over New Orleans, signaling our control of the territory, on December 20.

And then Jefferson did that third important thing I wanted to mention, which was to send Meriwether Lewis and William Clark to explore the Pacific Northwest and come back with a full report on all the good things we had there for ourselves. I don't think many people realize or remember that Lewis was Jefferson's personal secretary and close friend and was chosen by Jefferson because he felt that the expedition was so important that he wanted somebody especially good to head it. Lewis in turn picked his friend William Clark to join him on the expedition, which they hoped would take them as far as the Pacific Ocean, and the body of men set out on a dangerous and difficult trip that lasted two and a half years, from May 1804 to September 1806, and covered eight thousand miles. They ended up back in St. Louis with a tremendous amount of valuable information about the areas they visited and the Indians who lived there, and they confirmed that an overland route was possible, opening the door to considerable additional exploration and settling of the lands by Americans. Lewis went on to become governor of the territory in 1807, but had a sudden and tragic end two years later; he was on his way from his headquarters in St. Louis to Washington to arrange for publication of the important journals of his expedition when he stopped at an isolated inn on the Natchez Trace, and he was found dead there the next morning, just thirty-five years of age. It's still debated as to whether it was a suicide or whether he was murdered. Clark was appointed superintendent of Indian Affairs, negotiating a number of important treaties, and then was governor of the Missouri Territory from 1813 to 1821, resuming his duties as superintendent of Indian Affairs until his death at the age of sixty-eight in 1838.

Jefferson was a very social sort of man, and when he left the presidency on March 3, 1809, he went back to Monticello and spent the rest of his life there, keeping busy by entertaining visitors and neighbors and corresponding with friends around the country. He hurried back there because most of his interests were centered in his home, and during the eight years he was president, he stayed in Washington only when it was necessary for him to be there. At all other times, he went quickly back to Virginia and relaxed in his lovely big house.

He was a very genial man, and a good man to have around in any company. He knew how to make people enjoy themselves. In fact, he was too much that way for the simple reason that the friends he entertained, while he was president and after he left the presidency, ate him out of house and home and he lost all of his properties except Monticello because he couldn't keep up with the expense of running things. His house was a kind of hotel, and when he left the White House, he was nearly $25,000 in debt. His indebtedness increased rather than decreased in the years that followed because there were no presidential pensions in those days, and his only income was from selling tobacco and flour and a few other items grown and manufactured at Monticello. He also had a tremendous number of family connections to whom he kept giving money because he felt responsible for them, and in one way or another, I guess he was. He was a good farmer after he left the White House, and he'd been a good farmer in his earlier days, growing just about everything that grows on a farm and being very successful at it; but he was so liberal that anything he accumulated soon disappeared to the people who were begging him to take care of them or expecting him to entertain them. But he managed to get along, and he enjoyed the last seventeen years of his life as a private citizen.

He was just a good human being, and he liked people, and he liked to associate with people, and he liked to get along with people, and he liked to discuss all questions with anybody who was willing to discuss them with him. He talked to visitors and friends on any subject they wanted to bring up, and this gave him constant enjoyment because he knew all the most intelligent people in Virginia and New York and Massachusetts, and in France and England, too, for that matter. Sometimes, of course, he had to make some pretty strong sacrifices to keep up his way of life. In 1815, for example, when we were at war with the British again and they burned down the Capitol, the fire wiped out the Library of Congress at the same time, and Jefferson agreed to sell the government his beloved collection of books to start up a new Library of Congress. It must have hurt his heart to do that—he'd accumulated 6,500 books by that time, and it took eleven big wagons to get the collection to Washington—but he needed the $23,950 he got for his books. There's a sad postscript to that, too; there are only about a third of those books still in the Library of Congress because there was another fire there in 1851, and two-thirds of Jefferson's collection was destroyed. Still, he remained a happy and gregarious man for the remainder of his life.

His heavy correspondence also accomplished another good thing: it renewed his relationship with John Adams and they ended up friends. I hope I've made it clear that I don't believe Adams was a bad sort of man. I don't think there was anything underhanded about John Adams; I think he was an honorable and upright man and an outstanding character of his time. But his political ideas were not in agreement with those of Jefferson—in which *I* believe, of course—and because of this I don't think he was a very effective president. As I've said, his idea of government, like Alexander Hamilton's, was that the country should be run by a special coterie of people who, in those days, were considered better than the general run of the population—that the welfare of the country was best served by people who had a situation in the world above the ordinary run of the population because the upper classes knew more about what was good for the people than the people themselves knew. Jefferson didn't agree with this at all, of course; he trusted the people.

I suppose much of the reason for Adams's viewpoint stems from the fact that he spent so much of his time abroad as a diplomat and foreign officer for the United States; he spent most of the ten years from 1778 to 1788 in France, Holland, and England, before becoming Washington's vice president in 1789 and president himself in 1796. His son, John Quincy Adams, in fact, was raised principally out of this country. They were in contact mostly with Europeans whose ideas were very different from the ideas of the people who were growing up and developing in the Colonies; and while Jefferson and others were inaugurating some of the great policies and beliefs that were included in the Constitution, Adams was acquiring notions that were not very proper notions in Jefferson's opinion, and in mine. And I think that, while Adams was a strong advocate of freedom from England, and did everything he could to help free the country from England, he still had those views in the back of his head when he entered the White House. Well, anyway, he wasn't president long enough to bring many of his programs into operation. People got tired of him before he had a chance to have a second term.

As I've mentioned, he was so disappointed at not being reelected that he left the White House at midnight so that he wouldn't have to ride in the same carriage with Jefferson to Jefferson's inauguration, and he also left in that bad-mannered way because he felt betrayed by many members of the Congress. There's no doubt that he was. Every president is. But the difference is that that was just the start of it, and people hadn't yet learned to understand it as a fact of life.

I'm sure that Jefferson was as outraged by Adams's behavior as I was by Eisenhower's, and I'm sure Adams never really got over the fact that Jefferson had clearly been a better president than he'd been. I don't think, incidentally, that Jefferson was ahead of his time in doing a better job than his predecessor. I think the work Washington had done was simply carried on by Jefferson after he became president. Adams hadn't made any real approach to the Constitution, hadn't really tried to understand and use it, so—as though Adams had never even been there— Jefferson was just carrying on the firm and stable government that Washington had created. Jefferson kept the government running.

But the smoldering anger between the two men was all smoothed over by their long correspondence, and Jefferson and Adams became the best of friends. When Adams died in Quincy, Massachusetts, on July 4, 1826, at about six o'clock in the evening, he was nearly ninety-one, making him the president with the longest life thus far. His final thoughts were on the United States and on Jefferson; his last words were, "The country is saved, and Jefferson lives." But that was also a final irony in the lives of the two men, because Jefferson was already dead. He died five hours before Adams, at twelve-fifty P.M., aged eighty-three. He willed the only thing he had left, Monticello, to his daughter Patsy, but his indebtedness had now climbed to a total of $107,274, and Patsy had to sell the house and auction off his furniture to pay his debts. Monticello was later bought by a naval officer named Uriah P. Levy and bequeathed by him to "the people of the United States." Even that generous act didn't help because a battle developed over the terms of his will, and it wasn't until 1923 that the mansion was renovated and refurnished and opened to the public.

TWENTY-FIVE
Madison and the War of 1812

THE three men who followed Thomas Jefferson into the presidency—James Madison, James Monroe, and John Quincy Adams—were all right, I suppose, but they were certainly nothing special. They weren't simpletons like Ulysses S. Grant or fools surrounded by crooks like Warren G. Harding, but we're still lucky that the country managed to stay on its feet during the twenty years, from 1808 to 1828, in which they served.

Madison, born in Port Conway, Virginia, on March 16, 1751, was a friend of Jefferson's and became president largely because Jefferson made it clear that Madison was the man he wanted to succeed him. Jefferson was so popular as president that a lot of people asked him to run for a third term, but he said that he felt that two terms were plenty, and that a man who was president might be tempted to stay on for his lifetime, and then we'd have a kingdom instead of a democracy, and he preferred to go home to Virginia and see James Madison in his place. There were two other men in Jefferson's party who also wanted the nomination: Monroe, also a close friend of Jefferson's, and George Clinton of New York, who felt that Virginians were beginning to make the presidency their personal property and wanted to become the first New Yorker to get the job. But Jefferson favored Madison because Madison had been his secretary of state during all eight years of the Jefferson administration, working so closely with him on the Louisiana Purchase and on foreign policy and other matters that it was sometimes impossible to tell which man had thought up which moves or which policies in some situations, and Jefferson felt that Madison as president was most likely to carry on the things on which the two men had worked together. Jefferson was also an admirer of Madison because Madison was one of the principal authors of the Constitution and wrote most of the final version, and he was more influential than anyone else in the Constitutional Convention in managing to get it through at last. And it wasn't an easy victory, either; it was passed by a narrow margin of eighty-nine to seventy-nine.

That's why Madison is known in our history as Father of the Constitution and Master Builder of the Constitution, and that's another thing that Jefferson and Madison had in common: their belief in the Constitution and the need for a strong federal government to run the country, and their increasing dislike of Patrick Henry because of his opposition to the Constitution on the grounds that it limited states' rights. Henry became such an enemy of Madison's that, when Madison tried to become a senator from Virginia early in his career, Henry use his very strong influence in Virginia to get him defeated, saying that there'd be a revolution in the state and "rivulets of blood" would run if Madison entered the Senate. And when Madison switched around and decided instead to run for the House of Representatives, Henry again opposed him bitterly, putting up James Monroe as Madison's opponent, and missed getting Madison defeated a second time only by a tiny margin. But Jefferson and Madison were so firmly entrenched by 1808 that Madison won the nomination and the presidency with ease. He was then able to defeat another New Yorker named Clinton, DeWitt Clinton, who was George Clinton's nephew, in 1812, getting eleven states and 128 electoral votes to Clinton's seven states and 89 electoral votes. (Clinton returned home to New York, which was a good thing, because he then went to work on getting the all-important Erie Canal approved and completed, a necessity for the country at the time. The canal ran from Albany to Buffalo and connected Lake Erie and the Hudson River, allowing Americans in those areas to trade and do business with each other instead of having to rely on Canadian sources.)

Madison didn't look like much personally. He was the smallest of our presidents, just five feet four inches tall, and he was so thin that he tipped the scales at a hundred pounds only when he was soaking wet or had a bunch of rocks in his pockets. He was so nervous that he suffered from an ailment called epileptoidal hysteria, whose victims don't really have epilepsy but nevertheless have similar problems including falling to the floor and frothing at the mouth. He also dressed somewhat too conservatively, wearing only black suits, which made him look smaller and thinner.

He was the first president to wear only clothing made in the United States rather than the dressier stuff that came from England and France. He was also the first president to refuse to wear knee breeches and other overly ornate items of clothing. Before that, they all wore knee breeches and silver-buckle shoes and long stockings. That is, the officials did; the common people didn't. Madison changed the presidential clothing style because everybody else, the general public, was wearing substantially the same sort of clothes that we wear today; he felt there wasn't any reason to follow the British customs of pomp and ceremony. (But can you imagine a president wearing knee breeches or other ceremonial things today, even on special occasions? It surely wouldn't work in this day and age. They'd laugh him right out of office.)

Madison also had sort of nondescript brown hair, pale blue eyes, a weak and trembly voice that couldn't be heard in the back when he addressed large audiences, and a nose that caught your eye because it had once gotten frostbitten and was permanently scarred.

But despite his unimpressive appearance and manner, he was a brilliant fellow with a crystal-clear mind, an excellent education at the College of New Jersey, which later became Princeton University, and a decent man who, like his friend Jefferson, was much more interested in the welfare of the average citizen than the privileged few. We also owe him, as a nation, a debt of gratitude because he was a meticulous sort of person and kept a very detailed record of what went on every day at the Constitutional Convention—details that, since the sessions were secret, would otherwise have been lost to our history forever. But the reason he wasn't an outstanding president is that, like many another man, and despite his considerable brainpower and education, he found it difficult to make decisions. As a president, the man who had to say yes or no and do this or do that, he was what we might call, in these days, a weak sister. He just couldn't make decisions. Some historians say he was overintellectual. He was certainly well-informed on history and government, and he was certainly an intellectual, but I don't think we want to blame his intellectualism for the fact that he wasn't a very good president. It was just that, when it came time for him to act like an executive, he was like a great many other people; when the time comes to make decisions, they have difficulty doing it.

And that was particularly unfortunate because he was president when the War of 1812 came along, of course, and that was one of the worst periods in our history. In a sense, one of the main reasons Jefferson wanted Madison as his successor was that he felt that Madison would continue to preserve peace in our country, but events made that impossible. In Congress, two young men, Henry Clay of Kentucky, speaker of the House of Representatives, and John C. Calhoun of South Carolina, chairman of the House Committee on Foreign Affairs, were gaining power every day, and they were leaders of a group known as the War Hawks. Clay was born in 1777 and Calhoun was born in 1782, so they had no personal familiarity with the agonies of the Revolutionary War, and the War Hawks agitated constantly for the United States to go to war against England or France; they didn't seem to care which, and in fact a majority of the War Hawks felt that we should go to war against both.

There were, without doubt, reasons and provocations for harsh feelings toward the two countries. Both British and French ships were stopping and boarding American ships and seizing their cargoes. The British, in particular, were feeling proud of themselves because of their victories over the French, being more and more convinced that they were the sole masters of the seas; so, you'll recall, they were going one very unpleasant step further than the French and also seizing American sailors and forcing them into the British navy. As far as they were concerned, the Americans weren't Americans at all; they were still British subjects no matter how much the sailors insisted to the contrary.

All this became worse and worse toward the end of Jefferson's second term, with practically every American ship on the seas being stopped and boarded; and in desperation, in 1807, Jefferson put an embargo on American ships, prohibiting them from leaving American ports without his permission. His notion was the British and French might then promise not to bother American ships because they needed American goods for their own people. It didn't do any good. The British, in particular, continued to board the relatively few ships that were allowed to leave America, figuring, I guess, that they'd get along with just the American goods they managed to steal, and American merchants complained that the embargo was putting them out of business and they wanted to take their chances with their ships, and the War Hawks became louder in their insistence that we declare war against Britain.

There were also a couple of other reasons that some people in the country wanted us to go to war, though these weren't stated quite as openly. One was that there were some questions about the exact part of Florida that had been acquired under the Louisiana Purchase, and some politicians wanted us to go down there and just grab all of it, including the part that was still controlled by Spain, which was Britain's friend and ally at that time. And some other people thought that a war might give us a good excuse to move in the opposite direction and take over Canada.

We weren't prepared for war at all. The United States had never developed a military force that was of any consequence, and Madison was also harassed with generals who didn't know what to do or how to do it, and harassed with a militia that didn't want to fight and was willing to surrender. Madison wasn't to blame for the situation because it was a development of the American attitude that had brought about the isolation of the government of the United States from the rest of the world. They didn't think they would ever be invaded or they would ever have to defend themselves, so, when the time came, they had no first-rate military minds trained to meet the situation. And Madison just didn't have all the support he needed to win a war. A lot of people wanted to save their property without doing anything about it. They thought it would protect their property if they didn't fall out with the British. They thought that maybe they wouldn't be taken over even if the British won the war.

This was the position in which Madison found himself at that time. The American Army consisted of about three thousand soldiers, many of them drunkards and petty criminals who'd chosen military service as an alternative to going to jail, and these men were supplemented by only about an additional seven thousand militia, some of these of the same caliber as the regular soldiers. The people who ran the Army were men like General James Wilkinson, the fellow who collaborated with Burr when Burr tried to start his own country, and who was corrupt and stupid, and General William Hull, who'd been a good soldier in the Revolutionary War but was now grossly fat and clearly senile. The Navy consisted of about two dozen ships. And because a lot of people were against the war, that gasbag Daniel Webster and others insisted that Madison's plan to draft men into the Army and Navy was unconstitutional; the governor of Connecticut refused to supply men for the services; the Connecticut assembly got so agitated that it announced that the state was pulling away from the United States and was "free, sovereign, and independent"; and other parts of New England also almost seceded. Naturally, the Federalists called it Mr. Madison's War. Well, they do that every time. The War Between the States was called Lincoln's War, and World War II was called Roosevelt's War, and I suppose also Truman's War though never in my presence. But I don't think the War of 1812 was any more Madison's war than it was most of the rest of the country's. A clear majority of the people wanted to fight the British because of the commercial situation with which the country was faced.

Madison just didn't know what to do, and he didn't get much in the way of advice from the people around him, either. His vice president was George Clinton, the fellow who had been one of his rivals for the presidency, and Clinton was so disgruntled at the fact that he was just vice president when he really wanted to be president that he made it clear he wasn't going to do a thing except draw his paycheck. (The only thing for which Clinton is remembered is that the Bank of the United States's charter came up for renewal in 1811, and there was an absolute tie in the vote in the Senate on whether or not to renew it. Clinton broke the tie by voting *not* to renew it. That was because Madison had made it clear that he wanted it renewed.)

Clinton was sixty-nine when he became vice president, and he died in office in 1812 and was replaced by Elbridge Gerry, whose principal qualification for being given the job was that he was sixty-eight and party leaders felt he was therefore probably too old to be any opposition to James Monroe, who was hoping for the presidency after Madison. Gerry also did little except die in office in 1814.

Madison's secretary of state was Robert Smith of Maryland, whose performance was so poor that Madison finally fired him in 1811, and he was replaced by Monroe. And Madison's secretary of war was William Eustis of Massachusetts, who was also fired for poor performance in 1812, to be followed by John Armstrong of New York, also fired for the same reason in 1814, and then followed by Monroe, wearing two hats as secretary of state and secretary of war. And his secretary of the navy was Paul Hamilton of South Carolina, whose alcoholism became so noticeable that he had to quit in 1812 and was replaced by William Jones of Pennsylvania. As you can see, it was quite a mess.

On June 1, 1812, Madison finally gave in and asked Congress to allow him to declare war on the British, and on June 18, Congress said that he could go ahead; the final vote was an unenthusiastic nineteen senators for it and thirteen senators against, seventy-nine representatives for it and forty-nine against.

The war was a disaster for us from the start, and the worst thing about it was that it could have been avoided completely because, on June 16, the British finally voted to stop harassing American shipping. But we didn't know anything about that because of the slowness of communications in those days, and we plunged blindly into battle. We were beaten at almost every turn. The plan was to start off the war by invading Canada, and even though the best British soldiers were still busy fighting against Napoleon, other British soldiers had no trouble at all preventing that from happening. As just one example of our defeats, an American army of about two thousand men led by fat old Bill Hull started in that direction, but an army of British soldiers and Indian allies approached them in Detroit, and even though the American army was larger, Hull gave up in terror without a shot being fired on either side. He was later court-martialed for the surrender and sentenced to death, but pardoned in view of his good service as an officer in the Revolutionary War.

The British also blockaded our east coast and prevented essential supplies from coming to us from other European countries for just about the entire war.

And our most humiliating defeat came in almost the same way as the business in Detroit, when the British, who were determined to retaliate because Americans had destroyed some public buildings in Toronto, which was then called York, decided to try to take our capital. They landed with about five thousand men near Washington, and even though the American commander, General W. H. Winder, sent an even larger force to meet them at Bladensburg, Maryland, the American soldiers turned and ran to hide in Washington after ten Americans were killed and forty were wounded. It was such a rout that a number of British soldiers, running closely after the Americans in the bright sunlight, were put out of action not by bullets but by sunstroke. The British then entered Washington and set fire to the Capitol Building and the White House, and Madison and his wife Dolley had to leave the White House in a hurry and head down into Virginia to keep from being captured. Dolley Madison ran around the building before they left to make sure that the pictures of George Washington and Martha Washington by Gilbert Stuart, which were part of the decorations of the East Room at the White House, were saved.

Madison was actually exposed to gunfire himself. He wasn't a coward by any means, and he took active charge of some of the battles. I think he was the only commander in chief who ever took the field. He did that because his generals weren't any good. He had to do it. The general in charge of Washington just backed up and backed up and then laid down, and the same was true of a lot of his other generals. The British took Washington so easily that British soldiers settled themselves inside the presidential residence and ate the hot meal that Dolley Madison had been cooking when she and her husband had to abandon the place and run away, and the only reason the British left the city after just one day is that a storm started up and they were afraid that their ships would be damaged and they went to move them.

There were some victories, of course, and a lot of heroic soldiers and sailors, too. The ironic thing was that, even though the British prided themselves, and with reason, on being in command of the seas, most of our victories were in sea battles, and so were most of the other memorable events of the war. The frigate USS *Constitution,* the one most American remember as *Old Ironsides,* won a number of battles in the War of 1812. Captain Oliver Hazard Perry got together a small fleet on Lake Erie, whipped the British soundly there, gained control of the Great Lakes, and sent a message that became a patriotic phrase repeated over and over during the war, "We have met the enemy and they are ours." Captain Thomas McDonough won another decisive battle against the British on Lake Champlain and kept a large British force from coming down from Canada. Captain James Lawrence, dying of wounds on the USS *Chesapeake,* also said something that Americans remember to this day, "Don't give up the ship!" Francis Scott Key, standing on a British ship on a mission to try to arrange a prisoner exchange, saw British guns pounding Fort McHenry but failing to subdue the fort, and he was moved by the sight of an American flag at the fort and wrote "The Star-Spangled Banner."

And on land, General William Henry Harrison, later our ninth president, managed to chase the British deeply into Canada at one point and killed Tecumseh, the Indian chief who was a British ally. And of course there was that big battle at New Orleans in which old Andrew Jackson kept the city from being captured by the British, and in which there were two thousand British casualties and only twenty-one American losses (though "only" is probably the wrong word for even a single loss in a war).

But mostly it was one defeat after another, and our big break was that Britain and France were still in bitter conflict and the British couldn't pay too much attention to fighting the war against the United States. The British were like the people of any free country after long years of war; they really didn't want to fight anymore. They sent over a lot of mercenaries and didn't take as serious a hand in the fighting here as they might otherwise have taken. They were tired, just as all the rest of the world was, of the continued wars that had been carried on by Napoleon and the British prior to that time, and they just didn't feel like coming over and trying to reconquer the colonies that had won their freedom. If it hadn't been for the Napoleonic wars, they probably would have taken us over, because they were perfectly capable of doing it.

That was all very lucky for us, and Madison was privately quite happy when Russia offered to serve as mediator between our country and Britain. John Quincy Adams had been sent to St. Petersburg in 1809 as our first United States minister to Russia, and he was there when Napoleon, still thinking he could conquer the world, invaded that country in 1812. That made a lot of Russians sympathetic toward Britain because France was now their common enemy, but Adams had become a good friend of Czar Alexander I over the years and convinced Russia to allow commercial American ships to enter Russian ports and do a lot of other things to help us out. That led to the Czar's offer to step in and try to end the war. Britain, however, didn't like the idea of dealing with a third party, and eventually direct talks started up between our two countries.

The United States was represented by Adams, Henry Clay, who was then Speaker of the House, Albert Gallatin, who was Madison's secretary of the treasury, and Jonathan Russell, our minister to Sweden and a very persuasive negotiator. The talks took place on neutral ground in the city of Ghent, located in what is now Belgium. And finally a peace treaty was signed on December 24, 1814.

There were two real O. Henry twists to the end of the war. The first was that our great victory at the Battle of New Orleans, which, though it made a national hero of Andy Jackson and led him in time to the presidency, and made Americans take pride in themselves all over again, was tragically unnecessary. It took place, as I've mentioned, on January 8, 1815, and that, as you see, was more than two weeks after the signing of the peace treaty—but news traveled so slowly in those days that neither the British nor the Americans knew it and went about trying to kill each other. And the second was the result of the war itself, which, like many, most, or possibly all wars, accomplished absolutely nothing.

First of all, there wasn't a syllable in the peace treaty about the British injustices that had brought about the war; no promise whatever that the British would stop boarding American ships or stop pressing American sailors into the British navy. Second, there wasn't even a mention of one other longtime American complaint, that many of the attacks by Indians on American settlers were the result of British financing and stirring up of Indian tribes that were British allies, and in fact fought alongside the British on many occasions during the War of 1812. And third, the war was ended in an agreement that is called *status quo ante bellum*, which simply means that each side gives up all captured territory and goes back to owning only what it owned before the war.

And again like most or all wars, there were plenty of negative results of this one. A total of 286,730 Americans had left their homes and their families to fight in the war, and nearly seven thousand men came back in different condition or didn't come back at all; the final count was 4,505 wounded and 2,260 dead. British casualties were considerably higher. Our national debt, already very high, became considerably higher because of the huge costs of the war. And a lot of merchants and companies went out of business, partly because most of their sales were based on supplying war materials, and partly because they couldn't withstand the return of competition from British goods now that the war was over, and in 1819 we had our first real American depression.

As some historians have put it, Madison left the White House in 1817 "with relief," more than happy to turn the job and the headaches over to someone else. (It was now really a white house. Its basic external material was gray sandstone, but this was blackened by smoke after the

British set the building on fire, as you'll recall, and the architect who did the job of repairing and refurnishing it, James Hoban, decided to paint it white to cover up the smoke damage. The place was little more than a shell when Hoban went to work on it, and it took about three years to get it back in shape again. During that period, the Madisons lived in a place called Octagon House, just as Mrs. Truman and Margaret and I lived to a certain extent out of suitcases at Blair House when the White House started to fall apart again.) The man who followed as president, James Monroe, had an overwhelming victory over the Federalist candidate, John Quincy Adams, and Madison returned to Virginia and lived there for nineteen years until his death at the age of eighty-five in 1836.

He outlived all of the friends who'd worked with him at the Constitutional Convention, but unfortunately, like Jefferson, he was pretty broke when he left the White House and relatively poor for the remainder of his life. This was partly because of continuously bad crops on his extensive land holdings, but also because, like Washington's wife Martha, Dolley Madison was a widow when she married Madison, and she brought to her marriage a son, John Todd, who was a kind of bum and kept building up gambling debts and other debts that Madison had to pay.

But the Madisons lived together quietly and happy at the Madison estate, Montpelier, for the remainder of Madison's life, interrupting his retirement only to serve on the board of regents with Jefferson at the University of Virginia and taking over as rector there after Jefferson's death in 1826. Madison became increasingly weak in the final month of his life, and I've heard stories to the effect that his physician, Dr. Robley Dunglison, gave him stimulants at his request so that he could die on July 4 like Adams and Jefferson. But on June 28, as he was eating his breakfast, he suddenly showed signs of difficulties in swallowing, and a niece who was breakfasting with him asked him if anything was the matter. "Nothing more than a change of mind, my dear," Madison said, and then he closed his eyes and he was gone.

Dolley returned to Washington after Madison's death and reentered the city's social life. She was seventeen years younger than her husband, having married him in 1794 when he was forty-three and she was only twenty-six, and she was still a good-looking and vivacious woman, and she loved parties and dances and good times even though she was born a Quaker and grew up under very quiet circumstances in North Carolina, Virginia, and then Philadelphia. Her first husband, a Quaker lawyer named John Payne Todd, whom she married in 1790, died three years later in a smallpox epidemic, and Madison spotted her shortly after that and asked a mutual acquaintance—Aaron Burr, of all people!—to introduce them.

Dolley was thrown out of the Society of Friends after her second marriage because Madison wasn't a Quaker, and she became a social force in Washington, first as official hostess for Jefferson because he was a widower, and then for her husband. She lived until the age of eighty-one and continued as the social leader in Washington, famous for her charm and wit and the magnificence of her parties, until her death in 1849, past Monroe's presidency and John Quincy Adams's and Jackson's. She didn't have a lot of money and eventually had to sell Madison's detailed record of the activities of the Constitutional Convention, which had been kept secret until then, to Congress for $30,000, and then sell Montpelier, but her parties remained the best in the country.

Don't underestimate the importance of her work as hostess or of social life in Washington in general, either. Social leaders are necessary because foreign governments are very much intrigued with social affairs, and one of the duties of the president of the United States is to act as the social head of the country. In doing that, he gives receptions and enter-tainments all the time, and it's a privilege for someone to be invited to the White House and to one of these functions as a guest of the president. These functions are usually held for the heads of states who are friendly with us, and for other visiting men and women who are important po-litically and socially in other countries. It's a genuinely important program that has to be carried on, and in the days of Dolley Madison, it was even more important than it is now because we were a very young country and working all the time at developing friendships and relationships with other countries and with influential people from those countries. Dolley Madison became so well liked and so important to her country, so much like what the Japanese call a Living National Treasure, that she was made an honorary member of the House of Representatives. She couldn't be-come an actual member of the House in those days, so she was made an honorary member, and I think it was both appropriate and an honor to which she was entitled.

As I've mentioned, Mrs. Truman never had any ambition to be glamorous or a great hostess, but we had to throw many a party ourselves when I was president, for the same important reason, so that certain things could be accomplished or discussed that might otherwise not hap-pen. A White House dinner is rarely purely social. Discussions take place in the Red Room and the Green Room and the East Room at all those functions. They're bound to. Whenever men of different interests are associated socially, they always discuss eventually what's going on, in the hope that something will happen or be said for their benefit. That goes on at the White House just as at any other social function. When there's a social event at the White House, at least when Roosevelt was there and when I was there, the president would usually sit around; if it was a dinner, the president would sit at the table and talk for fifteen or twenty minutes with the men who were at the function. Then he would leave, and it was time for the rest of the men to have their own conversations. At that point, the guests were available to each other and could discuss anything they wanted to discuss. The guests were often foreign dignitaries, and in instances where heads of foreign states were there, the leading senators and representatives, and the chairmen of various committees, were always at these functions, so quite a lot got said and done.

Other parties in Washington are also often important because things frequently got worked out by senators and representatives and other members of the United States government at those times. Those functions are sometimes very interesting and entertaining, and when I was in the Senate, I used to attend them frequently and had a good time there.

The president usually doesn't attend these parties, because, when there's going to be a party or a dinner that includes the president, nobody could put on that function except the president himself, and he usually puts on enough of those on his own hook. But fortunately, there's always been some rich dowager in Washington who likes to hold dinners and parties and functions of that kind, so there are plenty of those as well. Evelyn Walsh McLean, the lady who owned the Hope Diamond, was the most outstanding hostess when I was president, and Gwendolyn Cafritz has now taken over since Evelyn died. The McLean parties were great parties, and I think one of the most important contributions to the development of our bipartisan foreign policy before, during, and after the war was Evelyn Walsh McLean's entertainments during that period.

I guess the First Lady in recent times who can best be compared to Dolley Madison is Eleanor Roosevelt, who, because of Franklin Roosevelt's physical disability, acted for him in many instances in matters that he would have handled himself under ordinary circumstances. She was a great lady, and she was exceedingly well thought of in both foreign affairs and domestic affairs, and I think she is more nearly analogous to Dolley Madison than any other First Lady who's ever been in the White House.

In policy matters, I think First Ladies have always had a great deal of influence, anyway, though I don't think presidents ever paid much attention to them on matters of appointments. But they had influence in policy matters because they looked into various matters for the president and made reports and discussed things with him. Franklin Roosevelt always discussed his policy matters with Mrs. Roosevelt, and in a great many instances, as everybody knows, she made foreign trips and trips all over the United States and furnished him with information on which he could rely completely. She was a Roosevelt before she was married, of course, I believe a sixth cousin of her husband and the niece of Teddy Roosevelt, and she was always interested in public affairs and very knowledgeable. Yes, a great lady, and I miss her. I would also like to have known Dolley Madison.

TWENTY-SIX
Minor Presidents: Monroe and John Quincy Adams

JAMES Monroe, our fifth president, didn't have any of the problems that Madison had, at least as far as his physical appearance and personality were concerned. Unlike Madison, our smallest president, Monroe was one of our biggest in size; he was over six feet tall and had big broad shoulders and big muscles that showed even when he was fully dressed. He was an outdoors type who preferred hunting and riding his horse to other kinds of pastimes, and I'd say, judging from portraits I've seen, that he was a particularly good-looking man, with plenty of wavy hair and a dimple in his chin and other attributes that might have made him a movie star instead of a politician if he'd lived a hundred and fifty years later than he did.

But he had plenty of other kinds of troubles. He was sent by Washington as minister to France, but got into so much difficulty there that Washington called him home and almost dropped him like a hot potato. He was sent by Jefferson as minister to Britain and did such a generally poor job there that, when he worked out a trade treaty with the British, Jefferson refused to okay it and wouldn't even send it on to Congress for study. Monroe was personally against slavery, but when Congress reached agreement to ban slavery in states being formed out of the Louisiana Purchase, he got so flustered over the question of whether or not Congress had the constitutional right to order such a ban that he decided to veto the whole tremendously important bill, actually preparing his veto message before he was talked out of it. In general, his principal problem was that he wasn't the brainiest man alive, and some history books I've read recently, fair-minded books, don't give him much space and dismiss him pretty fast with descriptions like "a commonplace man" and "neither his talents nor his achievements measured up to those of his predecessors" and even "one of our most dull-minded Chief Executives."

Like Washington, Jefferson, and Madison before him, Monroe was a Virginian, born on April 28, 1758, in Westmoreland County, and was a direct descendant of King Edward III. The first Monroe to come to this country didn't come voluntarily; he was Monroe's great-grandfather, Andrew Monroe, who was an officer in Charles the First's army when King Charles went up against Oliver Cromwell at the Battle of Preston in 1648, and he was captured in that battle and exiled to Virginia. By the time James Monroe was born, the family was pretty rich, with a large plantation and about a hundred slaves, and when Monroe's father, Spence Monroe, died in 1774, James inherited everything, even though he had an older sister and three younger brothers. (That was because of that ridiculous business of primogeniture, that medieval law under which a man's land and other properties descended automatically to his oldest son on the theory that all property owners were knights holding their land under military control at the king's pleasure, and the oldest son was best equipped for any necessary military action. As I've mentioned, Jefferson finally got rid of that one.) Monroe was only sixteen at the time, of course, and the estate was controlled by his uncle, Joseph Jones, for a while, but he grew up in luxury and went on to study law under Jefferson.

I'm sure you've gathered from what I've already said that his career prior to the presidency was distinguished but not in the class of the presidents who preceded him. He joined the Continental Army as a lieutenant at the age of eighteen and fought in a number of major battles, and he was promoted to captain and cited for bravery when he led an assault and captured a pair of cannons at the Battle of Trenton and was wounded and nearly died. In addition to his military service, he served in the Virginia Assembly and in the Continental Congress, but then left politics for a while and practiced law in Fredericksburg, Virginia, and then took that beating when he ran for United States Congress against Madison and was appointed senator with the help of his friend Patrick Henry.

It was in 1794 that Washington sent him to France, choosing him mostly because, like Jefferson, he was known for his enthusiasm for that country, but he messed up by overdoing things. Washington insisted on absolute neutrality by the United States in the war between England and France, but instead Monroe began to praise France and condemn England so loudly that Washington's secretary of state at that time, Edmund Randolph, reprimanded Monroe publicly. Then Monroe went to work in France to get Thomas Paine out of that French prison, which was all right, I suppose, especially since Monroe was under the mistaken impression that Paine was dying, but Paine immediately went to work as a free man at his chosen mission of attacking Washington all over the place. And then John Jay came up with a treaty with England, which Washington favored, despite a lot of flaws because we just weren't equipped for any new fighting with the former mother country or anyone else, and which Monroe was expected to back while going to work as a soothing influence with France. But instead Monroe spoke long and loud against the treaty, calling it "the most shameful transaction I have ever known," and Washington, in disgust, told him to come on home.

The same kind of thing happened when Jefferson sent Monroe to England in 1803. I suppose Jefferson should have known better in view of Monroe's much-expressed hostility toward England, and in view of his poor performance in France, but Jefferson's main interest was to get England to stop pressing American seamen into the British navy, and perhaps he thought that big, strong-looking James Monroe was just the tough fellow who could do it. Monroe didn't succeed at all, of course. Instead, he put together that trade agreement that didn't say a word about the impressment problem, and Jefferson tossed it into the trash can.

In 1807, Monroe came back to the United States and ran successfully for governor of Virginia the next year. He made Madison angry as the devil by opposing him for the presidential nomination in 1808, but went back to Virginia after Madison got eighty-three votes to his three, and was reelected governor of Virginia in 1811. But then Madison, who wasn't a man to hold a grudge for very long and was now ready to forgive and forget, offered him the position of secretary of state, hoping that Monroe's experience in Europe, despite the failures, might help prevent the war that was threatening with England. Monroe resigned as governor and took the job immediately. The War of 1812 wasn't prevented, of course, but Monroe served as Madison's secretary of state from 1811 to 1817, and after the war got underway, as I mentioned earlier, served simultaneously as Madison's secretary of war in 1814 and 1815, and did well enough in both jobs so that both Madison and Jefferson urged the other political powers and the public to make Monroe president when Madison left office in 1817.

It didn't look like a shoo-in at first. Monroe had a strong opponent for the nomination in his party, a man from Georgia named William H. Crawford, who'd served as secretary of war in Madison's cabinet for most of the final two years of Madison's administration, and then became, briefly, Madison's secretary of the treasury. A lot of the leaders of the party were also beginning to feel that it was time to end what was being called "the Virginia dynasty" by choosing a candidate from some other state. And then a need was being felt for a particularly strong candidate because the Federalists were putting up a very strong man, Rufus King of New York, a senator who had also been minister to Britain, working in that post from 1796 to 1803. But Monroe beat Crawford for the nomination 65 to 54, and then, with Daniel D. Tompkins, the governor of New York, as his running mate, received 183 electoral votes to King's 34.

There were nineteen states involved at that point in our history and Monroe took sixteen of them: Georgia, Indiana, Kentucky, Louisiana, Maryland, New Hampshire, New Jersey, New York, North Carolina, Ohio, Pennsylvania, Rhode Island, South Carolina, Tennessee, Vermont, and Virginia. King took only Connecticut, Delaware, and Massachusetts.

And he did even better when he ran for a second term in 1820. John Quincy Adams had followed his father into politics on the Federalist side, and he was now Monroe's opponent when Monroe ran for reelection, but Monroe annihilated him with the greatest of ease. There were twenty-four states involved this time, and Monroe beat Adams for electoral votes in every single one of the twenty-four, getting 231 votes to one lonely vote for Adams. In fact, the only elector who voted against Monroe was William Plumer, the governor of New Hampshire, and I've read somewhere that the only reason Plumer voted as he did was because he was a traditionalist and wanted Washington to remain the only president elected unanimously by the electoral college. (On the other hand, I've also read somewhere that that wasn't the reason at all, and that Plumer voted the way he did because he felt that Monroe was nothing more than a good-looking sap. But what does it matter? The point is that Monroe swept into office as though he had run unopposed.) Adams then became Monroe's secretary of state.

As far as Monroe's accomplishments as president are concerned, well, there were several, of course, as there nearly always are even with mediocre presidents.

One of the most important, naturally, was the Monroe Doctrine, the message that warned foreign powers not to attempt to establish new colonies in the Western Hemisphere, making it clear that we wouldn't tolerate Russia's plan to move down from Alaska into Oregon and Spain's and France's thoughts about recapturing some of their own former territories. As I've mentioned, this wasn't a separate pronouncement but just part of Monroe's regular message to Congress in 1823, and it shouldn't be credited solely to Monroe because John Quincy Adams wrote a lot of it and convinced Monroe to come out with it. And it didn't have very sharp teeth because we weren't really strong enough yet to do much about it if any of the other nations decided to challenge our viewpoint. But at least it made our viewpoint clear, which was that the Western Hemisphere was no longer open territory for European colonization, and that we'd consider any move on the part of a European nation to involve itself in Western Hemisphere affairs as an act unfriendly to the United States. And it did a world of good toward making European rulers understand that the United States was a country that was separate and independent from all others, and a country that was increasing in power, strength, and determination.

Monroe's other major accomplishment was the Missouri Compromise. This wasn't really Monroe's personal accomplishment, either; this was, in fact, the one that he practically vetoed, but at least it got passed during his administration.

The difficulty began to show itself mostly because Alabama, which until then had been part of Georgia, and the area that became my home state of Missouri, wanted to be given statehood. Nearly everybody liked the idea of getting more states into the Union, but the problem was that the admission of those two states was opposed by legislators from free states because admission of Missouri and Alabama would tip the scales in favor of proslavery forces. Up to that point, you see, there were more antislavery men than proslavery men in the House because, of course, the number of members of the House from each state depended on the population in that state, and the biggest population centers were in the North, and the same was true of the Senate, even though senators were set at two from each state regardless of population, since the last state admitted to the Union at that point, Illinois, which came in 1818, was a free state and that made it eleven free states and ten slavery states. But Alabama got its land grant from Georgia on condition that it remain a slavery area, and a majority of the people in Missouri had slaves or favored slavery, so the admission of Missouri and Alabama would make it, in the Senate at least, two more proslavery men than antislavery men.

A lot of bitter arguments started up, and a number of proposals were put forth, but none of them worked. A member of the House from New York, James Tallmadge, suggested doing nothing about the slaves already in Missouri but banning additional slaves from being brought in and freeing the children of slaves when they reached the age of twenty-five, which would after the passage of a lot of years end slavery there, but neither side in the Senate liked that one enough and it was turned down. Then another man from New York, John W. Taylor, proposed barring slavery entirely in the whole area of the Louisiana Purchase, but the proslavery people managed to get that shot down. Then antislavery people tried to get a plain and simple law passed requiring that new states be admitted only if they banned slavery entirely, which would have been great, but the other side defeated this by pointing out that, since all previous states had been admitted without this prohibition, Congress didn't have the power to make different rules for new states.

This went on and on for a couple of years until Henry Clay, who was beginning to be known as the Great Compromiser, managed to get both sides to agree to the Missouri Compromise, which let Missouri come in as a slave state but simultaneously allowed Maine, which until then had been part of Massachusetts, to come in as a free state. Alabama came in as a slavery state, but it was agreed that all future states carved out of the Louisiana Purchase above the southern boundary of Missouri must be free states. None of this was wonderful, but it increased our population and structure and strengthened the country. And perhaps it did a little, though just a little, to move toward the eventual end of slavery. It's such a shame that the thing was allowed to develop in the Western Hemisphere in the first place, but a lot of southerners wanted it because slavery provided free labor for them, and a lot of New Englanders did, too, because they were the importers of slaves and sold the slaves to the South, and it finally brought on the Civil War. There were always people opposed to slavery, of course, but just not enough of them in those days.

To sum things up, I consider Monroe a pretty minor president. In spite of the Monroe Doctrine. That's the only important thing he ever did more or less on his own, when you really got down to it.

Monroe was another man who was entirely destitute when he came out of the presidency in 1825. His wife, the former Elizabeth Kortright of New York, whom he married in 1786, when he was twenty-eight and she wasn't quite eighteen, was a beautiful woman but sickly most of her life, and they didn't have very much time together after he left office. There hasn't been too much written about the nature of her illness, but I think it must have been some kind of epilepsy that kept her from functioning at social gatherings most of the time while her husband was president, and she was so sick when he left office that he had to stay on in the White House for three weeks because she couldn't travel. In 1826, she had a sudden and violent attack and fell into a fireplace and nearly burned to death. They were living in their estate, Oak Hill, in Loudoun County, Virginia, at that time, but Monroe was $75,000 in debt and he kept begging Congress for repayment of money he said he had spent on his duties as president, but it took a long time to come through, and even then he ended up getting only part of the amount he requested.

When his wife died in 1830, aged sixty-two, Monroe had to sell Oak Hill and go to New York and live with one of his two married daughters, Maria Gouverneur. (Maria's husband, Samuel Gouverneur, was postmaster of New York City and her first cousin, and their wedding in 1820 was the first marriage ceremony ever held at the White House. Monroe's other daughter, Eliza, who was sixteen years older than her sister and bossed Maria around so much that the two women eventually stopped talking to each other, was married in 1808 to George Hay, the attorney who prosecuted Aaron Burr unsuccessfully when Burr was tried for treason in Richmond, Virginia. When her father and her husband died, she became a Catholic and spent the rest of her life in a convent in France.) Monroe died a year after his wife, on July 4, 1831, the third president to die on Independence Day.

Before I leave Monroe, I want to say a word or two about how disgraceful it was that the United States ignored Monroe's poverty to the point where he had to depend on his daughter and his son-in-law for food and shelter. I'm sure it's clear that I'm not one of Monroe's greatest admirers, but that's beside the point. A president's home life has everything to do with his ability to function as chief executive, and sometimes to serve his country in other ways after he leaves office. And though I'm not saying that the principal reason Monroe wasn't an outstanding president, and didn't do much after he left the presidency, is because his home life was inadequate, there's certainly no question about the fact that he shouldn't have been required to live the way he lived during the final years of his life. I think, for example, that every president should have a home provided for him after he leaves office. Some places in which some of the presidents had to live afterwards were pretty terrible, especially by contrast with the lovely White House. The new home needn't necessarily be in Washington, but wherever the man and his wife want to live. I've got mine right here in Missouri, so it makes no difference to me. But every single head of state of every other great country has that prerogative and that benefit, and yet we don't do it here. In fact, until not so very long ago, there wasn't even such a thing as a presidential pension. They just turned the presidents out to grass and let them starve to death.

It's principally, I suppose, because, in a republic where the people are in control of the government, they assume that the heads of state will be well enough off to take care of themselves and their families, but that hasn't always been the case. Some presidents, of course, were rich men when they went in there, but not necessarily when they came out. Jefferson died pretty much a pauper and he was a rich man earlier in life, and Monroe had been a rich man and died a pauper—I think he left something like six thousand dollars to Maria, which wasn't big money even in those days, and a little bit of property to Eliza—and several others had the same thing happen to them because they wouldn't exploit the fact that they'd been president of the United States. Presidents either had to go to work for industry or assume a position of special privilege or they were allowed to die in poverty. Well, I can understand the refusal of that special privilege business because I've been offered all sorts of things that I've turned down because I knew they were being offered only because they wanted a pet ex-president on hand or on their letterheads, so I'm glad it's a better situation now for former presidents. But it can be made better yet for future presidents, and much more fair and decent, by making sure they have good homes along with their pensions.

I'll go on now to John Quincy Adams. The single really interesting thing about Adams, I'm afraid, is that he was the only son of a president in our history to become president himself.

And even that happened almost by accident. During the final months of Monroe's second term, Adams and four other men emerged as possible presidential candidates, the other four being W. H. Crawford, Monroe's secretary of war and secretary of the treasury, John C. Calhoun, also Monroe's secretary of war for a period of time, Senator Henry Clay, and the man you know is one of my favorite people, Andy Jackson. This was before the days of political conventions and strong political parties, and presidential candidates were still being chosen by caucuses of members of Congress, and the congressional caucus selected Crawford. But this time various state groups objected and put up the other four men as candidates, and it ended with Calhoun's dropping out, saying he'd prefer to be either Adams's or Jackson's vice president if either man won, and with the other four men running against each other without party labels.

Adams didn't think very much of his three rivals; he kept a diary most of his life, and he wrote in his diary that Clay was a man whose "morals, public and private, are loose," Jackson was quarrelsome, and that Crawford was a man of "corrupt character" and the only man in America who has "risen so high . . . upon so slender a basis of service." But a lot of people liked the other men more than he did, and that's what I mean when I say that Adams became president almost by accident; this strange election split the votes four ways, naturally, and Adams didn't get the majority of *either* the electoral or the popular votes.

The real winner, in fact, was Jackson, who got ninety-nine electoral votes and 152,901 popular votes, which was 42 percent, to Adams's eighty-four electoral votes and 114,023 popular votes, which was 32 percent. The other two men split up the remaining votes, Crawford getting forty-one electoral votes and 46,979 popular votes, representing 13 percent, and Clay got thirty-seven electoral votes and 47,217 popular votes, also adding up to 13 percent. That threw the final choice into the House of Representatives, and on the night of January 9, 1825, as they used to say in old-fashioned novels, a mysterious event occurred. Old John Quincy forgot the things he'd said about old Hank Clay in his diary and asked Clay to come over for a friendly powwow. The next day, Clay told his supporters in the House to give their votes to Adams, and Adams became president and Clay became his secretary of state. Andy Jackson didn't like this much; he said sadly that "the Judas," meaning Clay, "has closed the contract and will receive thirty pieces of silver." But I'd prefer to be charitable here and believe that it was Adams's familiarity with foreign affairs, the fact that he had so much experience in foreign policy because he was in the foreign service almost up to the time he became president, that caused the House of Representatives to choose him over Jackson.

All in all, it's pretty clear that Adams's life was one without a whole lot of joy. His father had been president of the United States, true enough, but was the only president up to John Quincy Adams's time to fail to get himself elected to a second term. And then John Quincy himself became the second president to have that happen to him. And his early life doesn't seem to have been all that happy, either, since his father was so busy in politics and in diplomatic service that John Quincy spent a lot of time alone and away from his native land.

He was born on July 11, 1767, in Braintree, Massachusetts, and was a nervous individual almost from the start, suffering all of his life from terrible headaches and insomnia. He grew up to be an unattractive-looking fellow, five feet seven inches tall and fairly fat at 175 pounds, and he started losing his hair early and ended up with hardly a hair on his head. His appearance in general was austere and unbending, and though he was aware of this and tried to behave otherwise when he went into politics and knew it was important to make friends, he couldn't seem to help himself from behaving as usual; he wrote in letters and in his diary, "I never was and never shall be . . . a popular man . . . I am a man of reserved, cold, austere, and forbidding manners . . . I am certainly not intentionally repulsive in my manners and deportment . . . but I have no powers of fascination."

In 1777, he went with his father to France, and he lived mostly in France and in the Netherlands for the next seven years. Then, in 1781, when he was only fourteen, he went to Russia as secretary to Francis Dana, who was our first minister to that country and hoped to get Russia to recognize us as an independent nation. But the ruler of that country, Catherine II, practically ignored Dana, and Adams left and spent the next five months traveling around Europe alone, as he was so often, before returning to this country to study at Harvard. He graduated second in his class of fifty-one men and was elected to Phi Beta Kappa. He wasn't dumb by any means, just not a very attractive or happy fellow.

He became a lawyer after that and then, when he entered public service, served as Washington's minister to the Netherlands and minister to Prussia, and then as a state senator in Massachusetts in 1802 and a United States senator from 1803 to 1808. Then he was Madison's minister to Russia from 1809 to 1814, Madison's minister to England from 1815 to 1817, and finally Monroe's secretary of state from 1817 to 1825. But his generally unhappy nature kept these appointments from meaning very much to him and prevented him from being any more enthusiastic about himself than he was later on about his opponents for the presidency. He said from time to time that death would have been welcome to him, and he wrote very sadly in his diary in 1812, "I am forty-five years old. Two-thirds of a long life are past, and I have done nothing to distinguish it by usefulness to my country or to mankind."

His personal life was also full of trouble and tragedy. When he was thirty years old, he was in London and met and married Louisa Catherine Johnson, the beautiful daughter of an Englishwoman and an American who had been a merchant and was now serving as an American consul there. But Catherine had been born in London and had grown up in England and France, and John Adams was at first bitterly (and I don't mind saying stupidly) angry at his son for marrying a foreigner and refused for a long time to accept Louisa into the family. (Her birth in England, incidentally, made her the only foreign-born First Lady in our history.) And when her father-in-law finally did accept her, she proved to be as unhappy and nervous an individual as her husband. She suffered from insomnia, just as John Quincy did, and fainted quite often. She was also so shy and reclusive that she accepted almost no duties as hostess in the White House, and she even wrote an autobiography dealing with her general unhappiness, which was never published because she never finished it.

Louisa and John Quincy had three sons, but there was more unhappiness in store for the couple with two of them. Their first son, George Washington Adams, born in 1801, was a brilliant fellow who also went to Harvard and became a lawyer, but he proved to be an erratic young man who got himself and a young woman into trouble when she became pregnant, and he went on buying sprees and got deep in debt. Then he became mentally ill, began to suffer from what would be called paranoia today, and on a boat trip from Boston to New York in 1829, he accused fellow passengers of plots against him. He suddenly disappeared and was found drowned six weeks later, and it isn't known if he fell overboard or jumped and drowned.

A second son, John Adams II, born in 1803, was a much more stable man, and also became a lawyer and worked as his father's secretary when John Quincy became president. He was the apple of his father's eye and John Quincy said about him, "A more honest soul or more tender heart never breathed on the face of the earth." But he, too, was in poor health during most of his short life, and he died suddenly in 1834, aged only thirty-one.

Only the youngest son, Charles Francis Adams, born in 1807, lived a long life, long enough to have a distinguished career. He edited the ten volumes of John Adams's papers and twelve volumes of John Quincy Adams's diaries, and wrote many articles and a book or two of his own. (Not all of John Quincy's diary has been published, incidentally, but it's now hoped that the rest will be published because the Adams family has turned over the papers of the two Adamses to Harvard University to be indexed and microfilmed. We have a first set, here in the Truman Library, of microfilms of the papers that have been finished, and they're well worth reading. Unfortunately, though, I understand that there isn't a word about that meeting with Henry Clay in any of the diaries.) Charles Francis was also Martin Van Buren's running mate when Van Buren ran unsuccessfully for a second term in 1841, and he was later Lincoln's and Andrew Johnson's minister to England from 1861 to 1868. He might even have become the third President Adams, because he was considered a strong candidate in 1872, when Ulysses S. Grant was running for his second term, and polled the most votes in the first five ballots at the convention in Cincinnati. But he lost out on the sixth ballot to Horace Greeley, who was beaten by Grant and died shortly afterwards.

(Now *there's* a really sad story, the way Greeley's life ended. Greeley had a long and successful career as editor and founder of the *New York Tribune,* and as a reformer who was often ahead of his time, but his try for the presidency seemed to turn his luck around completely. He was the subject of brutal attacks and caricatures in newspapers all around the country during his election campaign, most of them calling him a traitor because he hated war and pleaded for peace at any cost during the Civil War, and also because he advocated amnesty for all southerners after the war. Then his wife died a few days before the election, and he was beaten decisively by that charismatic but incompetent fellow Grant, and the two blows one after the other caused him to become mentally ill. He was totally insane when he died soon after the election on November 29, 1872.)

Charles Francis Adams lived on for fourteen more years, doing the editing of his father's writings from 1874 to 1877. He's also remembered as the man largely responsible for persuading England to stick with the United States during the Civil War and not recognize the Confederacy, which they were close to doing.

Adams was opposed again by Jackson when he ran for a second term, and this time Jackson was elected overwhelmingly and went on to serve two terms. Jackson got 178 electoral votes to Adams's 83, and 647,292 popular votes, 56 percent, to Adams's 507,730 votes, 44 percent. Adams refused to attend Jackson's inauguration, a sore loser like his father, and then went back to Massachusetts and ran successfully for the House of Representatives, the only former president to serve as a congressman. He served in the House for seventeen years. He died in the Capitol Building, still serving his country. He had had a minor stroke in 1846 while walking with a friend in Boston, and on February 21, 1848, he had a sudden, second, massive stroke at his desk in the House, falling almost into the arms of the congressman next to him, David Fisher of Ohio. He remained in a coma after that and died two days later, and another colleague, Senator Thomas Hart Benton of Missouri, said quietly, "Where could death have found him but at the post of duty?"

He was a conscientious and well-meaning man, and I wish I could say more about his achievements than the couple of things I'm going to put down here. But there are really only two things that can be credited to him, and those only in part. One is the Monroe Doctrine, which, as I've said, he had such a large hand in thinking out and developing and writing that it should probably be called the John Quincy Adams Doctrine or at least the Monroe-Adams Doctrine. He also had a lot to do with our purchase during Monroe's administration of the parts of Florida that Jefferson didn't get in the Louisiana Purchase; Adams negotiated the treaty under which Spain gave us the rest of Florida in return for our writing off $5,000,000 they owed us. And he was also a capable and hard-working member of the House during those seventeen years after he left the White House. But practically nothing was accomplished in his own administration. He was the first president to think hard about improvements within our own country and advocated, among other things, a national university, an astronomical observatory, and countrywide roads that connected with each other. Congress, however, passed none of these things while he was president. So I've got to put him down as another minor president with very good intentions but no results.

I realize that some historians won't agree with this assessment, especially since so much of the history of that period was written by John Adams and John Quincy Adams themselves, and since so many other and later members of the Adams family became historians and wrote extensively about American history. John Quincy's grandson, Charles Francis Adams, Jr., was a railroad executive and president of the Union Pacific Railroad for six years, but also wrote a number of books on history and politics; Brooks Adams, another grandson, wrote a number of good books on history and economics, and as early as 1900 predicted in a book that the United States and Russia would end up as the two strongest world powers; and a third grandson, Henry Adams, became a professor of history at Harvard and the best-known historian of the family. His most famous books are his autobiography, *The Education of Henry Adams*, and *Mont-Saint-Michel and Chartres* and his study of our country during the time of Jefferson and Madison, which runs nine volumes. And of course a lot of the recent books coming out on the Adamses and related subjects have been written by other New England historians.

Well, they have a right to their prejudices, but it's important to take what they have to say and study it and compare it with what actually happened according to other reports. I just don't think there were any events in Adams's administration that were very outstanding.

TWENTY-SEVEN
My Favorite President: Andrew Jackson

AND that brings me to my personal favorite among our presidents (after Franklin Roosevelt, of course), Andrew Jackson.

There have been a great many books written about Jackson, and some of them are favorable and some of them aren't. Despite the books in that second category, he stands out in my mind as one of the seven or eight very great presidents of the United States. Each of the great ones was great for a different reason, but they were all great men, and the main reason I put Jackson in this category is that he knew what was right for the country and for the average man and woman, and he went to work to try to accomplish what was right even when his action wasn't very popular.

I remember one of the great things he did was when they were having a meeting in Washington, a political dinner, and Jackson got up and made a toast, and it almost upset the apple cart because his toast was that the Federal Union must be preserved. That wasn't what they expected from a southerner and a slaveholder, but it was typical of Jackson because he knew that the preservation of the United States was the most important thing for people from every part of the country, and he came right out and said it.

It's always been my opinion, in fact, that Maryland and West Virginia and Kentucky and Missouri refused to secede when the Civil War started because Jackson and his fellow Democrats worked hard at preventing them from going into the Confederacy. I can give you a concrete example of how hard that was to accomplish, since there was such a division of opinion even among family members who thought alike on most other subjects, and often the majority was on the Confederate side. If my memory serves me correctly, there were ninety-six thousand Kentuckians in the Confederate army and ninety-four thousand in the Union army. In Missouri, there were one hundred eighteen thousand Missourians in the Confederate army and one hundred sixteen thousand in the Federal army; those may not be the exact figures, but you get the general idea. Those were the states where so often families were against families. I also remember that there was one situation in Tennessee where there was a colonel in the Federal army who had two sons who were captains in the Confederate army. That didn't happen only in the border states, either. But I feel certain that it was as a result of Jackson's efforts to preserve the Union that those states stayed in, and of course the preservation of the Union was what Lincoln devoted his life to accomplishing a bit later on.

The campaign between Adams and Jackson was the first personal and partisan campaign for the presidency, the first really bitter campaign, and some very nasty things were said. Most of these were said about Jackson; I don't think there was so much said about Adams. You see, the times had become such that privileged people were in more complete control than ever under Adams and Henry Clay. They were both economic royalists, which is just a fancy phrase for rich people wanting to control everything and behave like kings. So Adams and other people on his side referred to Jackson as a man who was illiterate and uncouth, and said and wrote a great many other abusive things about him. And that same sort of slander was carried on against Jackson nearly all the time he was president of the United States, though they watched themselves and didn't go over the line and get *too* personal because they knew the old man might shoot them if they got too personal.

There are still books coming out which say that about Jackson, but he accomplished a lot of important things and had a number of important offices before he became president, and he was nothing like that picture some people have of him. He didn't go to Harvard or Yale or Princeton or any of the Ivy League colleges; he was educated in Tennessee, and mostly by a couple of clergymen, Dr. William Humphries and the Reverend James White Stephenson because his mother wanted him to become a Presbyterian minister before it became clear that he was too tough a citizen for that kind of thing. But he became a lawyer and a prosecutor for the western district of North Carolina, which was later separated away from the rest of the area and became the state of Tennessee, and he was very well thought of as an authority on law and legal procedure in that part of the country. He also became a plantation owner, just as the Virginians did when they first came to Virginia. He was a man of high standing in his community, and his advice was sought, and his help was sought, by all the people who were his neighbors. They all liked him; he was a good neighbor and a good man. And then he became a United States congressman and a senator and a superior court judge in Tennessee, so he was no ignoramus. He knew what he was doing all the time. (He was also a real authority on horses and knew how to pick a winning horse in a horse race, but that's another matter entirely.)

He didn't spell very well and his syntax was pretty bad. But the same was true of George Washington; he couldn't spell and his syntax also wasn't very good. And I've just finished reading a book in which the writer laughs at Jackson's successor, Martin Van Buren, and calls him an uneducated man because "he couldn't even spell." Well, you could also say that about Chaucer; Chaucer couldn't spell, either, though of course I'm only joking here and do realize that that was because spelling and other aspects of our language hadn't yet become standardized. But people like that writer just ignore the fact that practically nobody understood how to spell the English language until old Noah Webster set up a dictionary so all of us could find out how to spell things, or at least so all of us could spell things in the same way.

Jefferson was the only highly educated president in that period who understood English construction as well as we understand it today, but our other early presidents were also well-educated men who knew the history of government from start to finish. Some of us don't know it today as well as Jackson and Van Buren did, and Jackson wasn't any more uncouth than the rest of the people of that day.

But there's no doubt that he was subjected to a lot of snobbery during his lifetime, and it makes me mad sometimes to see that it's still going on in some books and in some magazine and newspaper articles and speeches where Jackson is mentioned. Fortunately, it didn't bother him very much because he was of the opinion that he was as good as anybody else, and he made it stand up. I suppose that's one of the reasons that the easterners didn't like him, although Harvard finally had to give him a degree because it came to the point where it was absolutely necessary to recognize him as a man who knew what he was doing and where he was going. His papers, though, still haven't received the attention, to this day, that they should have received. They're in the Capitol Building at Nashville, Tennessee, and I don't think they've been completely and thoroughly edited or completely gone over and indexed as they should be. The only plan for all of those papers is under a law that has been passed by the Congress to index and microfilm all presidential papers. That's in the mill right now, but it will take a long time to get it done. Meanwhile, his papers and everything else he wrote have never been published or edited by one of those New England historians, that whole army of New England historians. That's what the difficulty is. All the rest of the papers that have been published have been edited by one of those men, and they were all papers by presidents from the East. If I sound irritated, and even prejudiced, in this regard—well, I guess I am.

Jackson was born on March 15, 1767, the same year as John Quincy Adams. There's always been an argument over whether he was born in North Carolina or South Carolina because his father, a Scots-Irish farmer and linen-draper who was also named Andrew Jackson and came to this country in 1765, was hurt when a big log fell on him and died a few days before Andy was born, and his mother, Betty Hutchinson Jackson, a red-haired, blue-eyed, self-reliant woman, decided to go and live with her sister, Jane Crawford, in Lancaster County, South Carolina, and have her baby there. Some books say she got to Lancaster County and had her baby, and Jackson always said he was born in South Carolina, but other books say that she made a stop to see another sister, Margaret McCamie, in Union County, North Carolina, and gave birth to Andy Jackson earlier than expected there. I can't see where it makes any serious difference either way, but I know that North Carolina certainly claims him, because I once dedicated a statue in North Carolina to the three presidents who are supposed to have been born there, and Jackson was one of them.

The one thing that's certain is that Jackson wasn't born with a silver spoon and had a hard life as a child. His family was so poor that, when his father died, the family couldn't afford to put a headstone on his grave. He had two older brothers, Hugh and Robert, both of whom were born in Ireland before the Jacksons came to this country, but then the Revolutionary War came along and both young men died as a result of the war. Hugh died of heat exhaustion following a battle in 1779, and Robert came down with smallpox while a prisoner of the British and died shortly after being freed in a prisoner exchange in April 1781. Jackson lost his mother as a result of the Revolutionary War, too; she worked as a nurse during the war, taking care of American soldiers on British prison ships, and got cholera herself and died when Jackson was fourteen.

Jackson was a soldier in the Continental Army himself, even though he was only thirteen when he joined up in 1780. His uncle, Major Robert Crawford, was commander of a militia company in South Carolina, and Andy and his brother Robert became part of that company. The following April, however, the two boys were captured by the British and held prisoner for a couple of weeks, during which time they both got the smallpox from which Robert soon died.

Jackson recovered from the disease, but one thing happened while he was a prisoner that he never forgot, and that, in a way, shaped the rest of his life. Some British officer tried to make the Jackson kids shine his shoes, and they absolutely refused to do it, and the officer went at them with his saber. He hit Andy over the head with the saber, not with the sharp edge of the saber, and cut his head only a little bit but also cut his pride. After that, Jackson hated any person who was trying to press down on the rights and privileges of the ordinary citizen. I think that's what gave him his principle of equality for everybody. (I don't want to make it sound like that British officer gave the boys a couple of love taps, or that the British behaved like gentlemen during the couple of weeks in which the Jacksons were prisoner. One of the whacks of that saber cut one of Jackson's hands right to the bone, and then the British soldiers marched the boys, still bleeding and given no medical care, to a prison camp forty miles away. And they were fed nothing but stale bread and dirty water until they were let go, which is probably why they both came down with smallpox. But it was the blow to his boyish pride that Jackson talked about the rest of his life.)

He spent the rest of his boyhood being shuttled between relatives, but he was a bright young man who learned to read pretty much on his own by the time he was five years old, and got to be so good at it that, since most of the adults in the community couldn't read at all, he was given a regular assignment of reading newspapers aloud to residents whenever papers arrived in the area. He also never forgot being asked, when he was nine, to read the Declaration of Independence aloud to the local citizens when a copy came to them in 1776. And in time, as I've described, he became a lawyer and a judge, member of the House of Representatives, and a senator twice. (Though he later said that he didn't like the Senate very much, particularly the first time he served in the Senate. It didn't move fast enough for him, and he resigned after only five months.) He was six feet one inch tall as an adult, and thin, weighing about one hundred and forty pounds, and with red hair and blue eyes like his mother.

He was always a prideful man, and sometimes too much so. When he was twenty years old and just beginning to practice law, he decided that an attorney on the opposite side had insulted him and challenged the man to a duel. Fortunately, the seconds on both sides calmed down

Jackson and his opponent, and both men fired into the air. Then, in 1803, while he was a judge, he challenged the governor of Tennessee, John Sevier, to a duel because he heard that Sevier had made an insulting comment about Mrs. Jackson, but again neither man was injured. Later on, however, in 1806, Jackson fought still another duel with another lawyer, Charles Dickinson, who was also supposed to have said something insulting about Mrs. Jackson, and Dickinson wasn't as lucky. The two men fought their duel in a forest in Harrison's Mill, Kentucky, standing only eight feet apart. Dickinson had the reputation of being the most skillful man with a pistol in Tennessee, a fact that didn't stop Jackson from challenging him the minute he heard about Dickinson's remarks, and Dickinson fired the first shot. It was a clear and visible hit, and the seconds actually saw dust fly out of Jackson's coat as the bullet entered his chest. But Jackson remained erect and his second insisted that Dickinson return to his position, where Jackson fired and killed him. Dickinson's bullet remained in Jackson's chest all of his life because the bullet was too close to his heart to be removed.

And in 1813, he got into another situation that left bullets inside him for a long time. He served as second for a friend who was dueling with a man named Jesse Benton, and Benton's brother, Thomas Hart Benton, the fellow who later became a senator from Missouri, made some nasty remark about Jackson. Jackson immediately promised to horsewhip both men if they ever showed up in his vicinity, and when he learned that the Bentons were in Nashville, he went right over to the hotel at which they were staying. He spotted Thomas Hart Benton first and went after him, but he didn't see Jesse Benton standing in back of him, and Jesse Benton fired a bullet right into him. Then, as Jackson lay on the ground, Thomas Hart Benton fired more bullets into him. Doctors insisted that Jackson's left arm had to come off, but he refused to permit them to amputate, and he carried bullets in that arm for nineteen years before an operation removed them. He was a tough man, all right, and he regained full use of his arm not too long after he was shot. I guess that's one of the reasons I admire him.

Those were pretty wild times in our country, and all I can say about those terrible events is that it's a good thing that people eventually became smart enough to stop fighting duels and just limited themselves to calling SOBs SOBs. But these things established Jackson's reputation as a hard-nosed fellow who was afraid of absolutely nothing, and certainly softened, to some extent at least, the things the press and his political enemies said about him when he entered politics.

The reason that Sevier and Dickinson and other people said those insulting things about Mrs. Jackson, and the reason many of the ugliest things said about Jackson during his presidential campaign were in connection with his wife and his marriage, were because his early relationship with the lady and their eventual marriage were unusual, to say the least. Mrs. Jackson, the former Rachel Donelson Robards, was already married to another man, Lewis Robards, but was living apart from him at a boardinghouse run by her parents near Nashville. Robards, a citizen of Kentucky, married Rachel when she was seventeen, at which time the Donelsons were living in that state, but Robards was pathologically jealous and kept accusing his wife of having affairs with other men.

Despite the fact that Rachel and everyone else made it clear that his fears were entirely imaginary, he finally sent her to Tennessee to live with her parents until he called for her, and it was then that Jackson came there as a boarder and the two young people, both aged twenty-four, met and fell in love. Robards soon heard that this time he had a real problem and insisted that his wife return to him in Kentucky, and she went. But again he began to behave irrationally and accuse her of having affairs with everyone in the area, and Jackson heard about *that* and went to Kentucky and took her away. Robards got the Kentucky legislature to allow him to sue for divorce, and Jackson misunderstood and thought a divorce had actually been granted—or at least he said he did; I'm sort of on the fence about that one—and married Rachel in 1791.

But there hadn't been a divorce, and as soon as Jackson and Rachel Robards started living together, Robards brought his action for divorce and was now able to do so on the grounds of adultery. The divorce was granted in September 1793, and Jackson, calling it a remarriage, married Rachel again early in 1794. He remained deeply in love with her for the rest of their lives, even though her youthful beauty soon left her, and even though she was sometimes embarrassing and backwoodsy, smoking a corncob pipe and insisting that the Old World was spelled Urope, while Jackson, despite that stuff about uncouthness, became sort of sophisticated and was known in time as one of the best-dressed men in Washington. But Jackson's political enemies kept raking up the charge of adultery and that meaningless first marriage ceremony, and some historians believe that the agony caused by these revelations finally brought about Rachel's death at the age of sixty-one. She developed heart trouble, and though Jackson tried to keep newspapers that contained the stories away from her, she learned about them and became increasingly ill and died on December 28, 1828, just weeks after Jackson's election as president. And Jackson said bitterly at her graveside, "I can and do forgive all my enemies. But those vile wretches who've slandered her must look to God for mercy."

It was as a soldier again, this time in the War of 1812, that Jackson established his reputation and became one of the most popular men in the country. He was appointed as a major general in the Tennessee Volunteers by Governor William Blount, and offered to start out with the 2,070 other volunteers under his command and take Quebec away from the British. He probably could have done it, too; I'm sure it's clear by this time that Jackson was a pretty aggressive fellow, and so were the young Tennesseans who volunteered to serve under him. They were what you might call the squirrel hunters; they liked to fight, and if they couldn't fight someone else, they liked to fight among themselves. But Jackson was in some political trouble at that point, and his suggestion was turned down. This was the time when Aaron Burr was setting out to start his own country, and Jackson made the mistake of believing Burr when Burr said that he was working under government orders to stop an invasion by the Spaniards; Jackson gave Burr a couple of boats and a lot of military information, which infuriated President Madison even though Jackson backed off the minute he knew the truth.

Then, when the British moved down from Canada and captured Detroit, Jackson offered to take his men there and recapture it, and this, too, was refused. Instead, he was told to move his men to Natchez, Mississippi, and wait there for a possible move into Florida. And when he got *there,* marching his men through a winter as bitter as the one Washington encountered at Valley Forge, he was told by the general in charge, that old scoundrel James Wilkinson, that they weren't needed and he could disband his outfit and tell his men to head on home by themselves. Jackson wouldn't do that exactly as ordered. He led his men back to Tennessee in the same orderly fashion in which they'd traveled to Mississippi, taking no special privileges and suffering through the still-icy winter along with them. It was the march to Mississippi and back, incidentally, that got Jackson his famous nickname; one of his men remarked that the old man was as hard as a hickory tree—he was forty-five at the time, which made him an old man to the boys he was commanding—and the name stuck and he became known as Hickory Jackson, and then, when his red hair turned grayer, as Old Hickory.

In October 1813, Jackson finally received a real assignment; he was told to go to Mississippi again and fight the Creek Indians, who had just attacked Fort Mims, in the section of the Mississippi Territory that is now part of Alabama, and killed two hundred people. Jackson was still recovering from the bullets fired into him by the Benton brothers, but he got out of bed and put an outfit of volunteers together again, this time with two thousand five hundred soldiers, and set out for Mississippi. He got little support because supplies and additional men promised to him failed to arrive, and some of his own men finished up the brief periods they'd agreed to serve and left for home, but he fought a battle near the town of Talladega against a thousand Indians led by Chief Red Eagle, killing three hundred Indians and sending the others scurrying. Then he followed them, and after allowing all Indian women and children to leave, he fought them again and defeated the Creeks completely, killing seven hundred and fifty Indians and losing only forty-nine of his own men. (Again I wish there were a better word than ''only'' in this context, and I use it just to show the big difference in the numbers.) As reprisal, the Creeks had to give the United States twenty-three million acres out of their land ownership. And in a typical Indian display of admiration for an effective enemy, they also gave Jackson three square miles of land for himself.

I'm going to go off on another tangent here, but it's a very important tangent because this seems to be as good a place as any to say a thing or two about the treatment that the original population of the continent received from the American people, which is as bad a blot on our history as our treatment of black people. That's about the only thing I hold against old Jackson—not his battles with the Creeks, because I suppose they were necessary to keep the Indians from going on and killing more people, but the fact that he didn't do anything to help the Indians when he was president. The Seminoles and the Choctaws were terribly mistreated when Jackson was president, and I do hold that against him. In fact, let me go off on a tangent here and discuss our treatment of the Indians in the next chapter.

TWENTY-EIGHT
America's Treatment of the Indians

SOMETIME or other I think I ought to write an essay about the dreadful treatment given the Indians. If I never get around to it, I'm hoping that somebody, someday, will write something that outlines the patriotism of those Indian chiefs who were only trying to save their own country from exploitation by the whites, who made treaties with the Indians and broke them every time they made one. *Somebody* certainly ought to take the story of all those great Indians who were fighting for their own people and their own country and make it perfectly plain that there never were a people who were more thoroughly mistreated. I don't agree for a second with the historians who say that Indians were dirty, cruel, and lazy. There were Indian tribes on the East Coast and in central New York—the Iroquois, for example, and the Algonquins in Canada —who were working toward an organization that, in the long run, I think, would have made them great statesmen and a great asset to our country if they'd been treated fairly, which they weren't, of course. I've just read an article about those tribes that was written by a couple of men who don't like Indians, but I came away from it thinking more than ever that the Iroquois and the Algonquins were great people.

There were certainly Indians who developed a hatred for white settlers and went on murderous rampages, slipping up and killing white people and scalping them. But that was because they felt that their lands were being taken away from them, and they were, no question about it, and without compensation. Whenever the whites infringed on one of those treaties that we made and then broke, why, the Indians would fight back. It was a terrible thing when some family would be massacred by the Indians, but the Indians were only protecting their ownership of the property that had been taken away from them.

The real displacement of the Indian began after the Civil War; it was then that most of the Indian tragedy took place, when one president after another, Grant and Hayes and Garfield and—for a minute I couldn't think of the name of the striped-pants boy who followed Garfield, but I remember now that it was Chester A. Arthur—offered discharged Federal soldiers homesteads on Indian land. That homestead business was to give former soldiers a means of livelihood so that the economy of the United States wouldn't be upset, and some former Confederate soldiers went out west for homesteads, too, and it worked. But nobody seemed to give much thought to the livelihood of the Indians; the whites just casually took all their hunting grounds and all the places where they'd lived for centuries away from them. The citizens of the United States, by way of the president, would declare an area as public land, and the whites would take it over.

But there was plenty of mistreatment of the Indians before the Civil War as well. The early settlers had a very different attitude toward the Indians than they should have had. Many of the Indians were inclined to be friendly to the whites and were perfectly willing to make treaties with them. But the attitude of the white settlers from Europe was that the Indians were savages and an inferior race, and therefore the settlers had a perfect right to chase them off the land and take it away from them, which is what we did eventually.

They weren't an inferior race at all, of course. They were wonderfully wise people, and there were Indian setups in the Western Hemisphere that were almost ideal systems of government. Take the Iroquois in New York: they were an organization of five tribes known as the Five Nations, and they were organized in such a way that their representative government was almost parallel with the government of the United States under the Constitution with its states and its representatives in the national government and its state governments.

And the Indians had some very great leaders. Some of the greatest leaders this country ever produced were the leaders of the Indian tribes,

men like Pontiac in Michigan and Wisconsin, and Tecumseh of the Shaw-
nees, and Geronimo down in the Southwest, and Chief Black Kettle of
the Cheyennes, and Sitting Bull and Crazy Horse of the Sioux, and Chief
Joseph of the Nez Percé, who performed one of the greatest military
maneuvers in the history of the world. He took his whole tribe—I think
it was something like eighteen hundred men, women, and children—and
outmaneuvered practically the whole cavalry of the United States, including one of the great strategists of the Civil War, General Oliver Otis
Howard, moving his people more than a thousand miles up toward Canada, going from the valley of the Salmon River out in Idaho to Montana
east of what is now the Glacier National Park, which is a record that has
never been equaled. Howard's outfit and another force of soldiers headed
by another general were four miles apart, and neither of those generals
knew where the other was, but Chief Joseph knew where both of them
were and he got his people all out.

Finally, after the cavalry kept chasing him and killed off many of
his people, he surrendered, but old Joseph outmarched them all. The big
dam out in Montana, the Chief Joseph Dam, was named for that great
old Indian who outmaneuvered the cavalry of the United States for over
a thousand miles, and they never did catch up with him, not really.
(Howard, incidentally, was a pretty good fellow in many ways. He developed considerable respect for Chief Joseph, even though they were
on opposite sides of the fence, and in 1881 wrote an admiring biography
of the Indian leader. And he was also one of the first white men to work
for the welfare of the black people. He was chief commissioner of the
Freedmen's Bureau, created by President Andrew Johnson in 1865, and
then he founded and was the president from 1869 to 1873 of Howard
University, that excellent school in Washington whose student body and
faculty are mostly black people.)

The Indians also had a high regard for the individual and the dignity
of the individual, even where the enemy was concerned. The individual
in the great Indian tribes was a man of dignity and poise and had a right
to his say before the council, and his rights were always respected. The
Indians also were very fond of children, and they were very good to their
youngsters as they grew up. They tried to train them, both male and
female, to the duties that they considered their proper place in life. I
don't like the fact that they made the women do all the heavy drudgery
that needed to be done, but after the women became old, they were placed
in the council as part of the government of the tribe. At least that was
true in the Iroquois tribes, and I think that women in the other tribes,
after they reached a certain age, were looked up to and respected as
councilors.

Mostly, Indian lands weren't individually owned. For instance, the

Sioux had hunting grounds in various places and followed the buffalo north and south. And Chief Joseph and his people, in the valley of the Salmon River and the Snake River out in Oregon and Idaho, moved various places during various times of the year for fish on the Columbia River and for hunting grounds wherever game was most plentiful. The Indians just felt that they owned the whole country, and I think they did because they were the first occupants. But it was finally decided that the West was a part of the United States, and the presidents issued orders in which titles were given to settlers who would go in and stay for a certain period of time, and it worked out that the people who got the worst of it were the Indians.

The local Indian governments were substantially independent of each other. Each tribe had a chief equivalent to our president, and a council equivalent to our cabinet, and they also had a separate war council, an organization of fighting men known as the war leaders, which was international in the sense that the tribes sometimes banded together for defense and protection, though, like the operation of the United States, civil control never got out of the hands of the civil government. They didn't have any compulsory military service. The fighting men were highly honored, and Indian youngsters were told practically from birth that it might be necessary for them to defend their own people when the time came, and it was considered the greatest honor in the world for the warriors to fight for the benefit of the whole tribe. It was a volunteer organization entirely, and that's the reason they were so highly respected.

But it was a losing battle almost from the start, and the Indians didn't really have a chance because of the superior weapons and the murderous approach that many white settlers made toward them. The list of mistreatment and treachery toward the Indians is almost endless.

Practically every great chief ended up murdered or a prisoner. Tecumseh was shot in the back. Black Kettle made several treaties with the Americans and did his best to live up to them, agreeing to move his tribe to a reservation, and then General George Custer, the showoff and the Douglas MacArthur of his day, attacked the tribe without warning and without reason and Black Kettle and his whole family were slaughtered. The man who ordered the actual killing was another officer and a gentleman, an old Baptist preacher who was also a colonel of a regiment out in Colorado. He was just a fanatic. That man did some things for the country during the Civil War and was pretty well thought of at the time, but I never thought much of a man who would kill an old Indian and his whole family when they were about to obey the law, and an unjust law at that.

Sitting Bull and Crazy Horse were called to a conference by General George Crook, a man who was perfectly named, and Crook quoted the president and said the Indians would get everything they wanted. They didn't get anything they wanted, and in the end they were both assassinated, killed by Indian police who were hired to work for the soldiers. And Geronimo, the Apache chief who was such a fierce fighter that they were all afraid of him, ended up practically under house arrest in Oklahoma. When I was stationed in Fort Sill in 1917, they showed me the little brick building in which he lived during the last part of his life. It's still there, and if you want to see it, they'll show it to you and brag about that's where Geronimo lived. At the same time, of course, they'll call him a murderer and a cutthroat, and he may have been in some ways, but he was only trying to protect his own territory for his own people. And I don't have anything against him for doing that.

And things weren't helped much when the government created Indian bureaus for the alleged protection of Indian rights. Every one of our Indian bureaus in Washington was saddled with crooks and cheats. Once in a while you would have an honest man on the job, and then the difficulties would be exposed, and for a short period things would be all right. But it never lasted. There were several men who tried their best to do justice to the Indians, but they didn't have much of a chance because the crooks were always standing at the door ready to take what was loose. The Indians didn't understand the approach of the white man in business dealings, and they got cheated every time they got into a trade with a white man.

And in a sense, you might even say that we had less excuses for our mistreatment of Indians than of blacks. Everybody with any common sense at all, no matter what his position was or where he lived, knew that slavery was wrong, but at least the flimsy argument could be made that they'd been brought into the country to serve as the laboring force of the South, and that many of the plantation owners tried to behave decently toward them and at least fed and clothed them properly. But there wasn't even that much of an answer to the way we behaved toward the Indians. It was total callousness and greed and nothing more. They were the owners and the occupants of the land, and they were treated as a conquered people, with their land taken away from them and distributed by the government of the United States to homesteaders and settlers.

The Spaniards were even worse in their treatment of Indians in North and South America. The slaughter of Indians by the Spaniards was another of the most terrible events in world history, particularly the slaughter by Cortez in Mexico and Pizarro in Peru. They were ruthless in their treatment of the people who had developed two of the greatest empires in history. They were wonderful people, both the Aztecs and the Incas, and the Spaniards enslaved them. In fact, the Spaniards were the first ones to introduce slavery on the American continent, not only by importing the blacks from Africa but also enslaving the Indians who were already here.

All I can say about the conquest of the two great empires south of us is that the people who point out Geronimo's house and talk about him as a cutthroat ought to do their talking about the *real* cutthroats, the men who murdered and enslaved the Aztecs and the Incas. All they were interested in was the gold those people had, and they got it by destroying civilizations that were far ahead of the Egyptian civilization we read so much about.

In North America, the French made friends of the Indians because they wanted them on their side against the British, and they treated them reasonably well. But the Spanish never did; they treated the Indians like dogs. And the attitude of the Spanish toward the Indians hasn't changed all that much over the years. There's been a certain amount of inter-marriage and absorption into a mutual society between Spaniards and Indians, but not to a very great extent. You'll find that the people who control the governments made up of the Peruvian empire, Peru and Ecuador and Colombia, are the Spanish citizens who kept their bloodline more or less clear, and that's also true in Venezuela.

The same thing is true in Argentina and Chile. In Brazil, the Portuguese did more mixing with the Indians than any other group in South America, but the white Spaniards are still on top and run much of the country. And it really isn't any different in Mexico. I've been in Mexico on occasion, and they're fine people, but I think you'll find that what might be called the Spanish strain still runs the government. Juárez was an Indian and brought about the freedom of Mexico from the French, who were in charge at that point, so there were times when people of Indian descent were important in Mexican history. Still, the people who run the Mexican government in almost every administration are those who claim direct Spanish descent.

But the citizens of the United States were bad enough, and I suspect that the only reason we didn't enslave the American Indians was because the American Indians wouldn't be enslaved. There was never any slavery in the Indian tribes; even when they conquered another tribe, they never tried to make slaves out of the people of that other tribe. And I think the only reason we didn't try to make slaves out of the people we conquered with our superior weapons is that we knew that an American Indian would rather die than be anybody's slave. An American Indian considered himself as good as any two white men, and in many instances they were.

In the end, of course, we did conquer the Indians, and most of them were herded onto reservations, driven out or marched out, and others just died out. In the Southeast, the Cherokees and the Chickasaws and the Osages were simply moved off their lands and brought over to Oklahoma, which nobody thought was any good at the time. (It turned out to be one of the richest lands in the world and made many Indians equally rich, but then the white man stepped in to cheat them of everything they had and succeeded in most cases.) The Iroquois Five Nations held out longer than most other tribes, but they also were finally put on reservations in New York and elsewhere and had their lands taken from them and given to whites; and the last time I looked it up, there were 16,000 Iroquois left and 11,500 of them were still on reservations. And the great Sioux tribe of the Northern Central Plains were pretty much wiped out, and so were the Apaches in Arizona, New Mexico, and southern California.

There were a few exceptions to our almost total injustice to the Indians. We never did succeed in conquering the Seminoles down in Florida. I saw their chief the last time I was in Florida as president, and he presented me with an Indian-style shirt and reminded me that they had never surrendered to the government of the United States. I told him I couldn't blame them. And up there in Niagara Falls, when they were trying to get the St. Lawrence Seaway through, they had to make a pretty good settlement with the Iroquois, at least what was left of them, and the Iroquois finally got what was owed to them. And if you go west of the Mississippi, you'll find a lot of Osage Indians who own big parcels of land and are maintaining their property and doing okay, because, even though they were pushed onto reservations, they eventually got the United States to allow them to own property individually like all other Americans. For this reason, since much of their land turned out to have oil under it, they're known as "the weathiest Indian tribe in America."

But even at that they should have done better, because, in addition to the fact that, as I've said, some of them were cheated out of their oil holdings, I gather that others were also talked out of their agricultural land holdings as well. As I understand it, there was a trader out there named Sibley, and he got the Osages to give him, and some other settlers west of the Mississippi, all of the land between the mouth of the Osage River and the head of the Kansas River, in western Missouri and eastern Kansas, in return for the privilege of their trading at Sibley's Trading Post. Now, I don't know whether that's true or not, but I think you'll find that many of the deeds to the land in this part of the country show that Chief White Hair, who was the head man of the Osages, made that deal. And I had an assistant secretary of the air force or the navy, darned if I remember which, whose name was Whitehair, who was a great-great-grandson of old Chief White Hair, and he told me that it old White Hair hadn't been so easy with Sibley and the rest of those people, he and the rest of his family would be millionaires because they had some of the greatest agricultural land in western Missouri and eastern Kansas.

It seems as though about the only thing we gave the Indians in return for everything we took from them was what we used to call consumption—TB. They're very susceptible to that disease, and some Indians have to stay indoors almost all the time. They were the healthiest race that anyone ever met up with when the white people first came over here, and that was the gift we gave them. You know how I'd mark our papers on the Indians? Zero minus.

Our conscience was finally awakened thirty or forty years ago, and we've had two or three Indian agents in this century who are really looking after the welfare of the Indians. Now we have a large number of Eskimos in Alaska who are being properly taken care of, I think, and the Indians in New Mexico and Arizona have the best reservations in the country and are being protected. Nobody's allowed to go in there and take it away from them. I think they're being treated justly now. I think it's as near justice as can be given to them after they'd been exploited to death.

I tried to look after Indian rights all the time I was president. Whenever any bill came up that looked to me like a new attempt to exploit them, it got vetoed. You'll find, I think, that at least three such bills were vetoed when I was president, because they were trying to take away the few lands that the Indians had left to them. I think one of them even affected old Chief Joseph's settlement in Montana, the place where he finally ended up. And I vetoed a bill that would have taken away everything the Indians in Nevada had left if Senator Pat McCarran of that state had gotten his bill through. McCarran was a man I disliked and distrusted when I was in office, both as a human being and as a public official, and this was typical of him, I'm afraid; he was trying to arrange it so that all the Indian lands around Lake Tahoe were turned loose for settlement. It was the old business all over again: just take it away from the Indians. But I vetoed it, and saved the Indians from that much, anyway.

TWENTY-NINE
Jackson, Champion of the Common People

GETTING back to Jackson, his victory over the Creeks brought him back into favor again in Washington, and a couple of months later, he was given the rank of major general in the regular army rather than the volunteers. Then he heard a rumor that Spanish officials were helping out their British friends in areas of Florida still held by Spain, and he sent a scout to Pensacola to see if he could get information about that. The scout reported back that the British were definitely being allowed to use Pensacola as a naval base, and Jackson moved down there immediately and captured the town.

Then Jackson learned that the British were planning to capture New Orleans and headed over there. In New Orleans, Jackson put through some extremely strict measures to make sure that the city and his men were completely prepared for the British assault if and when it came; he dismissed all local officials, including the state legislature, and placed the city under martial law, and he also ordered the execution of some American soldiers who deserted and were then recaptured, saying in effect that he expected the British force to be much larger than his own and had to prevent his army from becoming even smaller through increased desertions. Some people felt he was only doing what he had to do, but others felt his actions were high-handed and excessive, and a federal judge finally served him with a writ of habeas corpus. (For people who don't know what "habeas corpus" means, which certainly included me during the early part of my life, it's a Latin phrase that translates as "you have the body," and it was used at first in situations when some person or some authoritative group might be imprisoning someone unlawfully —holding the prisoner without telling him the charges against him or without a proper trial or something of that sort. The judge issued a writ of habeas corpus to require the person or the people doing the imprisoning to produce "the body of the prisoner" to determine if he was receiving due process. Habeas corpus was then broadened to allow judges to ask questions in any situations where liberties were possibly being violated or reduced beyond the needs of an existing emergency, and that was the situation with the writ in Jackson's case.) Jackson, however, ignored the writ, and the judge fined him $1,000, which he paid.

But he was absolutely right in his information about the impending British assault on New Orleans, and in his prediction that the British force would be much larger than his own. On December 23, 1814, a combined force of British soldiers and soldiers led by General Sir Edward Michael Pakenham, an outstanding officer who had served under Wellington and helped him defeat the French in Europe, landed a few miles east of New Orleans and headed toward the city. Ironically, as you've probably already realized, this was just one day before the Treaty of Ghent was signed, and the terms of the treaty had already been worked out and agreed upon by both sides; but communications were so slow in those times that neither the British nor the Americans facing each other near New Orleans knew it, and fighting was fierce and continuous.

Jackson and his men managed to stop the British for a while, but then they retreated to an old, unused canal four miles outside New Orleans and built a defensive wall out of logs and mud alongside the canal. British soldiers and sailors kept arriving until Pakenham had about ten thousand men, as compared to Jackson's less than five thousand soldiers, and that including every fighting man Jackson could round up—even the young pirate Jean Lafitte and his followers. The British had approached and offered LaFitte £30,000 and a commission in the British navy if he served with them, but he chose instead to help out the Americans in return for a pardon for himself and his men, and Jackson accepted at once.

On January 8, 1815, a thick fog developed, and the British decided to take advantage of the fog cover and move on New Orleans. But again, as the British had done in some battles in the Revolutionary War, they marched forward in strict formation and in their bright uniforms, and

Jackson and his men were ready for them behind their mud and log wall. In the battle that followed, Pakenham was killed and 2,600 of his men were killed, wounded, or taken prisoner, as compared to eight Americans killed and thirteen wounded.

Pakenham's body was sent back to England for burial, and Franklin Roosevelt told me a story about that in the White House one day, but I think I'd better ask people to skip this paragraph if they're squeamish. When they went to ship the body back to Britain, according to the story, they pickled Pakenham in alcohol and tied the barrel of alcohol in which he was pickled to the mast. But the sailors down below found out that there was a barrel of alcohol attached to the mast, and they took a gimlet and bored a hole in it and got the alcohol out and drank it, so Pakenham was not in any condition to be buried when he got back to England. That's the story told to me by Franklin Roosevelt. I don't know where he got it, or whether it's true or not, but it's an interesting story. I think it's probably true. I don't think there's any doubt that if those sailors found out that there was a barrel of alcohol attached to the mast on the main deck, they wouldn't have hesitated to bore holes in it to get the alcohol regardless of what else was in the barrel.

Anyway, the Battle of New Orleans was the only real American victory of the War of 1812, and even though it was an unnecessary battle because the war had officially ended two weeks previously, it made Jackson famous and admired throughout the United States. Congress even gave Jackson back that thousand-dollar fine, though, to tell the truth, he didn't actually collect it until thirty years later.

When Monroe became president in 1816, he offered Jackson the job of secretary of war, but Jackson turned it down and said he preferred to stay on in active military service. The Seminoles were attacking American settlements in Florida frequently at this time, coming out of the Spanish parts of Florida and with fugitive slaves fighting along with them, and Jackson was sent to see what he could do about the situation. Monroe instructed Jackson to enter Spanish territory only if it was absolutely necessary to do so because he was "pursuing the enemy," but Jackson told Monroe that there'd always be trouble in that part of the country if Florida remained under Spanish control to give sanctuary to Seminoles on the warpath there, and he also pointed out that there were British residents in Spanish Florida busily stirring up the Indians against United States citizens. Jackson hinted that it might not be a bad idea to try to take Florida away from the Spanish while he was down there fighting the Seminoles, and the result was that he got permission to do a lot more than the official orders if things pointed in that direction. So again Jackson went a lot further than expected and did what some people thought was only his duty and others thought was excessive; he took over some Spanish forts, threw out the Spanish governor of the territory and put in one of his own officers as governor, and ordered the execution of two British citizens, Robert Ambrister and Alexander Arbuthnot, as ringleaders in plots to get the Seminoles to attack Americans. And again he found himself in plenty of trouble.

The ringleaders in *that* movement were the two men that Jackson later came to despise more than anyone else in the world, John C. Calhoun and Henry Clay. (To get ahead of the story just a little bit, Jackson was asked, after he left the White House, to name two things he had left undone that he thought he ought to have done. He said that he should have hanged John C. Calhoun and shot Henry Clay. If you're wondering about the distinction between the different ends he yearned to give the two men, the answer is that Jackson thought he should have fought a duel against Clay for insulting Mrs. Jackson and shot him, and he thought he should have hung Calhoun as a traitor.)

At this point, Clay was speaker of the House and asked that Congress condemn Jackson's actions in Florida, and Calhoun was Monroe's secretary of war, the job Jackson had refused, and went to Monroe and suggested that Jackson should be arrested, though he asked Monroe not to make it public that the suggestion had come from him. Spain also put up a considerable protest, saying it would declare war on the United States if its forts and control of its territory weren't returned immediately. But Congress refused to censure Jackson and Monroe refused to have him arrested, and Jackson found himself more popular than ever. We straightened things out with Spain by buying their Florida territory for $5,000,000, and Jackson was appointed governor of the territory in 1821.

Jackson stayed in that job just long enough to make sure that things in Florida were running smoothly, and then, in 1823, he became a senator again. You'll recall that I mentioned that the first time he was in the Senate, which was back in 1797, he was so bored by what he considered the snail's pace of that august body that he quit after five months, but this time he lasted two years before quitting again. There were a couple of interruptions or almost-interruptions: in 1824, President Monroe offered him the job of minister to Mexico, and Jackson thought about that for a while before turning it down, and then, of course, later that year, as you'll also recall, he ran for president against John Quincy Adams and did better in both electoral and popular votes than Adams but lost out when the House of Representatives picked Adams. After that happened, Jackson stayed on in the Senate into 1825, then resigned again to devote himself full-time to building up alliances and increasing his popularity even more so that he'd win for sure over Adams the next time, in 1828.

When Jackson was in the Senate that second time, incidentally, an interesting bit of irony occurred the first time he showed up to take his seat and his desk. The fellow at the desk right next to his was Thomas Hart Benton, the man who'd pumped him full of lead back in 1813, and now a senator from my home state of Missouri. Jackson knew, of course, that Benton was now in the Senate, but he didn't expect to find his old enemy sitting inches away from him. For a minute, the two men stared at each other, and then Jackson, who respected strong enemies as much as the Indians he'd fought a while back, reached out and shook Benton's hand. In time, even though Jackson still had Benton's bullets in his body, the two men became close friends, and Benton campaigned all over the place for Jackson when Jackson ran again in 1828.

In those days, it wasn't considered proper for a presidential candidate to campaign for himself; the candidates were expected to stand on a pedestal, aloof from the hurly-burly of politics, and let other people tell the country how good they were. But Jackson considered that tradition nothing more than a bunch of baloney, and when he was invited to New Orleans in 1828 to celebrate the thirteenth anniversary of his victory over Pakenham and his soldiers and sailors, he hurried down there and did a lot of talking, in that city and on the way down, about his presidential hopes and plans.

He also took the advice of experienced politicians in his party and accepted John C. Calhoun as his running mate, despite his personal dislike for Calhoun, because his advisors felt that Calhoun was needed to bring in southern votes. The reason was that Jackson and some of his followers had given halfhearted support to a protective tariff bill, a bill that northerners liked because it helped the growing textile industry by reducing foreign competition, which would be reluctant to bring in textiles and pay a tariff on the goods brought in, but that southerners hated because they felt that foreign manufacturers would retaliate by refusing to buy cotton and other raw American goods. The Jackson people really expected the bill to fail, which would give them points with northerners for trying and not offend southerners too much because the bill hadn't gotten through anyway. But the bill surprised everybody by passing and reduced Jackson's popularity in the South even though he was, of course, a southerner himself.

He didn't learn until after the election that Calhoun was the man who tried to get him arrested back in 1818, or I doubt that he would have agreed to his party's choice for the vice-presidential candidate despite the political value of the man. He also didn't guess that Calhoun thought the opposite of the way he thought on practically every issue and would oppose him on practically everything. But the Jackson/Calhoun ticket was an extremely strong one, particularly since they were up against the aristocratic John Quincy Adams, running on the National Republican ticket, and the equally aristocratic fellow he picked as his running mate, Richard Rush, the son of a signer of the Declaration of Independence, Benjamin Rush, and a former attorney general of Pennsylvania, comptroller of the United States Treasury, and attorney general in Monroe's cabinet and secretary of the treasury in Adams's cabinet.

In a sense, the election came down to a contest between the symbol of the privileged upper class of the East, as represented by Adams, and the symbol of the average working man of the North and South and the settlers of the West, as represented by homespun Andy Jackson. And there were a lot more of the latter than the former. Jackson received 647,286 popular votes to Adams's 507,064 votes, 56 percent to 44 percent, and 178 electoral votes to Adams's 83. Jackson received the majority of electoral votes in fifteen states—Alabama, Georgia, Illinois, Indiana, Kentucky, Louisiana, Mississippi, Missouri, New York, North Carolina, Ohio, Pennsylvania, Tennessee, South Carolina, and Virginia—and Adams received the majority in nine states—Connecticut, Delaware, Maine, Maryland, Massachusetts, New Hampshire, New Jersey, Rhode Island, and Vermont. In those days, as you know, the vice president was voted for separately in the electoral college, and Calhoun did almost as well, receiving 171 electoral votes to Rush's 83, with another fellow, William Smith of South Carolina, getting the other 7. And the Democrats were now in charge.

It was a return to real Jeffersonian democracy when Jackson came into power. Jackson was a great admirer of Thomas Jefferson, and he thought that Jefferson's idea that the everyday man ought to have a hand in the government was the right thing. And that's what he tried to do. The people who voted for Jackson were strongly in his corner because they felt he was interested in the welfare of the little man, the small farmer and the small businessman and other people like that, and he did his best to justify that belief in him. People have to have a leader, and when a leader senses what the people want and need and tries to help them in that direction, they'll always stay with him. Jackson was a man who understood what the people wanted, and he tried to give it to them. The presidents after Jefferson became mixed up with special privilege, and Jackson was trying to break the stranglehold on the ordinary man in the programs he planned to help the average person get along in his or her life. And people always look forward to a man who'll arrive on the scene and try to do that.

The southern plantation owners and the eastern industrialists had every reason to be suspicious of Jackson and to dislike him, because he was determined to take their special privileges away from them. That's the reason they were suspicious of him. The rich and powerful people in the country had control of the money interests up to that point, and Jackson's objective was to take that control away from them and see that the people who had little businesses, little farms, were properly taken care of. He wanted to help the people who needed help.

The country was ready for that sort of change, and Jackson was straightforward and honest and clearly for the people who had no real representation at the head of the federal government. The Declaration of Independence uses almost the exact words that Lincoln used in his Gettysburg Address, that all men are created equal, but it wasn't practiced, fundamentally, in many of the policies of the various governments, city, county, state, and national. But Jackson made a really sincere effort to give the common people the place in the government where they belong. He was no demagogue. His policies were a development of the Democratic party and of Jackson's ability to understand what the country needed at that time. He wanted sincerely to look after the little fellow who had no pull, and that's what a president is supposed to do. Jackson was a practical man, working for the welfare of the whole country, and I think he succeeded in his purpose, to a great extent if not entirely. There's the theory that Jackson showed no prior signs of being the kind of man he was as president, but I don't agree with that at all. He was always for the common people. He always made it clear, when he was a judge and a member of the House of Representatives and a senator, that he represented the man with a hole in his pocket just as much as he represented the big shots; and when he became president of the United States, he followed through on the policy he had always followed.

To tell the truth, Jackson didn't look much like a man ready to take charge when he finally got in in 1828. He was sixty-one years old but he looked a lot older, and he was suffering now from tuberculosis, sick in body from that disease and sick in heart from the sudden death of his wife. But I guess another reason I admire him so much is that he was a take-over man who always knew what he had to do and went to work right away at the job of doing it. Some people, even some of the people who supported him when he was running for president, felt he looked so bad when he was sworn in that he wouldn't last more than a year or two, but he surprised the worriers by working like a demon for eight full years in office and getting all sorts of good things accomplished.

As I've said, he didn't get any help at all from Calhoun. The principal difference between the two men was that Jackson thought in terms of the welfare of the whole country, whereas Calhoun was much more concerned with the rights of the individual states, and particularly the southern states. Calhoun was for nullification, a belief that the Constitution could be interpreted as saying that states had rights that overrode federal rights, so that, for example, if a state like Calhoun's South Carolina didn't like a bill such as that protective tariff bill, which they certainly didn't like, they could insist that that bill be nullified, meaning canceled out as though it didn't exist. Jackson felt that the federal government spoke for all states and all parts of the country, and that, if the Congress passed a bill, the law created by that bill had to be obeyed by everybody, and that included all states which might not like that law.

Calhoun felt that the South was being neglected or ignored by the federal government because southern states were largely agricultural and northern states were largely industrial, and he thought the government was favoring the North in its lawmaking because federal lawmakers believed that northern manufacturing and industry were more important to the financial health of the country than farming and agriculture. Jackson maintained that the government was dealing fairly and equally with all areas and elements of the country. Calhoun became more and more an apologist for slavery, and early hints that the South might consider separating itself from the United States, if a lot of states weren't admitted to the union as slave states, showed up in some of his actions and statements.

Later on, he helped get Texas admitted to the Union as a slave state and fought to keep California out because it was coming in as a free state. His theory in trying to prevent territories coming in as free states was that the federal government didn't really own those territories but just held them as a sort of trustee; the territories, he said, were owned jointly by all the states, so individual states could quite legitimately object to their property being allowed in as states if they wanted to do so. A nonsensical theory at best. And after he died, two books of his political philosophy were published, and they openly advocated secession "if necessary."

Jackson, of course, like Lincoln a few decades later, felt that secession should never be necessary or permitted under any circumstances whatever, and that the Union should be preserved at all costs. When he made his famous statement to that effect at that dinner, which incidentally was a dinner celebrating the eighty-seventh anniversary of the birth of Jackson's idol, Thomas Jefferson, he stared at Calhoun with that cold hawk-stare of his as he said it.

Jackson didn't get a whole lot of help from his cabinet during his first term in office, either, and the reason had very little to do with politics or government policy; it was mostly the result of another marital scandal that must have reminded Jackson constantly of his own problems regarding Mrs. Jackson. His campaign manager when he was running for the presidency was Senator John Eaton of Tennessee, who had been married to Jackson's ward, Myra Lewis, and Jackson made Eaton his secretary of war following the election. (The Jacksons had no children of their own, which is why Myra Lewis, a distant relative, became Jackson's ward. The Jacksons also adopted a nephew of Mrs. Jackson's and named him Andrew Jackson, Jr.) But Eaton was now a widower, and sometime before the election, he had an affair with a young woman named Margaret O'Neale Timberlake, who was the daughter of the couple who owned the boardinghouse in Washington in which Eaton lived, and who worked as a barmaid in the tavern attached to the boardinghouse. (Most senators in those days didn't have the funds to live in the equivalent of those beautiful Georgetown houses in which a lot of senators live today.) Jackson knew Peggy Timberlake because he had lived in that same boardinghouse when he was a senator himself, and he liked her, but the trouble was that she was married; her husband was John Timberlake, a purser in the Navy. And the scandal grew worse when Timberlake died at sea, possibly a suicide because he'd learned of his wife's affair with Eaton.

Jackson urged Eaton to cool down the scandal by marrying Peggy Timberlake quickly, especially since he was so much in love with her, and the Eatons were married two months before Jackson entered the White House. But the wives of most of the cabinet members stuck up their noses and wouldn't invite the Eatons into their homes, partly because the affair had been such widespread public knowledge before the marriage and partly because of Peggy Eaton's low social position as a former barmaid, and Jackson did another of those foolish, hotheaded things he sometimes did: he ordered his cabinet members to order their wives to socialize with Peggy Eaton and asked for the resignation of all cabinet people whose wives wouldn't cooperate. The cabinet members refused to talk to their wives or to resign; they told Jackson calmly that they had no control over the social activities of their wives. And the leader of the cold-shoulder movement against Mrs. Eaton—as you might have guessed, it was the wife of that enemy in Jackson's own camp, John C. Calhoun—redoubled her efforts to keep people away from Eaton's wife.

It got to the point where Jackson and his cabinet practically weren't talking to each other, and the situation worsened when cabinet members wouldn't back Jackson in his move against the Bank of the United States, which I'll discuss in just a minute. But the result of all this trouble was something that presidents have used to great advantage ever since that time, the employment of advisors outside government staff. Jackson just stopped calling cabinet meetings for a while, which was a bad thing, but it made him turn more and more to people he knew would be loyal and honest to him—a group of men who became known as his kitchen cabinet. Jackson was loyal to his friends, just as all of us have been during our administrations, and I hope all presidents will be that way. And Jackson knew that he needed people who were loyal to him in turn in order for him to have a program that he could carry through.

Fortunately, the people with whom he began to have policy meetings were some of the best minds in the country, including Francis Preston Blair, the editor of the *Washington Globe,* who later started another paper, the *Congressional Globe,* which became the *Congressional Record,* and whose residence, Blair House, I lived in when the White House was being fixed up; another newspaperman Jackson knew and trusted, Duff Green, former editor of the *St. Louis Enquirer* (though eventually Green sided with Calhoun on nullification and became more and more involved with southern rather than with national issues); Jackson's adopted son, Andrew, Jr., who also served as his secretary, and of course John Eaton. Another member of Jackson's real cabinet who became part of his kitchen cabinet was Martin Van Buren, former senator and former governor of New York and then Jackson's secretary of state, who had no hesitation about accepting the Eatons socially, possibly because he was a widower and had no wife to snub them. He subsequently, of course, followed Jackson into the presidency.

But the problem of the Eatons remained a thorn in Jackson's side, and in 1831 Eaton resigned as secretary of war, after which he challenged three members of the cabinet to duels, which they all refused. Eaton eventually became governor of Florida and minister to Spain. Then Van Buren resigned, a self-sacrificing move since he felt he'd also become too controversial because of his support of the Eatons and because he'd joined Jackson in showing his distaste for Calhoun. Jackson then appointed Van Buren minister to England, but Congress split evenly on approving the appointment, and this gave Calhoun the deciding vote, which he cast, spitefully, against Van Buren, despite the fact that Van Buren had been an excellent secretary of state and would almost certainly have been an equally excellent minister to England. As you can see, Calhoun, who was known in his day as the Gentleman from South Carolina, was no gentleman in a lot of ways.

Three other cabinet members also left in 1831, resigning on their own or finally succumbing to Jackson's repeated suggestions that they leave: Samuel D. Ingram of Pennsylvania, the secretary of the treasury, John M. Berrien of Georgia, the attorney general, and John Branch of North Carolina, the secretary of the navy. That left only one member of the original Cabinet, William T. Barry of Kentucky, the postmaster general; the job of postmaster general was a brand-new addition to the cabinet, and Barry stayed on until 1835. And then, early in 1832, as Jackson and Calhoun grew more and more at odds on the nullification question and on other things, and when Jackson made it clear that Van Buren and not Calhoun was going to be his running mate for his second term and his choice to follow him as president, Calhoun left the administration himself, the only vice president in our history to resign.* That brought in an almost completely new cabinet of men who were much more loyal to Jackson and worked with him to get his program through. And later in 1832, Jackson ran for his second term, with Van Buren as his running mate, opposed by Henry Clay on the National Republican ticket, with a fellow named John Sergeant of Pennsylvania, the lawyer for the Bank of the United States, looking for the vice presidency, and Jackson won again without difficulty. He got 687,502 popular votes to Clay's 530,189 votes, 55 percent to 42 percent with the other 3 percent going to minor candidates, and 219 electoral votes to Clay's 49, the other 19 electoral votes also going to minor candidates. Clay took only Connecticut, Delaware, Kentucky, Maryland, Massachusetts, and Rhode Island, with South Carolina's eleven votes going to a fellow named John Floyd and Vermont's seven going to a fellow named William Wirt. Van Buren had to run on his own, of course, in those days when the presidential and vice-presidential jobs weren't sewn together, and also did well, getting 189 electoral votes to Sergeant's 89, and 48 other votes going to others.

The most important thing Jackson accomplished in office, I believe, was his opposition to Calhoun's advocacy of nullification—not just because of that one interpretation of the Constitution, but because Jackson made it really clear for the first time that "United States of America" wasn't just a name but a country of people who were truly united and weren't going to allow themselves to be torn apart permanently for any reason whatever. And many years later, when South Carolina and other states seceded at the time of the Civil War, they still understood the presidential position that the United States was a going concern and would not be allowed to be broken up by a minority.

Calhoun didn't leave things alone, of course. Even when Jackson made that toast at that dinner, Calhoun responded with a countertoast that didn't go down too well with Jackson and other people there: "The Union—next to our liberty, the most dear!" And after Calhoun walked out of the vice presidency, he went back to South Carolina and got the legislature there to pass a law that said flatly that they had the right of

*My father was not here in 1973 when Spiro T. Agnew became the second. Aside from their resignations as vice presidents, of course, there's no comparison between the two men. Calhoun had plenty of faults, but after resigning as vice president, he went on to serve as a senator again and as secretary of state under President John Tyler in 1844 and 1845. Agnew left office one step ahead of the sheriff, accused of accepting bribes as vice president and of income tax evasion, and was fined $10,000 and placed on three years' probation. He was also ordered to pay $268,000 to the state of Maryland for various deeds committed while he was governor there, before becoming our vice president. He then went on to write a best-selling spy novel, which my agent, Scott Meredith, who also handled the rights to the Agnew novel, says wasn't too bad, and after that showed up doing mysterious jobs for various Arabs. Later on, he announced that he was bankrupt. MT

nullification and would obey only the federal laws they wanted to obey and nullify the laws they didn't want to obey, and one thing they weren't going to obey right off the bat was a tariff law Jackson had gotten passed in 1832, even though it was a milder tariff law than the one that had been passed in 1828. And if the United States didn't like it—why, they were prepared to secede from the United States.

Jackson didn't take long to make it clear that he didn't like it and wasn't going to let it happen. Right after he was reelected, he issued a Proclamation on Nullification in which he stated that any attempt at secession would be considered treason, and he ordered thousands of former soldiers back into active duty and got Congress to allow him to send these troops into South Carolina if necessary. South Carolina soon postponed and then dropped their secession plans, and on March 15, 1833, which happened to be Jackson's sixty-sixth birthday, they also canceled their nullification law.

The other important thing that Jackson achieved was his battle to dissolve the Bank of the United States, which was run by a Philadelphia financier named Nicholas Biddle, and even though it was a private enterprise, acted as financial agent for the country and controlled most of the country's money. The bank had been started back in 1791 by Alexander Hamilton, who felt that a central bank was necessary to keep the country on a sound economic basis, but went out of business in 1811, and started up again in 1816. Jackson, however, hated the idea of a central bank in general and the Bank of the United States in particular; he pointed out that the bank was strictly for big-time industrialists, quick to make big loans to big companies but hostile and even contemptuous when asked for loans by farmers and small businessmen. He also felt that the idea of a private company that controlled so much of the country's money gave that company too much power over the country and its lawmakers, and he also disliked the fact that the Bank of the United States also pretty much controlled the other banks around the country, small banks, because those banks had to borrow money from the big bank, and the Bank of the United States could then punish them at will or even put them out of business by suddenly calling in notes on loans.

Just after his reelection, therefore, Jackson went to work to take the financial control of the country away from the Bank of the United States. The Bank's charter ran until 1836, but Clay decided to make the matter a campaign issue and talked Biddle into making an application for early rechartering of the Bank during the preelection period, assuring Biddle that he'd support the application if he was elected, and convincing Biddle that it wouldn't matter even if Jackson won because Biddle's pals in the Senate would get the new charter through. Clay also pointed out to Biddle that so many people owed money to the Bank of the United States and to other banks under that bank's thumb—hell, he reminded Biddle, he even owed money to the Bank of the United States himself, or maybe Biddle reminded *him* of that in telling Clay that he'd better be nice to the big, powerful bank if he became president—that legislators and other people wouldn't *dare* to oppose the new charter because they might then be called upon to repay their loans immediately if the Bank of the United States was going out of business.

And after Jackson won, the Senate *did* pass a bill okaying the new charter, but they forgot how tough Jackson could be when he felt it was necessary. He immediately vetoed the bill, pointing out that the Constitution never gave the government the right to charter a central bank in the first place, and saying in his plain-spoken way that when laws "make the rich richer and the potent more powerful, the humble members of society, the farmers, mechanics, and laborers, have a right to complain of the injustice of their government." The Senate couldn't muster up enough votes to override his veto, and Jackson followed up by withdrawing eleven million dollars of government money from the Bank of the United States and spreading the money out in various state banks.

He ran into plenty of opposition here, too. Louis McLane, who became secretary of the treasury after Ingram left in 1831, refused Jackson's order to transfer the money, so Jackson transferred him to the post of secretary of state; Jackson then put William J. Duane in the job, but he also refused to transfer the money, and Jackson fired him; Jackson then moved his attorney general, Roger Taney, to the job of secretary of the treasury because he knew that Taney was as much opposed to the Bank of the United States as he was. But Clay was still a power in the Senate even though he'd lost the presidential election, and he managed to get the Senate to say no to the appointment, the first time in American history that a cabinet appointment had ever been rejected. Jackson finally took his secretary of the navy, Levi Woodbury, and made him secretary of the treasury, and Woodbury moved the money.

Clay then got the Senate to censure Jackson for moving the money without congressional approval, but the House of Representatives showed that it was on Jackson's side by passing resolutions approving Jackson's actions and calling for an investigation of the bank, and the censure was expunged from official records in 1837. The Bank of the United States went out of business when its charter ended in 1836, though it later turned up as a private bank until it finally collapsed entirely in 1841, and Biddle was indicted for fraud but wasn't convicted.

It was a great thing that Jackson did, seeing to it that the government rather than private and outside interests controlled the finances of the country. And he wasn't really undoing Hamilton's work. He was meeting the situation as it developed, eventually, out of Hamilton's work. No matter how good any situation is, or how good any organization, it can be turned into a racket if there isn't somebody watching to see that that isn't done. And that's what Jackson accomplished when he enabled the United States government to regain control of our finances.

It wasn't an instant or miracle cure for the country's banking problems, of course; like most solutions to problems, it brought some new problems of its own. The state banks, rich with all the money that Jackson poured into them, became far too easy and careless in giving out loans. They felt that Jackson's comments about the difficulties the average man had encountered in getting loans, when the Bank of the United States was in control, gave them a sort of mandate to loan out money quickly and at high interest charges, using the government money as a financial base and multiplying it by issuing paper money of their own.

Hundreds of other banks sprang up, so-called wildcat banks because they really had no resources at all, and they too issued carloads of paper currency and thrived by loaning out their own funny money. All these newly rich banks didn't just give out loans for genuine need or solid business expansion, either; they began to give more and more loans for land speculation in the West, which became wilder every day. Between 1832 and 1836, land values in the West increased by more than a thousand percent, and inflation gripped the country.

To counteract this, Jackson issued a proclamation he called the Specie Circular, which required that henceforth public lands could be bought only with hard currency—meaning gold and silver. That slowed down inflation and curbed wild land speculation, all right, but it also caused a lot of runs on banks by people who were nervous about the banks anyway or now wanted gold or silver to pay for their land speculation, gold and silver that the banks didn't have. Within a short time, more than nine hundred banks went out of business, and this in turn, combined with a number of major crop failures around the country, brought on a terrible depression that lasted until 1843 and made Van Buren one of the most unpopular presidents in our history, even though it was hardly his fault.

But even this did some good in the long run, because it caused Van Buren to introduce some worthwhile financial measures of his own. He felt that the federal government should control government finances on its own, rather than banks of *any* kind, and he developed the system of subtreasuries around the country to hold federal funds. And eventually we also prohibited the issuance of currency by any institutions other than the United States itself, and instituted the policy of watchdogging all banks that exists today.

* * *

There were other major accomplishments by Jackson as well, and one of these helped once again to make it clear, as we had to do frequently in our early history, that we were becoming a stronger and stronger country and wouldn't always be a weak, upstart little nation that had to kowtow to the big European powers. This all happened because France had damaged a lot of American vessels during the Napoleonic Wars, and of course, Jackson asked France for reparation to the United States and to the shipowners. France, however, didn't pay up and apparently expected Jackson to forget all about it. But Jackson didn't forget it; he just broke off diplomatic relations with France and mobilized our army and our navy. France quickly sent payment in the form of four installments that Jackson had told them were past due.

I'll just mention one other thing, and this was something that Jackson accomplished on his very last day in office. The territory of Texas was then owned by Mexico, as you know, but the people of Texas had been trying to separate themselves from Mexico for a number of years, and it all came to a head during Jackson's administration. Mexico had itself been a sovereign nation only since 1823, when they broke loose from Spain; but when Texas tried to do the same kind of thing, Mexico sent large forces of soldiers into the territory to quell what they considered a revolution.

In particular, one man, Antonio López de Santa Anna, who became president of Mexico in 1833, was particularly tough; he sent more and more soldiers into the territory, and when Texans fought back, the Mexicans captured three hundred men in a battle at Goliad and then killed them instead of imprisoning them, and then, as everybody remembers, wiped out the Texans at the Alamo, killing Davy Crockett, Jim Bowie, and about a hundred and eighty other men. But "Remember Goliad!" and "Remember the Alamo!" became rallying cries for Texans, and on April 21, 1836, Sam Houston, who had served under Jackson during the fighting with the Creek Indians in 1814, managed to turn the tables on the Mexicans. In a battle at San Jacinto, he not only defeated the Mexican Army but captured Santa Anna himself, and Mexico gave up the Texas territory. It became an independent republic and then asked to become a territory of the United States.

Jackson was undecided about the situation for a while, wanting Texas on the one hand but hesitating on the other hand because Texas was a slave territory and a lot of northerners opposed any kind of alliance with the territory for that reason. (There was no question about Texas's attitude toward slavery; the constitution of the Texas Republic was patterned after our own Constitution in most ways, but it also contained language expressly accepting slavery.) But on Jackson's last day in office, he decided

to recognize Texas's independence officially, regardless of northern opposition, and this led to Texas's eventual entry as a state. It became our
twenty-eighth state in 1845, during James K. Polk's administration.

Jackson left office on March 4, 1837, and had the satisfaction of
seeing his friend and supporter, Martin Van Buren, follow him into office.
The campaign in 1836 was again very bitter and nasty, with Jackson's
and Van Buren's enemies calling Van Buren "Martin Van Ruin" and a
puppet of "King Andrew the First," and contrasting Van Buren unfa-
vorably with his principal opponent, William Henry Harrison, saying that
Van Buren was a man who grew up in wealth and luxury and Harrison
was an honest, homespun fellow who grew up in a log cabin. The truth
was that Harrison grew up in a mansion in Virginia, where his father, a
signer of the Declaration of Independence and governor of Virginia from
1781 to 1784, owned a large plantation, while Van Buren was a self-
made man whose father owned a small farm and a tavern in Kinderhook,
New York.

And there were also some problems with the man chosen by Jackson
to run for the vice-president's job, Richard Mentor Johnson, a controversial and flamboyant fellow who was badly wounded at the Battle of
the Thames during the War of 1812 and claimed to have killed Tecumseh,
the Shawnee chief who allied himself with the British during the war,
personally in that battle before he fell himself. (This was a big battle
between an American force led by old William Henry Harrison and a
British force led by a British general, Henry A. Proctor, plus about twelve
hundred Indians led by Tecumseh. It took place at the Thames River—
not the one in England, of course, but another Thames River in Chatham,
Ontario, Canada.) Johnson was also hated by southerners because he'd
taken a slave as his common-law wife and brought up their mulatto
daughters as free people who, he said, were as good as anybody else.

None of these problems mattered in the end, anyway, for two reasons. First of all, both men were Jackson's stated choices, the most
important factor of all. And second, the opposition was pretty much in
disarray; they'd re-formed as an entirely new party, the Whigs, but they
couldn't seem to agree on their presidential choice. They finally settled,
if it can be called settling, by running their separate choices: the western
faction put up Harrison, the easterners put up Daniel Webster, and the
southern faction put up a man from Tennessee named Hugh Lawson
White. There were also two separate Whig candidates for vice president,
Francis Granger of New York and John Tyler of Virginia. The result was
that Van Buren got more popular votes than his three opponents combined,
765,483 to 739,795, and 170 electoral votes to Harrison's 73, White's

26, and Webster's 14. (A fellow who wasn't even running, Willie P. Mangum of North Carolina, got the remaining 11 electoral votes.)

Johnson had a bit more trouble; he would have had a majority of electoral votes if he got Virginia's votes, but the state's electors refused to vote for him and gave their votes instead to a man named William Smith. This created a contest between Johnson and Granger—Tyler got only 47 electoral votes and was out of it—and put the matter in the hands of the Senate, the only time this has ever happened in a vice-presidential race. Well, the Senate finally gave Johnson 33 votes and Granger 16 votes, and that was that.

Tyler, incidentally, happens to have been my great-great-uncle, and I guess you know that he finally became president himself in 1841, our tenth president, though he certainly wasn't one of our great ones. My family never thought much of him because they said he had a mean disposition, and that all the family had mean dispositions as a result of being related to him. But he did some good things as president, and he established a couple of precedents that are still a part of the policy of all the presidents of the United States, which I'll mention in a couple of sentences a little later on, so I guess I have a sort of soft spot for him. He was a stubborn son of a bitch in many ways, and I suppose that's what's called having a mean disposition. But when a man is stubborn and believes what he believes and carries it out, I think it's a good trait. And when old John Tyler had to make some keynote decisions, he made the right ones.

Jackson returned to Tennessee after he left office and lived the remaining eight years of his life at the Hermitage, his twelve-hundred-acre plantation. It wasn't a period free of troubles for him. His tuberculosis had gotten worse and he only had one functional lung; he was also blind in his right eye because of a cataract and had a case of dropsy that distorted his face. He was in such constant pain that he was unable to lie down and had to sleep sitting up in bed. But his good, tough old mind was as strong as ever, and when he was dying on June 8, 1845, his last thought was for the relatives and servants he heard crying nearby. "Please don't cry," he said. "Be good children, and I hope to see you all in heaven, both white and black, both white and black." And then he was gone.

THIRTY

Van Buren, Tyler, and a Great President— Polk

MARTIN Van Buren lasted only one term because of the depression, even though he had about as much to do with it as you and I did. That depression, as I've said, was caused partly by crop failures but mostly by all the speculation in land that had been opened up for settlement—paper speculation that made the depression inevitable and probably unavoidable.

Some writers have even wondered in recent times why Van Buren became president at all, when there were other people around who seemed more brilliant—Calhoun, Webster, and Clay, for instance. Well, one reason Van Buren was elected, of course, was that the Democrats were the popular party in the country at that time and there were few other prominent men in view on the Democratic side at that point—Webster and Clay, as you know, being in the other party. Another reason, and the main one, was that he was Jackson's vice president and he was elected because Jackson wanted him to be elected president; it was a time when it looked as if the country had reached the heights of prosperity, which was the way it appeared just before the Panic of 1837, and he was supported by old Andy Jackson, so he got elected. And a third reason is that in that day, in the period from about 1820 to about 1850, the man who had the most outstanding career as a member of the House of Representatives or as a United States senator or as vice president of the United States was the man most certain to become president—because of his former position and because he displayed the fact that he probably understood better than anyone else what the government stood for.

And the truth is that none of those other men were better qualified for the job than Van Buren. Van Buren had a distinguished career in New York and in Washington, and then he became Jackson's closest advisor, and I don't think he ever gave Jackson any bad political advice or bad advice on any other subject. The other three men, on the other hand, developed their reputations mostly on the grounds of their ability to make speeches. Webster, for example, is remembered to this day mostly because he was such a great orator, and he was certainly always making orations, but that's just another way of saying he was an old windbag, and he certainly wasn't much else. It's also coming out now that he was in the pay of the United States Bank all the time he was in the United States Senate, which I guess he had to be in order to pay his bills. It's true that he later served as secretary of state for Harrison, Tyler, and Millard Fillmore, and I imagine he was a good secretary of state if three different presidents kept putting him into the job, but he was still a windbag. Calhoun had some good points, too, but he was such a states'-rights man that he was all too ready to push for destruction of the Union. And Clay had good points, too, but I think he was tainted permanently by that sneaky deal he made with John Quincy Adams.

I'm not saying, you understand, that Van Buren was a great president or even a good president; on the contrary, I've got to say that our country would have done just as well not to have had Van Buren as president. But my reasons are different from the fact that that catastrophe came along in the form of a depression while he was president. My particular reason for not thinking much of him is that he was just too timid and indecisive. I don't know whether or not he even had any personal philosophy on the role of government; I think he was a man who was always worrying about what might happen if he did this or that, and always keeping his ear to the ground to the point where he couldn't act as the chief executive, and for that reason he was just a politician and nothing more, a politician who was out of his depth. He was known as the Cautious Dutchman, and he *was* a cautious Dutchman. But he was just *too* cautious; he was always too busy listening to what people told him about what might be the result of what he might do, when what he should have done was gone ahead and done what was necessary to be done, and then listen to what happened.

One example is that depression, which Van Buren might not have been able to prevent, but which he could almost certainly have shortened. When the panic of 1837 came along, he just wasn't there with remedies for the situation. As I've mentioned, old Andy Jackson arranged things so that he paid off the national debt, and it was a great thing to do, but there's one advantage of having a national debt under certain other conditions, which is that it shows the people that the government is functioning and has the funds and the ability to make loans at a time of real emergency. And if Van Buren had just gone ahead and taken the bull by the horns and restored that debt to prevent the panic or at least bring it to an end, I don't think he would have had any trouble, but he didn't have the nerve to do it. Maybe it was a little too early in our history to expect a president to be capable of meeting a situation of that kind, but I don't think so.

And another example was his inability to make up his mind on the admission of Texas as a state of the United States. He kept hesitating and kept hesitating because he didn't know which side popular opinion would be on. If he had any conviction on what ought to be done, he would have ended up all right, but there he was again, trying to find out what people wanted so he could give them what they wanted, instead of having a policy of his own and telling people that it's the best policy. And you can't behave that way when you're in a position of responsibility, as he was; you've got to make up your mind on the basis of what *you* think is right and then go ahead with it. All the South voted against him on that account, and that's another reason he was defeated for reelection.

Van Buren ran against William Henry Harrison again, with my stubborn old great-great-uncle as Harrison's vice-presidential candidate, and this time the Whigs got in, with Harrison getting 1,275,017 votes, representing 53 percent, to Van Buren's 1,128,702 votes, which was about 47 percent. Harrison got 234 electoral votes and Van Buren got 60. For the first time in our history, the campaigns for both candidates were as brassy as the ones we have today, with political posters, campaign songs, and all the rest, and as I've mentioned, with Van Buren pictured as a rich old dandy and Harrison as a plain fellow in a log cabin even though the exact opposite was true. (For the record, Harrison's boyhood home in Virginia, the Berkeley plantation, was one of the largest and most elaborate in the state, and his house in North Bend, Ohio, his residence while he was running for the presidency, was a structure with a mere twenty-two rooms. He was a very rich man for his time, and the family was a well-known and powerful family. Harrisonburg, Virginia, was named for the family.)

Anyway, as you'll recall, Harrison didn't last very long as president. One of the principal campaign slogans on the Whig side was "Tippecanoe and Tyler, Too,'' because Harrison had been a general fighting against the Indians in a battle near the Tippecanoe River, which is above Lafayette, Indiana, on November 7, 1811, and had won that battle, and he'd also fought in a battle or two in the War of 1812. And Harrison was a show-off and insisted on riding to the White House on a white horse and in his fancy uniform. He wouldn't wear an overcoat because that would conceal the uniform, and he wouldn't wear a hat or gloves either, and it was a particularly cold March day with an icy wind blowing. And he caught cold on the way to the White House and died a month later, and Tyler was president.

Harrison was the oldest man ever to be elected president,* aged sixty-eight and two months when he died on April 4, 1841. But that isn't all that old, and he probably would have survived a little icy wind except for the fact that he also showed off in other ways. He read the longest inaugural speech ever read by an incoming president; he spoke for about an hour and three-quarters and got everybody tired out, including himself, and even Daniel Webster, who had difficulty quitting during his own speeches, said that Harrison killed off two or three Roman councils and a Roman emperor or two in that message, it was that long. And then they had two or three inaugural balls that night, and he kept going from one to the other in his uniform and with no overcoat. And it killed him.

The Whigs had no platform at all during the campaign; Harrison was nominated and elected on the false premise of Van Buren's prosperity and his own poverty, and on the fact that he was a military hero and he was against everything that had gone before. (Yes, Virginia, ''aginners'' sometimes win. It's happened in our own times as well.) And of course, Harrison didn't accomplish a thing during the month he was in office. He made no contribution whatever. He had no policy. He didn't know what the government was all about, to tell the truth. About the only thing he did during that brief period was see friends and friends of friends, because he was such an easy mark that he couldn't say no to anybody, and everybody and his brother was besieging him for jobs. He had to get up early in the morning because people were sitting on his doorstep and sleeping on the White House grounds in order to get to see him. That wasn't unusual, of course; it was the same way during Jackson's and Van Buren's administrations and continued for a long time. People just showed up and asked the president personally for jobs after he was in office. That continued all the way up to the time of Grover Cleveland, when the civil service bills were passed. Up until then, the president was

---

*Ronald Reagan eventually beat that record. He was born on February 6, 1911, and was two weeks short of his seventieth birthday when he delivered his inaugural speech on January 20, 1981. I can't remember whether or not he wore an overcoat. MT

always importuned for all kinds of jobs. It hasn't been so bad since then, but it's bad enough, as I know from experience.

I mentioned that I was going to devote a small amount of space to old John Tyler, and here it comes.

I guess the reason I have a certain amount of grudging respect for old Tyler is that he knew his own mind and stuck to his decisions. He was the first vice president to take over when a sitting president died, and the decision he made at that time is the best example of what I mean. Daniel Webster was the secretary of state at that point, and Webster wanted it to appear that Tyler was just acting president; Webster, in fact, wanted Tyler to call himself acting president. Well, I think I've made it clear that I'm not too impressed by Dan Webster, even though he's probably better known to the general public today than some of our past presidents because he was from New England and those New England historians gave him a lot space in their writings. As far as I'm concerned, he was just a ballyhoo artist, and my old great-great-uncle shut him up pretty fast. He let Webster know that he knew the Constitution just as well as Webster did, and he said, "The Constitution provides that I'm the president of the United States when the president passes on, and I'll function in that capacity. And for that reason I'm president and not acting president, and I'll call myself president, period."

He even sent back letters that came addressed to Acting President John Tyler; he wouldn't even open them. He was the first man who followed through on that constitutional directive, and there have been six others who've done the same since, including me, of course. Webster backed down immediately because he knew that was Tyler's attitude at all times: "As long as you support me, you can stay, but as soon as you feel you can't support my policies, you're free to resign. And if you don't resign, I'll kick you out." That's another thing I like about him, because disloyalty is one of the things I despise most in life; I always tried to be loyal to people around me and expected loyalty in return from them.

And an even stronger example than Dan Webster's foolishness about the acting-president business showed up in August and September 1841, just a few months after Tyler became president. Tyler came into the presidency as a Whig because he ran as vice president with Harrison, but he was really a Democrat, and he was an admirer of Jackson even though he didn't agree with all of Jackson's policies by any means. So when Henry Clay pushed through a bill to bring the Bank of the United States to life again, Tyler vetoed the bill, and when Clay followed up with a bill to create a Fiscal Corporation, which amounted to the same thing, Tyler made it clear that he felt that the president and not some outside organization should have the final say on the fiscal policies of the country and vetoed that one, too. He vetoed that second bill on September 9, and two days later his entire cabinet resigned—all except Webster, who liked his job and wanted to keep it for a while, though he, too, finally left in 1843 and eventually returned to the senate. Webster felt he was particularly qualified for the office, and the people who hired him apparently felt he was, too, but I never thought so. Anyway, the mass resignation was all right with Tyler, and he just put in other people he thought were as good or better.

Webster also tried to convince Tyler that it was the custom for each member of the cabinet to have one vote and the president also to have one vote, and therefore, if the president was outvoted by his cabinet, that should be it. And President Tyler informed Webster very carefully that if the cabinet had five or six or seven votes or a million votes, and the president's one vote went the opposite way, then *that* would be it. Lincoln carried that through in the very same way when his cabinet voted on the Emancipation Proclamation. The whole cabinet voted against it, and Lincoln said, "The ayes have it. There's one vote for it and that's the vote of the president of the United States." And the cabinet began to find out that they're employees of the president of the United States, and the president's decision is the one that counts.

Tyler was also the president who finally brought Texas into the Union. He tried to accomplish it at first by signing a treaty of annexation with Texas in April 1844, about eleven months before he left office, but the Senate wouldn't ratify the treaty. But later that year Polk began to campaign and made the admission of Texas one of the strongest planks in his platform, and he was supported and elected so enthusiastically that the members of Congress finally saw the light. They passed a joint resolution okaying Texas's entry into the Union, and on March 1, 1845, two days before he left office, Tyler signed the important piece of paper. Two days later, on his very last day in office, he signed another important piece of paper that made Florida part of the United States.

Those are some things I admire about Tyler, but there were also plenty of things that weren't so admirable. He wasn't overly strong for labor; he thought labor ought to be kept in its place. He had a superior attitude toward the ordinary fellow; he was a big landowner in the state of Virginia, and all those big landowners thought the small farmer was beneath consideration, so he was very careful to see to it that the ordinary fellow who had a small farm didn't have much of a say in the community. And he was a states'-rights man all the way and finally joined the Confederacy, though he didn't do so until Virginia seceded and he went along with his state. It was a bad thing to do, but as I've said, he was a stubborn and contrary old son of a gun, and he had his own beliefs and stuck to his beliefs.

Tyler almost died in office himself. On February 28, 1844, he went with a lot of other people to inspect and cruise along the Potomac on the *Princeton,* a new warship that was very modern and advanced for its time, and a terrible accident occurred that took a lot of lives. One of the things they all went to inspect was a big gun called the Peacemaker, which was the largest naval gun in the world at that point in history, and the gun was fired twice for the visitors without incident. But on the third firing, the gun suddenly exploded, killing Tyler's new secretary of state, Abel P. Upshur, who took over the job when Webster left, his secretary of the navy, Thomas W. Gilmer, his valet, a close friend, David Gardiner, and a number of other people. Tyler himself was belowdecks at that moment and wasn't hurt, and he helped carry Gardiner's twenty-three-year-old daughter, Julia, to safety on a nearby rescue vessel. Four months later, he and Julia Gardiner were married, even though he was thirty-one years older than his bride.

Tyler had had a very happy marriage with his first wife, the former Letitia Christian—the marriage lasted twenty-nine years and gave them eight children—but he had been a widower for about seventeen months at the time of the accident, and he didn't like the single state. The papers laughed at the couple because of the difference in their ages, but they went on to have seven more children, making Tyler the president with the largest number of children in our history. I admire him for that, too.

Tyler made no effort to run for reelection when he completed his single term on March 4, 1845. He was disavowed by the Whigs because of the stands he'd taken against Whig policy on financial matters, and he knew he wouldn't be chosen as the Democratic candidate because he was officially a Whig president, so he thought briefly about running as a third-party candidate and organized a party that he called, and I'm not joking, the Democratic-Republican Party. His main motive was to oppose Henry Clay, who was going to run for the third time and as a Whig, and to oppose Martin Van Buren, who seemed likely to run again on the Democratic side, but then the Democrats nominated James K. Polk, and Tyler dropped out because he didn't want to take votes away from Polk and give the election to Clay. He went down to Sherwood Forest, his twelve-hundred-acre plantation about thirty miles away from Richmond, Virginia, and had those seven more children, five boys and two girls, and lived there happily until his death on January 18, 1862.

In one of those believe-it-or-not incidents, Julia Tyler predicted her husband's death. He was a member of the Confederate House of Representatives at that point, and the House was meeting in Richmond and Tyler was staying at the Exchange Hotel in that city, and Julia was busy with her family and not planning to join him. But she had a nightmare in which Tyler was mortally ill, and she hurried into Richmond. Tyler assured her that he was feeling fine, but two days later he became dizzy and nauseous, and he fainted suddenly in the hotel's dining room and died soon after that. He was seventy-one years old. No official notice was taken of his death because he was the only president to join the Confederacy and he was considered a traitor. Well, he had those few good points, but all things considered, I think I was right in listing him as one of the presidents we could have done without. And I think maybe I would have listed the man he replaced, William Henry Harrison, as another president we could have done without if he had lived long enough.

Anyway, Polk managed to follow Tyler into the presidency, though he didn't win by a tremendous margin. Clay was still a very popular fellow around the country, and even though an even more popular fellow, Andrew Jackson, was a good friend of Polk's and campaigned hard for Polk throughout Tennessee, which was also Polk's home state, Clay still managed to win the state. (Jackson and Polk were so close and thought so much alike about so many things that Polk was nicknamed Young Hickory. Politics is a funny business, though, and Jackson's support and the fact that Polk's residence was in Tennessee still didn't help enough.) But when all the counting was over, Polk had 1,338,464 votes, representing 50 percent of the popular vote, and Clay had 1,300,097 votes, representing 48 percent, with a splinter candidate, James G. Birncy of the Liberty-Abolitionist Party, getting 62,300 votes, the remaining 2 percent. Polk racked up 170 electoral votes, and Clay got 105.

Polk was forty-nine when he became president, our youngest president up to that point. (Eventually other presidents were elected who were even younger. Teddy Roosevelt, for example, was forty-six when he was elected in 1904. John F. Kennedy was only forty-three when he was elected in 1960. That was essentially a young men's contest. Nixon was forty-seven in 1960, though I thought those jowls of his and his unshaven appearance made him look about sixty when I watched him on television.) Polk was also supposed to be the first of our dark horse presidents to be elected, but that's hooey—or at least, if he was a dark horse president, he wasn't such a *dark* dark horse. He'd certainly been around, and visible on the political scene, long enough despite his relative youth.

He was born in 1795 and was a member of the Tennessee House of Representatives by the time he was twenty-eight, a member of the House of Representatives in Washington from 1825 to 1839 and in fact speaker of the House for the last four years of that period, and then governor of Tennessee from 1839 to 1841. He had his upsets, of course—he was defeated by a Whig named James C. Jones when he ran for reelection as governor in 1841, and Jones beat him again for governor in 1843—but he was definitely being considered seriously for either the presidency or the vice presidency when the Democratic Convention started up in Baltimore in May 1844. I guess the reason he's thought of as a dark horse is that he was a sort of compromise candidate, and it took nine ballots to get him picked. Van Buren was back in the running and led on the first ballot, but it would have taken a two-thirds majority to end it right there and he didn't get that much; and then Van Buren's vice president, Richard M. Johnson, started to pick up steam, and so did old James Buchanan and another fellow, Lewis Cass, who had been our minister to France and later became a senator from Michigan.

By the fifth ballot, Cass was in the lead, and Polk didn't get a single vote right through the first eight ballots. But then people began to line up behind Polk, and on the ninth ballot, he received 233 votes while Cass got only 29 and Van Buren only a miserable two. Polk's running mate was George Mifflin Dallas, a former mayor of Philadelphia, senator from Pennsylvania, minister to Russia, and after his term as vice president under Polk, minister to Great Britain. I've also been told that Dallas, Texas, was named after George Dallas, though I'm not sure why because I've read a number of things about the man and didn't see any mention that he ever went near the place.

The news of Polk's nomination, incidentally, was telegraphed to Washington, the first official use of Samuel F.B. Morse's newfangled invention. But nobody believed it because they were so sure that Van Buren or Cass would get the nod.

People always look surprised when I mention that I consider Polk one of our greatest presidents. In fact, you can almost see them thinking, "James *Who?*" as though they hardly recognize the name. Well, I suppose I can understand that reaction, because Polk wasn't one of the presidents who had a hundred books written about him, but there are a lot of reasons I feel the way I do.

I've already mentioned the main reason, which is that he was the ideal chief executive in the sense that he knew what he wanted to do and had to do, and he did it and left, and in the sense that he said that his program could be accomplished in a single term and *was* accomplished in a single term. But let me expand on that a little bit.

Polk became president at a particularly crucial period in our history. First, he followed a whole string of weak presidents, Van Buren and

Harrison and Tyler, and he had a lot of catching up to do because of the lack of activity of his predecessors, who hadn't really measured up to the presidency. And I think he suspected that the same situation might develop, with more mediocre presidents, after he left office, particularly since he knew that two of his generals, Zachary Taylor and Old Fuss and Feathers Winfield Scott, both of whom were Whigs, had presidential ambitions. Polk didn't think much of either man; he referred to them as "superpampered" and living high on the hog and loving their lives of luxury, and I'm sure he got a certain amount of satisfaction out of putting them to work when the Mexican War came along. He made them disturb themselves: old Winfield Scott in particular didn't want to go to Mexico and command our troops down there, but he had to go.

And Polk was right about those presidential ambitions, of course. Both men became candidates for president, and though Old Fuss and Feathers never got his ambition accomplished, Taylor became the next president of the United States in 1848. (Scott ran against Franklin Pierce in 1852 and was defeated.) Polk was also correct if he did have that suspicion about the quality of the presidents who followed him. Exactly the same situation occurred after Polk's administration as had been the case before it; we had four presidents who were just there. And then, when Lincoln came along, he had to catch up on all the rest of them to save the Union.

We had some very, very poor sticks as presidents during that period. Taylor was a military man and nothing more, and the only reason he didn't do a whole lot of harm is that he didn't last very long; he died a little over a year after he got into office, aged sixty-five. There are conflicting theories on the cause of Taylor's death. Some reports say he died of typhoid contracted while he was in Mexico; other reports say he died of heat prostration because he sat in the sun for hours listening to some long speeches at the Washington Monument, which was being built at the time; still others say he ate a whole bowl of cherries and drank a whole pitcher of milk after those speeches, which was a dangerous thing to do because sanitary conditions were terrible in Washington in that period and dairy products and raw fruit were usually avoided. I guess, in view of the way I sometimes felt after listening to long speeches, I'd pick the middle explanation.

That put his vice president, Millard Fillmore, into office, and Fillmore was a nonentity who'd only been put on Taylor's ticket because he was a Know-Nothing and the Taylor people wanted to pick up that part of the vote. The Know-Nothings, for those of you who aren't familiar with that sorry bunch, were a political group of people who were anti-immigrant and anti-Catholic. The official name was the Native American

Party, which sounds like some of those hate organizations that sprang up in our own time.

Then along came Franklin Pierce, who was an easy-going, good-looking fellow who liked to be considered a friendly man to everybody, and who liked everybody in sight provided people didn't try to make him work too hard. And after that came James Buchanan, who was an old bachelor from Pennsylvania and believed that the president had no power to lead the country, and that the principal or sole role of the president was to enforce existing laws without considering changing situations.

That's one of the reasons, incidentally, that South Carolina was allowed to secede without interference, when the Civil War was getting ready to happen during Buchanan's administration. There are always people in Congress who'll try to hedge in the president and keep him from doing his job if he'll let them, and the presidents I've just named were perfectly willing to let someone else do the work. They just didn't want to do the work themselves. It's fortunate that Polk was an outstanding president, but he was the *only* outstanding president of that whole long period, until Lincoln came along.

It was also a difficult period for Polk because the condition of the nation was a peculiar one at the time, with southern states and northern states struggling against each other to gain control of the Senate. And of course, the entry of Texas into the Union, one more slave state that might upset the balance between North and South, exacerbated things. But Polk was interested strictly in what was good for the country as a whole, not in the wishes of one part of the country or another, and he felt very strongly that it would be the best thing for the country if the whole southwest corner of our area could be made part of the United States. The movement of pioneers and settlers into the West and the Southwest was taking place and increasing all the time, and he was all for an increase in the size of our country.

Around that time, a fancy phrase began to be used around the country. The phrase was "manifest destiny," and it expressed the belief of many of our citizens at that time that our country was destined, I suppose by God, to rule the area from coast to coast. Well, I don't like that phrase, and I don't think I'd have believed in it if I had been alive during that period, either; I think we were lucky in having people in the areas around us who wanted to become part of the United States, and I think we were smart in buying up some of those areas around us when we had the opportunity to do so.

Nor do I like the use of that phrase to define the difference between the way some other countries behaved over the years and the way we behaved. Here, for example, is something I've just read. "Imperialism implies the conquest of colonial people who would then be kept in a state of permanent subserviency to the mother country, but manifest destiny, on the other hand, proposes the annexation of adjacent territories whose people would then be elevated to a point where they can enjoy the benefits of the American Constitution.''

Well, it's certainly true that, when we took other territories into the United States, we did so with the idea that the people would have exactly the same privileges that people had in other parts of the country. But I don't care much for that ''elevated'' stuff, since the people we took in were just as good as we were to begin with, and I don't think ''manifest destiny'' has anything to do with it. I think we were just doing what's right.

Polk was a strong supporter of Texas's entry into the United States, both as a candidate and as president, so of course he was blamed when our war with Mexico started up about a year later. The plain fact, however, was that he had to meet the situation or lose Texas right after we'd gained it, and so he met it. Our annexation of Texas made Mexico our bitter enemy for a while; diplomatic relations broke off between our two countries, and we began to snarl at each other, with the United States insisting that our southwest border extended to the Rio Grande and Mexico insisting that it extended to the Nueces River, giving us much less territory. There was also a growing problem because many Americans had claims of various kinds against the Mexican government and kept pressing Washington because the Mexicans just ignored those claims.

Polk tried a peaceful approach first. He sent John Slidell, who had been minister to Mexico before the two countries broke off diplomatic relations, into Mexico, and Slidell carried in his pocket an offer to pay Mexico for the disputed territory, and at the same time pay additional money for the areas comprising New Mexico and California, which had become populated more by American settlers than by Mexicans. But the Mexican government wouldn't even give Slidell an audience, and Polk decided that the only thing to do was to send an American military detachment headed by Zachary Taylor into the controversial area between the Nueces and the Rio Grande.

It wasn't a big military force, just thirty-five hundred men, but everybody knew that it represented about half of the entire United States Army at the time, and the Mexicans viewed the arrival of Taylor and his men almost with amusement. On May 9, 1846, they sent a much larger force of Mexican soldiers across the Rio Grande and attacked Taylor's men immediately. This caused Polk to ask Congress to declare war on Mexico, and Congress made it official on May 13.

The vote to declare war on Mexico was passed by a big margin, 40 to 2 in the Senate and 174 to 14 in the House, but that didn't mean that Polk's decision was popular with everybody. He was called a warmonger and a militant expansionist, particularly by the Whig press, but every good American president has been an expansionist to a certain extent. One Whig newspaper even said it was such a wicked war that they hoped that all the soldiers sent down to fight would drown in the ocean and the country would be rid of them. Didn't some people say the same thing about our soldiers in Korea later on? The thing that was really bothering the Whigs, of course, was the fear that the accumulation of territory in the Southwest would make the Northeast less powerful, particularly since Texas had come in as a slave state and some other new states might come in the same way. Even Lincoln, who was then thirty-seven years old and an obscure congressman from Illinois who probably didn't think much about eastern power, was pretty vocal on the subject of the war because he was a Whig at the time and against anything Polk wanted to do. He called the war unconstitutional and an act of aggression and a very dirty business. And then he was the most unconstitutional president we ever had when he got there himself, because he had to be.

It's the sad truth that political parties, important as they are in certain ways, sometimes impede progress rather than advance things. You've got to have a leader with ability and strength to work out the welfare of the country in spite of what any party wants to do for its own purposes. And as far as I'm concerned, Polk was the perfect president for the period because what was needed was a man who was strong enough to meet the existing situation and carry through the program that he felt was right, and that's what Polk did. The Whigs were perfectly willing to vote a lot of money for matters that involved business, particularly big business, but didn't want to vote money for men and armaments even though the money was clearly needed. It was just like it is today. There isn't any difference. The Republicans are just Whigs all over again.

You've heard Nixon say that the Democrats always made war and Republicans always kept the peace. Well, that's just political conversation, nothing but political conversation.* Whenever it was necessary for a country to go to war, it didn't make any difference who was in power. How did the Spanish-American War come out under a Republican administration? It was a situation that had to be met and it was met. Why did the War Between the States take place, when Lincoln—also, of course, a Republican—wanted to preserve the Union? There isn't any difference in the situation when emergency comes—it makes no difference which political organization is in control of the White House. The

---

*My father originally used a shorter word here, but then decided to change it. MT

president has to make up his mind and decide what he wants to do and do it.

And Polk was living in an age when the terrific burdens of making decisions in a war were entirely in the hands of the president. And when that came about, he decided that there were much more important things than going to parties and shaking hands with people, and he became our third real commander in chief. Washington was our first commander in chief when we were still a collection of colonies and, when he became president, had to make it clear to the British that we intended to be a real country, and then Madison was commander in chief during the War of 1812, and Polk became our third. He acted both as president and as commander in chief because that's what it took. He insisted that all matters of consequence had to be approved by him, and he didn't delegate any real authority to anyone else, and he conducted the war right from the White House.

And he did a good job, even though I'm sure it was a terrible strain and helped contribute to his death at the early age of fifty-three, just three months after he left office. I know exactly how he must have felt, but in my time there were more able and informed people around to help the president, and that made a difference.

So Polk managed in time to get better artillery than the Mexicans and more soldiers than the Mexicans, and it didn't take too long to win the war once that was all accomplished. Old Fuss and Feathers Scott followed Taylor down into Texas, this time with ten thousand men, took Veracruz, and beat Santa Anna at Cerro Gordo. Taylor beat the Mexicans at Palo Alto, Resada de La Palma, and Monterrey. And then Taylor moved deep into Mexico and in September 1847, captured Mexico City, and the Mexicans asked for peace and signed a treaty early the next year.

The treaty was ratified by the Senate on March 10, 1848, and the Mexicans now took essentially what Polk had tried to offer them before the war. The Mexican government wasn't happy about selling the territory to the United States, of course, and encouraged Britain to bid for it. Russia was also in the picture for a while. But Polk insisted that our purchase of the area was an essential part of the treaty that ended the war and finally prevailed. The United States paid Mexico $15,000,000, just about what Jefferson had paid for the Louisiana Territory, and agreed to take over and pay any legitimate claims that American citizens had against Mexico, which eventually cost our government an additional $3,500,000. In return, we received an area of about a half-million square miles, meaning about two-fifths of Mexico's original territory. The agreement was that American territory would now extend from the mouth of the Rio Grande to the New Mexico line, then west to the Gila River, then along the Gila River to the Colorado River, and then along the boundary between Upper California and Lower California all the way to the Pacific Ocean.

And in time, that area formed all of California, all of New Mexico, and substantial parts of Arizona, Colorado, Nevada, and Utah. As you'd expect, some of the usual carpers of the period said he overpaid, but he was perfectly right in deciding that it was the best thing for the country if the whole southwest corner of the United States could be made a part of the nation, and of course, nobody can find fault with that arrangement at the present time. If you include Texas, the settlement with Mexico gave the United States an additional 918,000 square miles.

Polk also used the Mexican War to settle another territorial dispute, this one in connection with the Oregon Territory and with Great Britain rather than Mexico. Both our country and Britain claimed that territory, Britain saying it was part of Canada and our government saying it was part of the United States, and both countries had soldiers and settlers in the area going as far back as 1818. The United States insisted that it owned the land all the way up to the extreme northern boundary, which was 54°40′ latitude—and one of the Democratic slogans during the election campaign was "Fifty-four forty or fight!"—while the British insisted that American territory ended well below that at the Columbia River. Privately, the United States was completely willing to accept a compromise arrangement that would give us the disputed territory from latitude 42° north to the 49th parallel, and in fact we kept suggesting this to the British going all the way back to John Quincy Adams's administration, but the British kept turning us down.

Finally, at around the time Polk was sending troops down in the direction of Mexico, he again approached the British and once more offered to settle the dispute at the 49th parallel, hinting strongly that we were just as willing to take on the British to settle major territorial problems as we were the Mexicans. And this time the British agreed, and we signed a treaty with them in June 1846. We got the area that eventually comprised the states of Oregon and Washington, and the British got the area that eventually comprised British Columbia, and we've been friendly with our Canadian neighbors ever since.

We've also been friendly with Mexico since that time, of course. During the Mexican War, the Mexican government changed several times, and at one point old Santa Anna was in exile in Cuba, and we helped him by letting him through our blockade at Veracruz and getting him back into Mexico, in return for a promise that he'd help end the war and convince Mexico to sell us the territory we wanted. He then proceeded to break that promise, when he became president again, by fighting us harder than ever. But I can't agree with people who call him a charlatan for this reason, because some parts of Mexico didn't go along with him, and it turned out that he didn't have the power he thought he had. And when he organized his people to fight against us, he felt he was just defending his country, which I think he had every right to do.

And as far as Mexico itself is concerned, my only thought, when I visited that country, is how happy I was about our friendship with the Mexican people. The secretary of state of Mexico rode along with me and asked me if I would be willing to put a wreath on a monument to the heroes of a battle there, and I said of course I would. I didn't see any reason why heroes, wherever they are, shouldn't be recognized by both their friends and their former enemies. The secretary of state didn't think I knew anything about the battle, or the fact that it was a battle against the United States, but I did.

Polk left office on March 4, 1849, planning to tour for a month or so through the South and then live out the rest of his life quietly in a house in Nashville he had just bought from Senator Felix Grundy, and which he and his wife, Sarah, renamed Polk Place. But there was a cholera epidemic in New Orleans, and Polk contracted the disease there and died at Polk Place on June 15. The Polks had no children, so he left his estate entirely to his wife, requiring only that all their slaves be freed upon her death. It was the right requirement, but it proved unnecessary. Sarah Polk lived until August 14, 1891, and died at the age of eighty-seven, long after the Civil War brought the much better result of freedom for all slaves.

THIRTY-ONE
Lincoln, Surrounded by Tragedy

Old Abe Lincoln is the president I want to look at next, and for me as with nearly all Americans, he's a president I admire tremendously. In a way, it's surprising that I feel the way I do about Lincoln, because I was born and raised in the South, of course, and a lot of southerners still don't feel that way about him at all. And that included the Truman family, all of whom were against him. Some of them even thought it was a fine thing that he got assassinated.

I realized even as a child that that was pretty extreme thinking or worse; let's just call it dumb thinking, or no thinking at all. But it still took me a while to realize what a good man Lincoln really was, with a great brain and an even greater heart, a man who really cared about people and educated himself to the point where he knew how government should work and tried his best to make ours work that way. I felt just the opposite of the rest of the Truman family after I studied the history of the country and realized what Lincoln did to save the Union. That's when I came to my present conclusion, and that was a long, long time ago.

I suppose, too, that I shouldn't even refer to him as *old* Abe Lincoln, because he really wasn't old at all at any stage of his career. He was only twenty-three when he was a captain of Illinois volunteers serving under Zachary Taylor, twenty-four when he got a job as postmaster of New Salem, Illinois, twenty-five when he was elected to the Illinois legislature, thirty-eight when he was elected to the House of Representatives, and only fifty-one when he became our sixteenth president. And saddest of all, he was only fifty-six when he was murdered by John Wilkes Booth.

Probably the most surprising thing of all about Lincoln is the fact that he became president at all, because, by every standard and every rule of the game, the odds were totally against him. His grandfather, also named Abraham Lincoln, was a totally uneducated man who settled in Kentucky because a pal of his of whom you may have heard, a fellow named Daniel Boone, told him that land could be bought there for just a few dollars, following which the first Abe Lincoln was promptly shot dead by an Indian. Lincoln's mother, Nancy Hanks Lincoln, was illiterate, too, and I've read in some books that she was also illegitimate. She died when Lincoln was only nine. The future president's father, Thomas Lincoln, was totally illiterate, too, a man who couldn't read or write, could only barely scrawl his name when he had to sign some paper or other, and spent his whole life scratching out a bare living as a farmer and occasional carpenter.

And though Thomas Lincoln survived his first wife by thirty-three years, living until the age of seventy-three, he wasn't an especially good influence on his son, either. He married for a second time a year after Nancy Lincoln's death, this time to a widow named Sarah Bush Johnston with three children of her own, and seems to have become more interested in Sarah's kids than his own two children. Abe Lincoln and his father became increasingly distant, and Lincoln didn't even attend his father's funeral when the old man died in 1851.

Lincoln also seems to have been beset by tragedy all of his life. His only sister, Sarah Lincoln Grigsby, died in childbirth, aged twenty-one. The great love of his young life, some historians say, was a red-haired beauty named Ann Rutledge, but she died of typhoid fever at the age of twenty-four, and those historians maintain that Lincoln never really got over it. (I do want to mention, though, that other historians say that that story was all hooey and that Ann Rutledge was actually engaged to a friend of Lincoln's named John McNamar. And the woman Lincoln eventually married, Mary Todd Lincoln, always insisted that the story was completely false and was invented mostly by William H. Herndon, Lincoln's onetime law partner and biographer, just to hurt her by hinting that Lincoln really loved the memory of someone else more than he loved her. It's certainly true that Mary Lincoln and Herndon's wife despised each other, and that the so-called evidence about the Lincoln-Rutledge romance presented in Herndon's book was full of contradictions. Well, you can make up your own mind about that one.)

But there's no question about the tragedy in Lincoln's immediate family. Only one of his four children, all sons, lived to become an adult; that was Robert Todd Lincoln, who died at the age of eighty-three in 1926. Lincoln's second son, Edward Baker Lincoln, died in infancy; his third son, William Wallace Lincoln, whom Abe Lincoln called Willie and perhaps loved most of the four boys, died at the age of eleven; and Thomas Lincoln, whom Lincoln called Tad, died at the age of eighteen.

As everybody knows, Lincoln himself also had practically no formal education; his entire schooling when he was growing up in Kentucky and Indiana amounted to attendance of about a single year. But he was fortunate in one way, which was that his stepmother wasn't the traditional ogre at all; Sarah Lincoln was a good-hearted woman who treated young Abe like one of her own children, and she believed in education and encouraged her stepson to do a lot of studying and reading on his own. (I'm sure you remember Lincoln's famous statement: "All that I am, or hope to be, I owe to my sainted mother." I believe that statement refers to Sarah Lincoln rather than Nancy Lincoln, who died so young that she just didn't have the time to be much of an influence on her son.) And it was certainly Lincoln's private studies of everything from Aesop's fables to law books to the Bible and the works of Shakespeare that eventually made him the well-informed, clear-thinking, eloquent man he proved to be as president.

And still totting up all those odds against him, he certainly showed no signs in his early life that he'd eventually achieve success. His father made it clear that he considered his son capable of being nothing more than a farmer or a laborer, frequently loaning him out to other farms when he wasn't using him personally, at salaries of around a quarter a day. When Lincoln served as a soldier, his military career wasn't exactly distinguished; he was a captain for only one month and was reprimanded twice, once for firing off a gun by mistake and once for letting his men get drunk, after which he reenlisted as a private but saw no action. He later entered politics and ran for the state legislature, but came out eighth in a field of thirteen candidates. Then he left politics and opened a grocery store but went bankrupt after a few months, an experience that reminds me of another fellow who once decided to open a haberdashery. It took me twelve years, incidentally, to pay off my debts from that store; it took Lincoln seventeen to pay off his debts.

Around 1831, Lincoln, who was then living in New Salem, decided to study law, a decision that required him to walk twenty miles to Springfield many times to borrow law books because there just weren't any in New Salem. He supported himself with various odd jobs like that one as postmaster, which wasn't too arduous because mail was delivered only once a week in that area, and in 1831, as a Whig, he tried politics again with another shot at the state legislature. This time he got himself elected and served four consecutive terms, and in 1836 he received his license to practice law and opened an office the following year in Springfield. But his defeats weren't over yet. In 1843, he ran for the House of Representatives and was defeated; then he tried again in 1846 and was elected, but as I've mentioned, he talked so bitterly against Polk that he embarrassed his supporters, who walked away from him and returned him to private life. And then in 1854 he decided to run for the Senate and lost once more.

Would you have guessed, after all that, that Lincoln would become president of the United States just seven years later? I certainly wouldn't have. But Henry Clay was gone by this time, having died in 1852, and so were all the other great leaders of the time, and we were left with people like those nincompoops Pierce and Buchanan. And meanwhile Lincoln, despite his defeats, was developing a bigger and bigger reputation as a lawyer and as a bitter opponent of the theory, held by a lot of people, that the only way to end the controversy over slavery was to split the United States into two countries, one that permitted slavery and one that didn't. He wasn't an abolitionist; he felt, in fact, that abolitionists were unrealistic and doing more harm than good, and that the individual states where slavery already existed should decide for themselves, rather than have the federal government decide, whether or not slavery should be continued there. But he hated slavery and was strongly against seeing it spread, a feeling that developed in his mind and heart when he was twenty two.

In May 1831, he took a boat trip to New Orleans, and the things he saw there stayed with him the rest of his life. Another young man who went with him—his name was John Hanks, and I believe he was a cousin of Lincoln's—later reported, "We saw Negroes chained, maltreated, whipped, and scourged. Lincoln saw it; his heart bled . . . was silent from feeling, was sad, looked bad, felt bad, was thoughtful and abstracted . . . It run its iron in him then and there. I have heard him say so often . . ." And in 1858, having left the Whigs and joined the Republican Party, Lincoln decided to run for the Senate, mostly because his opponent would be the incumbent senator from Illinois, Stephen A. Douglas, who was running for reelection, and Douglas didn't seem to care whether slavery spread into the new states or not.

The contest between the two men brought on the famous Lincoln-Douglas Debates, a series of seven debates that took place in the small

Illinois towns of Alton, Charleston, Freeport, Galesburg, Jonesboro, Ottawa, and Quincy. On the surface, Lincoln and Douglas weren't all that far apart in their viewpoints. Both men hated slavery but felt that the preservation of the Union was more important than ending slavery, or at least ending it right away. Lincoln, in fact, stressed that in his speech accepting the senatorial nomination, his famous "House Divided" speech. "A house divided against itself cannot stand," he said. "I believe this government cannot endure permanently half slave and half free. I do not expect the Union to be dissolved; I do not expect the house to fall; but I do expect it will cease to be divided. It will become all one thing or the other. Either the opponents of slavery will arrest the further spread of it, and place it where the public mind shall rest in the belief that it is in the course of ultimate extinction, or its advocates will push it forward until it shall become alike lawful in all the states, old as well as new, north as well as South."

And even during the war, on August 22, 1862, he wrote a letter to Horace Greeley in which he said, "If I could save the Union without freeing *any* slave, I would do it; and if I could save it by freeing *all* the slaves, I would do it; and if I could do it by freeing some and leaving others alone, I would also do that."

Both men—unpleasant when you think about it today, but not surprising for the period, especially since some of the same kind of thinking continued right up into modern times—wanted black people to be free but not necessarily equal; Lincoln, for example, stated openly in the fourth debate that he was against intermarriage between blacks and whites and against allowing blacks to vote, hold office, or be jurors. Both men felt there was a basic difference between the two races and wanted whites to continue to rule the roost, though Douglas indicated that he felt that that was the natural right of the white man and Lincoln admitted that he preferred it because he was white himself. "There is a physical difference between the two," Lincoln said, "which, in my judgment, will probably forever forbid their living together on the footing of perfect equality; and inasmuch as it becomes a necessity that there must be a difference, I . . . am in favor of the race to which I belong having the superior position . . . But there is no reason why the Negro is not entitled to all the natural rights enumerated in the Declaration of Independence—the right to life, liberty, and the pursuit of happiness."

Speaking for myself, I could never see, even as a child, any more "physical difference" between whites and blacks than between people with brown eyes and blue eyes or black hair and blond hair, and as a friend of mine once said, none of us ask to come into the world and darned few ask to be allowed out of it, and we all look the same a few months or a few years after we're out of it anyway. But that was the way both Lincoln and Douglas felt. The big difference between *them,* however, is that Douglas was pretty cagy in expressing his feelings about slavery, never really coming out and saying that slavery was atrocious and evil, and being willing to allow new states to make their decisions about coming in as free states or slave states; whereas Lincoln, though his "House Divided" speech left it to the American people to reach the final decision on the subject, made it absolutely clear that the only correct and moral decision was an end of slavery, and therefore new states must come in only as free states. He defined slavery and the acceptance of slavery in wonderful language. "It is the same spirit that says, 'You toil and work and earn bread, and I'll eat it.' No matter in what shape it comes, whether from the mouth of a king who seeks to bestride the people of his own nation and live by the fruit of their labor or from one race of men . . . enslaving another race, it is the same tyrannical principle."

Lincoln lost the debates, I suppose; at any rate, Douglas took fifty-four state districts to Lincoln's forty-six and was reelected, though there was a lot of talk at the time that Douglas won the election only because there had been some altering of district borders before the election to favor the Democrats. But Lincoln's speeches made him famous nationally, and it was different, of course, when he again opposed Douglas, this time for the presidency.

Lincoln didn't just walk into the nomination: he was opposed by Senator William Henry Seward of New York, a very popular fellow who had also twice been governor of his state, and Seward beat Lincoln on the first two ballots, though not by a large enough margin to end the voting. But Lincoln won the nomination on the third ballot, and with Senator Hannibal Hamlin of Maine as the vice-presidential candidate, didn't have too much trouble beating Douglas and his vice-presidential candidate, Senator Herschel V. Johnson of Georgia. In the popular voting, Lincoln got 1,866,352 votes, representing 40 percent, Douglas got 1,375,157 votes, representing 29 percent, and two splinter candidates, John C. Breckinridge of the National Democrat Party, who had been old James Buchanan's vice president, and John Bell, candidate for the Constitutional Union Party, got 845,763, or 18 percent, and 589,581, or 13 percent, respectively. In the electoral votes, Douglas did much more poorly, carrying only one state, Missouri; Lincoln got a total of 180 electoral votes, Breckinridge 72, Bell 39, and Douglas 12.

Seward became Lincoln's secretary of state, as I'm sure most people remember from their reading and their history lessons. Douglas, who wasn't a bad fellow in many ways, put his strong support behind Lincoln, once he knew he wasn't destined to be president himself, and went on a speaking tour to try to help hold the country together. But he came down with typhoid fever after a speech in Springfield, Illinois, and died in Chicago on June 3, 1861.

The official starting date of the War Between the States is April 12, 1861, when South Carolina soldiers captured Fort Sumter and Lincoln declared war and called for 75,000 Northern volunteers. But as a practical matter, the war really began a couple of months before Lincoln walked into the White House on March 4. On December 20, 1860, immediately after the news of Lincoln's election reached the South, the South Carolina legislature voted unanimously to secede from the Union, and the Mississippi legislature followed on January ninth with a vote of 84 to 15, Florida on the tenth with a vote of 62 to 7, Alabama on the eleventh with a vote of 61 to 39, Georgia on the nineteenth with a narrower margin of 164 to 133, Louisiana on the twenty-sixth with a vote of 113 to 17, and Texas on February first with a vote of 166 to 8. The seven states immediately began to take over forts, arsenals, and outposts within their territories, and on February fourth, representatives of six states met in the state capital at Montgomery, Alabama, to form their own government, excluding only Texas, which couldn't get there in time. And on the ninth, Jefferson Davis of Mississippi was named president of the Confederate States of America and Alexander H. Stephens of Georgia was chosen as vice president.

Then Lincoln entered the White House, rushed in by train at night because there was already talk of plots to assassinate him, and said in his inauguration speech that he wasn't going to try to end slavery in the South but wouldn't tolerate secession by southern states. And then he learned that Fort Sumter, deep in the heart of South Carolina, had only a few weeks' worth of supplies and rushed more supplies down there, and South Carolina soldiers kept the supplies from getting there by firing on the fort, causing Fort Sumter to surrender. And the shooting war was on.

Virginia, the richest and most prestigious of the southern states, hesitated for a while about joining the Confederacy, but finally agreed to secede by a vote of 88 to 55 on April seventeenth; and even then, some pro-Union counties refused to accept the vote and formed their own state, West Virginia, which was formally admitted to the Union almost two years later, on January 1, 1863. Arkansas joined the Confederacy on May 6, 1861 and North Carolina on May 20. The three border states, Kentucky, Maryland, and my own state of Missouri decided to stay in the Union, though a lot of men from Kentucky and Missouri went and joined the Confederate forces on their own. And Delaware also decided to stay in the Union even though it was a slave state.

In May, the Confederacy made its first big mistake by moving its capital from Montgomery to Richmond, Virginia, which moved it closer to northern forces and therefore easier to capture. But though I know that Civil War buffs would be happy to argue this with me from dawn until dusk, they really didn't have a chance to win. The white population in the North was more than four times as large as the white population in the South, twenty-two million white northerners and five and a half million white southerners; there were nine Confederate states and twenty-two Union states when the war started, and that doesn't even include Kansas and West Virginia, which joined the Union later on. And the basically industrial North had far more money and far better transportation and communications facilities—22,000 miles of railroads in the North, 9,000 miles in the South—than the basically agricultural South, and a very much better navy.

The South probably had better generals, especially Robert E. Lee and Thomas Jonathan Jackson, who got the nickname of Stonewall Jackson because another commander, General Barnard Bee, said that he and his men stood like a stone wall at the Battle of Bull Run; but the North had some very good men, too. The best, of course, was old Ulysses S. Grant, who was, as I've said before, a failure and a drunk as a soldier in the Mexican War and in peacetime posts after that, a failure as a farmer and a real estate salesman and as a clerk in his father's dry-goods store when he left the Army for a while, and an even worse failure as president after the Civil War, but a really first-rate commander during the war. But there were others, too: General Phil Sheridan, for example, who cut off Lee's final retreat at Appomattox Courthouse, Virginia, and at last caused Lee to surrender; Admiral David G. Farragut, who bottled up New Orleans, the Confederacy's biggest city, with his fleet and caused its surrender, and then did the same thing to the port of Mobile, Alabama; and General George B. McClellan, who was only thirty-four years old but another damn good officer, though perhaps not as tough and courageous as he should have been.

I say this because he beat Lee in a battle at Antietam Creek, Maryland, on September 17, 1862, a battle that was probably the bloodiest day of the war and brought about a total of 23,000 deaths of men from both sides, but then let Lee retreat back into Virginia instead of chasing and capturing him. And a lot of historians believe that the war might have ended right then and there, with a tremendous saving of lives, two and a half years earlier than it did, if McClellan had had the courage and the sense to go after Lee. I know that's Monday-morning quarterbacking, but this time I think the quarterbacks are probably right. McClellan, incidentally, became Lincoln's Democratic opponent when Lincoln ran for reelection in 1864, but got only 1,808,725 votes, representing 45 percent, to Lincoln's 2,216,067 votes, representing 55 percent.

On July 13, 1862, Lincoln told the two men who were closest to him in his cabinet, Seward and his secretary of the navy, Gideon Welles, that he'd written a document that, he said, would announce his decision on what must be done about slavery. This was, of course, his Emancipation Proclamation, but it wasn't quite the sweeping or perfect decision that some people today half-remember it as being. Abolitionists had been urging Lincoln to free all slaves the moment the war started, and to a certain extent even before that, but Lincoln resisted doing so on the grounds that he didn't want to upset the slave states that remained in the Union. And then, when he finally made his move in that direction, he limited it to the third alternative he had indicated in his letter to Horace Greeley, a gradual move that freed some of the slaves, with only the hope that all slaves would eventually be freed.

The Emancipation Proclamation freed only those slaves in states or parts of states that were still "in rebellion" against the United States at the time the proclamation became law, using as a flimsy excuse for its limitations the fact that Lincoln was only able to do even that much by using his powers as commander in chief "as a fit and necessary war measure for suppressing said rebellion," but it allowed the slave states loyal to the Union—Delaware, Kentucky, Maryland, Missouri, and Tennessee—to keep their slaves—and even allowed slave owners in recaptured areas to do the same.

Lincoln read a preliminary draft of his proclamation to his cabinet on July 22, but then went along with Seward's suggestion that he hold it back until Union forces had won a substantial victory over the Confederates. That came on September 22 with the Union victory at Antietam, and Lincoln then read a revised draft of his Emancipation Proclamation. It became law on January 1, 1863, but there was no real way to enforce it while the war was going on, and Jefferson Davis and Robert E. Lee, desperate for reinforcements for the Confederate Army, countered it by inviting slaves to join up with the implied promise of freedom after the war if the Confederates won.

They didn't win, of course, and it took the Thirteenth, Fourteenth, and Fifteenth Amendments to the Constitution to end slavery forever in this country. The Thirteenth Amendment, adopted on December 18, 1865, abolished slavery without payment to slave owners. (That was an important financial consideration, since the government, already hard hit by the costs of the war, would have had to pay plenty if they had to compensate slave owners. In the years just before the war, the average price for a field hand in places like Missouri and Louisiana ranged from $1,200 to $1,600, and in one slave auction, a horrible phrase, the average price for "a prime field hand" was $1,900, with one particularly strong man going for $2,850.) The Fourteenth Amendment, which became law on July 28, 1868, stated that no state could "deprive any person of life, liberty, or property without due process of law." And the Fifteenth Amendment, which became law on March 30, 1870, gave all citizens the right to vote without considerations of "race, color, or previous condition of servitude."

There have been plenty of abuses of those laws, of course, and slavery continued in other parts of the world for a long time after that and is still continuing. In Brazil, for example, slavery wasn't abolished until 1888. And as recently as 1950, I saw a survey which estimated that there were four million men, women, and children held and working as slaves in Yemen, Saudi Arabia, Ethiopia, and other places.

The Civil War finally ended on April 9, 1865, with Lee's surrender at Appomattox. Lee was a truly great general; the only other generals who were under consideration to head the Confederate Army when the war started, and who stayed in the war until it was over, were Pierre Beauregard and Joseph E. Johnston—both graduates, like Lee, of West Point, though Lee graduated first in his class and I think the other two were a little further back in the ratings—but I don't think either of them could have handled the Confederate Army as well as Lee did, particularly in his campaigns in Virginia.

But when Lee moved into Pennsylvania and was driven back after those three horrible days of battles, from July 1 to July 4, 1863, at Gettysburg, and Grant took Vicksburg on that same July 4 and split the Confederacy by controlling the Mississippi River, that had more to do with ending the war than all those military maneuvers in Virginia. The bulk of the resources outside the area before that had been coming in from New Orleans, and of course that also cut Texas and Arkansas and Louisiana off from the Confederate government, and it was really the beginning of the end of the whole effort of the South to win the war. And when Lincoln delivered his Gettysburg Address on November 10 of that year, he talked as though the outcome of the war was still in doubt, but the truth was that the North had already won even though the war dragged on for another year and a half.

The cost on both sides was horrible: 359,528 men dead on the Union side, 258,000 dead on the Confederate side, with hundreds of thousands additional wounded. The bitterness between North and South continued for many decades, and no candidate for president from the Deep South has been elected to this day.* And five days after the end of the war, Lincoln was shot to death by John Wilkes Booth.

*The unofficial ban ended on November 2, 1976, with the election of Jimmy Carter. Carter is, of course, from Georgia. MT

* * *

I was once asked if I'd classify Lincoln as a liberal or a conservative. I don't like either of those terms, particularly in connection with Lincoln. I'd rather just say that he was a good president who worked for the benefit of the people and for the preservation of his country, and you can put him in any class you want—with the common people and the slaves and everybody else. He did everything he possibly could to save the Union, and he was willing to save the Union under any compromise if he possibly could, and he did save it.

He certainly wasn't a man of indecision, as some people said at the time. He was a man who wanted to get all the facts, and when members of his cabinet told him what he ought to do in this situation or that, he'd listen and make no statement, and that's the way he got that reputation with some people of being unable to make a decision. But the simple fact is that he was able to make a decision, all right, but he wouldn't make it until he had all the information he thought he ought to have. Then, when he finally got all the facts together, he made his decision. That's the difference, and there's a big difference between a man of indecision, and a man who assembles all necessary information before making his decision. Lincoln *had* to make decisions and take chances, and he studied each situation and made decisions that he felt were best for the people of the United States and for the rest of the world, and that's the reason he turned out to be a great president.

He was called a dictator and a tyrant, and that's why Booth shot him, but I don't think he ever went beyond the scope of the Constitution. He was a man who understood the Constitution, and he understood its intentions and the powers that aren't put down in writing, aren't in the actual language, but are there to be used by a president in emergencies. And he knew how much he could stretch it, stretching it to the point where it almost cracked, but he never actually cracked it.

During the emergency of the Civil War, he had to sidestep the things that were hampering him in his job, but it was absolutely necessary that he do that. He suspended habeas corpus, permitting military authorities to arrest and try people suspected of interfering with Union troop movements or otherwise helping the South, and he ordered the arrest of writers, publishers, and public speakers who wrote things or said things against the government or the government's operation of the war—actions I would never have taken, nor would any other modern president, but which Lincoln felt were unavoidable because there was so much bitterness, so much secret help to southern friends and relatives by northerners, and so much opposition to things the government was already doing, like the first military draft in our history, that he didn't want the situation inflamed still further.

But even with those extreme actions, I don't think he ever went beyond the scope of the Constitution; I think he just met the existing situation with emergency measures, and the Constitution provides for that. Suppose he hadn't? Suppose he just hung around, not knowing what to do and ending up doing nothing, and one of those northern generals, Grant or old Bill Sherman or someone else, was willing to say that this or that has got to be done and we'll take over the government and do it, and marched into the White House with his people? Lincoln maintained and used his authority as commander in chief of the armed forces, and I don't think he ever went outside his authority as commander in chief and president in doing the things that were necessary to save the Union. He worked with a Congress that was often hostile to him, and he worked with a hostile Supreme Court, and with a cabinet that was hostile most of the time, and he also had to fire four or five generals before he got one who won the war for him. But he managed to get around the obstacles and smooth things over so he could get things done that were absolutely essential.

His cabinet was particularly bad. His secretary of war during most of the Civil War was Edwin M. Stanton, and Stanton was everything and anything, just a chameleon. He was whatever was in. If you'll read an outline of his history, you'll find that he was for whatever he thought would help Stanton, and he didn't give a damn about principle at all. Seward was so-so; he was so egotistical that he once wrote, "It seems to me that if I am absent only three days, this Administration, the Congress, and the district would fall into consternation and despair," and Lincoln had to remind him from time to time that the name of the president was Abraham Lincoln and not William Henry Seward. Salmon P. Chase, the secretary of the treasury from 1861 to 1864, disagreed with Lincoln on almost every financial matter and kept quitting until Lincoln finally accepted his resignation. About the only really good man in the whole administration was Gideon Welles, who was a funny-looking old fellow with funny whiskers, but who was totally honest and loyal and smart. Welles's diary, incidentally, tells a lot about the character of every man in that cabinet, and it's worth reading.

Lincoln also had one of the balkiest Congresses that any president ever had. The Congress even set up a thing called the Committee on the Conduct of the War, also called the Committee of Fifteen, as a watchdog organization to make sure the president didn't do anything wrong. I'm very familiar with their activities because I was interested in the subject and read everything I could find after I organized a committee of my own during World War II; but there was a big difference because my committee consisted of people I picked myself to help me out, whereas that Committee of Fifteen was made up of the most antisouthern members of the period, and let me tell you, they were a real thorn in Lincoln's side. In particular, there was an old fool named Benjamin F. Wade, a senator from Ohio, and a senator named Zachariah Chandler from Michigan, and a fellow from Massachusetts whose name was Kootz or something like that, and they should have been tried for treason, all three of them, though they weren't.

But Lincoln knew how to handle people. He was a good lawyer and he always represented his clients well because he knew how to put forth the fundamental basis of his cases in a manner so that the jury understood him and he could win his cases. He knew how to win an election. He knew how to win over the people after he was elected. So he was patient with people and listened to what they had to say, and although that Committee on the Conduct of the War interfered with the conduct of the war no end and was a thorn in Lincoln's side all the time, he still managed to make the operation work in spite of them. And that's one of the gifts that a man has to have when he's in that sort of situation.

There's no doubt about the fact that Lincoln had to sidestep some things that were hampering him in the job that had to be done at the time, but Franklin Roosevelt did the same thing in World War II; he had to, when we had some of the same difficulties. He went ahead and accomplished the important purpose, to save the free world, and I had some of the same difficulties and did some sidestepping myself. I'll say a few words about that in the final chapter of this book, but as far as Lincoln was concerned, there's just one simple point: he saved the Union. And that's the important thing.

The Union forces allowed Confederate soldiers to keep their horses and their weapons when they returned home, but they weren't quite as courteous to Jefferson Davis. It was customary in those days to keep a fellow in chains when he was put in jail for a major crime, and Davis was captured in Irwinville, Georgia, in April 1865 and kept in chains in Fortress Monroe in Old Point Comfort, Virginia, for two years. Ironically, Davis's real popularity came after the southern surrender, after the war was over. During the war, his popularity went down all the time. He had trouble with the southern governors, he had trouble with his generals, he had trouble with his Congress, and he was not a conciliatory person. He always wanted everybody to agree with him, and if they didn't agree with him, there was trouble. But after the surrender, after they threw Davis in prison in chains, his popularity began to rise. The Committee of Fifteen was still calling the shots, and they did every dirty thing they possibly could, and of course it ended up making Davis the most popular man in the South. He was finally released on bail in May 1867, but the government never proceeded further against him, and he lived quietly and peacefully until his death in 1889.

I don't think Lincoln would have allowed them to do what they did to Davis, if he'd been alive, but of course he was gone himself by that time. No American, perhaps no person of any nationality, will ever forget that tragic event, but I'll describe it because it's possible to forget some of the details. It happened, of course, on April 14, 1865, Good Friday, when Lincoln and Mrs. Lincoln went to Ford's Theater in Washington to see a comedy, *Our American Cousin,* starring a popular actress named Laura Keane. Two friends were already in the presidential box, Major Henry Rathbone and Clara Harris. The Lincolns arrived late, and the performance was stopped to allow the audience to rise and cheer them. Then the play continued for ninety more minutes, reaching the second scene in the third act. At this point, Lincoln's single bodyguard, a man named John F. Parker, walked away for a moment, and John Wilkes Booth appeared suddenly in the presidential box and shot Lincoln in the back of the head with a single-shot .44-caliber derringer.

It was part of a plot to assassinate Lincoln and others in his administration, and at about the same time two other conspirators, David E. Herold and Lewis Thornton Powell, who was also known as Lewis Payne, went to Seward's house and stabbed him and three other people repeatedly, though all eventually recovered. Andrew Johnson, who became Lincoln's vice president in his second term, was also on the hit list, but the man assigned to that sorry job, George A. Atzerodt, lost his nerve and never approached Johnson.

Booth was a member of a famous acting family; his father, Junius Brutus Booth, was one of the world's best-known actors, almost as popular as Edmund Kean, and he had two brothers who were very famous, too, Junius Brutus Booth, Jr., and Edwin Booth. John Wilkes Booth was a popular performer as well. Most members of the Booth family were Union sympathizers, but John Wilkes Booth went the other way and constantly expressed enthusiasm for the Confederate cause even though he continued to act throughout the North during the war. Shortly before the end of the war, on March 20, Booth joined in a plot to kidnap Lincoln and take him to Richmond, Virginia, but when Lincoln failed to appear where Booth and six other men hid and waited for him, the assassination plan was set up.

After he shot Lincoln, Booth jumped down to the stage, shouting, "*Sic semper tyrannis! The South is avenged!*" He caught his foot on the flag of the presidential box as he jumped, breaking his left leg as he hit the stage, but he managed to escape from the theater and jump onto a horse that the other conspirators left for him. Then he joined Herold at a place called Garrett's Farm near Bowling Green, Caroline County, Virginia, but soldiers found the farm after two weeks of searching. The two men were hiding in a tobacco barn on the farm, and Herold gave up immediately, but Booth refused to surrender and the soldiers set fire to the barn and later found Booth shot to death in the rubble.

One of the soldiers, a man named Boston Corbett, claimed to have fired the shot that killed Booth, but some historians say that Booth probably committed suicide by shooting himself. Atzerodt and Powell were also captured soon afterwards, and Herold, Atzerodt, and Powell were sentenced to death and hanged. Two other men, Samuel Arnold and Michael O'Laughlin, both of them former Confederate soldiers from Maryland, took part in the kidnapping plan but not in the assassination and were given life imprisonment at Fort Jefferson in Dry Tortugas, Florida. And Edward Spangler, a stagehand at Ford's Theater, was convicted of helping Booth escape and given a six-year prison sentence.

There were also two miscarriages of justice connected with Lincoln's murder. The boarding house in which Booth lived while he and his friends were plotting was run by a widow named Mary Eugenia Surratt, and her twenty-one-year-old son, John Harrison Surratt, joined the other men in the kidnapping attempt, but went into hiding when that attempt failed and didn't take part in the assassination. Despite this, Mrs. Surratt was arrested along with the other people because "she knew about the assassination plan and didn't tell the authorities," and even though it's now pretty clear that she took no part in the assassination at all, she was hanged along with Herold, Powell, and Atzerodt.

The other unjust sentencing was that of Dr. Samuel Alexander Mudd, who set Booth's broken leg, for which he was tried along with the conspirators and sentenced to life imprisonment. Mudd was a Confederate sympathizer, but had nothing whatever to do with the assassination, and the sentence was unquestionably overharsh, particularly in view of the fact that a more active participant, Edward Spangler, got only six years.

John Surratt was captured and tried on June 10, 1867, for his part in the conspiracy, but probably because people now understood the injustice in the case of his mother, the jury voted eight to twelve in favor of acquittal. He continued to be held in prison, but was finally released a year after the trial and lived quietly until his death in 1916. Michael O'Laughlin died of yellow fever in prison in 1867, and President Johnson pardoned Mudd, Spangler, and Arnold in 1869.

The bullet that entered Lincoln's head was made of brittomia, an amalgam of antimony, copper, and tin, and it split in half as it entered, one part lodging in the brain and the other in the right eye socket. There was a physician in the audience that night, Dr. Charles Leale, and he was rushed to Lincoln's side and got rid of a blood clot to relieve pressure on the brain, but he said immediately that the president would not recover. Lincoln was carried across the street to Peterson's Boardinghouse and put down on a bed, which was so small that it wouldn't hold his six-foot-four-inch frame and he had to be laid down diagonally, and he died the following morning. It was a sad end to a short life that might have continued for many more years, years in which I'm sure Lincoln would have done many more good things for his country.*

Lincoln's widow, Mary Todd Lincoln, never really recovered from his assassination as she sat alongside him, and from the other tragedies in her life. Her little eleven-year-old son, Willie, had died in the White House just three years before, as I mentioned earlier, and now her husband was brutally murdered; and then in 1871 her youngest son, Tad, died, aged only eighteen. She also suffered terribly during the Civil War because she was a southerner herself, born in Lexington, Kentucky, on December 13, 1818, and had a brother and three half-brothers in the Confederate Army. It's no real wonder that, in 1875, she began to behave irrationally, saying that people were trying to kill her, and her sole surviving son, Robert Todd Lincoln, had to place her in an institution in Batavia, Illinois. But she was sufficiently recovered after three months to be released to the care of her sister, Mrs. Ninian Edwards, in Springfield, Illinois, and the following year she was declared entirely competent to handle her own affairs. The tragedies certainly shortened her life, however, and she died on July 16, 1882, at the age of sixty-four.

I read a book about Lincoln one time in which the author commented that Lincoln never said a kind word about Mrs. Lincoln in his life. I don't think that's true at all. One of the reasons that Lincoln remains an enigma in some ways, one of the reasons you can't tell a whole lot about what was really in Lincoln's mind, is because an immense number of his personal papers were destroyed by his son. Nicholas Murray Butler, who was president of Columbia University for a long time—from 1902 to 1945, if I remember correctly—ran up to see Robert Lincoln one time at Lincoln's summer home in New Hampshire, and there was Lincoln just deliberately throwing his father's papers into the fire. Butler stopped him, of course, and Lincoln left some papers over in a trunk that was to

---

*The sad truth is that my father is probably mistaken here. In 1978, Dr. Harold Schwartz, a noted physician associated with the USC School of Medicine, studied twenty years of medical evidence and research on Lincoln's physical condition and determined that Lincoln was suffering from a disease called Marfan's syndrome, a hereditary ailment that affects the heart and alters bone growth. Dr. Schwartz pointed out in a medical journal article that Lincoln's unusually long arms, fingers, and legs, and his visibly sunken chest, were typical of people afflicted with Marfan's syndrome, and so was a symptom that Lincoln himself described, an occasional involuntary twitching of his left foot, which is also typical of the disease. Dr. Schwartz's conclusion was that Lincoln was near death at the time of his assassination. MT

be opened twenty-five years after he passed on, but there was nothing of interest in the trunk when it was opened. But I think that, if we had the letters and papers and documents that were destroyed by Lincoln's son, we'd find that that comment in the book was entirely wrong, because Mrs. Lincoln's character was assassinated after Lincoln died, not before.

I was still in the Senate when that trunk was opened, and I was mad at the time about the loss of Lincoln's papers and I'm still mad about it. And the same kind of thing happened to Millard Fillmore; his son burned all his papers, and that's an outrage. Those papers, presidential papers, are really the property of the people and ought to be turned over to them as soon as a man comes out of the White House. If old Robert Todd Lincoln had done just that, that stuff about his father's attitude toward his mother would, in my opinion, have been gone forever. I don't believe a word of it.

The simple fact is that I've never believed most of the stories about Lincoln's marital problems, because I think Lincoln was the sort of fellow who, when he entered into the most sacred contract that a man can make, the marriage contract, which calls on husband and wife to love and respect each other for the rest of their lives, would have lived up to the letter and spirit of that contract to the end. I've read the things which say that Lincoln was not exactly attracted to Mary Todd when he met her at a dance in Springfield in 1839, when she was living with her sister there, and that he didn't show up at their wedding, and it took a while to bring him back to the marriage. I also know that he was supposed to have written to a friend, "I feel as if I'm being led to slaughter." (It's too bad that, when his son was destroying all those papers, he didn't destroy that one.) I've read these things, and I think a lot of it was nothing more than plain old marital jitters.

That didn't stop him from having a sense of humor about the marital state, either. I heard another Lincoln story one time that has never been published as far as I know. The Spanish ambassador was having an affair one time with one of the ladies in Washington, and they had a big iron fence around Lafayette Park, and the ambassador got locked in the park. Lincoln went inside the White House and got a ladder and helped him out. As far as I know, that's a true story, as true as some of the other stories that are told about Lincoln, anyway. It certainly fits in with his sense of humor, because he probably thought the Spanish ambassador's dilemma was funny.

Stop and think about the personal life of the Lincolns for a minute. Mary Todd Lincoln was twenty-three when she was married, at which time Lincoln was thirty-three and already a quiet, retiring fellow who was bound to be nervous about getting married. And Mary Todd was no wallflower when he met her at that dance; she was the daughter of a banker, an extremely well-educated and cultured young woman who spoke French fluently and went to the best schools, where she studied music and dance and a lot of other things. And think about some of the things that some biographers list in support of the theory of her mental instability. Her mother died when she was seven and she didn't get along with her stepmother, which is why she was living with her sister when Lincoln met her. Well, the world is full of fairy tales and true stories about stepchildren who didn't get along with their stepmothers and vice versa, and Lincoln had rare good luck that his own stepmother was such a wonderful woman. Mary Todd Lincoln was also a spendthrift, and to an excessive extent, but that doesn't make her crazy; I'm sure she was spoiled to a great extent by her rich father and began some of her bad habits that way. She's also supposed to have yelled at her husband a lot. Well, an awful lot of wives do that, though mine is a happy exception.

I think a lot of misinformation came about because of that nasty book by Lincoln's former law partner, and the libel was also carried on by a mean, radical segment of the press that didn't like Lincoln. Too bad; some of them ought to have been shot, and if old Jackson was still around, he would have shot some of them. (I don't really mean that.) But as a result of Herndon's book and that newspaper publicity, I think Mrs. Lincoln became one of the most mistreated and misrepresented women who was ever in the public eye.

Fortunately, there have been a number of good books published recently that have been both kind and careful in outlining the history of the Lincolns, and I think that, if you'll read those books, you'll find that there was nothing wrong with Mrs. Lincoln at all except for that brief period when the world and the sadness in her life got to be too much for her. She was like a lot of other wives. She didn't really understand what the limelight in the White House was going to be like, but there have been a great many other First Ladies exactly like that, and that's no real reflection on them at all. I don't think she had anything to do with urging him and pushing him to seek the presidency, as some books have said, though I think she had a great deal to do with urging him to keep it after he had it, particularly when he became discouraged about the job as all of us have at times, and I think she was very well satisfied and very happy in the White House in spite of what the *Chicago Tribune* and the *New York Tribune* and the *New York Herald* had to say at the time. In those days, the papers run by Horace Greeley and Charles A. Dana and James Gordon Bennett were the influential press of that day, but they were often mean and scurrilous and far from accurate.

I even read a book once that said that *both* the Lincolns were lunatics, that Mary Todd Lincoln was paranoid all her life and Abe Lincoln suffered from melancholia to the point of madness. Well, I don't believe that Mrs. Lincoln was paranoid all her life, and though I'm sure Lincoln suffered from bouts of melancholy, he controlled them sufficiently so that he didn't have them in public. He was bound to suffer that way; it goes with the job, especially in his situation where there were thousands of men being killed on both sides. I think his heart was just as strong for the men on the Confederate side as on the Union side, and it must have made his heart very, very sorry and sad when he heard the reports of battles and deaths.

This same stupid book even tried to hint that Lincoln was a secret drunk because the two men who followed him, Johnson and Grant, were such heavy drinkers. Well, as I've mentioned, I've never thought much of Grant drunk or sober, but Johnson wasn't a drunkard at all. His critics accused him of being erratic as a result of drinking because he was slightly tipsy at his inauguration, but that was because he was in poor physical condition when he was inaugurated, and he drank just a little brandy and got that way. He didn't drink any more at other times than the average fellow does in the White House. And as far as Lincoln is concerned, I don't know whether Lincoln drank or not, but he was certainly no heavy drinker. I imagine he used some of the good product that came from his home state. I think it's been said in other books that he didn't like the stuff. Well, that's all right if true. It's a very good thing when a fellow doesn't like it. I don't like it, either.

I'll end this chapter by saying again that Lincoln was a great and wonderful man in every way. He didn't believe in putting up a front. He always showed up as plain, decent Abraham Lincoln, and he always showed up as the man who happened to have the job of president of the United States and was therefore in charge of things, and that's the sort of man I admire. There's nothing in the world I dislike more than a stuffed shirt who tries to put on a front and make people think he's something that he isn't. Stuffed shirts can always have a pin stuck in the shirt, and then the wind comes out and you find that they're counterfeits. I don't think it was a pose on Lincoln's part. I think he was just plain Abraham Lincoln all the time, in public and in private, and that's just what a man ought to be, just himself, no matter what job he has, even if he's president of the United States or king of a great country. If he's himself, he'll be all right. King George VI was the same sort of man, an honest, straightforward public servant. It doesn't make any difference what position he may hold; if he's that kind of man, he won't have any trouble being a good man in this world of ours.

THIRTY-TWO

Woodrow Wilson—
Too Smart to
Be President?

IF you're very young, you've probably never even heard of a fellow named Champ Clark, but he was a very important man to Missourians and to a lot of other people back in 1912. He was speaker of the House at that time, and he seemed much more certain to become our twenty-eighth president than a relatively obscure former college professor named Thomas Woodrow Wilson.

I was fairly young myself in June 1912, twenty-eight years of age, and I was helping my father out and cutting wheat in the field at home, on our hundred and sixty acres where there's a big business development now, while the Democratic National Convention was going on in Baltimore. There was a little telegraph station in a field about a quarter of a mile away, and information would come in the form of short little bulletins, and somebody would tell me that a new message was in and I'd run over there. I'd bring the binder around there and tie the lines around the brake and go over and find out what was going on. My father was for Champ Clark, practically all Missourians were; as you've gathered, old Champ was a Missourian himself, and he would have been the first president ever from Missouri, so we all hoped he would be nominated and elected. And we were sort of stunned when we finally learned that the Democratic party had nominated Wilson instead of Clark.

In that election, the Republicans were fighting with each other, their official candidate being President William Howard Taft, up for reelection, while Teddy Roosevelt ran as an independent on the Bull Moose ticket, so the Democratic choice was just about certain to get in, and just about the whole country assumed that the Democratic choice would be Champ Clark. Clark was an old war-horse politician who was born in 1850 and served in the House of Representatives from 1893 to 1921 with just a single brief break in 1896. The more progressive members of the Democratic party considered him just a touch too cautious and slow-moving in most of his policies, but he was a very popular man and seemed certain to get the nomination.

Among other reasons, there was no one else around as well-known to the voters as he was. Wilson was in the picture, of course, with a growing reputation for intelligence and efficiency as a man who rose from a salary of $1,500 a year as a professor at Bryn Mawr to become president of Princeton University and then governor of New Jersey; but he also had a reputation of being a stiff-necked professorial type, still very much the aristocratic president of a great university, a man who found it hard to get along with people who he was sure didn't know as much as he did. That's where his trouble lay: he knew many things better than most people who came in contact with him and couldn't help but show it, and that doesn't work too well with congressmen and senators with whom a presidential candidate and president has to get along. And William Jennings Bryan was still around and in many ways was still one of the strongest people in the party, but Bryan had run for president three times and been beaten by McKinley in 1896 and 1900 and by Taft in 1908 and wasn't likely to be put up again.

These days, about the only thing people seem to remember about Bryan is that he was on the wrong side in that nonsense in Dayton, Tennessee, in July 1925, when young John T. Scopes was put on trial for teaching, in his biology class, the Darwin theory about man's being descended from apes, and thereby contradicted the biblical explanation of man's creation. But that was just a bit of silliness that Bryan himself came quickly to regret, and in many other ways Bryan was one of the best people in the country and certainly one of the best men associated with Wilson. I truly think that Bryan might well be one of the most misunderstood and underestimated men in American history. He was in a class by himself from about 1896 on, the man who was in the forefront for the welfare of the common, everyday fellow who didn't have any real representation of any other kind.

If it hadn't been for Bryan, there would have been no truly liberal program continued in the United States; the things Bryan suggested and wanted, financially and in every other way, were the things that came into effect when Wilson was president, and were the stimulant for the even more liberal programs that came into effect with Franklin Roosevelt twelve years later. The idea of the Federal Reserve Board, which was set up under Wilson in 1913, was to arrange things so that there was enough circulating medium to enable the ordinary man to carry on his business and his life, and that's all Bryan ever wanted in that area, and he was also in the forefront in agricultural reform and labor reform and child labor reform and a lot of other things. These things were mostly the result of influence exerted by William Jennings Bryan. That's absolutely correct, and in my opinion, history will tell it that way.

Well, Bryan knew that he didn't have a chance personally in the 1912 election, and he went to the convention strictly with the idea of supporting Clark. But the situation at that point in our history was that the finances of our country had developed to the point where the bankers were in total control, and Bryan wanted to be sure that that would change if, as seemed certain, the Democrats would get in this time and displace Taft and Teddy Roosevelt and all the other Republicans.

To understand the question of financial control of our country, and to put it into the simplest terms, you've got to keep in mind the fact that the Federal Reserve Board was set up with the plan of increasing the circulating medium, of issuing more currency so that there would be more money around for business loans and for transacting business in general. But you've also got to keep in mind the fact that those dollar bills had to be based on something valuable so they wouldn't just be meaningless pieces of paper, but rather, a sort of promissory note backed by something of value. In those days, the valuable thing backing our currency was gold, with the issuing of currency dependent on the amount of gold in the country, and our finances became a controlled proposition because the New York banks cornered most of the gold in the country and thereby controlled most of the currency in the country, and that made money scarce because the banks kept raising interest rates on loans and only very big firms could afford to borrow money at those rates.

Eventually, of course, Franklin Roosevelt took us off the gold standard entirely. His point was that gold was artificial backing, too, just a piece of metal in the way that the dollar bill is just a piece of paper and doesn't mean anything unless it's backed itself by commodities—corn and wheat and oats and automobiles and factories and everything else that makes up the industrial center of the country. Goods of every kind. Things were to be handled in a way so that the financial backing of the currency in circulation wouldn't be gold alone, but gold backed by commodities; thereafter, gold would be used only on a very small percentage basis, and the real backing would be the whole commercial and commodity strength of the whole United States. That would make our currency much sounder than when just backed by gold, and the cornering of the gold market couldn't in any way affect the currency of the United States. The government would base the issuance of currency on the economic strength of the country, trying to make sure that enough money was around so that it would be available to everybody and not just to the biggest and strongest business organizations.

But gold was still the backbone of our currency in Wilson's day, and the idea of the Federal Reserve Board was to increase the circulating medium but with absolutely sound backing, by controlling gold and setting up twelve regional Federal Reserve banks—in New York, Philadelphia, Boston, Cleveland, Atlanta, Richmond, Chicago, Minneapolis, St. Louis, Kansas City, Dallas, and San Francisco. These would in effect be banks' banks, issuing Federal Reserve notes and loaning out money to banks to loan to the public and to business more painlessly and cheaply, the money to be given out more freely when times were tough and loans were really needed and tightened up when it seemed necessary to try to control inflation. As an example, the circulating medium back in the twenties was about three and a half billion dollars, and I think it's now up around thirty billion. If the big banks had had their way, they would have kept currency to the point where they could choke off credit whenever they felt like it. The objective of the Wilson administration for the Federal Reserve Bank, in short, was to make credit available in all sections of the country on the basis where it would increase building programs and help industry, and in particular help the small merchants and small businessmen.

That was the kind of thing that Bryan wanted, and he set out to talk to Clark about it, but then Clark made a terrible tactical error; he shut himself up and wouldn't talk to Bryan or anyone else on the subject. (I'm not sure why he behaved in that stupid way; the people who supported Clark never forgave him, and they're still talking against him to this day. And I don't blame them.)

Bryan was a delegate from Nebraska, and the Nebraska delegation was instructed for Clark and voted for him in the early balloting. But Bryan was a particularly important supporter because he was the head of the Democratic party, and he wanted to be sure that control of the country's finances didn't remain in the hands of the bankers; and when Clark wouldn't see him and talk to him about the matter, he kept thinking about it and thinking about it and finally decided that he just couldn't support Clark.

In the beginning, Clark had a clear majority of the votes locked up, but not the two-thirds majority needed to give him the nomination. On the first ballot, Clark got 440½ votes, Wilson got 324, and a congressman named Oscar W. Underwood, a man from Alabama who was supported by conservative southerners, got 117½. The amount needed to give one of the candidates the nomination was 726 votes. Things continued pretty much the same way for eight more ballots, and then, on the tenth ballot, the Tammany Hall delegates gave their support to Clark. This Tammany Hall support brought Clark's total up to 556, still not enough for the nomination, but it convinced Wilson that he had no chance and he might as well throw in the towel. But just as he was ready to give up, one of his strongest supporters, a fellow named William Gibbs McAdoo, who later married one of Wilson's daughters and also became the first chairman of the Federal Reserve Board, called him and begged him not to quit, and Wilson decided to stay in a while longer.

And it was a good thing he did, because Tammany Hall's support of Clark had a different effect on Bryan; as far as he was concerned, Tammany Hall was New York and New York was Wall Street and the bankers who controlled credit and currency flow and all the rest, and he got up and made a speech against August Belmont, who was the head of the Tammany organization. Belmont was immensely wealthy and a member of the famous old New York family, but he was also just a hack Tammany politician, and in a sense Bryan's speech was also a speech against Champ Clark. He looked old Belmont right in the eye and pointed to him as he spoke, and then he would turn and look contemptuously at Clark, and then back at Belmont again. Just about everybody in the country was overwhelmed by that speech, and I think it was reported that they got something like five hundred thousand or six hundred thousand telegrams. It took quite a while longer, and the voting continued all the way from June 27 to July 2, but that was the end of the situation as far as Clark was concerned. Wilson began to move closer and closer to Clark after Bryan endorsed him officially, moving ahead of Clark in the thirtieth balloting. He had 633 votes in the forty-fifth balloting, and then everybody moved into his corner and he won the nomination in the forty-sixth tally with 933 votes. Even my father and I decided that Bryan was right and Wilson was the right man.

All this made Wilson technically a minority candidate, of course, since the majority of the delegates at the convention, and the general public behind them, had started out by supporting Clark, but it made very little difference. It made about half as much difference as it did when Lincoln came in as a minority candidate, because a lot of people in Lincoln's party continued to oppose him after he was nominated, and even after he was elected president, whereas most Democrats rallied behind Wilson and continued to support him after he was nominated. But there's certainly no question about the fact that he was an unusual and unexpected man to be chosen.

He was certainly no professional, knowledgeable politician. Back in his student days, Wilson said in his Ph.D. dissertation that leaders like governors and presidents should make decisions alone and not be influenced by hidden party machines or political bosses, and he tried hard to adhere to that philosophy when he went into politics himself. When he agreed to run for governor of New Jersey in 1910, he did so on the strict condition that nobody try to tell him which bills to support or which people to hire to run the state, and in the brief time he was in that job, he got through a number of laws designed to keep politics on the up-and-up, including a law that required political candidates to file financial statements on their campaigns and prohibited corporate contributions to those campaigns, and a law that simplified and improved voting methods. He even fired the top political boss in New Jersey, a fellow named James Smith, when Smith tried to tell him what to do. And at the Baltimore convention, Wilson made it clear that he wanted the nomination strictly on merit and not on the basis of a collection of little private deals, warning his associates that they'd be dropped if they even hinted at the possibility of a political office or other job to anyone, making it clear that "not a single vote . . . will be obtained by means of a promise."

But he was also a practical man, and he learned pretty quickly that life just wasn't that way, and he had to go to work and agree with political bosses on some things in order to get elected and then reelected. He couldn't separate himself totally from the political bosses. Why, of course he couldn't, because he'd never polled a precinct in his life, and he never had anything to do with the ordinary day-by-day fundamentals that make up politics like getting people out to vote, and he just didn't have anybody down on the ground to go around and talk to people, to the general public. Politics is the ability to get along with people, and politics is government, and some of the so-called bosses are just people who understand the political situation from the ground up. Wilson had to make his peace with them in order to get into office and stay in office, and he never would have been nominated if the bosses at the Democratic Convention hadn't been in control of certain parts of the organization that would nominate him. He still believed in personal leadership by men like himself, but leaders have to have an organization behind them or they don't get to lead.

The other thing that surprised some people about Wilson's quick political popularity and his nomination, his move in just a couple of years from Princeton University to the White House, was that very fact—the fact that he was a college professor, and a college professor who was extremely liberal in his political thinking at that. Nobody really expected an intellectual like Wilson to become president. Well, as far as his liberal political thinking is concerned, I've said several times in this book that I truly don't like hanging those labels on people because they're often misleading and mean different things to different folks; but if you want to call him a liberal, well, then he was a commonsense liberal. He wasn't one of these synthetic liberals. He was a liberal who was for the welfare of all the people around in your neighborhood and my neighborhood. And when the time came for a decision between the special interests as represented by Belmont and Tammany Hall, and the people as represented by Wilson, the convention and then the country went for Wilson.

He was certainly also a college professor; in fact, he was the first professional educator to become president of the United States. (Of course, the last president, as I write these lines, was a college president, too, but we're talking about very different kinds of people here. Wilson had great knowledge and a great mind.) Getting back to real educators, a great many presidents taught school, of course. Garfield taught school, and several others taught school, but they were not the executive heads of great universities; Wilson was the first one, I think, in that position. And he was a lot more than "a mere college professor," as some people called him at the time. He had written a history of the United States that's still one of the basic sources of information on government in the United States from the beginning, and he'd studied history thoroughly and knew what it was all about. And he'd made it clear in his history, and in his speeches, that his dream and his plan was to set up a program that would continue the ideals of the Constitution, and of course everybody liked that idea.

And of course, he was obviously and visibly one of the smartest people in the country and possibly in the world. Wilson had the idea that he was *the* smartest man in the United States, and as I've mentioned, of course people associated with him didn't like that attitude, but it's probably the truth. His speeches and his messages stated his case clearly and in a language that the people could understand, and he could always get his audience to be with him.

As I mentioned earlier, he was the first president in a long time to go down to the Congress personally and read his State of the Union message, and it made a big hit with the Congress. He knew his messages by heart; he didn't read them, he delivered them. I was talking to a fellow recently who used to sit behind Wilson when he was making his speeches, and he said Wilson would keep one hand behind him, and every time he would go through a point he would put his thumb on his first finger on the next point, and the next point, and the next point, and the fellow said he followed his speeches through and he never changed a word in his delivery of his points after he'd written them. It takes a genius to do that. He was a great man, a truly great man. I'm certain that history and historians will mark Wilson down as one of our greatest presidents, and in a sense, this book is in some ways a history book and I'm doing that right now.

I think the country had pretty much made up its mind that it didn't want any more of the Republican program by the time Wilson received the nomination and began to campaign for the presidency. Teddy Roosevelt had been a pretty popular president from his start in office on September 14, 1901, after McKinley had been shot on the sixth and died a week later, until the end of his second term on March 4, 1909; and Taft was also popular during his single term after Teddy Roosevelt finished up and said he wanted Taft to succeed him, but people were just sick of what the Republicans had accomplished, or rather, failed to accomplish. The plain fact is that we had a backward-looking program in regard to the welfare of the country and the world from Cleveland's second term in 1892 to the end of Taft's term in 1912, and it was obvious that Wilson was determined to change all that. So when the time came to make a decision about who should be our next president, and Bryan got on Wilson's bandwagon, that did it.

Wilson went up against three pretty strong opponents. The three were Taft, the Republican candidate, who was a strong contender because he was the incumbent, which always helps, and because he was a big, fat, hearty fellow who weighed 332 pounds and was always smiling, and whom most people liked on sight; Teddy Roosevelt, who came back from a highly publicized African safari saying that he'd made a mistake in backing Taft because Taft had proved too conservative in his actions as president, announcing that he was going to run himself on the Progressive Republican, or Bull Moose, ticket; and Eugene V. Debs, the Socialist candidate.

Teddy Roosevelt was often more bull, without the moose, than substance. As I've said earlier in this book, he talked an awful lot about breaking up trusts but broke up darn few of them. He also talked a lot about serving the needs of the little man, but never really succeeded; I suppose he tried to a certain extent, but just couldn't succeed because the controls at that time were again in the hands of the people who believed in special privilege. And up to 1912, he kept saying that he was absolutely against a president's serving for more than two terms, but he now explained away his candidacy by saying that he meant a president shouldn't serve more than two *consecutive* terms. To be completely honest about it, I think the best thing old Teddy ever did in his life was break up the

Republican party and get Wilson elected. And when people went to the polls, their preference for Wilson over the other three men was pretty obvious.

Wilson ended up with almost as many popular votes himself as the combined total of his three opponents, and more than four times as many electoral votes. Wilson got 6,286,820 votes, representing 42 percent, to old Teddy's 4,126,020 votes, 27 percent, Taft's 3,483,922 votes, 23 percent, and Debs's 901,255 votes, representing 6 percent. And in the electoral vote, Wilson got 435 votes to Roosevelt's 88 and Taft's 8; he carried forty states out of the forty-eight we had at the time, giving only California, Michigan, Minnesota, Pennsylvania, South Dakota, and Washington to Roosevelt and only Utah and Vermont to Taft. And in Wilson's bid for reelection in 1916, when he was opposed by Charles Evans Hughes, later the Chief Justice of the Supreme Court, and where things were much closer because Teddy Roosevelt stayed out personally this time and reunited the Republicans by throwing his support to Hughes, Wilson still managed to win with 9,129,606 popular votes to Hughes's 8,598,221 votes, and 277 electoral votes to Hughes's 254.

Wilson also had trouble in that second election, incidentally, because he had to take some strong action against Mexico in the years between 1913 and 1916, which made a lot of Catholics decide that Wilson was anti-Catholic and vote against him. They were dead wrong, of course, because the fact that Mexico's population was mostly Catholic had absolutely nothing to do with it. At that time, we were not on very friendly terms with the Mexican government. A fellow named Porfirio Díaz was the head of the government for a very long time—from 1877 to 1911, in fact—and Americans invested around a billion dollars in Mexican business; and then there was a revolution and a man named Francisco Madero took over and didn't do a thing to protect Americans and American money; and then Madero was assassinated and another man, Victoriano Huerta, grabbed power by military means, not by election, and was even less friendly to Americans and to the United States, particularly after Wilson said he wouldn't recognize a government built on assassination.

Things got bad when Mexican soldiers arrested some American sailors in Tampico, Mexico, even though they released them right away, and then got worse when a fellow whose real name was Doroteo Arango, but who called himself Francisco Villa and then was nicknamed Pancho Villa instead of Francisco, and who pretended to be a Mexican patriot but was really nothing more than a bandit and a gangster, invaded Columbus, New Mexico, and killed a number of Americans. Wilson had to send naval forces to shell and occupy Veracruz and Army forces under

General John J. Pershing into Chihuahua after Villa, which is why he lost all those Catholic votes.

Huerta eventually resigned and left Mexico, lived in Europe for a while, and then came to the United States and died of alcoholism in an El Paso, Texas, jail. Pershing never caught Villa, who lived on for a number of years but was finally murdered by some of his own people in 1923. (Pershing's expedition made him famous, however, and resulted in his becoming commanding general in World War I. And I served under him, of course.) But in more recent times, even though there was another Mexican president named Huerta, Adolfo de la Huerta, who came in by revolutionary means some years after that first one, Mexico has now had five or six duly elected presidents, and has followed a program of government on the basis of a chief executive and legislative and judicial branches, and it is as fine a government as there is anywhere in the world, including our own.

I don't think Wilson's intervention into Mexico was an act of aggression, not at all. He had no territorial ambitions. He was trying to keep peace on the border and prevent a dictator from going outside his prerogative as president of Mexico. And the successors of that regime, at least the more recent successors, have all been friendly to us, and they've been statesmen and the finest kind of men. I know from personal experience, because I've been acquainted with nearly every one of the men who's been in there since Wilson's time. I think, in fact, that Wilson's actions helped stabilize the Mexican government. I think that was his real intention. When those things were done, there was terrible turmoil going on in Mexico, but that's been straightened out, and they now have a peaceful approach to elections and to everything else that takes place in that country. I don't think Wilson had any intention of infringing on the prerogatives and powers of the Republic of Mexico. I don't think his action was contrary to his policies of peace. Wilson was trying to achieve peace in the Western Hemisphere, and his efforts finally succeeded.

I think I ought to stop at this point and say a few things about Wilson's personal life, so that you know a bit more about the man who served as president during the crucial period of the first of the two terrible world wars. And I guess as good a way as any to start is to express my personal opinion that he should have continued to call himself Thomas Woodrow Wilson, or possibly even just plain Thomas Wilson if he was bent on dropping one of his names, because he was an austere-looking fellow all his life, and I think he'd be remembered more affectionately if people could think of him as Tom Wilson the way you think of Lincoln as Abe Lincoln. "Woodrow" always struck me as an awfully fancy name, but that was apparently the way Wilson wanted it, since he started calling himself T. Woodrow Wilson right after college, and then dropped his first name and that initial entirely.

He really wasn't as cold and reserved as he looked in his photos and public appearances, and he wanted almost desperately to help people and improve the world around him, but he was no bundle of laughs, either. He was essentially a serious type, possibly because he was descended from and surrounded by church people. His maternal grandfather, Thomas Woodrow, after whom he was named, was a Presbyterian minister; so was his father, Joseph Ruggles Wilson; one of his two sisters, Marion, married a minister, Anderson R. Kennedy; and his first wife, Ellen Louise, was the daughter of a Presbyterian minister, Samuel E. Axson, and granddaughter of another minister, I.S.K. Axson. But Wilson had a sense of humor, too, and because he had a thin face and wore glasses from the age of eight and considered himself an ugly man, he once wrote a limerick about himself that I still hear people quoting from time to time, even though I don't think that most people remember that it was the work of our twenty-eighth president:

For beauty I am not a star
There are others more handsome by far
But my face I don't mind it
For I am behind it
It's the people in front that I jar.

Wilson was of Scotch-Irish descent; his maternal grandfather came to this country from Paisley, Scotland, in 1835, and his paternal grandfather, James Wilson, came here from Strabane, Ireland, in 1807. Wilson's father grew up in Ohio and served as pastor in churches in Virginia, Georgia, and North Carolina, and his mother, Janet Woodrow Wilson, whom people called Jessie, also grew up in Ohio, and attended the Chillicothe Female Seminary before settling down with her husband and raising a family. The Wilsons had four children: Marion, who was the oldest, Annie next, then Thomas Woodrow, and finally Joseph, who became a newspaperman in Nashville and then an insurance man.

Wilson, who was born on December 28, 1856, in Staunton, Virginia, where his father was then serving, worried his parents as a child because he seemed almost retarded and didn't learn to read until he was nine, and he remained baffled by mathematics throughout his life. But he managed to get through his preliminary schooling and enrolled in the College of New Jersey, which later became Princeton University, in 1875, and graduated with a ninety average, after which he entered the University of Virginia Law School. He had to drop out due to illness, but studied at home and was admitted to the bar in 1882. But he didn't really care for law and went back to school, entering Johns Hopkins and earning a Ph.D. in political science in 1886. (He's the only president in our history, incidentally, with an earned doctorate. As I say, the man had quite a brain.) And then he taught law and political science at Bryn Mawr, history at Wesleyan in Middletown, Connecticut, politics and jurisprudence at Princeton, and finally became president of Princeton and president of the United States.

Wilson met Ellen Louise Axson in April 1883 and became engaged to her in September, but their marriage was postponed until June 24, 1885, so that he could get through Johns Hopkins and get that job teaching at Bryn Mawr, which was just then starting up as a brand-new college for women. The Wilsons were married for twenty-nine years, and they had three daughters: Margaret, born in 1886, who never married, but was first a singer with the Chicago Symphony Orchestra, then an advertising executive and stockbroker, and died of uremic poisoning in 1944 in a religious retreat in Pondicherry, India; Jessie, born in 1887, who was a social worker before she married a law professor named Francis B. Sayre, and died in 1933 of complications after an operation for appendicitis; and Eleanor, born in 1889, who married Wilson's friend William Gibbs McAdoo in 1914, but the couple were divorced twenty years later, and she lived out her life in California and died in 1967.

The Wilsons had a good marriage, and Ellen Wilson supervised happily the marriage of her two daughters in the White House. But then she came down with Bright's disease, the official name of which is glomerulonephritis, a kidney ailment that is nearly always fatal, and she died on August 6, 1914, aged only fifty-four. Wilson was prostrated by her death; he told his close friend Colonel Edward Mandell House that he hoped someone would assassinate him, and House believed that his death wish was sincere. But just eight months later, one of Wilson's cousins, Helen Bones, who took over as White House hostess after Ellen Wilson's death, introduced Wilson to a forty-three-year-old widow named Edith Bolling Galt, a lively and good-looking woman who was the daughter of a Washington judge and a direct descendant of Pocahontas. Wilson fell in love immediately with Mrs. Galt, and the next month asked her to marry him.

The press began an immediate and fierce attack on Wilson, saying that Wilson was behaving with extreme disrespect to his late wife in courting a woman so soon after his wife's death. There was also a typographical error in a *Washington Post* story that was so pointed, though it was apparently unintentional, that the *Post* hurried to call back all copies of the edition, but some got out and became collector's items.*

Wilson and Mrs. Galt were engaged officially in July, but the furor over their alliance became so severe that Wilson offered to let her out of their engagement if she wished it. She didn't, and they were married on December 18, 1915. The second marriage was as happy as Wilson's first, and Wilson's last word was a calling out of his wife's name when he died nine years later, on February 1, 1924. The second Mrs. Wilson lived on for thirty-seven years and died at the age of eighty-nine on December 28, 1961—coincidentally, you'll notice, Woodrow Wilson's birthday. She remained active all her life, attending Franklin Roosevelt's and John F. Kennedy's inaugurations and other functions, and was still quite a good-looking woman even in old age. My daughter Margaret stood next to her at the Roosevelt inauguration and was quite impressed with her good looks, even though she was already well into her seventies.

Thinking about it now, many years later, it's really astonishing that Wilson was able to put through so much reform in so short a period, far more than most other presidents managed to accomplish during their administrations. A leader who has a program that's worthwhile, as Wilson did, can put his program over, and if it hadn't been for the First World War, and the things that forced us into that war, I think the Wilson administration would have been considered one of the best we've ever had, second perhaps only to Franklin Roosevelt's. Well, the country was ready for it—I guess that's the principal reason. The country had all sorts of difficulties and problems at the time, and when Wilson came along, he appealed to the people in a way that no other president had appealed to the people since—well, I'd say since the time of Grover Cleveland, though I suppose that Teddy Roosevelt had a certain amount of appeal in his earliest days. And when a program appealed to the country, why, the Congress went along with it.

In the beginning, Wilson had practically no trouble at all with the Congress. He had no problem at all in getting along with the various senators and representatives during his first term. But when we became involved in the war, and then when he later made a terrible and exhausting trip around the country to promote the League of Nations and his health broke down as a result of that trip, then the Congress began to figure out who was going to be in next, and you know how Congress is. Their

---

* My father was embarrassed about giving details of the typographical error, but as a longtime writer of mystery novels, I believe that you've got to be fair to the reader and be sure to name the killer once you've described a murder. I've also got to confess that I think the typo was pretty hilarious. The line was supposed to read, "The President spent much of the evening entertaining Mrs. Galt." The way it came out was, "The President spent much of the evening entering Mrs. Galt." MT

attitude toward him changed so much that it was almost like limiting the term of the president, almost like limiting the period of the Wilson administration. But he still managed to get such a lot done during his eight years, and that's the incredible thing.

He also had quite an excellent cabinet. His relationship with his cabinet wasn't always very cordial because he hated to delegate responsibility; he just didn't like to delegate responsibility. He also had a tremendous number of different men in his cabinet because of constant turnover. I think he was always listening to his people, but then he'd make up his own mind, and it was all too frequently in exactly the direction opposite to the one on which he'd just been advised. But just as frequently, the members of his cabinet ended up influencing his thinking despite his initial reaction against their suggestions, and before they quit, because so many of them were first-rate people.

Bryan, for example, became secretary of state, and Wilson was smart enough to take over all the things that were right in what Bryan wanted to do and put them into effect, and that, of course, is what Wilson did with the Federal Reserve Board and other things. The separation between the two men came about because of the World War. Wilson was in general agreement with Bryan until the time came that it was absolutely necessary for him to meet the situation. Wilson tried hard to keep us out of the war; he took a neutralist position, and so did Bryan. But when the time came that the ugliness of things being done by the Germans forced us into the war, when the sovereignty and the welfare of the United States was in danger, Wilson had to do what he did, and I think he did the right thing.

Other good people in Wilson's cabinet were William McAdoo, the fellow who told him to hang in there during the Democratic Convention and became his son-in-law, and who was his secretary of the treasury from 1913 to 1918 and a damn good one. Then Carter Glass took over the job and had a lot to do with helping Wilson set up the Federal Reserve System. And Newton D. Baker was Wilson's secretary of war, a man who was a pacifist but was capable of swinging into action when necessary, and managed to get our Army up to four million men, the strength needed to enable us to win the war. James C. McReynolds was the attorney general before he left to become a Supreme Court justice, and he was very helpful in pressing antitrust laws against AT&T and the New Haven Railroad and a lot of other companies that were getting to be too greedy. And just to name two more good men, the secretary of the navy was Josephus Daniels, who later became our ambassador to Mexico and a very efficient one, and as you may remember, he was helped out while running the Navy by a bright young assistant secretary named Franklin Delano Roosevelt.

Wilson also had some people around him who weren't so good, of course. Like almost everybody in politics, Wilson became involved with some unfortunate associates. The man most people remember is Colonel Edward Mandell House, who was a pretty minor politician in Texas— that "colonel" is a strictly honorary Texas title—until he latched onto Wilson and became Wilson's closest friend and constant advisor; but Jim Smith, that fellow who ran the New Jersey political machine, was worse. Smith was the worst man ever associated with Wilson, but fortunately, Wilson soon realized that he had to throw Smith over if he was going to do an honest job, and he did throw him over quickly and early in the game.

I guess House is remembered because he was associated with Wilson for a much longer period, and another not-too-wonderful fellow associated with Wilson for quite a while was George Harvey, or Colonel George Brinton McClellan Harvey to give him his full handle, the editor and publisher of a magazine called *North American Review* and later editor of *Harper's Weekly* and another one he started himself and called *Harvey's Weekly,* I suppose in the hope that people would become confused and buy it thinking they were buying *Harper's*. (His "colonel" was another honorary title given a fellow who never got any closer to any army than watching soldiers parade on holidays.) Harvey was one of the first people to suggest to Wilson that he ought to try for the presidency, so we can thank him for that, and House also deserves some thanks because he did some wheeling and dealing at the Democratic Convention and helped Wilson get the nomination, but that's about it.

Both men later exploited their positions as special advisors to the president, not for the benefit of President Wilson or the country but to make themselves more and more important and influential, and in the end Wilson had to get rid of them, too. Wilson took on House because he thought he could trust him, and he also became close to Harvey for the same reason. A man in the job of president, as I've said before, has to have people he can trust who aren't part of the cabinet or in other official jobs, special associates who are in a position to give the president information that the president is not able to get in any other way. A president has to have associates like that because he's got to have information from every direction, and in order to have that information, he's got to have people who aren't restricted to information sources within their own official circles. And it isn't a dangerous thing to have connections of that sort because the president is always in control.

But when House got to the point where he thought he was greater than the president, where he thought he *was* the president, why, then Wilson had to pull the rug out from under him and let him go, just like every president has had to do with some of his confidants. And the same thing happened to Harvey. House went around after that telling people that Wilson was "the most prejudiced man I ever knew," and Harvey launched a whole series of bitter attacks on Wilson in that magazine of his, that *Harvey's Weekly*, but nobody paid a whole lot of attention to the two fools.

I've already mentioned the Federal Reserve Board and some of the other things Wilson accomplished while in office, such as the first child labor laws in the country and the antitrust laws that legalized strikes and collective bargaining. But the two most important things accomplished by Wilson, of course, were the winning and ending of the war, and though it didn't work out in the end, the starting of the League of Nations.

As I've mentioned, Wilson tried hard to keep us out of the war when it first started on July 28, 1914. He appealed constantly to prowar groups to calm down and issued a Neutrality Proclamation giving the reasons our country should stay out of the war; and even when a German submarine sank the *Lusitania,* which was a British passenger ship, without warning on May 7, 1915, and on which 128 Americans were among the 1,195 men and women who died that day, Wilson still pleaded for neutrality, telling an audience of just-naturalized citizens a few days later, "There is such a thing as a man being too proud to fight. There is such a thing as a nation being so right that it does not have to convince others by force that it is right." At the same time, however, Wilson protested bitterly to the German government, and for a while German submarines stayed away from American ships. As late as January 1917, Wilson was still hoping to keep the United States out of the war, and that month he made a speech that pleaded with the warring countries to accept "peace without victory." But the response from the Germans was a contemptuous announcement that they'd stayed away from American shipping long enough, and that, starting February 1, German submarines would sink without warning all ships, including American ships, doing business with the Allies.

Two days later, Wilson appeared before a joint session of Congress and announced that the United States was breaking off diplomatic relations with Germany. He still hoped to keep our country out of the war, but later that month, a message from Germany to Mexico was intercepted in which Germany promised Mexico that it would return Arizona, New Mexico, and Texas to Mexico if Mexico joined Germany in attacking the United States and helped Germany win the war. Wilson didn't tell Congress about that message at first; he asked only that he be allowed to arm American merchant ships, revealing Germany's offer to Mexico only when the House gave permission but the Senate held back. Then, on March 18, German submarines sank three American merchant vessels, and we entered the war two weeks later.

Our entry into the war turned the tide toward an Allied victory. As I've mentioned, Newton Baker got our Army up to four million men, and Josephus Daniels got our Navy up to a half million men; in March, 80,000 men were sent overseas, in April, nearly 120,000 more men were sent, in May, nearly 250,000 more men were sent, and by August there were over 1,000,000 Americans in France and 1,750,000 men there by October.

Teddy Roosevelt also tried to get into the act, or at least into the newspapers, by announcing that he was eager to command a division in France. But Wilson wouldn't agree to it because he thought it was a political maneuver, and in all probability it was. I think Roosevelt might have made a good division commander, but like Wilson, I believe it was a political proposition all the way, and Wilson didn't have any political generals. The generals who were placed in command of the divisions and all the other units in the First World War were selected on the basis of efficiency and military education and knowledge, not on the basis of being famous or an ex-president.

By the end of May, the Germans had moved to within fifty miles of Paris, but then the Allies stopped the German advance at Château-Thierry, Americans recaptured Belleau Wood and took Cantigny, and then captured thousands of German prisoners and mountains of German supplies and weaponry at Marne and St. Mihiel. Late in September, more than a million Americans fought and won in the Meuse-Argonne offensive, terrible battles in which there were 120,000 Americans killed or wounded. More than a third of the total American casualties of the war occurred during that offensive. But it resulted, finally, in making the Germans and the Austrians ask for peace, and as everybody knows, the armistice was signed on November 11, 1918. Over 100,000 Americans died and another 200,000 were wounded in the eighteen months we were in the war, and a conservative estimate of total casualties for all nations, which I saw just after the war ended, counted over 10,000,000 dead and over 20,000,000 wounded.

Wilson began to plan for the end of the war soon after we were in it, and on January 8, 1918, addressed both houses of Congress with a speech that became known as the Fourteen Points because it named fourteen things that he felt were necessary to achieve lasting peace and a settlement that all nations could accept. The speech was just wonderful; it was idealistic but also practical, and the language was as memorable in its way as Lincoln's Gettysburg Address. And it did a lot to hasten the end of the war because it made it clear to the German people, already sickened by the worldwide slaughter and as anxious to see an end of it as the people everywhere else, that the Allies, or at least the United States, didn't intend to occupy Germany or otherwise behave the way many victorious nations behaved in the past toward nations they conquered.

The first five points were general: they called for "open covenants, openly arrived at"; complete freedom of the seas for all nations, both in wartime and peace; elimination of all economic barriers between nations; drastic reduction of armaments worldwide to no more than the amount necessary for protection and safety; and settlement of colonial claims based on the desires of the people living in those colonies. Then he dealt with eight specific things: restoration of conquered territories to Russia, restoration of conquered territories to Belgium and maintenance of Belgium as a separate and sovereign nation, France to be given the Alsace-Lorraine territory that Germany had been demanding, Italian borders to be changed to give territories to those nations that had the most people of those nationalities in those territories, division of Austria-Hungary based on nationalities, division of Balkan countries according to principal nationalities, Turkey to control only Turkish people and allow all others to set up separately, and with unlimited access to the Dardanelles for vessels of all nations, and independence and access to the sea for Poland. And Wilson's fourteenth point was the one I consider the most important of all, a concept that still gives me hope, the establishment of "a general association of nations . . . for the purpose of affording mutual guarantees of political independence and territorial integrity to great and small states alike."

Wilson's first message to Congress, in which he described the things he wanted to try to do for his country, is, I think, one of the greatest and most eloquent documents in the history of this country, but his speech on the fourteen points is even more so because it described what he was trying to do for the world. I believe that that great speech will always live on in the history of the world because, aside from the points that were necessary at the time for the peace of the world, he set out that concept of the League of Nations. And in his concept of an organization like the League of Nations, he was on the right track and brought something to the presidency that no other president had brought before him. I'm glad that it isn't necessary to say "before him or since," because Franklin Roosevelt tried to continue the program that Wilson started with his support of the United Nations. And the fact that the League of Nations didn't work out in the end, or that the United Nations is ineffective in many ways and beset by many other problems, doesn't diminish the importance of the concept by one iota, because at least it's a start toward joining nations together to try to deal with injustice in the world.

As I mentioned earlier, Wilson decided to go personally to the Paris Peace Conference, the first time a president in office ever went to Europe, but he made the serious error of not including any Republicans or any senators from either party in his delegation. This was an especially major mistake because his personal popularity had eroded during the war, and the Republicans managed to regain control of both the House and the Senate in the 1918 elections. So when Wilson got back to the United States, he discovered that the acceptance of the treaty worked out at the Paris Peace Conference, which included the plan to work out the League of Nations, wasn't going to be as easy to sell to some resentful and irritated Washington legislators, and some segments of the general public, as he thought it was going to be.

Then Wilson made another tactical error. Some senators and congressmen just didn't like the idea of an association of nations because they had prejudices against some other countries and didn't care to join together with them on *anything,* and some legislators had objections to other aspects of the treaty; and in particular one very influential Republican, Senator Henry Cabot Lodge of Massachusetts, was chairman of the Senate Committee on Foreign Relations, and a very conservative fellow who later headed the group of Republicans pushing Harding's nomination, and had quite a number of objections to the League and to other things in the treaty. But none of the complaints about the treaty were really all that major, and Wilson could unquestionably have mustered up the necessary two-thirds majority to get the treaty through if he were willing to add some language to "guarantee the United States' sovereignty." But he wasn't, and the Senate became just as intransigent and childish and refused to ratify the treaty.

That was when Wilson decided to take his cause to the people and went off on a speaking tour that took him eight thousand miles around the country and all the way to the West Coast, and that brought about his collapse from exhaustion on September 25, 1919, and a stroke on October 2 that paralyzed his left side and made him an invalid for the rest of his administration and the rest of his life.

Wilson was able, after a while, to walk with a cane and to speak, though somewhat unclearly, and he spent the last year of his second term mostly in bed and in a wheelchair, so much out of things that Edith Wilson checked every item of government and decided which matters to bring to his attention and which ones to skip. He left office on March 3, 1921, staying on in Washington and opening a law office in partnership with a man named Bainbridge Colby, who served as secretary of state during Wilson's final year in office, but he was now almost totally blind and so sick that he did little more than have occasional conferences with Colby and others in his house on S Street. And on February 1, 1924, he told his wife, "I'm a broken piece of machinery," and two days later, aged sixty-seven, he called out for Edith Wilson, lapsed into a coma, and died. It was a sad ending for a very fine man.

The United States never joined the League of Nations, though Wilson was awarded the Nobel Peace Prize in 1920 for proposing the League and for his other work. Warren Gamaliel Harding was elected president on November 2, 1920, and in his bumbling way let a lot of the good things advocated or achieved by Wilson go out the window, and Franklin Roosevelt had to put them back when he became president. The League of Nations continued until 1940, at which time it was down to a skeleton staff, and then it disappeared entirely.

THIRTY-THREE
FDR (and Me)

PRESIDENTS of the caliber of Jefferson and Lincoln don't tend to reappear, but we had one in the nineteen thirties when Franklin Delano Roosevelt took over. He was a great, great president. He had the ability to make people believe he was right and go along with the things he wanted to do, and he was also very daring in his actions. He surrounded himself with people who were knowledgeable historically about the things that had happened before their time and understood how to use past experiences in current circumstances, and he knew how to make the thinkers of the country work for him. That's always necessary for the head of a government. He must know how to stop the overly radical thinkers before they take over, and he must know how to make use of what they can contribute and use it for the benefit of all the people and not for just a few. And Franklin Roosevelt certainly did.

People are always asking me what I thought of Roosevelt as a person, aside from his presidential abilities. Well, I'm sorry to have to disappoint people who love gossip and are hoping that I'll have something unpleasant to say, but I liked him. I liked him a *lot*. He was a very easy person to like because he was a very, very pleasant man and a great conversationalist, with marvelous flashes of humor in almost everything he said, and he had a personality that made people feel close to him. For those reasons, as well as for my tremendous admiration for him as our president, I was very fond of him. And when he died so suddenly and so quickly on April 12, 1945, just sixty-three years of age, I felt truly overwhelming sorrow—not just because he had done so many wonderful things in his administration and I wanted to see him complete his fourth term and finish the job, but as though I'd lost a close relative or my closest friend.

He had defects, of course, both as chief executive and as a human being; every president does. It's a difficult thing to talk about defects I saw in Franklin Roosevelt, and particularly difficult for a successor to try to say that something better could have been done under this set of circumstances or that because nobody—remember this—nobody, not even the vice president, knows all the facts on which a president makes his decisions. And if other decisions come to mind that might have been better, they're Monday-morning decisions, made after the fact. I think Roosevelt did the very best he could do under each set of circumstances and made the right decision at each moment it had to be made.

But I'll try to talk a little about defects in order to make this a balanced account. For one thing, he was a first-rate executive, never afraid to make those decisions he made, but he wasn't a good administrator because he just wasn't able to delegate authority to anybody else. He wanted to be in a position where he could say yes or no to everything without anyone's ever arguing with him or questioning him, and of course you can't do that in our system of checks and balances. And I was always of the opinion that he ought to have restraints, as every president should have, and I sometimes argued with him myself when he wanted to go too far or when he set out to do something strictly on his own and without the agreement or help of others.

For example, I didn't disagree at all with his proposal that he be allowed to add a Supreme Court justice, up to a maximum of six, for each present justice who was at least seventy years of age and had served for at least ten years. Under Roosevelt's plan, each of those older judges could either choose to retire at full pay and be replaced by a new man, or elect to stay on in the job with Roosevelt having the right to appoint new men, up to that maximum of six, who would be assistant justices but would have full voting rights to counterbalance the remaining people. Some good people on both sides of the aisle *did* oppose Roosevelt's plan, and in some cases violently, including George W. Norris and my friend Bennett Clark and Roosevelt's own vice president at the time, John Nance Garner; but the problem was that many of the justices had been appointed by the long string of Republican presidents who preceded Roosevelt—

Taft, Harding, Coolidge, and Hoover—and something just had to be done because ultraconservative justices like George Sutherland, James McReynolds, Pierce Butler, and Willis Van Devanter kept shooting down everything Roosevelt tried to accomplish. I also felt, as Roosevelt did, that many of the justices were much more concerned with the interests of big business than with the needs of the average man and woman suffering from the terrible depression, and I knew from my studies of history that the Supreme Court had varied from five to ten members over the years and didn't think there was anything magical about the number nine. I expressed my feelings very bluntly at the time. "The cry is that the President wants to pack the Court," I said. "I say the Court is packed now, and has been for fifty years, against progressive legislation."

But I didn't agree at all with Roosevelt's obvious feeling that he had become so popular and so powerful that he could go ahead and push through anything, even an unprecedented plan like that one, without help and without bothering to try to convince people opposed to the plan that he was right. There was no question about his popularity and his strength when he began to talk about his Supreme Court plans early in 1937. He had just beaten old Alf Landon by winning forty-six states to Landon's two, Maine and Vermont, racking up 523 electoral votes to Landon's 8, and the House had 334 Democrats to 89 Republicans and the Senate had 75 Democrats to a mere 17 Republicans. But there was much stronger general opposition to the plan than Roosevelt estimated, and more resentment at what was considered his high-handedness than he realized, and arguments kept on and kept on from February to July. And then the man who was doing the principal pushing for Roosevelt, Senator Joseph Taylor Robinson of Arkansas, the Senate majority leader, died of a heart attack, and the bill vanished along with Joe Robinson. And the United States lost a bill that might have been very helpful to the American people because Roosevelt's ego misinformed him and made him believe he could win on his own.

I guess that was his principal defect, that growing ego of his, which probably wasn't too minuscule to start with, though perhaps it was his only flaw. It was also his ego, I think, that prevented him from even listening when, in the months between the day of Herbert Hoover's defeat in the 1932 election and the day Roosevelt actually entered the White House, Hoover suggested that he and Roosevelt get together and close the banks jointly for a brief period. I think there should have been more consideration given Hoover when FDR took over, and more help accepted from him because he was bound to have observed and learned some things that Roosevelt just didn't know when he first entered the Oval Office; but the campaign had been a pretty rough one, and so many people were blaming Hoover for the depression as though he'd caused it all by himself, calling cardboard shanties Hoovervilles and empty pockets Hoover flags and things like that, that Roosevelt decided that he was smarter than Hoover in every way and Hoover just didn't know what he was talking about when he suggested closing the banks.

But the bank closings were an absolute necessity; people in every state in the union were pulling out their savings and closing their accounts and sticking their few dollars under their mattresses, and more than half the national banks in the country were either out of business or refusing to allow withdrawals. And ego or no ego, Roosevelt finally had to close the banks himself so that government auditors could go in and see which of the banks still in business were solvent and safe and which weren't. The delay actually increased the problem—not a serious increase, but it would have been better if it had been done when Hoover suggested it be done instead of a little later on. After the auditors' examinations, the banks that were determined to be okay were allowed to reopen, and that made people feel better and a bit confident and helped to a certain extent. And in time the Roosevelt administration passed banking acts in 1933 and 1935 that prohibited banks from selling stocks and bonds, and then set up the FDIC, the Federal Deposit Insurance Corporation, and that helped a lot more.

And as a final example, it was also Franklin's ego, I suppose, that caused him to run for a third term, and then a fourth term. Generally speaking, I'm against more than two terms for a president, and always have been, because I think that two terms are usually enough. But the reason I'm also against that Twenty-second Amendment, and the reason I think it's as bad in its way as that idiotic Eighteenth Amendment, the Prohibition Amendment, and testified to that effect to the House of Representatives and to Congress, is that a president is like any other executive and shouldn't be required by statute to step down at a time when events are such that it would be better if he continued to stay on the job a while longer. And I wasn't against Roosevelt's decision to run for a third term because, in that instance, I thought it was a good idea; we were in a situation of another world war, and it was good that the situation was being met by someone who had been on the ground for years and was continually familiar with what was going on.

I'm certain it wasn't his original intention to try to stay on for more than two terms. In fact, I've been told that he'd already signed a contract to become chief roving editor for *Collier's* at the end of his second term. I think he would have been a good one. And he obviously had every intention of going through with it, since he'd signed a legal document. So I think it's silly when people ask me what happened that made him change his mind and decide to go on for a third term. The thing that happened was that he was anxious to see the free world win the Second

World War. That's all it was. That's all he had in mind. A contract with a magazine meant nothing when he became committed to Churchill and France and all the other countries that were anxious to escape the Nazi control of that part of the world. And the only thing I'll say about the charges that he plotted to bring us into the war is that they're ridiculous in the extreme. I think he did everything he possibly could to keep us out of the war—until he realized, just as Wilson did, that our entry into the war was inevitable and unavoidable. We just had to pitch in and help, and that's why there are monuments to Wilson in London, Paris, and Rome, and monuments to Roosevelt being put up everywhere as I write this. There's one for Roosevelt in London right now; I was there just a short time after it was unveiled. And there's a monument to both Wilson and Roosevelt in Paris, and a street in Nice named Woodrow Wilson Boulevard. The two men are in the same great class.

Don't forget that Roosevelt sent men over to talk to Hitler about stopping the slaughter, and Churchill also tried. Roosevelt and Churchill were alike in many ways, particularly when they worked together during the war; I believe Roosevelt's support made Churchill great and Churchill's support made Roosevelt great, so it was a mutual proposition, and each had influence on the other that was very helpful in the end to the welfare of the world. I don't think the early effort with Hitler was blindness or failure to recognize Hitler for what he was. I think it was a desperate effort to avoid what eventually came about. I think both Roosevelt and Churchill were desperately anxious to prevent a Second World War. Well, they didn't succeed, and we won the war, so why argue about it?

But in a way, I was also a little bit concerned about Roosevelt's decision to run for a third term, and then a fourth, because I thought there might have been a partially wrong reason involved: that he wasn't doing it only because he felt it was best to keep the same experienced man in place, but that he might also have felt that he was the *only* possible man who could lead our country to victory in the war. I think he began to feel that way more and more the longer he stayed in office, and it isn't hard to understand; it was natural for him to feel that the majority of the people were behind him in view of his unprecedented four terms. And they were. But part of the reason the people were backing him was that we had an emergency that had to be met, and they were afraid they wouldn't be able to find another man who could meet it. That happens whenever a strong president is in office. But the president himself should be realistic enough and objective enough to realize that no chief executive, no matter how good he is, is irreplaceable, and that our country will always survive, and eventually flourish, despite changes in management. In Franklin Roosevelt's case, of course, the day came when he was no longer there, and thank heavens, even if I do say it myself, we made it all right.

But that slightly swollen ego of his was just about his only fault, and let's not forget for a minute that he was the man who restored the economic health of this country and saved the free world by winning the Second World War. So don't ever ask me, as someone once did, if it's true that he wasn't a great originator of ideas or a philosopher like Jefferson or others of similar standing. I can't even judge whether or not he was a great philosopher in the Jefferson tradition because I'm not one myself. But Roosevelt was the man who brought about the recovery from the terrible depression we had in 1929 and 1930 and 1931, and he was the man who persisted in the manner that won the Second World War. Isn't that enough to make us think of him almost as a god? It certainly is in my book.

And don't think that I agree for a second with the people who say that the good things Roosevelt accomplished during his administration were counterbalanced by his one terrible mistake of helping the Russians and even kowtowing to them. I don't think our policy toward the Russians in his administration *or* mine was a mistake at all.

I don't want to give you the impression that I loved Stalin and some of the other Russians with whom I dealt; I didn't and I don't. I place a lot of the blame on Stalin for the Second World War, and particularly the length of the war and part of the terrible total of losses in the war, because he made a deal with Hitler. Any talk on Hitler's part about making a deal with England was just pretense, and very transparent pretense at that, because I don't think he liked England. All those Continental countries have always been afraid of England. And I don't see how Churchill, all by himself, on that little island across the English Channel, could have done other than what he did do—try to talk some sense to Hitler even though he realized that Hitler was a lunatic, and then fight like hell, when it became necessary to fight. But if Stalin hadn't made that deal and had stayed with his friends, if a big, strong country like Russia had showed strength instead of cowardice, Hitler might still have been controlled. But Stalin didn't have the sense to stay with his friends. At the time we're talking about, France had folded up, Holland, Belgium, all Western Europe had folded up, and Stalin then folded up too and made a deal with Hitler. He went and met this guy and made a deal with him, and then, as soon as the time became right for Hitler to knock Stalin's ears down, Hitler went back on the deal. You can almost be glad and say that it served Stalin right, except for the fact that it wasn't anything to be glad about because we were affected so much by the fact that he made the deal in the first place.

But the simple truth of the matter is that, though Russia needed us when Hitler double-crossed Stalin, we also needed Russia. Roosevelt felt, and I agree, that without the participation of Russia, there was a good chance that we couldn't have won the war. If the Russians had stayed with Hitler, and if Hitler had been smart and kept the Russians on his side, there's certainly little chance that we could have won the war in Western Europe. Russia had seven million men in the field and we only had one million six hundred thousand. Do your own figuring. I believe that despite all our mobilization, and despite all the tremendous industrial might that the United States was about to turn on, we still couldn't have done it without Russia. If Russia wasn't on our side, I truly feel that the war might not have been won. And that's not just because Germany had Japan on its side. We did manage to whip Japan eventually, even though it took terrible measures to do it. But if Hitler had used his head, I'm not so certain that we could have whipped the Germans. Don't forget that Hitler conquered France and all of Western Europe. If he had stayed out of Russia, he would have had the world by the tail because he had that deal with Stalin. But then, luckily for us and the rest of the world, he went crazy, or crazier than ever, and he made the same mistake that Napoleon made. And that's when we were able to put him out of business.

Roosevelt has also been criticized about the meeting with Stalin at Yalta, in the Crimea, in February 1945, during which postwar plans were discussed and Roosevelt and Churchill agreed to give Russia a strong position in Germany after the war by dividing that country into four zones—American, British, French, and Russian, of course—and also agreed to restore Port Arthur, in China, to its former status as a Soviet naval base, which it had been before the Russo-Japanese War in 1904, plus some other concessions. In return for this, Russia agreed to join us in the war against Japan, and also join a new organization that would be called the United Nations. And the argument here was that we really didn't need Russia to win the war against Japan, and didn't need them in the new organization, so why make concessions to them?

Roosevelt has even been criticized about Yalta on other grounds: that he shouldn't have gone to Yalta personally because it was "demeaning" for an American president to make that big trip, and because he was a very sick man at that point and lacked the strength to negotiate forcefully. Well, I saw Roosevelt immediately after he got back from Yalta, and I made the arrangements for his appearance on the Hill, and he was as spirited and clearheaded as ever. He certainly showed his physical deterioration and weakness, and I think he surprised some people when he addressed Congress for the first time from a wheelchair, but he'd been growing weaker physically for some time and it affected in no way his ability to function and to negotiate. People who interpreted his physical appearance to mean that he hadn't fared well in his negotiations with Stalin were absolutely misreading the situation.

I think Roosevelt made a good deal at Yalta, and all I can say is that everybody ought to read the protocol and agreement that was made there, and then read the protocol and agreement that was made at Potsdam, and they'll find that they would have been just fine if the Russians had kept the agreements. We wanted the Russians to feel they were part of our team in Germany because we didn't want any belated thinking on their part that a new Russian-German partnership, using German technology and Russian military strength and physical resources, might be very nice—and don't think there was no danger of that even at that late date. And we also felt, as I still feel, that the United Nations will eventually bring about world peace, and that the organization would be incomplete and almost pointless without a major country like Russia in it.

And the same answer applies to people who felt that it was unnecessary or demeaning for the president of the United States, in his frail condition, to go all the way to Yalta to meet Stalin. That had been the policy all along. Roosevelt had been to Casablanca and to Teheran and to Cairo, and the trip to Yalta was just a continuation of the effort to achieve world peace. Would I have gone if I'd been president at the time? Under the circumstances, of course I would have. Not to accommodate Stalin. To accommodate myself and try to get peace in the world. Roosevelt didn't go to accommodate Stalin. He went with the idea that he was going to win world peace and keep it with the United Nations, that's what he went for. We had to have Stalin's support. I had to send a man to Stalin myself to get Molotov to agree to the United Nations charter after it was made up.

The trouble, of course, was that Russia *didn't* live up to the agreements, but nobody could really have predicted that in advance. Roosevelt certainly didn't show any signs of discouragement when I saw him after he came back from Yalta. I don't think he was in any way of the opinion that Stalin wouldn't keep his agreements, and after talking to Roosevelt, I felt the same way when I went down to Potsdam.

Potsdam was a meeting for the purpose of implementing agreements with Russia that had been begun all the way back in Quebec, early in the game. I went there with the expectation that everything would be in shipshape condition. I didn't go to make any new agreements; I went there for assurance that there'd be no modification of previous agreements. I went for confirmation of what had been done at the four meetings previous to Potsdam, and when the Potsdam Conference was over, everything had been agreed to and all of us had confidence that Stalin would keep his engagements. There was no indication at all at the time that

Stalin would eventually behave the way he did. You had to believe someone, and Stalin was speaking for Russia.

It was easy to make agreements with Stalin, and it wasn't until later that we all found out that the reason it was so easy to make agreements with him was that he didn't intend to keep the agreements. Later on, Churchill was very critical of Russia, but that was just hindsight; he was right there with Roosevelt at Yalta and with me at Potsdam, and he was certainly willing to make agreements, wasn't he? Churchill felt the same way that Roosevelt and I did. He was there and made the agreements in both instances. He thought the Russians were all right, and so did I, and so did everybody else who was there.

There was no thought about our ideological differences on the part of the Russians while we were saving their skins, not after the Germans approached within reach of Moscow and Leningrad. The objective of the Russians then was to get with the people who could save them. And we did save them; we sent equipment—six and a half billion dollars' worth of equipment—through the Caspian Sea and the Persian Gulf. If it hadn't been for that approach, the Russians would have been pulverized by Hitler. I don't in the slightest way share the opinion some people developed in retrospect that we made a mistake in helping Russia because we had to save Russia to save ourselves; if Hitler had succeeded in pulverizing Russia at the time he had a chance to do it, where would we be?

It's a pity, of course, that the Russians showed their ingratitude so quickly. But it's that way with so many people you help when they're down; they get up and find they're working again and working well, and they think they did it all themselves. The Russians obviously decided they did it all themselves, and after Potsdam, Stalin began to break every agreement he'd made. He broke twenty agreements he'd made with Roosevelt, and he broke thirty-two with me. I don't know how you're going to be able to tell in advance that a man is going to make agreements and then break them; I guess you just can't. Perhaps, thinking about it, he really even intended to stick by his agreements up to and including the time of the Potsdam Conference. He'd certainly appeared to be a friend of the West at Casablanca and Cairo and Teheran, and at Yalta and Potsdam as well. But he changed dramatically after Potsdam. Perhaps he came to the conclusion that he was independent and out of danger and could do as he damn pleased—that he was now comfortably in a position where he could gain his objectives without the help or the friendship of the West, and that's what brought it about.

The Russians began to ignore promises they'd made in connection with Berlin, Greece, Turkey, and the Near East, and if we hadn't met the problems effectively and decisively, I think we might have been in a bad fix. For example, they'd agreed to withdraw their troops from Azerbaijan, and they didn't do it. So we ordered a fleet into the Persian Gulf and told the Russians we were sending in divisions, and they moved out. The same thing happened with Tito at Trieste, when he made up his mind that he was going to take over Trieste. And I sent him word that all right, come on, we have divisions and fleets there to meet him, and he didn't come. That seems to be the only kind of language some people understand. It's a shame that it's so, but it's the truth. And when the Japanese surrender took place, I made it a point to be careful to keep the Russians out of Japan in view of the way they'd behaved in Western Europe. I definitely didn't want them in on the occupation of Japan.

Well, I've delineated Franklin Roosevelt's faults, and as you can see, they didn't amount to a hill of beans. But if you're still wondering why I consider him perhaps our greatest president, my heavens, all you have to do is look at the incredible number of things accomplished in his fruitful years in office.

The Emergency Relief program, which kept people from starving in the streets, was established during his administration. The FDIC, the Federal Deposit Insurance Corporation, which insures deposits in savings banks and keeps them safe, was established during his administration. The FSLIC, the Federal Savings and Loan Insurance Corporation program, which insures deposits and keeps them safe in savings and loan institutions, was established during his administration. The WPA, the Works Progress Administration, to give employment to people who didn't want to subsist on handouts, and which resulted in the building of 75,000 bridges, 650,000 miles of highways and roads, and 125,000 national and local government buildings, and helped develop some of our country's best artists, musicians, actors and actresses, and authors, was established during his administration. The Social Security Act, which made sure that elderly people had at least a minimum amount of money on which to live after they stopped working, was established during his administration.

And so was the TVA, the Tennessee Valley Authority, which used the Tennessee River and other waters to bring electricity and other advantages to seven especially depressed states; and the SEC, the Securities and Exchange Commission; and the Wagner Act, which prohibited employers from discrimination against unions and union members and allowed workers to bargain collectively; and the CCC, the Civilian Conservation Corps, which gave healthy outdoor jobs, things like tree-planting and road-building and flood control, to over three million young men who would otherwise have been idle and bitter on city streets; and the FHA, the Federal Housing Authority, which guaranteed mortgage loans and kept the building of homes going instead of grinding to a halt;

and the REA, the Rural Electrification Administration, which brought electricity to hundreds of areas previously ignored by the big utility companies because they were sparsely populated and considered potentially unprofitable by those companies; and dozens of other programs along similar lines. It's hard to believe that these essential programs weren't around before Roosevelt came along, but they weren't. And many of these things are still with us, of course, so is it any wonder that I feel about him as I do—or that you should, too?

And then all at once, on that terrible spring day in 1945, Franklin Roosevelt wasn't with us any longer. He was in Warm Springs, Georgia, planning to remain there for a three-week vacation, and the day was particularly relaxed. Franklin was working on a speech, an artist named Elizabeth Shoumatoff was looking over at him and working on his portrait, and his cousin Margaret Suckley was sitting and crocheting. Then suddenly the President said, "I have a terrific headache," and lapsed into unconsciousness, and at 4:35 P.M. he was dead of a cerebral hemorrhage. The words he'd written before that were both memorable and typical of his thinking: "The only limit to our realization of tomorrow will be our doubts of today. Let us move forward with strong and active faith." It was a simple restatement of his famous philosophy: "The only thing we have to fear is fear itself."

And then, just as suddenly, *I* was president of the United States.

Sam Rayburn, the speaker of the House, had asked me to come over to his Capitol office that afternoon and discuss some bills on which the Senate and the House weren't seeing eye to eye, and when I got there, Sam was sitting and talking with two other men, Jim Barnes, a White House legislative assistant, and Lew Deschler, the House parliamentarian. Sam started to mix us some drinks, and then mentioned, almost as an afterthought, that Steve Early, the President's press secretary, had called and asked that I call him as soon as I got there. Sam obviously didn't think it was anything important, and neither did I, but I returned the call, of course. And Steve told me, "Please come over here"—to the White House, that is—"as quickly and quietly as you can."

· I went over immediately, stopping only to get my hat and tell one of my secretaries where I was going, and I walked out to my car and driver so quickly that the Secret Service didn't know where I was and spent some frenzied minutes catching up with me. But I still didn't have the faintest guess of what had happened. And I wrote to my mother and to my sister, Mary, a few days later, "I thought that the President had come to Washington to attend the funeral of the Episcopal Bishop Atwood, for whom he was an honorary pallbearer, and who was his good friend. I thought that possibly he wanted me to do some special liaison work with the Congress . . .'' Then I was taken up to Eleanor Roosevelt's study on the second floor of the White House, where she was with Steve Early, her daughter Anna, and Anna's husband, John Boettiger. And then I knew, from the look on their faces, what had happened even before Eleanor put her hand on my shoulder and said, "Harry, the President is dead." And when I asked her, "Is there anything I can do for you?" her answer was, "Is there anything we can do for *you?* You're the one in trouble now."

Just the day before, I'd joked about being the vice president when I addressed a group of newspapermen covering the Senate. One of them called me Mr. Vice President and I said, "Smile when you say that," and I told them that the Senate was the greatest place in the world and that I wished I was still a senator. "I was getting along fine," I said, "until I stuck my neck out too far and got too famous. And then they made me VP and now I can't do anything." But now I wasn't the vice president any longer, and there was plenty to do.

I won't deny that, at first, I felt plenty of fear myself at the added and overwhelming responsibilities that had come to me so suddenly. I tried to deal with it lightly, telling Mrs. Truman that I thought I'd make a good president because Abraham Lincoln and I had so much in common. And when she looked hard at me, probably wondering if I was turning pompous in my old age, I told her that I wasn't comparing myself to Lincoln in terms of intelligence or administrative ability or anything really significant like that. But at least, I said, Lincoln and I had three other things in common.

First of all, I said, Lincoln and I were alike in that we both didn't like to hunt and didn't like to fish. He didn't like to kill anything, and I didn't like to kill anything, either. Second, I said, I think Lincoln and I both had a sense of humor; and, I told Mrs. Truman, a sense of humor is a tremendous help to any man in a position of authority. Because when a stuffed shirt tries to tell a man in a place of responsibility what he ought to do, the best way to settle the argument with him is to stick a pin in him and let the wind out—and if you have a sense of humor, you'll have a good time doing it. And third, Lincoln and I both went broke in business. Lincoln's partner went broke in business, and Lincoln ended up owing eleven hundred dollars. Lincoln also didn't mind the store because he was always lying behind the notions counter reading newspapers and books to keep himself informed. Well, my old partner, Eddie Jacobson, says that when our business was going broke, customers would come in all right but I was always in a corner reading about Andrew Jackson. I'll admit that I've probably read more about Jackson than anyone else in the country. It took us a long time to pay off our creditors, too. It was 1935 before they were all settled and taken care of.

I also thought a lot, in those early days, about my start in politics and the road that had taken me to where I was right then. I guess that my political career started around 1912, when Wilson became president of the United States and I became postmaster of Grandview, Missouri, population around three hundred people. It was also my first experience with bipartisan politics. That part of the country was unanimously Democratic; there were about 230 voters, and the Washington Township precinct for Grandview was the voting place for Grandview, and I don't suppose there were over forty Republicans in the whole layout. But of course they had a Republican postmaster during the Republican administration, before Wilson came in, and that was a girl who was the secretary of the Eastern Star and all that kind of business, and a good friend of my sister's, and also the daughter of a man named L. C. Hall, who ran a threshing machine in the neighbourhood and threshed all the wheat and everything else and was one of the best friends that my father and I had. Well, when Wilson was elected, they wanted a Democratic postmaster, and they couldn't think of anybody better, so they made me postmaster.

But I was also the road overseer in Washington Township along with my father; he was the road overseer and I was his deputy and did most of the work until he died in 1916, so I appointed the Hall girl deputy postmaster and she just kept on running it as she had during the Republican administration. I guess I was postmaster three or four years. And then I went into the First World War as a lieutenant in the artillery and she continued to run things at the post office even though she was a Republican, so you see what I mean about bipartisanship.

And then, after the war and after I opened a men's clothing store in Kansas City, Missouri, with Eddie Jacobson, who had been my partner in running the canteen at Camp Doniphan, Oklahoma, during our training days, and we went bust, I was back in politics again and managed to get myself elected judge of the eastern district of Jackson County, Missouri, with the help of Tom Pendergast. Pendergast, incidentally, was not at all the kind of political boss like Tweed of New York or Big Bill Thompson of Chicago. He was sincerely for the welfare of the people, and whenever a man wanted to do the right things, Pendergast supported him in doing right. There's no question about the fact that sometimes, when there was a man or an organization who wanted to get votes by an underhanded program, Pendergast might support them, too. But when he found a man who wanted to do right, he always supported him, and I think I'm a good example of that.

And then, in 1926, I was elected presiding judge of Jackson County, and reelected in 1930, and in 1934 I ran for senator from Missouri and won. And in 1944, of course, I was the candidate for vice president when Roosevelt ran for his fourth term.

So now there I was, at 7:09 P.M. on the evening of April 12, 1945, as Chief Justice Harlan Fiske Stone swore me in as president of the United States in the Cabinet Room at the White House, underneath a portrait of Woodrow Wilson. And as I've already admitted, I was plenty scared. But scared or not, and prepared or not, I promised myself one thing that evening, and in the days and nights that followed: that I'd work damn hard and try damn hard to be a good president.

I think most people will give me that much: that I tried hard to be a good president. And I hope that some people, at least, will feel that I succeeded.

AFTERWORD

WHILE this book was still being edited, a small excerpt was published in *Parade,* the Sunday supplement that appears in hundreds of newspapers in the United States and Canada. The excerpt was the section in which my father lists his choices for the eight best presidents and the eight worst. Shortly after the excerpt appeared, *Parade*'s editors sent over a pile of letters that came in response to the piece. I'll admit that I opened the letters with a certain amount of nervousness, expecting that my father had stepped on some toes in naming his "worst" choices, one or two of whom might turn out to be other people's favorites. To my relief and pleasure, there were no letters like that at all. Instead, virtually every letter said exactly the same thing, and I'll quote one of these, from a gentleman in Illinois, which is typical of all the rest. "There's a terrible omission in the Truman article," the letter said. "He forgot to list one of the best presidents of all: Harry S. Truman

Or, if he insisted on being modest, why didn't he just make it nine best presidents and include himself in that way? And definitely not at the bottom of even that exalted list." You'll get no argument from me on that subject.

MT

Index